Folklore
of Canada

Edith Fowke
Folklore
of Canada

M&S

First printed in paperback 1982

Reprinted 1992

Canadian Cataloguing in Publication Data
Main entry under title:
Folklore of Canada
Includes bibliographical references.
ISBN 0-7710-3204-8
1. Folklore in Canada. I. Fowke, Edith, 1913-
GR113.F65 1990   398.2'0971   C90-094073-5

Illustrations by Laszlo Gal

Printed and bound in Canada

McClelland & Stewart Inc.
The Canadian Publishers
481 University Avenue
Toronto, Ontario M5G 2E9

CONTENTS

ACKNOWLEDGEMENTS

We wish to acknowledge with thanks the generosity of Mr. Nicholas J. Fodor and Electrovert Limited, who have lent their support to this project in honour of the company's twenty-fifth anniversary.

Quote from Marius Barbeau in the introduction by permission from *Funk and Wagnalls Standard Dictionary of Folklore, Mythology, and Legend*, ed. Maria Leach, ©1949.

"Origin Legend" and "The Girl Who Established Peace" from *The Ojibwa Indians of Parry Island, Their Social and Religious Life* by Diamond Jenness; "The Magic Flute," "The Clever Daughter," and "The Live Statues" from *Folk Narrative Among Ukrainian Canadians in Western Canada* by Robert B. Klymasz; "Local Anecdotes from Lunenburg" from *Folklore of Lunenburg County, Nova Scotia* by Helen Creighton; and "Superstitions and Popular Beliefs in Nova Scotia" from *Folk-lore of Waterloo County, Ontario*" by W.J. Wintemberg. Reproduced by permission of the Canadian Centre for Folk Culture Studies, National Museum of Man, Ottawa.

"The Seven Stars" and "Blueface" collected by Kenneth Peacock, and "The Farmer and the Little Bird" and "The First Night of Christmas" collected by Magnús Einarsson. Printed by permission of the Canadian Centre for Folk Culture Studies.

"The Blind Singer" by permission of Mrs. Marius Barbeau.

"Chansons franco-ontarien" by permission of the Centre franco-ontarien de folklore, Université de Sudbury.

"Le Sergent" and "Le Vieux Sauvage" by permission of Father Anselme Chiasson.

"Parlour Games from Ile Verte" ("Nous irons jouer dans l'île") by permission of Maurice Tremblay and the American Folklore Society.

"In Quest of the Ballad" by permission of Mrs. W. Roy Mackenzie.

"Superstitions and the Supernatural in Nova Scotia" from *Folklore of Nova Scotia* by Mary L. Fraser, by permission of the Librarian, Xavier College, Sydney, Nova Scotia.

"Celtic Tales from Cape Breton." Reprinted from *Studies in Folklore*, W. Edson Richmond, Editor. Copyright © 1957 by Indiana University Press, Bloomington. Reprinted by permission of the publisher.

"Newfoundland Riddles" by permission of Elisabeth B. Greenleaf.

"Larry Gorman and the Cante-Fable." Reprinted from *Larry Gorman, The Man Who Made the Songs* by Edward D. Ives. Copyright © 1964 by Indiana University Press, Bloomington. Reprinted by permission of the publisher.

"Pat and Mike Jokes from Nova Scotia" from *Folklore from Nova Scotia* by Arthur Huff Fauset by permission of the American Folklore Society.

"Tall Tales and Other Yarns from Calgary, Alberta." © 1945 by the California Folklore Society. Reprinted from *California Folklore Quarterly*, Vol. 4, No. 1, January 1945, pp. 29-49, by permission of the Society and Herbert Halpert.

"Songs of the Great Lakes" by permission of Mrs. Ivan H. Walton.

"Ontario Calls and Fiddle Tunes" by permission of Mrs. J.D. Robins.

"The Cattle Round-up, 1906" by J.O. McHugh by permission of the Alberta-Glenbow Foundation.

"Western Vernacular" by John D. Higinbotham by permission of the Alberta Historical Society.

Thanks to Jay A. Anderson, M. Carole Henderson, Ruth Rubin, Susan Smith and Gerald Thomas for their original material.

INTRODUCTION

Folklore is a difficult term to define. For one thing, it refers to both the materials involved and the method of studying them. Also, there are several different approaches, with the result that you can get almost as many definitions as there are folklorists. When the Englishman William Thoms introduced the term in 1846 to replace the older "Popular Antiquities," he intended it to cover "manners, customs, observances, superstitions, ballads, proverbs, etc., of the olden times." Since then many have tried to define it more exactly, but some modern folklorists are still reduced to listing the things they mean when they talk of folklore. However, the emphasis now is less on "the olden times" and more on the traditions that continue into the present.

Some define folklore as "oral literature" or "the verbal arts," but it also includes some things that are not transmitted orally. One fairly widely accepted definition has it that "folklore is the material that is handed on by tradition, either by word of mouth or by custom and practice." Another, more simply, says that it is "everything that we don't get out of books."

The Standard Dictionary of Folklore, Mythology, and Legend gives twenty-one different definitions by as many folklorists. The only Canadian among them was Dr. Marius Barbeau who wrote:

> Whenever a lullaby is sung to a child; whenever a ditty, a riddle, a tongue-twister, or a counting-out rhyme is used in the nursery or at school;
>
> Whenever sayings, proverbs, fables, noodle-stories, folktales, reminiscences of the fireside are retold;

Whenever, out of habit or inclination, the folk indulge in songs and dances, in ancient games, in merry making, to mark the passing of the year or the usual festivities;

Whenever a mother shows her daughter how to sew, knot, spin, weave, embroider, make a coverlet, braid a sash, bake an old-fashioned pie;

Whenever a farmer on the ancestral plot trains his son in the ways long familiar, or shows him how to read the moon and the winds to forecast the weather at sowing or harvest time;

Whenever a village craftsman – carpenter, carver, shoemaker, cooper, blacksmith, builder of wooden ships – trains his apprentice in the use of tools, shows him how to cut a mortise and peg in a tenon, how to raise a frame house or a barn, how to string a snowshoe, how to carve a shovel, how to shoe a horse or shear a sheep;

Whenever in many callings the knowledge, experience, wisdom, skill, the habits and practices of the past are handed down by example or spoken word, by the older to the new generations, without reference to book, print, or schoolteacher;

Then we have folklore in its own perennial domain, at work as ever, alive and shifting, always apt to grasp and assimilate new elements on its way. It is old-fashioned, grey- or white-headed perhaps, fast receding from its former strongholds under the impact of modern progress and industry; it is the born opponent of the serial number, the stamped product, and the patented standard . . . .

Some scholars may question certain aspects of that definition because it stresses the past, but it does give a good picture of the range of our subject.

The aim of this anthology is to present a representative cross-section of the various kinds of folklore found in Canada. Some genres, notably folk song, have inspired many books, but most types are sparsely represented and often buried in obscure or out-of-print sources. We must have more collecting and research before we can form a clear picture of all our traditions, both past and present, but in the meantime this sampling will give some idea of our unwritten lore.

Genuine folklore should be given in the form in which it is used by the folk, not as reshaped by writers seeking to popularize it. Many of the Canadian books loosely labeled as folklore are what Richard Dorson terms "fakelore": rewritten, bowdlerized, and romanticized versions of folktales. (This applies particularly to many of the books for children based on Indian legends; most genuine Indian tales are not considered suitable for children.)

I have tried to draw the material in this volume from authentic sources representing genuine folk traditions. Except for the fact that some items are translated, the texts are faithful to the original sources. Prefaces to each item give some background information, and the notes at the end of the book indicate the exact sources and give references to similar material found elsewhere.

Although some national anthologies arrange the material by regions, in Canada it is more practical to arrange it by ethnic origin; hence there are sections on the native peoples, Canadiens, Anglo-Canadians, and the Canadian mosaic. The Anglo-Canadian section includes all peoples from the British Isles: Irish, Welsh and Scots as well as English. It also includes a few items drawn from groups of varied ancestry. Some will criticize the proportion devoted to each group, for the Anglo-Canadian section is by far the largest, although more folklore has been collected from the native peoples and the French Canadians. However, a wealth of French-Canadian lore is already in print, and many books and articles explore the Indian and Inuit cultures, while much English-language Canadian folklore has so far been neglected.

All the texts are printed in English. The sections on the native peoples and the cultural minorities were already available in English, and some of the French-Canadian material had also been printed in English. I had planned to give both the original French and English translations for the French sections but economic factors made this impractical. However, the translations are quite literal, and the notes indicate where the French texts may be found. The songs, which do not translate well, are given in the original French as well as in English.

Most of the items deal with the verbal arts: folktales, songs, language, riddles, jokes, and rhymes. Only a few represent the broader field of folklife, but this area is well documented in many books about pioneer times and local history. Nor have I attempted to cover folk arts and crafts: again, many books with extensive illustrations are readily available. The bibliography lists some of the major books devoted to folklife and material culture.

In some items the tale type and motif numbers (from Aarne-Thompson, *The Types of the Folktale* and Thompson's *Motif Index of Folk Literature*) and reference numbers to other standard collections of riddles, superstitions, and jokes have been added in parentheses. These are explained in the Notes and the indexes at the back of the book.

The largest part of our folklore came to this country with the early settlers and was handed down from one generation to another. This book includes some samples of this old-world lore, but it gives priority to native Canadian traditions: material composed or adapted in Canada, rather than the tales, songs, beliefs, and customs imported from the old world. I have also tried to avoid reproducing material easily found elsewhere. Some of the earlier articles are drawn from sources that are

11

obscure or out of print, and quite a few sections present previously un-published material: the Blood Indian tales, the Newfie jokes, the songs of the Great Lakes, the discussion of French-Canadian foodways, the square dance calls, the autograph verses from Saskatchewan, the discussion of the Sasquatch and the Ogopogo, the urban legends, and the Yiddish tales.

Here, then, is a varied sampling of our folk culture – what Dr. Dorson has termed "the hidden submerged culture lying in the shadow of the official civilization about which historians write." In the search for our national identity surely this folk culture deserves more recognition than it has so far received, and I hope that this collection will give its readers some insight into its many and varied elements.

Edith Fowke

I The Native Peoples

I The Native Peoples

The folklore of the native peoples of Canada has been very extensively documented. The first to note the Indian tales were the Jesuit priests: during the second half of the seventeenth century they recorded a number of Huron and Algonkin tales in the *Jesuit Relations*. Later priests such as Father Lacombe and Father Petitot noted tales of the western and northern tribes.

The first to record any tales in English was Henry Rowe Schoolcraft who served as Indian agent among the Ojibwa of the Great Lakes between 1812 and 1842. His writings inspired Longfellow's *Hiawatha*, although that was based on a confusion of the Ojibwa culture hero, Manabozho, with Hiawatha, a historical Iroquois leader of the sixteenth century.

In the half century after Schoolcraft, many others followed his example: Indian agents, missionaries, doctors, and teachers noted down the tales they heard and printed them, sometimes translating the narratives literally, more often retelling them in a style they thought would be of greater interest to the reading public. Then toward the end of the nineteenth century the amateur collectors were succeeded by the specialists: anthropologists, ethnologists, and folklorists, who published literal translations of the tales they collected from particular tribes.

The items of this section have been chosen to represent different aspects of the folklore of the native peoples: accounts of the Shaking Tent of the medicine men, and The Last Sun Dance of the Cree, and a few tales from each of the major groups: the Indians of the West Coast, the Plains, the Central Woodlands, and the Eastern Woodlands, and the Inuit of the north. These are only token samples of a rich and varied lore.

1. THE SHAKING TENT
Alexander Henry

Much has been written about the rituals associated with the Indian medicine men, but none has aroused as much interest as the mystery of the shaking tent. As Rex Lambert notes in Exploring the Supernatural, *"For over three centuries white men of all kinds – soldiers, missionaries, traders, and travellers – pried into the secret of the Shaking Tent. Some scoffed or pronounced it a trick. Others admitted themselves completely baffled. No one, however, whether sceptic or believer, could explain satisfactorily how the phenomena were produced – the quakings and shudderings of the stout poles and their coverings; the weird lights that sparkled above the tent top, the eerie wailing voices that seemed to come from far and descend from the sky in a rushing wind upon the medicine man within; and lastly, the oracular forecasts of the future that he uttered in his trance."*

Champlain observed the phenomena in 1609; Father Paul LeJeune, head of the Jesuit Mission to the Hurons, gave an eye-witness account of an Indian sorcerer's seance in the Jesuit Relations *in 1634; the artist Paul Kane, who traveled through western Canada in 1848, and many less famous travelers have also described it.*

One of the most detailed accounts is that of the trader, Alexander Henry the Elder (1739-1824). At the end of the Seven Years' War, Indians under Pontiac rebelled against the British, and Henry found himself virtually a prisoner of the Ojibwa at Sault Ste. Marie. When Sir William Johnson, the British Indian agent, invited the Ojibwa to send a deputation to Fort Niagara to conclude a peace treaty, Henry urged the Indians to accept. Their chief told him that they did not know whether the invitation was a trap or not so they would consult the Great Turtle, their master spirit. What follows is Henry's account of that ceremony.

For invoking and consulting the GREAT TURTLE the first thing to be done was the building of a large house or wigwam, within which was placed a species of tent, for the use of the priest, and reception of the spirit. The tent was formed of moose-skins, hung over a frame-work of wood. Five poles, or rather pillars, of five different species of timber, about ten feet in height and eight inches in diameter were set in a circle of about four feet in diameter. The holes made to receive them were about two feet deep; and the pillars being set, the holes were filled up again, with the earth which had been dug out. At top, the pillars were bound together by a circular hoop, or girder. Over the whole of this edifice were spread the moose-skins, covering it at top and round the sides, and made fast with thongs of the same; except that on one side a part was left unfastened to admit of the entrance of the priest.

The ceremonies did not commence but with the approach of night. To give light within the house, several fires were kindled round the tent. Nearly the whole village assembled in the house, and myself among the rest. It was not long before the priest appeared, almost in a state of nakedness. As he approached the tent the skins were lifted up, as much as was necessary to allow of his creeping under them, on his hands and knees. His head was scarcely inside, when the edifice, massy as it has been described, began to shake; and the skins were no sooner let fall, than the sounds of numerous voices were heard beneath them; some yelling; some barking as dogs; some howling like wolves; and in this horrible concert were mingled screams and sobs, as of despair, anguish and the sharpest pain. Articulate speech was also uttered, as if from human lips; but in a tongue unknown to any of the audience.

After some time, these confused and frightful noises were succeeded by a perfect silence; and now a voice, not heard before, seemed to mani- fest the arrival of a new character in the tent. This was a low and feeble voice, resembling the cry of a young puppy. The sound was no sooner distinguished, than all the Indians clapped their hands for joy, exclaim- ing, that this was the Chief Spirit, the TURTLE, the spirit that never lied! Other voices, which they had discriminated from time to time, they had previously hissed, as recognizing them to belong to evil and lying spirits, which deceive mankind.

New sounds came from the tent. During the space of half an hour, a succession of songs were heard, in which a diversity of voices met the ear. From his first entrance, till these songs were finished, we heard nothing in the proper voice of the priest; but now, he addressed the multitude, declaring the presence of the GREAT TURTLE, and the spirit's readiness to answer such questions as should be proposed.

The questions were to come from the chief of the village, who was silent, however, till after he had put a large quantity of tobacco into the tent, introducing it at the aperture. This was a sacrifice, offered to the spirit; for spirits are supposed by the Indians to be as fond of tobacco as themselves. The tobacco accepted, he desired the priest to inquire, Whether or not the English were preparing to make war upon the Indi- ans? and, Whether or not there were at Fort Niagara a large number of English troops?

These questions having been put by the priest, the tent instantly shook; and for some seconds after, it continued to rock so violently, that I expected to see it levelled with the ground. All this was a prelude, as I supposed, to the answers to be given; but, a terrific cry announced, with sufficient intelligibility, the departure of the TURTLE.

16

A quarter of an hour elapsed in silence, and I waited impatiently to discover what was to be the next incident, in this scene of imposture. It consisted in the return of the spirit, whose voice was again heard, and who now delivered a continued speech. The language of the GREAT TURTLE, like that which we had heard before, was wholly unintelligible to every ear, that of his priest excepted; and it was, therefore, that not till the latter gave us an interpretation, which did not commence before the spirit had finished, that we learned the purport of this extraordinary communication.

The spirit, as we were now informed by the priest, had, during his short absence, crossed Lake Huron, and even proceeded as far as Fort Niagara, which is at the head of Lake Ontario, and thence to Montreal. At Fort Niagara, he had seen no great number of soldiers; but, on descending the Saint Lawrence, as low as Montreal, he had found the river covered with boats, and the boats filled with soldiers, in number like the leaves of the trees. He had met them on their way up the river, coming to make war upon the Indians.

The chief had a third question to propose, and the spirit, without a fresh journey to Fort Niagara, was able to give it an instant and most favourable answer: "If," said the chief, "the Indians visit Sir William Johnson, will they be received as friends?"

"Sir William Johnson," said the spirit (and after the spirit, the priest), "Sir William Johnson will fill their canoes with presents; with blankets, kettles, guns, gun-powder and shot, and large barrels of rum, such as the stoutest of the Indians will not be able to lift; and every man will return in safety to his family."

At this, the transport was universal; and, amid the clapping of hands, a hundred voices exclaimed, "I will go, too! I will go, too!"

The questions of public interest being resolved, individuals were now permitted to seize the opportunity of inquiring into the condition of their absent friends, and the fate of such as were sick. I observed that the answers, given to these questions, allowed of much latitude of interpretation.

Amid this general inquisitiveness, I yielded to the solicitations of my own anxiety for the future; and having first, like the rest, made my offering of tobacco, I inquired, whether or not I should ever revisit my native country? The question being put by the priest, the tent shook as usual; after which I received this answer: "That I should take courage, and fear no danger, for nothing would happen to hurt me; and that I should, in the end, reach my friends and country in safety." These assurances wrought so strongly on my gratitude, that I presented an additional and extra offering of tobacco.

The GREAT TURTLE continued to be consulted till near midnight, when all the crowd dispersed to their lodges. I was on the watch, through the scene I have described, to detect the particular contrivances by which the fraud was carried on; but, such was the skill displayed in the performance, or such my deficiency of penetration, that I made no discoveries, but came away as I went, with no more than those general surmises which will naturally be entertained by every reader.

2. THE LAST SUN DANCE
Richard Hardisty

Some form of sun dance was traditional with most Indian tribes. As Gertrude Kurath notes, "The most famous and spectacular sun dance, that of the Great Plains, is a votive rite centred about a consecrated tall pole. It is a combination of a buffalo rite and sun sacrifice, and retains the buffalo associations in its paraphernalia."

An eye witness of "The Last Sun Dance" of the Cree Indians of Alberta was Richard George Hardisty (1871-1942), the first white child born in Rupert's Land. His parents were Richard Hardisty, a chief factor of the Hudson's Bay Company and the first Senator from the Northwest Territories, and Elizabeth McDougall, daughter of the famous western missionary, Rev. George McDougall. Their son had a colourful career: at seventeen he joined the Hudson's Bay Company; later he ranched near Edmonton, established geological camps in the north, spent three years in Africa, and returned to Edmonton to become one of Alberta's leading businessmen.

The Cree, the most northern of the Plains tribes, are thought to have derived their sun dance from the Assiniboines who lived in the area just south of them. The initiation of the braves that Mr. Hardisty describes was typical of the voluntary torture that characterized the dance among all the Plains Indians. The gambling games that followed the dance are similar to those played by several West Coast tribes.

I shall never forget my boyhood impressions of an Indian festival of which I was an eye-witness when the Last Sun Dance was held on the river-flats in the heart of the area now known as the City of Edmonton. Prior to the time of which I shall speak civilization had been slowly but surely creeping into the west, yet at that time with the exception of the employees of the Hudson's Bay Company, there were not more than ten white men between Fort Garry and the Rocky Mountains, and they were mostly missionaries. Civilization had already affected the Indians,

18

sometimes disastrously, for thousands had died of smallpox and scarlet fever, and contacts with Hudson's Bay officers and missionaries had already modified some of the tribal rites and customs. The Sun Dance, which but a few years earlier had been a savage and gruesome pagan rite, was becoming a more peaceful and social gathering.

Up to the early eighteen-seventies there had been a practically constant state of war between the Crees and the Blackfeet . . . At last the tribes met in a great peace conference near where Wetaskiwin now stands . . .

A few years later a great gathering of Cree Indians at Fort Edmonton staged the last Sun Dance, and though I was but a youngster at the time, the picture is still clear in my mind's eye after all these years. For more than a week the Indians had been coming in, and the river flats below the Fort were dotted with tepees of buffalo hide. The encampment was about three quarters of a mile east of the Fort . . . After sunset, camp fires glowed, the banks of the river, covered with pine and spruce, making an intensely dark background below the skyline, made the camp fires bright and dotted the plain with brilliant light. The beating of drums, the howling of dogs joined the voices of those keeping time to the drum beat. This religious gathering had been for ages an annual event at which were featured the making of sacrifices and the enduring of self-inflicted torture. The conjuror rehearsed his medicine hymns – looked to his medicine bag – fixed his rattles and bells and retouched his ghastly costume. The warriors burnished their war dress. The women made ready their finery, though all they had, such as beaded leggings, a leather girdle – decorated with brass tacks – would be contained in a small bag made of calfskin.

The selection of the tree to be used as the "Idol Pole" was carried out with great ceremony. This "Idol Pole" was set up in the centre of the enclosure. For walls, small poles were set in the ground, sloping inward, and covered with leafy branches, making a good shelter from rain or sun. The walls formed a large circle with the pole standing about thirty feet high in the centre. One opening was left as an entrance, but this was closed with a buffalo robe during the ceremony. The "Idol Pole" was decorated with different coloured clays and streamers of red and blue tape or braid. Long pieces of shaganapie, reaching from the top of the centre pole to the circumference of the lodge, carried small bells, dried bones, and in former days the scalps taken in their last battle. Strong lines made from buffalo hide swung loose to the ground from the very top of the centre pole.

The enclosure would hold, seated on the ground, about a hundred braves. No women or children were permitted to enter during the ceremony. They, however, sat outside encircling the enclosure and taking part in the pow-wow, raising shrill but musical voices to the high heavens, keeping time to the rhythm of the drum beats. This all took time – it took preparation and rehearsal. The festival lasted for six days with but one performance a day and that at noon, by the sun.

In former days any of the warriors who desired to call upon the Sun God to favour him against his enemies in war and to supply his needs to maintain himself and family, took part in the ceremony, by sacrifice and self-inflicted torture. At this time, however, the Sun was invoked to witness only the cruel ordeals of youths who desired to become warriors and be recognized as men. In this last Sun Dance, twelve young men qualified as braves daily. The warriors, led by the chiefs and headmen, gathered in full war paint, naked but for a breech cloth – brass rings hanging loose on their ankles; dozens of brass rings on their wrists and forearms – strings of bear claws and elk teeth round their necks. They move towards the temple, led by conjurors and medicine men, the medicine men chanting, in doleful notes and in unknown tongues, petitionary and sacrificial hymns, their faces and bodies painted in alternate streaks of white and yellow – their ornaments around neck, waist, and ankles are human bones. The drums beat and the medicine men dance, going forward. The chief walks quietly behind, but the warriors, sounding the tribal war whoop, go through all kinds of contortions. They enter the enclosure and sit on the ground, their bodies moving and swaying, their voices raised to the beat of the drums.

The medicine men, now opposite each other, dance back and forth, chanting their incantation to the Sun to bless the gathering, working themselves and the warriors up to a frenzy of excitement. In the meantime, the women and youngsters have taken their place on the outside, and their voices blend with the warriors' and the drums beat louder.

About fifteen minutes before noon six young men, clean, their copper skins glistening in the sun – they are naked but for the breech cloth, no ornament, no paint – enter and dance the war dance, facing outward from the centre pole. They look fearlessly into the eyes of the warriors as they circle several times. Proud they are, for they have become experts in the use of bow and arrow, in tracking game, in trapping, in wood and prairie lore and all the many activities of the hunter and provider. Now they are to go through the test of courage and endurance to become warriors – taking their place in councils of the tribe – winning the privilege of seeking the hand of some girl – their eyes having no doubt already caught the eye of one girl.

The drums continue, the women's and children's voices grow shriller and shriller, war whoops fill the air. Three of the boys stop before one medicine man, standing erect, their chests thrown out. Three others face the medicine man on the opposite side. The medicine man produces two short pieces of red willow, prepared for the occasion, looking some-what like the skewers butchers use to fasten the roast of beef. The stick is about four inches long with one end pointed – the point hardened by fire and then scraped. Now the medicine man gathers as much of the flesh on the youth's chest as he can between his thumb and forefinger, forcing the stick through the flesh. The second stick is placed in the same manner on the opposite side, an equal distance from the centre of the youth's body. A loop of deer hide, about the width and length of a boot lace, is then fastened to each of the sticks. The youths face about, when all are skewered, and to the loops are attached one of the rawhide ropes hanging from the centre pole – the loops when tied are about six inches from the youth's chest, directly in the centre of his body. The drums beat, the medicine man cavorts, the war whoop rings out, there is a frenzy of movement and sound. The young men, their legs extended, their bodies thrown back, their weight carried by that portion of their flesh punctured by the stick, sway back and forth, blood streaming down their bodies from their wounds, sweat pouring from them. They leap and tumble, but utter no sound. The agony must continue until the flesh is torn through and they are free.

As each frees himself, he rushes from the enclosure, into the midst of his family – mother, cousins and aunts – each prepared to minister to his suffering torn flesh. The wound is covered with the fine brown powder taken from dried toadstools, which to my own knowledge will stop bleeding, and is soothing and healing. It has taken less than fifteen minutes for the six to complete their ordeal; immediately six others take their place.

At the same time, daily, for six days, the test is carried out, not one of the forty-eight young men failing to qualify as warriors. It is a great disgrace to the young man should he fail to pass the test, for in that event he is compelled to help the women-folk around the camp gathering wood, making fires, cleaning game, drawing water – not for such as he are the pleasures of the hunt or the thrill of war. The young girls avoid him.

At the conclusion of the trials for the day, the visiting, feasting, and drinking begins and continues day and night. The older women have kept the pots boiling; buffalo, moose, bear fat, beaver tail, deer tongues, ducks, geese, partridges, saskatoons and cranberries fill the pots. Tea – tea on the boil day and night. Drums beat, boys and girls shout and romp, young boys with bows and arrows aim at targets of interwoven willow hoops, which are thrown and shot at while rolling and seldom missed.

Continual movement, family to family, lodge to lodge, eating and drinking everywhere, young braves singing and dancing. To increase the potency of the boiled tea, blackstrap and other tobaccos, saskatoons, and cranberries are added. These cocktails, with the added excitement of the drum beats and noise, bring out actions very similar to present-day cocktail parties – the difference only the surroundings – instead of chesterfields or bed, the bare ground, the same ideas, however, lying down wherever sleep overtakes them – waking – eating – drinking.

The dancing lodges had been erected where dancers took their turns. The program was made up of but four dances – the "Wood Partridge," the "Prairie Chicken," the "Medicine Rattlers," and the "Kid Fox." Each in turn to vocal and drum music went through their movements. The dances are imitations of birds and animals dancing, resembling somewhat the quadrille and the lancers.

This band of Crees were prosperous – the winter catch of furs had been large. They were well provided with trade goods, chief of which were Hudson's Bay four-point blankets. The blankets, much lighter in weight than a buffalo robe, were used in place of it as part of gambling paraphernalia. The game was between two contestants who endeavoured to hide three articles in their hands or under the blanket which covered each of the contestants' knees as they sat on the ground facing each other. The wagers were for wearing apparel, pipes, dogs, horses, and in a crisis – wives. Sharpened stakes were used for chips. Each contestant had a friend responsible for moving the stakes to the winner's side.

The manipulator shows his opponent the three articles, then he makes passes behind, before, and under the blanket, then exposes them. This goes on for some minutes. He suddenly stops – both closed hands extended in the direction of his opponent. The drums are silent. The opponent claps his hands together and by certain movements of his fingers and hands indicates where he thinks the three articles are hidden. These hand signals appear to have been adopted by the present day buyer on the floor of a stock exchange.

When a correct guess was made, the three hidden articles were transferred to the winner. When a wager is won, another is made, and so continued for several nights and days till one or the other is cleaned out. Should either of the players become weary, a friend is ready to substitute for him. Their women provide them with food and drink.

These festivities are repeated night and day for the duration of The Last Sun Dance. I had spent much of the time during the week running about, taking in everything to be seen. Yet on the morning following the last day of the festival I was up early and out on the balcony of the Big House. I looked over the flat, there was no sign of life – the flat was deserted. Nothing but the skeleton of the Sun Temple was to be seen.

The Camp had moved at dawn.

3. TAHLTAN TALES
James A. Teit

The mythological tales of the North American Indians usually feature a culture hero who secures various things for his people. Stories about the theft of light and fire are very widespread, and are particularly popular along the west coast where the culture hero is the Raven. The Raven stories follow a fairly constant pattern in which Raven steals fire, sunlight, and water, and travels about transforming animals and objects so they have their present characteristics.

James A. Teit (1864-1922) was a Canadian anthropologist renowned for his work with the Indians of the interior of British Columbia. Born in the Shetland Islands, he came to Canada and settled at Spence's Bridge, British Columbia, near a village of the Thompson Indians. He learned the language of the local tribes and studied their culture in detail. When he died, Franz Boas wrote: "His collections are almost the only ones that give us a picture of the life of the Indians of that region."

Among the lore he collected were a number of tales from the Tahltans, a tribe inhabiting the interior of northern British Columbia along the Stikine River. The following samples are typical of the multitude of Indian myths about their culture heroes. The Latin passage in the second story illustrates how anthropologists tended to handle sexual references in a more straitlaced era. An English translation has been added in brackets. The last tale illustrates the trickster element which is characteristic of most Indian culture heroes.

THE BIRTH OF RAVEN

A number of people were living together near the sea. Among them was a man, gifted with magic power, who did not live with his wife. He did not allow any other man to go near her, and watched her very closely. He had a married sister, who gave birth to a boy who grew very rapidly. When he was old enough to travel about, his uncle asked his mother for permission to take his nephew hunting, and she consented. They went out to sea in a canoe. When they had gone some distance, the man told the boy to sit on the prow of the canoe. Then he rocked it, and the boy fell into the water and was drowned. The man returned home and told his sister the boy had fallen overboard and been drowned.

His sister gave birth to another son; and when the latter had grown a little, his uncle asked the boy's mother to let him go hunting. He drowned him in the same way. Thus he killed every son to whom his sister gave birth. At last she gave birth to another son. This was Raven. He played in a manner different from other children. He was fond of carving wooden toys representing canoes, people, fish, and other things, and played with them. When he was still a small boy, his uncle asked his mother to allow him to go with him hunting. She refused several times, saying, "He is my last child, and I do not want to lose him." At last the boy said to his mother, "Let me go! I shall not meet with any harm." She then assented, and he went. Before leaving, he hid a toy canoe under his blanket.

His uncle asked him to sit on the prow of the canoe, and rocked the canoe until the boy fell into the water. He remained underneath for some time; then, after coming to the surface, he made the toy canoe assume large proportions, and paddled home in it. His uncle had preceded him, and told his sister that her son had been drowned, and that he was just as foolish as her other sons had been. Soon afterwards the boy arrived, and told his mother all that had happened. He said, "Uncle killed my brothers in the same way that he tried to kill me." She was glad that he had returned, for she had given him up as dead.

After some time the uncle asked the boy's mother to allow him to go again. She consented, and the boy went. His uncle tried to drown him, but he escaped in the same manner as before. A third time he asked him; but this time he refused to go, saying, "You always try to kill me." His uncle went alone; and when out at sea a considerable distance, the boy ran to his uncle's wife's house and played with her. He noticed that she always kept her arms down. He tickled her to make her lift her arms. At last he clutched her abdomen, and then she raised her arms. A bluejay flew out from one armpit, and a woodpecker from the other. She died immediately. Her husband knew at once that something was wrong, and came home. When he found his wife dead and the birds flown, he became very angry, and chased the boy, intending to kill him. The latter put his small canoe on the water. At once it assumed large proportions, and the boy embarked and escaped.

After this he became Raven. He began to travel over the world, and never returned to the place where he had been born.

ORIGIN OF DAYLIGHT

At this time there was no daylight, or sun, moon, or stars. Raven went to a village and asked the people if they could see anything. They said, "No, but one man has daylight, which he keeps in a box in his house. When he takes off the lid, there is bright light in his house." The people could not work much, for it was night continually. Raven found out where Daylight-Man lived, and went to his house. This man also had control of the sun, moon, and stars. Raven went into the house and came out again. He planned what to do to get daylight for himself and the people.

Daylight-Man had many slaves, and a daughter who had been a woman for three years, but she was still undergoing the ceremonies encumbent on girls at puberty. She lived apart in the corner of the house, in a room of her own, and was closely watched. She drank out of a white bucket every day, and she always examined the water before drinking to see if there was anything in it. Slaves always brought the water to her. Raven changed himself into a cedar-leaf in the bucket of water the slave was bringing. The girl noticed it, and before drinking threw it out. He assumed his natural form again. Next day he transformed himself into a very small cedar-leaf, and hid in the water. The girl looked in the water, and, seeing nothing, she drank it all, and thus swallowed Raven. Mense sequente menstrua non habuit. Tribus post mensibus tumuit et ejus mater hoc animadvertit. Mater eam rogavit an persisteret menses habere et ea dixit eos non habuisse tres menses. Mater dixit, "Deinde gravida es et cum viro fuisti." Ejus parentes eam rogaverunt sed negavit se cum viro fuisse; [The following month she did not menstruate. After three months she began to swell. Her mother noticed this and asked her if she was still not menstruating. She said she had not menstruated for three months. Her mother said, "You are pregnant; you have been with a man." Her parents questioned her, but she denied that a man had been with her;] and they did not see how she could have been, as she had been so closely watched. After nine months she gave birth to a son. Her parents said they would rear the boy and acknowledge him as their grandson, even if he had no father. They said if she told who the father of the child was they would agree that he marry their daughter, they would treat their son-in-law well, and all would be well; but she persisted in saying that she had never seen man.

The boy grew very fast and soon was able to walk and talk. His grandfather loved him dearly. One day he cried very much and wanted to be allowed to play with the moon. His grandfather ordered the moon to be taken down and given to him. The boy was pleased, and played with it until tired; and then they hung it up again. After a while he got tired of the moon and cried much, saying he wanted the sun. It was given to him; and he played with it until tired, then gave it back, and the people hung it up again. After a while he became tired of the sun, and cried for the Dipper (stars). Now they allowed him to play with these things whenever he wanted. After a long time, when he felt strong, he cried for the daylight. His grandfather was afraid to give it to him, because it shed so much light; besides, whenever it was lifted up, the sun, moon, stars, and everything worked in unison with it. It was their chief. At last, however, the boy was allowed to have the daylight, but his grandfather was uneasy when he played with it. When the boy lifted up daylight, much light would come; and the higher he held it, the brighter became the daylight. On these occasions, when the boy held the daylight high, the old man would say, "Eh, eh!" as if he was hurt or extremely anxious. The boy balanced the daylight in his hands to get used to carrying it.

At last, one day, he felt strong enough for the feat he intended to perform. He put two of the toys in each hand and balanced them. He felt he could carry them easily. Then, at a moment when the people were not watching, he flew out of the smoke-hole with them. He threw daylight away, saying, "Henceforth there shall be daylight, and people will be able to see and work and travel. After dawn the sun will rise; and when it sets, night will come. People will then rest and sleep, for it will not be easy to work and travel. Then the Dipper and moon will travel and give light. These things shall never again belong to one man, nor be kept locked up in one place. They shall be for the use and benefit of all people." He threw daylight to the north, the sun to the east, the moon to the west, and the Dipper to the south. Since the introduction of daylight, people and game rise with daylight, and go to sleep with nightfall.

RAVEN PAINTS THE BIRDS

Now Raven called all the birds to a great feast. He painted each one a different way – the hawks, the owls, the eagles, the jays, and all birds, great and small. He painted Robin red in the breast. He painted Bluejay blue, and tied up his hair in a knot on his head. He tied up Ruffed-Grouse's hair in a knot. He painted Bald-Headed Eagle white on the head, neck, and back, and the rest of his body black. And thus he painted all the birds in different ways. He told the birds, "I called you to a feast. Now I will cut up the bear and feast you." Now he changed his mind about feasting them, and instead he worked himself up into a passion and wanted to fight them. They became afraid, and all ran away. So they have kept the colours in which he painted them until the present day. Those who had their hair tied up now have crests on their heads.

THE ORIGIN OF BIRTH AND DEATH

Once the Tree and the Rock were pregnant and were about to give birth. The Tree woman held on to a stick or bar, as Indian woman do, while the Rock woman used nothing to hold on to. Her child, when half born, turned into a rock and died. Raven came along shortly afterwards, and found the women. He said, "I am very sorry. I have come too late. Had I been here, this would not have happened. Now people must die because Tree gave birth, and Rock did not." If Rock had given birth, and Tree had not, people would never die. People would have been like rocks, and lasted forever. As it is now, people are like trees. Some will live to be very old, and decay and die, as some trees do; while others, when only partly grown, will die like young trees that die without decay and fall down. Thus death comes to people at all ages, just as among trees, and none lives very long.

RAVEN LOSES HIS NOSE

The people had lines set in the sea, but they could catch no fish. Their bait and even their hooks and lines disappeared. One night some of them watched by sitting in their canoes and holding the lines in their hands. One of them felt something, jerked his line quickly, and caught Raven in the nose, for it was he who had been eating the bait. The people pulled the line up into the canoe so quickly that Raven did not have time to disengage his nose; and, as he did not want the people to get him, he pulled back and broke off his nose. The people found they had caught some one's nose, but they did not know to whom it belonged. They took it to their village and gave it to one of their chiefs, who was a wise and wealthy man. Every one went to his house to see it, but none recognized it.

Raven put on a lump of pitch for a nose, shaped and coloured it, and then, pulling his hat down over his face, went to the village. He entered the first house. The people said, "You are a stranger"; and he answered, "Yes, I have come from a different place." They asked from what country and why he had come. He answered, "Oh! I have come from a distant country because I heard something." They asked him what he had heard. He said, "I heard you caught something." They answered, "Yes." He said, "I hear it is a very strange thing. I want to see it. I have come a long way to see this curious thing." They directed him to the next house. Thus he went through all the houses, asking and being answered in the same way. At last he entered the chief's house. There were many people there. The chief showed him the nose, and asked him if he could recognize it. He held it in his hand, and examined it very thoroughly and slowly, at the same time making remarks expressive of his wonder at the curious object. At a moment when the people's attention was diverted, he flew up with it through the smoke-hole, and sitting down on the high branches of a tree, he put it on. This is why the raven's nose now has a mark as if it had been broken off.

4. OJIBWA TALES
Diamond Jenness

Next to the Raven cycle of the west coast, the Manabozho stories of the Ojibwa form the most extensive Indian myth. The Ojibwa or Chippewa, probably the most numerous of the Indian tribes, occupied the eastern woodlands north of Lake Huron and Lake Superior and west as far as Lake of the Woods. These samples of their tales were collected from the Ojibwa Indians of Parry Island by Diamond Jenness (1886-1969), a native of New Zealand who first came to Canada in 1913 to join the Canadian Arctic Expedition led by Vilhjamur Stefansson, and later became director of the Anthropological Section of the National Museum.

The origin myth begins with twin brothers who are thought of as both human and animal: Nenibush (sometimes White Rabbit) and Wolf. (The culture hero here called Nenibush was more commonly called Manabozho or Nanibozho.) When Wolf is drowned by evil manitous Nenibush's lamentations call him back to earth and lead to the formation of the Grand Medicine Lodge. Nenibush's revenge leads to the flood and the escape on a raft, and this in turn leads to the Earth Diver myth which is present in the creation stories of nearly every Indian tribe. In the end, like so many gods and heroes, Nenibush departs for the west. This version was told by Jonas and Tom King.

The second tale of "The Girl Who Established Peace" is an example of the local legends which incorporate some elements from the tribe's history. Here an ancient war between Mohawks and Ojibwa has inspired a story about an Ojibwa Joan of Arc who triumphs with the help of great serpents. It was told by Mary Sugedub.

ORIGIN LEGEND

Wolf, the brother of *Nenibush*, was so skilful a hunter, and killed so much game, that the *manidos* became angry and plotted to destroy him. Now it happened that Wolf was camping with *Nenibush* and his grandmother *Nokomis*, "Earth," on the edge of a frozen lake. Every morning *Nenibush* would go outside his wigwam and discover the track of some animal that had passed during the night; Wolf would then pursue it and towards evening bring the carcass back to camp. Now *Nenibush*, knowing that the *manidos* were plotting his brother's death, warned him never to cross the lake, however late at night he might be returning. Early one morning, however, the *manidos* sent an exceedingly fleet-footed caribou past their camp. *Nenibush* told Wolf, who pursued and killed it after a very long chase. It was then so late in the evening that Wolf decided to leave the carcass until the next day and return to camp across the ice; but the ice broke when he was half-way across the lake and he drowned.

Nenibush, waiting in vain for his brother, realized at last what had happened. He lay on the ground, covered his head with his blanket, and wept for four days and four nights. All the birds and animals from the sky, and all the birds and animals from the water, came to comfort him, but without avail. At last they said, "Wolf had better return." So on the fourth day Wolf came out of the water and approached his brother's camp. But as he drew near *Nenibush* called, "Do not enter the camp. You must go far away and preside over the dead in the west." So now Wolf rules the dead in the far-away land of the west.

Still *Nenibush* refused to rise from the ground. At last there approached him beings called *mede manidos, mede* spirits, who set up wooden images of human beings, four in a row. While one spirit drummed, the others danced in front of the images, wearing in their belts bags of muskrat and other skins. *Nenibush* looked up at the sound of their singing and dancing, and the sight pleased him. He rose to his feet, and offered one of the dancers a *skibdagan* or medicine-bag made of skin. The spirits then disappeared, saying to one another, "What will *Nenibush* do now?" They covered the sky with dark clouds so that *Nenibush*, looking up, saw all the portents of a heavy rainstorm. He said to *Nokomis*, his grandmother, "Those things are trying to deceive me"; and, setting the wooden images in place, he himself danced and sang in front of them, pointing an otter skin with weasel and muskrat appendages towards the sky just as *medes* do now to ensure fine weather for the Grand Medicine rites. Quickly the clouds disappeared and the sky became clear again.

Nenibush now determined to punish the *manidos* that had killed his brother. He wandered all over the land, but could not find them, for they were water-serpents. Then one day he discovered them sleeping in the sun on a sandy beach. He tried to draw near them, but they recognized him and retreated into the water. Early the next morning he returned to the same place and transformed himself into a stump. The serpents emerged from the water, led by their leader who was as white as a winter rabbit. They were suspicious of the stump, and sent "tiger" to investigate it. He clawed it, and when it did not move returned to his companions and said "It is only a stump." Still suspicious, they sent a big snake, which wound itself all around the stump. Still *Nenibush* did not move, and the snake, like the "tiger," reported that he was only a stump and that they could sleep in safety on the beach. But as soon as the animals slept *Nenibush* changed himself into a man again and shot an arrow through their leader's heart. Leader and all, they leaped into the water, which rose rapidly and flooded all the land. *Nenibush* fled to the top of a mountain and climbed a tall pine tree. The water followed him until it reached to his neck, but it receded again to its proper level. *Nenibush* then descended, built a large raft in case it should rise again, and resumed his travels.

One day he met in the woods an old woman who carried a bag on her back, weeping. "Why are you weeping?" he asked; and she answered, "Our chief has been shot by *Nenibush* and is near to death. I am looking for a medicine to cure him." "What do you do when you enter his house?" he asked. "I administer my medicine alone, admitting no one, and sing over him." Straightway *Nenibush* killed her, dressed himself in her clothes, set her bag upon his back, and went to the chief's house. The people took no notice of him when he entered, for they thought he was the old woman. Then he killed the chief with his knife, skinned him as he would a deer, tied the skin into a bundle, and fled to his raft. The serpent people pursued him, and the water rose so rapidly behind him that he had barely time to reach the raft. Animals and birds of all kinds took refuge with him, for the water covered even the mountain tops, and this time did not subside. *Nenibush* said to them, "We had better create some land. Let some one dive down and bring me up a little sand." Otter went down. He could not reach the bottom and was almost drowned; but *Nenibush* pulled him on to the raft again and revived him. Loon dived, and failed also. Then they sent down muskrat, who rose at last so near to death that *Nenibush* had difficulty in reviving him. "Did you see any land?" he asked; and muskrat replied, "Yes. When I was nearly dead I saw it. I couldn't gather any of it in my mouth but I scratched up a few particles in my claw." *Nenibush* planted these particles of sand on the water, and laid on them the smallest ants, which ran around and made the land grow larger. Then he placed the rats on it, and as it grew, larger animals. Last of all, when the land had the form that we know today, he released the moose and the bear.

Nenibush finally went west and joined his brother. There he remains, and a giant cedar tree grows from his head. He wanders no more.

THE GIRL WHO ESTABLISHED PEACE

At the time of the wars with the Mohawks a young girl named Odobidodge went into seclusion. There she dreamed that she heard Grandmother Moon say to her, "My Granddaughter, you shall establish peace throughout this wide land." She gave the girl two brooms and added, "With one of these brooms you shall sweep up all the dirt. Leave the other at home, for you will need it in the ages to come. Now follow me and I will show you this wide land that you must clean up." The girl followed her invisible guide, whose voice alone she could hear, and they visited all the Indian camps scattered throughout the country. At certain camps Grandmother Moon said to her, "These are the trouble-makers whom you must sweep away." She then conveyed the girl back to her wigwam, and told her that after four days she would die, and four days later would come to life again.

Four days later the girl died. As she lay in her wigwam, dead, she saw all the harm that the trouble-makers were inflicting on her people. She saw the Mohawks and their allies destroying her countrymen and roasting little babies alive. She felt a call to lead the warriors to victory, to sweep away all the pestilent Mohawks with her broom. Then Grandmother Moon visited her again and said, "You were only sleeping and dreaming of the misery your countrymen endure at the hands of the trouble-makers. Now go forth in secret and warn the people that all the *manidos* throughout the land have summoned you to lead them to victory and peace. Call *Nzagima*, the boss of the serpents, the guard of the buffaloes. He will come to your aid."

The girl told her parents of her vision, and her parents announced it to their countrymen, who gathered together a war-party. She then summoned *Nzagima*, and heard his voice asking, "What is it you want?" "The Mohawks and their allies are destroying our people and intend to exterminate all our bands," she replied. "The great *manidos* have therefore decreed that they shall be swept away, and that victory and peace shall follow our arms. Go forth and proclaim the news that we are about to drive our enemies from the country."

"That is what I wish also, something to devour," said *Nzagima*, as he sped away in fury. The path that he and his fellow-serpents travelled became a mighty torrent that flooded a portion of the land and gave the canoes of the Ojibwa quick transit to their enemies. Some of the Mohawks met them on the water, but the great serpents overturned their canoes and drowned them. At Rama, and again near Toronto, the Mohawks attempted to make a stand; their thunder held at bay the thunder of the Ojibwa and killed many warriors until *Nzagima* attacked and destroyed it from beneath the earth. Then the Mohawks retreated eastward as fast as they could travel, and the Ojibwa pursued them. At last the girl commanded *Nzagima* to retire and remain quiet. Had she not done so all the Mohawks would have been destroyed.

5. MICMAC TALES
Silas T. Rand

Characteristic of the tribes of the Northeast Woodlands, and particularly of the Micmacs of Canada's Maritime Provinces, are the many sacred legends about Glooscap. Unlike most Indian culture heroes, he appears always as a man, not as an animal, and does not share the usual trickster traits; but the tales about him are otherwise similar to those of other Indian heroes: his wanderings create various physical features of the landscape, he tames the winds, and secures water and food for his people.

The first to collect the Glooscap tales was Silas Tertius Rand (1810-1889), a native of Nova Scotia who entered the Baptist ministry and worked for many years among the Micmacs. He translated much of the Bible into the Indian language, and compiled a Micmac grammar and dictionary. The following selection from his Legends of the Micmacs *contains many elements common to other Indian legends.*

GLOOSCAP, KUHKW, AND COOLPUJOT

The tradition respecting Glooscap is that he came to this country from the east – far across the great sea; that he was a divine being, though in the form of a man. He was not far from any of the Indians (this is the identical rendering of the Indian words used by my friend Stephen in relating the sketches of his history here given). When Glooscap went away, he went toward the west. There he is still tented; and two important personages are near him, who are called Kuhkw and Coolpujot – of whom more anon.

Glooscap was the friend and teacher of the Indians; all they knew of the arts he taught them. He taught them the names of the constellations and stars; he taught them how to hunt and fish, and cure what they took; how to cultivate the ground, as far as they were trained in husbandry. When he first came, he brought a woman with him, whom he ever addressed as Noogumich (Grandmother – a very general epithet for an old woman). She was not his wife, nor did he ever have a wife. He was always sober, grave, and good; all that the Indians knew of what was wise and good he taught them.

His canoe was a granite rock. On one occasion he put to sea in this craft, and took a young woman with him as a passenger. She proved to be a bad girl; and this was manifested by the troubles that ensued. A storm arose, and the waves dashed wildly over the canoe; he accused her of being the cause, through her evil deeds, and so he determined to rid himself of her. For this purpose he stood in for the land, leaped ashore, but would not allow her to follow; putting his foot against the heavy craft, he pushed it off to sea again with the girl on it, telling her to become whatever she desired to be. She was transformed into a large, ferocious fish, called by the Indians *keeganibe*, said to have a huge dorsal fin – like the sail of a boat, it is so large and high out of the water.

The Indians sometimes visit Glooscap at his present residence, so says tradition; this is in a beautiful land in the west. He taught them when he was with them that there was such a place, and led them to look forward to a residence there, and to call it their beautiful home in the far west – where, if good, they would go at death.

The journey to that fair region far away is long, difficult, and dangerous; the way back is short and easy. Some years ago, seven stout-hearted young men attempted the journey, and succeeded. Before reaching the place, they had to pass over a mountain, the ascent of which was up a perpendicular bluff, and the descent on the other side was still more difficult, for the top hung far over the base. The fearful and unbelieving could not pass at all; but the good and confident could travel it with ease and safety, as though it were a level path.

Having crossed the mountain, the road ran between the heads of two huge serpents, which lay just opposite each other; and they darted out their tongues, so as to destroy whomsoever they hit. But the good and the firm of heart could dart past between the strokes of their tongues, so as to evade them. One more difficulty remained; it was a wall, as of a thick, heavy cloud, that separated the present world from that beautiful region beyond. This cloudy wall rose and fell at intervals, and struck the ground with such force that whatever was caught under it would be crushed to atoms; but the good could dart under when it rose, and come out on the other side unscathed.

This our seven young heroes succeeded in doing. There they found three wigwams – one for Glooscap, one for Coolpujot, and one for Kuhkw. These are all mighty personages, but Glooscap is supreme; the other two are subordinates. Coolpujot has no bones. He cannot move himself, but is rolled over each spring and fall by Glooscap's order, being turned with handspikes; hence the name Coolpujot (rolled over by handspikes). In the autumn he is turned towards the west, in the spring towards the east; and this is a figure of speech, denoting the revolving seasons of the year – his mighty breath and looks, by which he can sweep down whole armies and work wonders on a grand scale, indicating the weather: frost, snow, ice, and sunshine. (Such was Stephen's very satisfactory explanation.)

Kuhkw means Earthquake; this mighty personage can pass along under the surface of the ground, making all things shake and tremble by his power.

All these seven visitors had requests to proffer, and each received what he asked for; though the gift did not always correspond with the spirit of the request, it oftentimes agreed with the letter. For instance, one of these seven visitors was wonderfully enamoured of a fine country, and expressed a desire to remain there, and to live long; whereupon, at Glooscap's direction, Earthquake took him and stood him up, and he became a cedar-tree. When the wind blew through its boughs, they were bent and broken with great fracas – making a thunder-storm by strong winds, which scattered the cedar-boughs and seeds in all directions, producing all the cedar-groves that exist in New Brunswick, Nova Scotia, and elsewhere.

The other men started, and reached home in a short time.

One of them had asked for a medicine that would be effectual in curing disease. This he obtained, but, neglecting to follow implicitly the directions given, he lost it before he reached home. It was carefully wrapped up in a piece of paper, and he was charged not to undo the parcel until he reached home. His curiosity got the better of his judgement; he could not see what difference it could make if he just looked at his prize as he was going along. So he undid the parcel, and *presto*! the medicine slipped out on the ground, spread and slid in all directions, covering up the face of the earth, and vanishing from sight.

On another occasion several young men went to see Glooscap in his present abode. One of them went to obtain the power of winning the heart of some fair one, which all his unaided skill had failed hitherto to do; an hundred times he had tried to get a wife, but the girls all shunned him. Many of the party who started on this perilous expedition failed to overcome the difficulties that lay in their way, and turned back, baffled and defeated; but several of them succeeded. They were all hospitably entertained; all presented their requests, and were favourably heard. The man who sought power to captivate some female heart was the last to proffer his petition. Glooscap and his two subordinates conferred together in a whisper, and then Earthquake informed him that his ugly looks and still more ugly manners were the chief hindrances to his success; but they must try to help him. So he was handed a small parcel, and directed not to open it until he reached his own village; this he took, and they all set off for home together. The night before they arrived, he could restrain his curiosity no longer; he opened the parcel, the foolish fellow! Out flew young women by the scores and hundreds, covering the face of the earth, piling themselves in towering heaps, and burying the poor fellow, crushing him to the earth under the accumulating weight of their bodies. His comrades had cautioned him against disobeying the mandate, and had begged him not to undo the parcel; but he had not heeded the caution. They now heard him calling for help, but he called in vain, they could not help him; and his cries became fainter and fainter, and finally ceased altogether. Morning came at last. The young women had all vanished, and the fragments of their comrade were scattered over the ground; he had been killed and ground to atoms as the result of his unbridled curiosity and disobedience.

In former days, water covered the whole Annapolis and Cornwallis valley. Glooscap cut out a passage at Cape Split and Annapolis Gut, and thus drained off the pond and left the bottom dry; long after this the valley became dry land. Aylesford bog was a vast lake; in this lake there was a beaver-house; and hence the Indian name to this day – Cobeetek (the beaver's home). Out of this beaver-house Glooscap drove a small beaver, and chased it down to the Bras d'Or lake in Cape Breton – pursuing it in a canoe all the way. There it ran into another beaver-house, but was killed; and the house was turned into a high-peaked island; Glooscap feasted the Indians there. A few years ago a heavy freshet tore up the earth in those regions, and laid bare the huge bones of the beaver upon whose flesh Glooscap and his guests had feasted – monstrous thigh-bones, the joints being as big as a man's head, and teeth huge in proportion.

In cutting open a beaver-dam at Cape Chignecto, a small portion of the earth floated away; and Glooscap changed it into a moose and set his dogs on it. The moose took to the bay and made off; whereupon Glooscap turned him back into land, made him an island – the Isle of Holt – and fixed him there. He changed the dogs into rocks, which may be seen to this day, seated on their haunches, with their tongues lolling out of their mouths; the plain is called Ooteel (his dogs). Spencer's Island is his kettle turned over; and the scraps he shovelled out when trying out his oil still lie scattered around, but turned into stone.

(Related to me Sept. 30, 1869, by Stephen Hood)

6. BLOOD INDIAN TALES
Kenneth Peacock

The Blood Indians formed one of the three tribes making up the Blackfoot nation – the strongest and most aggressive of the Plains Indians. Kenneth Peacock collected these tales on the Blood Indian Reserve in Saskatchewan while on a field trip for the Folklore Division of the National Museum in 1968.

Whereas the tales of Raven, Glooscap, and Manabozho illustrate the Indian creation myths, these Blood stories are more like ordinary folktales: the März*chen or wonder tales of Europe. The first is one of a*

35

large group of etiological tales that purport to explain the origin of the Pleiades. It is also closely related to a very widespread Plains tale usually identified as "The Bear Woman." Like the sister here, the bear woman attacks her family; they flee, delaying her by throwing magic objects behind them, and finally kill her by discovering one vulnerable spot.

The second tale is similar to one Stith Thompson calls "The Piqued Buffalo Wife" which is found among most Plains tribes. The mating of humans and animals is a feature of many Indian tales: here it is indicated symbolically.

These tales also illustrate the fourfold repetition that is characteristic of American Indian culture: four is their ritual or sacred number just as the number three predominates in Indo-European culture. In the first story the boy shoots the arrow forward four times; in the second the buffalo dance four times.

THE SEVEN STARS

A woman was all alone with her youngest brother. She told him, "Go out shooting so you can kill birds." His older brothers were away on a hunting party. What the older sister was really doing was preparing to murder the boys. One day when the woman's youngest brother returned from shooting birds he peeked into the dwelling. The woman was still, talking to an elk and a plume. "If they can hit this feather, only then will they be able to kill me."

He looked and started to run away. On the way he met his brothers and told them their sister had vowed she would kill all of them. He said to them, "We will begin fleeing." And they began running away.

When the boy did not return to his sister she realized that he knew of her plan. She prepared herself and started chasing them. The boys looked back and saw that she was gaining on them. The youngest boy told his brothers, "Let's run into one of these gullies." When they had run into one, he said to them, "Close your eyes." His brothers closed their eyes and he shot one of his arrows ahead, and after doing this he told them, "Now open your eyes." All of them were standing where the arrow had hit the ground.

They continued running, and when their sister caught up with them again, the boy did the same thing and shot his arrow ahead again. Four times he shot the arrow forward, and they managed to reach a valley where they all climbed a tree. The youngest boy sat highest in the tree. Their sister came upon them and said, "Damn you, Okina, damn you. I was going to kill you."

The boy sitting closest to the ground was shooting at their sister but

36

was unable to kill her. The sister killed him with one shot. All (were killed) except Okina, who was left alive. A bird glided around him and said to him, "All right, Okina, the plume!" He bent forward, took careful aim, but his shot only scratched the plume. The woman became dizzy and nearly fell down. The bird encouraged him again with the same words, and this time his shot broke the plume, and his sister was killed.

He cut open her chest, took out her heart, and cut it into slices. When the meat was dry he burned the pieces. As the smoke from the meat reached the six brothers of Okina they all came back to life and sat up.

They walked away from the spot and began to make plans. "All right," they said, "let us discuss our future." The oldest brother said, "We will be seven buffalo." Okina told him, "That is not good because we will all be killed by the people." Another said, "We will be seven deer." Okina argued, "That, too, is not so good. We will still be killed." Another said they should be wolves. Okina argued again, "We will be trapped by the people."

Still another suggested being seven trees, all standing side by side. Okina argued, "That is not good. Children will climb us when the people are camping beside us. The buffalo will also come and use us to scratch themselves until we become old."

Another suggested turning into lakes, all lying close together. "We will be mistreated. Women will taint us and the children will swim in us, the buffalo will drink us, urinate and move their bowels in us. We will finally dry up, and that is not good."

Still another said, "We will be rocks, all close together." "Oh, we will suffer. Children will climb upon us, and women will use us to pound their cloth. We will be chipped so they may scrape their deer hides with us."

"All right," they said, "You have disagreed with everything we have suggested. Now what's your plan?" "Yes, we will sit as we are sitting right now but in the sky. In the future new generations will tell tales about us. The new people will tell our story."

"Yes, you are right," they agreed, and it was so.

BLUEFACE

A young man was just travelling about one day when he came upon a female buffalo which was stuck in a mud pond. He wanted to help it get out of the pond so he took a long stick and prodded the buffalo with it. Finally it was able to jump out and run away.

The man went back home and a long time passed.

In the spring, all the little buffalo were born by their mothers, including the one which had been stuck in the mud pond. Her little one would join with the other calves, but they would all butt him with their little horns and tell him, "You are a child of a man."

Finally the little calf told his mother, "My friends tell me this." The mother said to her calf, "We will look for your father then."

They went and travelled a long time. They came upon a village in a valley. Where there was a thick growth of trees on a hillside, they went. The young calf would take on human form and join all the village children in their games. When the children left him and went home, he would go back amongst the trees. All the village people could not find out who he was.

Someone became curious and told the children to ask the boy (the calf) who his father was. The children when they again came to play asked him, "Why are you travelling around?" "I am looking for my father," he said.

The people told each other and said, "Bring the child around and make him pass each lodge."

When all the members of a family were gathered in their lodge, the boy would come by. "See if you can find your father here," they would tell him. He would see and tell them, "He is not here."

Finally, all the men without wives were united to a lodge, and when the boy looked in, he said, "There is my father." He circled all those sitting inside and sat by a young man. All of them were fed, but the young man was given more so that he might eat with the child. The man thought, why is he sitting beside me?

The meal did not take long and the host announced, "We have stayed long enough." When they got out, the child said to the man, "Come with me." They went and when they were out of the village he told him, "I have now found my father. You are he!"

The man couldn't figure it out! I never had any relations with a woman! he thought. On the side of his face, the man had a blue mark. When he examined the boy closely, there was a similar mark just a little closer to the hair. But I never had any relations with a woman!

"My mother said to go and get her," the child said. "She sees you, don't run away because she will charge at you. When she is just about to hit you, hold her by the horns."

They went to the woods and when they reached the clearing, "There she is. Go into the opening," the boy told him. When he did, the buffalo jumped up and charged him. Just as she was about to hit him, he caught her by the horns. Suddenly a woman was standing before him, who told him, "Let me go." And then she told him, "This is how it is. When I was stuck in that mud pond a long time ago, you came along and prodded me with a stick. I was able to get out and be free. That is how that child is yours, my son. He is the one standing there. He has your blue face."

Then the man understood. He thought, But I only touched her with a stick! It's miraculous how he is my child. As if reading his mind, the woman said to him, "Yes, you know he is your son."

"Well then come home with me," he said. So they went to his home and Blueface had a wife. They lived together a long time.

Blueface had two pets – a crow and a magpie. They grew to love the child a lot, and he in turn loved them. When he was outside running and playing each one would sit on his shoulders.

The woman warned Blueface, "You can hit me with anything, you can beat me if you want to, but one thing, don't ever try to hit me with ashes. And also, don't try to hit me with anything sharp. These are the two things I tell you not to hit me with. Do anything else you want." "Okay," he said.

So a long time passed, and one day the man got angry for some reason.

The child's grandparents (Blueface's parents) also loved him very much. The old man was always carrying him on his back with the crow and the magpie perched on the boy.

So one day the man got angry for some reason, and took a burning wood from the fire and scared his wife with it. When she saw it, both she and the child could not get out of the lodge fast enough. The man ran out after them, to tell them to stop. They had returned to buffalo, with the calf running ahead of his mother. All the dogs barked at them as they went over the hill and out of sight.

The grandparents – the old man and the old lady – were always walking about, crying and longing for their grandson. The crow and the magpie were always flying amongst the children looking for the baby.

Blueface's mother told him, "Oh you have done something bad to my grandson. Your wife warned you. Because she was miraculous, she warned you." He told his mother, "All right, I will look for them. If I don't return after a while, send my pets after me and if they bring back even the tiniest object, put the thing on my bed and cover it. Then put some tobacco in your pipe and smoke, saying 'Blueface, this is your smoke.'"

So Blueface went. After a long time he found a great herd of buffalo which covered a lot of land. When he searched and looked over on the herd, he saw a female and her calf sitting by themselves. "Oh I hope that is my wife," he said.

He put buffalo dung on his body and crept to their water hole where he made a hole and crawled in. He was in there and the buffalo started coming to drink from the well. Then after they were finished, all the calves started drinking and then when the last one came, Blueface looked to where the single female and her calf had been. The calf was gone! So he jumped up and caught the young calf. It was his son. It was so happy to see him. It said, "I will go and tell my mother to come."

The calf ran up and told his mother, "My father is here." The female

39

came down. He told her, "I came to get you." She answered, "I will go and ask the leader. If he agrees, then I will go home with you. You put us in a very bad way. Ashes we are very scared of, and also knives. You really put us in a bad way."

The calf went to the leader and asked him if they could return with his father. When the calf returned, he told his father, "The leader said that there will be a dance. If you can guess which one I am four times, we can all go home."

When all the buffalo gathered for the dance, Blueface's son told him, "When I dance the first time, I will have my tail curled. That's how you'll know which one I am. On the second dance, I will not use one of my front feet. On the third dance, my ears will be down. On the fourth one, my eyes will be closed."

The man picked his son the first three times; however on the fourth, all the calves closed their eyes, and he caught the wrong one. All the buffalo ran over him and crushed him to death. When there seemed to be nothing left of him, the buffalo dispersed.

When Blueface had been gone a long time, the old woman untied his pets. A while later they came back with a tiny speck of meat. The old lady took it and covered it in his bed. She then smoked the pipe outside saying, "Blueface, this is your smoke." When she had said it four times, Blueface came out of his lodge. "Well I could not do anything, I could not bring your grandson back."

(That's how the story was told to me.)

7. ESKIMO TALES
Franz Boas

The two most widespread of all Inuit tales were first collected by the famous anthropologist, Franz Boas (1858-1942), very early in his career: he published them in 1888. The first is the major Inuit myth which is told in slightly varying forms throughout all the northern tribes. It accounts for the Inuit goddess of the underworld and the creation of various sea creatures; other tales tell how Sedna created the walrus and reindeer during a famine, and give elaborate descriptions of her home in the world of the dead.

The second story, another etiological tale, is also very common among northern tribes. The trick by which the sister identifies her clandestine lover turns up in folktales from other countries, including a Hindu tale from India.

SEDNA AND THE FULMAR

Once upon a time there lived on a solitary shore an Inung with his daughter Sedna. His wife had been dead for some time and the two led a quiet life. Sedna grew up to be a handsome girl and the youths came from all around to sue for her hand, but none of them could touch her proud heart. Finally, at the breaking up of the ice in the spring a fulmar flew from over the ice and wooed Sedna with enticing song. "Come to me," it said; "come into the land of the birds, where there is never hunger, where my tent is made of the most beautiful skins. You shall rest on soft bearskins. My fellows, the fulmars, shall bring you all your heart may desire; their feathers shall clothe you; your lamp shall always be filled with oil, your pot with meat."

Sedna could not long resist such wooing and they went together over the vast sea. When at last they reached the country of the fulmar, after a long and hard journey, Sedna discovered that her spouse had shamefully deceived her. Her new home was not built of beautiful pelts, but was covered with wretched fishskins, full of holes, that gave free entrance to wind and snow. Instead of soft reindeer skins her bed was made of hard walrus hides and she had to live on miserable fish, which the birds brought her. Too soon she discovered that she had thrown away her opportunities when in her foolish pride she had rejected the Inuit youth. In her woe she sang: "Aja. O father, if you knew how wretched I am you would come to me and we would hurry away in your boat over the waters. The birds look unkindly upon me the stranger; cold winds roar about my bed; they give me but miserable food. O come and take me back home. Aja."

When a year had passed and the sea was again stirred by warmer winds, the father left his country to visit Sedna. His daughter greeted him joyfully and besought him to take her back home. The father hearing of the outrages wrought upon his daughter determined upon revenge. He killed the fulmar, took Sedna into his boat, and they quickly left the country which had brought so much sorrow to Sedna. When the other fulmars came home and found their companion dead and his wife gone, they all flew away in search of the fugitives. They were very sad over the death of their poor murdered comrade and continue to mourn and cry until this day.

Having flown a short distance they discerned the boat and stirred up a heavy storm. The sea rose in immense waves that threatened the pair with destruction. In this mortal peril the father determined to offer Sedna to the birds and flung her overboard. She clung to the edge of the boat with a death grip. The cruel father then took a knife and cut off the first joints of her fingers. Falling into the sea they were transformed into whales, the nails turning into whalebone. Sedna holding on to the boat more tightly, the second finger joints fell under the sharp knife and swam away as seals (*Pagomys foetidus*); when the father cut off the stumps of the fingers they became ground seals (*Phoca barbata*). Meantime the storm subsided, for the fulmars thought Sedna was drowned. The father then allowed her to come into the boat again. But from that time she cherished a deadly hatred against him and swore bitter revenge. After they got ashore, she called her dogs and let them gnaw off the feet and hands of her father while he was asleep. Upon this he cursed himself, his daughter, and the dogs which had maimed him; whereupon the earth opened and swallowed the hut, the father, the daughter, and the dogs. They have since lived in the land of Adlivun, of which Sedna is the mistress.

THE SUN AND THE MOON

In olden times a brother and his sister lived in a large village in which there was a singing house, and every night the sister with her playfellows enjoyed themselves in this house. Once upon a time, when all the lamps in the singing house were extinguished, somebody came in and outraged her. She was unable to recognize him; but she blackened her hands with soot and when the same again happened besmeared the man's back with it. When the lamps were relighted she saw that the violator was her brother. In great anger she sharpened a knife and cut off her breasts, which she offered to him, saying: "Since you seem to relish me, eat this." Her brother fell into a passion and she fled from him, running about the room. She seized a piece of wood (with which the lamps are kept in order) which was burning brightly and rushed out of the house. The brother took another one, but in his pursuit he fell down and extinguished his light, which continued to glow only faintly. Gradually both were lifted up and continued their course in the sky, the sister being transformed into the sun, the brother into the moon. Whenever the new moon first appears she sings:

Aningaga tapika, takirn tapika qaumidjatedlirpoq; qaumatitaudle.
Aningaga tapika, tikipoq tapika.
(My brother up there, the moon up there begins to shine; he will be bright.
My brother up there, he is coming up there.)

II Canadiens

II Canadiens

In a 1961 survey of "The Present State of French-Canadian Folklore Studies," Luc Lacourcière noted:

> From the beginning of Canadian history to the middle of the nineteenth century, folklore and oral tradition were in what we could call *un âge d'or*. They continued developing naturally and spontaneously. Even the Seven Years' War and the cession of Canada to the English offered no obstacles; quite the contrary, these important historical events created a new climate in which the peasant's attachment to the soil became more pronounced and his French traditions more deeply rooted. Because of the attitude of the king of France who never allowed the establishment of a press in New France, and the English Government which consistently after the conquest of Canada used English as an instrument of propaganda for introducing that language and Protestantism, there was a complete lack of publication in French and a scarcity of French schools. This period, which appears to some historians as a new dark age, was truly the golden age of oral literature.

The lore preserved through that golden age has provided a rich field for study. The first to draw upon it were the early French-Canadian writers who incorporated many traditional customs and legends in their books. Then Ernest Gagnon collected a hundred songs and published them in 1865 as *Chansons populaires du Canada* – the first book of genuine Canadian folklore. Half a century later Dr. Marius Barbeau began his long and fruitful collecting of French-Canadian tales and songs for the National Museum and gradually recruited a group of enthusiastic and talented collectors to work with him. Much of the material they collected appeared in special Canadian issues of the *Journal of American Folklore*.

Dr. Barbeau's disciples included Carmen Roy who succeeded him as director of the folklore division at the Museum, and Luc Lacourcière who in 1944 began to teach folklore at Laval University and to organize its Archives de Folklore. Since then he and his colleagues have been carrying out a massive task of collecting and analyzing the entire body of French folklore in North America. In a preliminary catalogue, Conrad Laforte classified some 38,000 variants of songs under 2,600 common titles, and the archive has identified more than 5,000 versions of tales which, as Lacourcière notes, "is probably the most important collection of folktales in any language in North America." Laval scholars are also studying all other types of folklore, and are publishing their findings in the periodical series listed as *Archives de Folklore*.

In addition to the extensive collections at the National Museum and Laval, Father Germain Lemieux has been finding a rich supply of tales and songs among the French Canadians of northern Ontario, and Le Centre d'études acadiennes at the University of Moncton has been exploring the lore of French Canadians in the Maritime Provinces.

1. THE BLIND SINGER
C. Marius Barbeau

The most important single figure in the history of Canadian folklore was Charles Marius Barbeau (1883-1969). As F. J. Alcock, chief curator of Canada's National Museum, wrote in 1950: "Dr. Barbeau has been responsible for the development of folklore research in Canada, and the wealth of folklore material in the possession of the National Museum of Canada was largely collected by him and the numerous students to whom he has transmitted his enthusiasm for this type of study."

What he achieved in one lifetime is almost unbelievable. In an age of increasing specialization, he ranged over the whole field of folklore and anthropology, collecting and studying and describing Indian myths, ceremonials, language, music, arts, and culture, and French-Canadian folktales, songs, art, handicrafts, and architecture. A prolific writer and completely bilingual, he published some fifty major books, as many more pamphlets and monographs, and almost six hundred articles in over a hundred different periodicals ranging from scientific journals to popular magazines and daily papers.

45

The following account of a French-Canadian singer and story-teller catches something of Barbeau's devotion to the lore of his people. Here in a few brief pages he sketched the society of rural Quebec and the personality of a gifted informant.

Isolation has long invested Charlevoix county with a peculiar charm. In this mountainous district along the St. Lawrence, the French-Canadian villages are unlike any other. Their people are quaint in their speech, their ways, and habitations. Something about them makes one think of the Kingdom of Saguenay of ancient wonderland. For two hundred years they have lived by themselves, and the spell of a fairy-like enchantment is not quite broken yet.

Anyone who, until recently, wished to visit this county was obliged to land from a river boat with large side-wheels either at Cap au Diable (Devil's Cape) near the Gouffre (Whirlpool), Baie St. Paul, Les Eboulements, La Malbaie and Pointe au Pic. This was the only means of approach in the mild season, and the whole district was ice- and snow-bound for several months every year . . .

When I first landed from the wheel-boat at Les Eboulements, fifteen years ago, my secret wish was at last fulfilled. For I had heard of this place since my school days. It was like venturing into the haunts of Merlin, whose fame as a wizard was familiar, or of Petit-Jean, the giant killer of ancient folk tales. I had come to collect tales and songs and had been promised a good harvest. The Lorette folk had told me, "My dear man, there is no place like the mountains beyond Cap Tourmente for this kind of fun. The people there still gather at night to sing folk-songs and tell fairy tales. And they drink good bootleg – jamaica, curaçao . . . "

Unlike Baie St. Paul, which I had seen at a distance in a deep bay, Les Eboulements sat sideways along the shore-line. Houses dotted the road close to the river; behind these, cottages on a high terrace glittered in their whitewash under the setting sun . . .

After a few days at Les Eboulements, I heard of Louis l'Aveugle (the Blind), a famous character, blind from youth, yet able to travel unaided, reading the road in front of him with his cane of red birch. He would go with his fiddle from house to house, not as an ordinary beggar – the term would have been an insult – but as a nomad in his birthright. With no home of his own, he owned no less than two counties, Charlevoix and Chicoutimi; and they were far from grudging him a subsistence. Always welcome, he knew that "the door is on the latch (*la porte est sur la clanche*)," as the saying goes. The fun he brought to his hosts was indeed worth a lot, for he was brimful of riddles, stories, and songs. This heritage he had received from his father, of whose name no one was sure – he was called Simard, like many others in that district. And he

46

carried his burden lightly, for no one was happier than he under the bright sun.

No sooner did Louis "the Blind" appear anywhere than the people started up and exclaimed, "*He*'s arrived!" *He* meant Louis, the jolly good fellow, the wizard. It could be no other; no one was like him. The children gathered in a circle around him, giving him no time to breathe. They wanted to hear him sing "Pyrame and Thisbe," a ballad-like song, accompanied on his fiddle. And he would instantly humour them.

He could go anywhere, stay with whomever he pleased, but he was discriminating. He chose the best places, the best table, and the finest feathered bed. And he had a good "stomach" memory (*mémoire du ventre*).

The night of his arrival, the folk gathered around him, wherever he stayed, for a "veillée." There he brought fresh news; he was an ambulant newspaper. And he knew everybody a hundred miles around. A child was born here, an old man had been buried there . . . ; he had lived on so many years that death had almost forgotten him. And so went the news. He lavished upon all gossip and entertainment. His wit and utter candour were disarming, and the storehouse of his yarns, his tales, and his songs was inexhaustible.

Like the others, I wanted to meet Louis "the Blind," but it was not easy to find out where he was. No one knew. Growing old, he was seldom seen and, in recent years, his visits were far between. The only clue at hand was that he usually came to Ste Irénée for the feast of Ste Anne on the 26th of July.

A few days before the feast of Ste Anne, I took my phonograph and went from Les Eboulements to Ste Irénée, on the chance of meeting the blind singer there . . . Soon after I arrived, I saw him walking slowly along the road, his cane feeling the ground in front of him. Though I had never met him, I recognized him by his long white hair and unusual oval face, his vacant stare – that of a blind man, and the quiet assurance of his demeanour. He owned the place and quite enjoyed coming home after a long absence. I spoke to him, and he seemed to know me: I was an old friend. He used the pronoun "tu" (thou) at me, as one does to a child or a familiar.

"Come in and sit down!" he said. We stopped right there, and walked into a house. Whoever were the hosts I did not know, but he did, and we sat down. He understood at once that I wanted folk tales and songs from him, like all the others, young or old. What else to expect! Yes, he would gladly tell me all I wanted to hear, from the time Adam and Eve partook of the apple under a tree! "But not just now!" he said, "in a few days, or perhaps a week."

"Why not now?" I wondered, for I had come a long way just to hear him. Must I go back disappointed?

I was not the only one from afar, he wished me to remember. He had come all the way on foot from Mille-Vaches, on the north shore towards Labrador, and that is not next door! He made this pilgrimage every year, returning to Ste Irénée where he was born, for the feast of Ste Anne, to confess his sins to the priest and for communion – really a serious affair. His house-cleaning, no less! This would change him into a cherub, all white, with a nimbus around his head! But the search for his sins and the scrubbing was all that he could undertake for the next days. Meanwhile no songs, no tales, no fiddle: they were worldly, if not a bit sinful.

I tried to coax him, offered him so much per hour in remuneration. But money went nowhere with him. I must wait until the following week. But now he would give me samples of what he could do, to whet my appetite – a few songs tossed overboard. He began to warm up, and might have spent the whole morning singing, had not our casual hostess brought our consultation to an end by offering us a cup of coffee. We parted for a few days.

As the district was new to me, I tried to find my bearings. The people at Ste Irénée were leisurely and old-fashioned. They greeted me as I went by. If I liked it, I could walk in and look at the homespuns, the bedspreads and *portières boutonnées* with lovely coloured designs. The flannel was brightly striped with red and apple green. Country chairs of maple retained their rich natural colour, but were mellowed with age; or they were painted lacquer red or sky blue – two tuneful colours that are the preference of rural Quebec . . .

The small villages inland, on the high plateau of the Laurentians, were also worth a visit. In the total absence of strangers, ancient customs thrived there, at Ste Angès, on two beautiful lakes; at St. Hilarion, on the hillside; at St. Paschal, where lived old Mailloux, the story teller; or in the valley up Whirlpool River (Rivière-du-Gouffre), which empties into the St. Lawrence at Baie St. Paul . . . Folk-songs were the fashion in those places – so I was told. People still gathered in "veillées" and revelled in the spell-binding tales of Père Mailloux, Marcel Tremblay, Jean Bouchard, and lesser folk entertainers.

So, to my entire satisfaction, I went up into the hills. For a week I lived there in fairyland, where the diet was poor and the beds made of straw. But it was all worth the experience. For, most of the time, I heard of enchanted kingdoms, some of them under the Red Sea, others on the Crystal Mountain, or a Thousand Leagues beyond the Sun . . .

When the day came for my appointment with Louis "the Blind," I wondered whether he would remember. Yes, he was there on the dot, his hair and beard neatly trimmed, but he was without a halo, quite the same as before. We sat down at once to work, I taking the narratives in shorthand and his songs on the phonograph. He seemed to enjoy this business-like way of dealing with his large repertory. Perhaps he felt flattered, as an artist, at this kind of tardy recognition from abroad.

One song followed another in quick succession, and I was greedy for more. All this was wealth to me. "Hola!" he would exclaim. "Friend, wait a minute! You mistake me for a song book. You turn the page and there is the thing! But here the devil is in the song (*le diable est dans la chanson*)." And he would turn his brain inside out to find the first line of the next song, which he knew well. The whole trouble was with the first word. Once he had it, the rest moved on like clockwork.

Before the end of the third day, my phonograph cylinders ran out, but ninety-three songs rested in my bag, and some of the best too. Never had I hoped for so many in so little time. As we had nothing to do for a few hours, Mme Simard, the hostess, decided to have "veillée." There I would hear more tales as they were usually told, with trimmings and the full gamut of histrionic work.

The "veillée" began early; even before dark all the guests had arrived. Père Mailloux was there, the most dramatic of folk tale tellers. His diction was fine and his delivery unmatched; he was a real artist. Mme Jean Bouchard, the singer of sad "complaintes," had come from Goose Cape (cap-aux-Oies); and several others were anxious to vie with each other in telling yarns and sharing in the fun.

Now the tale was told of the Princess du Tombozo, a princess that tricked Petit-Jean out of his magic treasures, but was the worse for her deceit in the end. Petit-Jean gave her plums from a fairy tree, which made her nose grow a foot long, for which reason she was named "Princess with a real nose." The next tales were of John the Bear, Birch Twister (Teur-Merisier), who could, as soon as he came of age, twist a birch tree between his fingers; Merlin, the hero of mediaeval literature; Red Heel (Talon-Rouge); and the Dragon with Seven Heads.

The people talked so much and so long that they grew thirsty. But there was only root beer to drink. Hm! not as in the good old days – the Golden Age not so long ago! The rum and the curaçao then flowed as if from a spring. Tears almost came to the eyes of those who had known better times. Bootleg pure and simple it was for sure, but the best and all of it so cheap, next to nothing!

The people along this coast were fine sailors. They used to travel long distances, to Anticosti, Newfoundland, and St. Pierre et Miquelon, and bring back barrels of fine spirits and liqueurs, which they hid in their barns. Then they passed it on to friends for a penny a drink. Bootleggers made quite a bit out of it, but never grew wealthy . . .

The "veillée" would not be complete without "the peg" and that meant one more tale from the blind nomad. Turning to him in jest, the folk exclaimed, "Ho hey! Louis, what are you doing there in the corner?

It's no time to pull a long face. Tell us that yarn about the haunted houses!"

He waited a moment, then began: "Haunted houses, hm! my young friends! But my throat is dry, it is parched!"

He stopped. It was time to give him a bit of whisky – an exception for him.

Clearing his throat, a mere habit, he said, "Now listen!" and you could not hear a breath. His audience was all ears . . .

2. CONTES POPULAIRES

The following are a few representative folktales from French Canada. Some of them reflect the long dominance of the Catholic religion in Quebec: French Canadians tell many religious legends, most of them dealing with the creation or the flood. The story of how God made the bee and the devil the toad, and the one about "The Winter of the Crows" are typical.

Those are examples of international legends, but the largest group of French-Canadian folktales are the "contes merveilleux" – the Märchen *or wonder tales classified as "Tales of Magic." They show little religious influence; indeed, many of them are thought to have their roots in a pre-Christian era. Most of their plots are widespread in Europe and Asia, and they illustrate the characteristics of the typical wonder tale: repetition by threes, an emphasis on trials and quests, the triumph of the youngest son, magic objects and supernatural helpers, marvelous transformations, and happy endings. In many, the hero is Ti-Jean – "Little John" – the French-Canadian counterpart of the Jack of the "Jack Tales" so popular in Anglo-American tradition. "Ti-Jean and the Big White Cat" is a good example of this large group.*

The next two tales are examples of a different category: "Jokes and Anecdotes." The religious influence is again evident in the story of Richard and his cards, and the story of the calf that was sold three times is a famous joke known throughout Europe. The last, "Jean Baribeau," is an example of a "Formula Tale" although it is somewhat more ingenious than the usual circular yarns.

THE BEE AND THE TOAD

When God had made the earth, the sun, the moon, and the stars, he put streams and trees and fruits upon the earth. Then he put Adam and Eve to live among them like a king and queen. They had everything they needed to make them happy. Among the thousand and one lavish sweet things, the bee should not be forgotten, this fine little insect that makes so much wax and honey. After the fall of the wicked angels, Lucifer, the leader of the infernal band, did everything he could to imitate or spoil the works of the All-Powerful.

One day when Adam and Eve were eating honey and delighting in this delicious food, Satan became jealous and looked for a way to spoil this source of their happiness. Creeping into their garden, he hid in a clump of briars near a beehive, and started to make a creature that would destroy the honey-bee.

As the good God had made the bee, which is the symbol of valour, of industry, and even of respect for authority (since the bees show so much respectful deference to their queen), that was a reason for Satan to want to destroy it.

He took a little earth and rolled it in his hands for a long time. When he had shaped this mud, he blew upon it three times, and muttered strange words, looking toward the beehive. Then he threw his newly-made creature in that direction.

But Satan was still new to the art of creation. He forgot to put wings on his new destructive friend which passed through the air and brushed against the honey-laden bees. They quickly lit on the branch of a tree, and the creature fell to the ground. Satan had made the toad. On falling it lay for a moment as though dead, and then it began to stir a little, then to gasp, and at last it breathed again.

Some bees who had left the swarm flew around in the air near the giddy creature; others soon followed to have a look at this new enemy unknown until then. The toad, waking up hungry, with the destructive instinct for which he had been created, started to jump and even managed to snap up some of the honey-bees that were circling around him.

From that day to this, wherever there are beehives, if you pass one in the evening at dusk and look carefully, you are sure to find one or more toads hidden near its mouth. They cannot help snapping as the bees enter and leave the hive. They are still ugly creatures, the living image of the devil who made them.

THE WINTER OF THE CROWS

After the patriarch Noah, following God's orders, had worked a hundred years to build the ark, he took on board it representatives of all the animal species on the earth, and lived there himself with his family.

Torrential rains fell from the sky and inundated first the valleys and plains and then the hills and even the highest mountains. The creatures living outside the ark perished down to the last one, save the fishes, and the ark, raised by the swelling waters, floated on the waves.

Much later, after the waters had gone back into the oceans, the lakes, and the rivers, Noah wished to make sure that the surface of the earth was again habitable. He opened a window and let out the raven, which until then had been the bird favoured from creation with bright and magnificent feathers and whose voice filled the air with joyful warblings.

"Fly over the surface of the earth," Noah commanded the raven. "If you find there any green trees, bring me a branch."

The raven saw some bodies floating in the water and, satisfying his voracious appetite, set out to devour them. He forgot his master's order, and no longer returned to the ark which had run aground on a mountain. Noah then cursed the raven for its faithlessness; his curse blackened the feathers of that bird and changed its warblings into a hoarse and plaintive croak.

The second time Noah sent the dove to look for green trees. The first time she returned with her beak empty; the second, she brought a green branch which bore fruit. The patriarch blessed the sweet messenger who became white and pretty, and who since has never ceased to be the bird beloved by all.

The time of liberation had come. Noah opened doors and windows and let out the captive species who spread out on all sides. As soon as he saw the crow, relative of the raven, flying past, he stopped it and, swayed by resentment, said to it: "You and your cousin the raven are condemned to travel forever without respite. Your tastes will be voracious and bloody, and your voices will break out in lugubrious cries. At your approach the elements will rouse up and by their anger chase you from their presence."

The crow, pursued by all the winged folk, fled uttering lamentable cries. It took refuge in a deserted spot, then wandered alone and abandoned. For nourishment it gulped down the flesh that remained on the dead bodies beached in the slime. It met one day its cousin the raven who, like it, nourished himself on carrion. The crow and the raven, knowing themselves forever banished from the presence of man, bound themselves in friendship in their misfortune, and driven by remorse went away far toward the north.

52

After a long and painful journey they perched to rest on a tree in the midst of a great forest of pine and fir trees where peace and silence reigned. This forest had been one of ours, in Canada, for a long time. The ground, covered by a mantle of snow, had not the customary gloom of their deserts. The rays of the sun had here and there pierced through this white mantle, making it spotted. Everything smiled on the fugitives, who believed themselves at last sheltered from the opprobrium of man and nature.

The illusion of the raven and the crow did not last long. Early the next day their awakening was painful. The north winds, stirring at their approach, blew up a storm, and the sky, filled with threatening clouds, made the snowflakes swirl. The cold, coming from the north, gnawed piercingly into the exiles. They resumed their flight in front of the protests of the forest which refused them asylum.

Every year since that time the crows emigrate toward Canada at the coming of spring, and the forest rises up against them because of the curse of Noah.

The old man who, one spring a long time ago, told this legend to Adélard Lambert, of Berthier, began by these words: "Today the weather is fine, but it won't last long. I've seen three crows; they passed on the wing, going south. They seemed pursued by an invisible phantom."

At this explanation his wife added: "By passing they announced the little winter. Poor crows! They are paying very dear for a folly that dates back so far that one has almost forgotten it. And to say that they are condemned to undergo this injury right to the end of time!"

The same evening she told at length the legend of the crows to the children who questioned her; and she saw, with satisfaction, in their eyes the impression that her tale made on her small audience. She finished with the words: "If God's anger falls like that on the simple birds who were cursed by Noah, how much more his punishments will weigh on the faithless man who disobeys his commandments and scorns his representatives."

TI-JEAN AND THE BIG WHITE CAT

There is a king who has three sons. One is called Jean, another, Cordon-bleu, and the other, Cordon-vert. One day the king says to them: "All three of you are now of age. The one who will fetch the finest horse will have my crown." The boys rig themselves up, go out and walk . . . When they reach the fork of three roads Cordon-vert says: "I take this road." Cordon-bleu adds: "And I, this road," and Ti-Jean finishes: "And I the other road." Before separating they agree: "On a certain day we will all return to the fork of the roads."

My Ti-Jean walks and walks right to the end of the road. There he takes a little path into the forest and walks. Arriving near a little straw hut, he sees a big white cat drawing water with four toads. He sits down and watches. The cat, having filled a tank with water, unhitches her four toads and *rrnyao, rrnyao*, dips herself in it. And from the tank comes a fine princess, such as Ti-Jean has never seen. She asks him: "What are you looking for?" "A horse," replies he; "we are three brothers, and our father the king has promised his crown to the one who leads back the finest horse." The princess tells him: "Tomorrow morning I will again be the big white cat that you have seen. You will go into my stable and take the finest of my toads. When you return to your father's you will harness him and the next day he will become the finest horse in the land."

Just like that, the next morning Ti-Jean takes the toad and rides it away, *patati, patata*. At the three roads he meets his brothers whose horses are very fine. Looking at Ti-Jean and his toad they say: "Don't show yourself like that to our father or you'll kill yourself." But he comes behind them, *patati, patata*, whipping his mount with a little willow switch. "Don't come with us," they say, "it's a real disgrace." "That doesn't matter, let's go." They arrive at their father's late in the day and put their horses in the stable. Ti-Jean uses the comb on his toad, *perarrar*. And his brothers say: "You're going to break our father's comb." "Papa can afford another one."

The next morning Cordon-bleu and Cordon-vert rise and go to show their fine horses to the king. "And Ti-Jean?" he asks. They reply: "Oh, him? He has a toad." "A toad? I must see it." Ti-Jean rises after the others. His toad is the finest horse that has ever been seen, with a silver mane and golden shoes. "Ah!" cries the king, "it's Ti-Jean who has won, he has the finest horse. But you know that a king has three tests. Now the one of you who will bring me the finest hand-woven cloth will have my crown." And the three go out on their horses. Reaching the fork of the three roads, Cordon-bleu says: "I take the same road." Cordon-vert also takes the same. "I also take mine," finishes Ti-Jean, and sets out. He walks and walks, reaches the little path, and from there to the little house covered with straw. The big white cat is still drawing water with her three toads. Ti-Jean sits down and watches them do it. Once the tank is full, *rrnyao, rrnyao*, the white cat dips herself in the tank and comes out a fine princess. She says, "This time, my Ti-Jean, what are you looking for?" He replies: "I'm looking for the finest homespun that my father has ever seen." "Tomorrow morning," replies the princess, "I'll again become a big white cat. You will look in my small chest of drawers and you will take the ugliest walnut that you find there and put

54

it in your pocket. When you reach your father's you will slit it with a knife and it will become thirty ells of the finest cloth ever seen."

Cordon-bleu and Cordon-vert meet at the three roads. Oh, what fine cloth they have! But Ti-Jean, having put the nut in his pocket, has nothing. One of his brothers asks him: "Ti-Jean, I think you have nothing?" To which he replies, "I think that with all the cloth you have, my father will have enough."

At their father the king's next morning, they rise and go to show their cloth. Their cloth is beautiful. That of Cordon-vert especially is unequalled. "As for Ti-Jean, I think he has nothing." But Ti-Jean arrives and gives the nut to his father, saying: "Split this on the table with a knife." The king splits the nut and it becomes thirty ells of the finest cloth that he has ever seen. He says, "It's Ti-Jean who has won again. But you know a king has three tests. Next there remains still one thing to do." "What is that?" they ask. "The one who will fetch the most beautiful woman will have my crown, and this time, it is the end." They all go out again, Cordon-vert and Cordon-bleu on their horses and Ti-Jean on his toad. Cordon-bleu says: "I'll take the same road again." Cordon-vert: "And me too." And Ti-Jean: "I also take mine." He walks and walks, and Ti-Jean reaches the little hut covered with straw, and sees again the big white cat drawing water with her toads. *Rrnyao, rrnyao*, the cat plunges into the tank full of water and comes out a beautiful princess. Ti-Jean falls on his back with admiration, so beautiful does he find her. "Tell me then, Ti-Jean, what are you looking for on your third trip here?" And he replies: "You know my father the king has three tests. He has said, 'The one who brings me the most beautiful girl, it's the last, he will have my crown.'" And he adds: "Now I have never seen on this earth one more beautiful than you." She says: "I am transformed, and I will become a princess again only if the king's son marries me." Ti-Jean says: "Good!" "Tomorrow morning," adds she, "I will again be a big white cat. You will hitch my four toads to my carriage, and we will go together."

The next morning, Ti-Jean rises and sees the princess transformed. He hitches the toads to the carriage and seats himself on the small seat, the big white cat beside him. In this way she brushes against him, walks on his knees, and rubs her cheeks against his, *rrnyao, rrnyao*!

His brothers reach the fork of the three roads. By God, they have beautiful girls! Then they look at Ti-Jean with his white cat and the four toads and say: "That's the limit. Ti-Jean is going to kill himself." And they are delighted. "With that old carriage and those four toads, he's nothing to us." "Let's go, then," replies he. There he is behind them, whipping the toads with a switch, while the white cat brushes against his face mewing *rrnyao, rrnyao*. The three brothers reach their father's, Ti-Jean leads the white cat into his room and goes to brush his toads, *bring, brang, brang*! "Ti-Jean, you're going to break your father's comb." "Our father can get another."

In the morning the king finds that Cordon-vert and Cordon-bleu have some beautiful girls. He asks: "Ti-Jean?" "Oh, he has a big white cat." "Be that as it may, I must see her." And my Ti-Jean comes in holding his princess by the hand. It isn't that the king can't believe it, he has never seen so beautiful a girl in his life. Having hitched the toads, Ti-Jean arrives with four unequalled horses and a carriage such as no one has ever seen. The three brothers go away together to marry their girls, Ti-Jean marrying the princess. "It's my Ti-Jean who has won my crown," says the king, and, raising it from his head, bang, he puts it on Ti-Jean's head.

And so it goes . . . I was at the wedding. But since then, I haven't seen those people, and I don't know how things go over there.

RICHARD'S CARDS

One day a man named Richard is passing a church and goes in to hear the holy Mass.

Richard goes to a pew by the wall where you hear and see the best. There, instead of taking a book of devotions from his pocket, he drew out a deck of cards. The constable's finger motions him to leave the church. But Richard does not move. The constable goes to him and says, "Instead of amusing yourself with a deck of cards, take a book of devotions." Richard replies, "After Mass I'll explain my deck of cards to you."

The Mass over, the priest and the constable come to reproach Richard, who replies: "If you'll let me, I'll explain my deck of cards." "Speak, Richard," replied the priest, "I'll let you." Richard draws the deuce and says: "The deuce represents to me the two Testaments." Drawing the trey: "The trey reminds me of the three persons of the Holy Trinity; the four represents the four evangelists; the five, the five books of Moses; the six represents the six days that God took to create heaven and earth; and the seven, the day when He rested, after the creation." Drawing the eight, he said, "The eight reminds me of the eight people saved from the Flood." Drawing the nine . . . (the nine ungrateful lepers). Drawing the ten: "The ten represents God's Ten Commandments." Drawing the Queen: "She reminds me of the Queen of Heaven." Drawing the King: "The King represents the only Master to Whom I owe obedience." Drawing the ace: "The one and same God Whom I adore."

The priest says, "Richard, I notice that you've missed the Jack." "Father, if you'll let me speak, I'll satisfy you." "Speak, Richard, I'll let you." "Father, the Jack represents to me a real rascal, just like your constable here."

THE CALF SOLD THREE TIMES

There was a poor devil of a habitant who ended by drinking all his wealth. He had left only a young spring calf. He goes out then to sell it, in order to have some money to drink.

On the way he meets the village doctor whom he knew well. He stops him and says: "Well, friend, won't you buy a fine calf this morning?" "How much?" "A sovereign." "Done." And the doctor pays for the calf and tells the habitant to bring him to his house for he was called to a patient and couldn't take him home at the moment.

The habitant continues on his way and soon meets the notary. "Well, friend, won't you buy a fine calf this morning?" "How much?" "A sovereign." "Done." And, like the doctor, the notary pays and tells the habitant to lead the calf to his place for he was called to an invalid's home to draw up a will.

Some distance before reaching the village the habitant meets the lawyer and says to him: "Well, friend, won't you buy a fine calf this morning?" "How much?" "A sovereign." "Done. Take him to my home for I have to go to the next village on pressing business."

The habitant goes then to the village, stops at a tavern, spends his silver, then climbs into his wagon, taking his calf home with him.

The doctor, the notary, and the lawyer were very surprised on returning to find that the habitant hadn't delivered the calf bought that morning. They spoke together and finally decided to arrest the dishonest habitant. The latter goes to find a lawyer in a neighbouring place and confides his case to him. The lawyer, listening to the account of the case that's been entrusted to him, says: "Your case, sir, is very difficult to defend. Your dishonest act is too clear. However, there's one way of winning this case. Each time that the judge or prosecutor asks you a question, you reply only with these words: 'Oink, oink, oink!'"

And so when the time of the trial comes, the judge, addressing himself to the habitant, questions him thus: "Sir, have you sold a calf to the doctor here?" "Oink, oink, oink," replies the habitant. "Also to the notary?" "Oink, oink, oink." "Is it the same calf that you sold to the lawyer?" "Oink, oink, oink." "But you haven't delivered your merchandise to these gentlemen." "Oink, oink, oink." "Why haven't you delivered what you sold?" "Oink, oink, oink." After several questions, the judge, receiving no other reply, says: "You see, sirs, that this man is crazy. I order that he be let go in peace."

The lawyer engaged to defend the habitant goes to find him and says joyfully: "Now that I've won your case, you're going to pay me for my work." "Oink, oink, oink," was the reply that he received. "See here, it's ten dollars, you're not going to be begged to pay me." "Oink, oink, oink." "See here, you can't put on that lunacy with me. It's I who have won for you." "Oink, oink, oink." "See here, must I get angry to make you pay?" "Oink, oink, oink." And the defender, no more than the doctor, the notary, and the lawyer, got no other satisfaction. Which proves that in this little case as in many others, the lawyer and the habitant had learned nothing about honesty.

JEAN BARIBEAU

Jean Baribeau was born to poor parents who were thieves. They who loved him with a most tender love drove him away from their house at the age of three. Then he headed toward the capital to complete his studies.

But the political struggles and the sorrows of love led him soon to the gates of the tomb. They called in the most renowned doctors, and thanks to their enlightened care he died. His fiancée erected a magnificent monument on which these words were carved: "Here lies Jean Baribeau, born of poor parents who were thieves. They loved him with the most tender love . . . . " (Begin again and repeat at will.)

(After some recriminations from the listeners that this repetition is boring, the story-teller pretends to leave the vicious circle in which he turns, and changes the story thus:)

His fiancée gave him the most magnificent funeral. Everyone wept; the chief of the firemen wept into his helmet. When his helmet was already full, a tear slid, fell, germinated, sprouted. The king's son, passing by, tripped, fell, killed himself. His father, who loved him to distraction, gave him a magnificent funeral. Everyone wept; the chief of the firemen wept . . . . (Begin again.)

(After having thus made fun of his listeners twice, the story-teller can usually enjoy a well-earned rest.)

3. LEGENDES

Where the "contes populaires" are recognized as fictional and use ancient plots known in many countries, the "légendes" or "anecdotes populaires" are told as true stories and are more closely linked to a particular area. They are local legends rather than international folktales, and hence reflect more closely the beliefs, traditions, and customs of the rural French Canadians. An assortment of one hundred anecdotes published in 1920 dealt with such subjects as hidden treasures, lutins *(goblins),* feux follets *(will-o-the-wisps), the* chasse galerie *(flying canoe),* loups garous *(werewolves), sorcerers, and encounters with the devil. Many of them use widespread motifs, but they are all nicely localized and told as true.*

Perhaps the most popular of all the French-Canadian legends is the one variously titled "Rose Latulippe," "Le Diable à la danse," or "Le Diable, beau danseur." The following version, which Dr. J.-E.-A. Cloutier of Cap-Sainte-Ignace, Montmagny, gave to Dr. Barbeau in 1919, came from several people in l'Islet, but mostly from the octogenarian widow of Joseph Caron. Dr. Cloutier's version is more detailed than most, and shows clearly the influence of religion on the local legends. It gives a good picture of social gatherings in rural Quebec, and includes many words and phrases from the local idiom.

The second legend, about the encounter with the devil in the form of a dog, illustrates the firm belief characteristic of legends, with the assurance that the narrator heard it from the very woman involved, and the third, about the competition between two wizards, is nicely localized in a farming community.

THE DEVIL AT THE DANCE

They were very good people in the home of François C . . . , not proud, religious, charitable to the poor, not haughty. They owned little. Besides, straight as the king's sword. And when they were selling they gave generous measure, always a good trait. They never spoke ill of anyone; and they never missed the First Friday of the month. Why, to tell all, they were first-class people.

It isn't often that they had a dance in this house. But the reason, this year, was that young François, their son, had just returned from a great trip to a distant country with Captain Basile Droy. They had to have a feast for his arrival.

Always at François C . . . 's home there'd be a great party the day after Twelfth Night. After supper a great many guests came, a lot of young people especially. They followed the great Dédé from the top of the island who was a fine fiddler and singer. It disturbed Mother Catherine when she saw many come who weren't invited, but she was too good natured to make a fuss. After all, they were all childhood friends of young François.

Toward nine o'clock the great musician took out his fiddle from its fine varnished case. He began to pass the rosin over the bow. Then *zing,*

zing, he started to chord. Ho, then, some hymn tunes, some songs: "Nouvelle agréable," "Ça bergers," "En roulant ma boule." After that it was some simple jigs, and then reels. Why, one could never miss the chance to hear such fine music!

Young François, with Germain Chiasson, little Blanche's suitor, and José Moreau, who was nicknamed "Golden Throat" because of his fine talk, went to call his father into the study to speak to him in private. There he asked permission to dance some rigadoons. There's nothing wrong with that, is there? Father François had to be begged because of the priest's sermons, and also the unexpected guests, some of whom smelled of liquor. He went to consult his wife. Why, it was too bad to refuse this to young François who'd just returned from such a long voyage. So he gave permission.

As soon as he agreed, they cleared the middle of the room. Everyone settled around the kitchen. Old François opened the dance with his wife Catherine, in a simple jig with not a few flourishes, I'm telling you. Of fine steps there were many. I tell you that for old people of their age, it wasn't easy to match them. It was Pierre, his son, who came to relieve them with his wife, Manda Berton. They were two fine dancers also, but they didn't beat Father François and his wife, oh, no!

The great Dédé played like one possessed, tapping his heel, which there was nothing so fine to hear. He wasn't controllable, this lad, when he had a little shot. They organized reels, *casse-reels*, cotillions, *spendys*, "*salut-des-dames*" . . . The great Dédé seemed set for twenty-four hours. Between dances he stopped just long enough to take a little shot, then hurrying back, played all kinds of things – dances, songs, hymns, even laments. It went like real wildfire!

At eleven o'clock there was a little lull to catch breath. Suddenly they heard some small bells, then the sound of a sleigh which slid over the ice. *Crunch*! it said.

After a little while there's a knock on the door. "Come in," says Pierre. The door opens, then they see a tall handsome man with curly hair and a fine black beard cut to a point. He had lively black eyes which seemed to throw sparks. He had a fine beaver cloak, with a fine sealskin cape. He also had very fine moccasins of caribou, decorated with beads in thirty-six colours, and porcupine quills, also dyed all kinds of colours. He looked like a real gentleman, indeed! Then, just imagine! A fine sleigh gleaming like a mirror, with fine buffalo skins, a fine glossy black horse, with a white harness that had cost five or six gold coins. He looked unbelievably vigorous, this horse. He was all covered with hoar frost. All the horse dealers went around him to have a good look, but no one recognized him. He must have come from a distance. They offered to unharness him for the gentleman, but he refused, saying it wasn't worth the trouble, that he'd just put the fur robe on his back. He wouldn't be long. When passing he'd seen that people were enjoying themselves and he came in to dance a couple of dances.

They offered to take his wraps. He took off his cloak and cap but he wouldn't remove his kid gloves. The young people thought that was to show off, like city gentlemen, who did that, it seemed. At all events, I tell you that he certainly looked nice, that unexpected guest, and I assure you that the young women were strutting around and eyeing him. They wanted to know who would have the honour of dancing with this fine cavalier. But as he was a great gentleman who knew how things were done, he went to ask the daughter of the house, Mamselle Blanche, who was not to be overlooked, you know. She was a fine-looking girl who had manners and a good bearing; she was a little shy at first; it took away some of her confidence. Imagine it, then, to dance with this gentleman before everyone, it was embarrassing. Also when he asked her like this: "Mademoiselle, will you do me the honour to dance with me?" she replied, blushing and trembling a little: "With pleasure, sir, but excuse me, I don't know how to dance very well." The little hypocrite, she knew very well that she was one of the best dancers on the island.

He wasn't only a beautifully dressed gentleman, this guest, my children; he was also a very fine dancer indeed, I assure you. Father François couldn't believe it and he was all dumbfounded: "My, my, what a fine dancer he is," he didn't tire of repeating to himself. He didn't know where he got all these steps. "He invents them, he invents them," he repeated endlessly.

He had begun by dancing a simple jig that lasted a good half hour. The fellow seemed infallible. After little Blanche, all the best dancers at the party were rising in turn to face him, but he was coping with them all. He didn't seem tired as he came to make his first bow to his partner.

Several young men tried to replace him, but they lost the step quickly and he signed to them by waving with his arms to return to their place. After that he jigged two or three fine flourishes which were really something to see.

One would say that there was a game between the fiddler and him, to see which would outlast the other. Dédé was starting to feel weak, he was finding the game a little hard. He was sweating heavily. He was much too proud to slow up. He seemed rather to catch fire little by little, one would say that he was getting inspired. I'm telling you, the dust was flying under his feet, and he was tapping his heels always without losing a beat.

But suddenly *crack*, a broken string! Oh, the wretch, he had done it on purpose. Luckily, he had some spare strings. Meanwhile, while he restrung, it gave him time to catch his breath a little. The guest of honour took advantage of it to organize a spendy, with the participation of course of the handsome stranger who during that time was flirting with all the girls.

At last the fiddle was restrung. Dédé, replenished with a good shot of rum, seemed as fresh as at the beginning of the party.

"Gentlemen, pray take your place for a spendy," cried José Moreau in his fine singing voice, and they form up with more enthusiasm than ever. All this commotion finally ended by waking Pierre's little boy who was two years old. As Manda, who was doing the honours of the house, was too busy to take care of him, Grandmother Catherine had taken him on her knee, and then to amuse him she sat with him right in the door of the bedroom where the little one could enjoy the whirling of the dancers. But each time the fine strange dancer passed before the child, he uttered cries of fright, and, gripping the old woman around the neck, he cried: "Bur . . . bur . . . burning, sir, burn . . . burning!" "I say, how strange he is this evening," Catherine said to herself. As these fits were repeated each time the dancer passed before the child, the old woman began to find this funny; then, suddenly she noticed that the stranger's black eyes pierced the child with looks full of hatred.

He was dancing at this time with a young girl who wore a fine golden cross on her neck. As he passed below her, Grandmother Catherine heard him ask the girl if she would exchange this cross for a fine locket decorated with diamonds and containing his portrait. She rose, ran into the bedroom where a small jug of holy water stood at the head of the bed. She dipped her trembling old fingers in it and, still holding the child in her arms, she came through the door, making a sign of the cross over the dancer. It was magical and frightening. The Devil – for it was he in person – leaped to the ceiling, uttering a hellish cry. He wanted to spring toward the door but he saw over it a temperance cross mounted on a holly bough. Mad with rage, Satan threw himself through the stone wall, leaving behind him a great hole in the dark stone. Then they heard a fearful uproar outside. The Devil and his horse disappeared into the night; a trail of flames flashed under the horse's feet.

Everyone came out appalled, and saw that the ice was completely melted where the infernal horse had touched. It hardly needs saying that the party broke up then.

Next day a bricklayer came to fill up the hole where the Devil had passed, but he never succeeded. Each stone that he tried to put in seemed possessed by an unknown force, and nothing would make it stay in place. They had the house blessed again, but the opening still remains, as if God wished to give a continual warning.

The old stone house stands today. Facing the hole in the room there is always a chest of drawers where they set holy candles, and outside the wall you see all year round a cord of stove wood piled.

But since then they never dance in the stone house of François C . . . .

THE BLACK DOG AT THE WICKED ROCK

The Wicked Rock (in Notre-Dame-du-Portage, Temiscouta) got its name from the tricks the Devil played. I heard one of the stories of these tricks told by the very people who knew what happened.

It was a woman who was married to Noel Perrault. At that time there was no doctor in the country, but there were some skilful women, mid-wives who had a special gift for healing. One fine day a birth was expected at the home of one of Mme Perrault's brothers, named Perron. The time come, Perron, whose house was near the Wicked Rock, went to look for Mme Perrault, who was staying with M. Michaud. Arriving there, he says, "My wife needs you; come quickly." They go in haste, together, down the bank. As soon as they pass the end of the road by the brook, a big black dog faces them. The man is frightened. It's terrible. The woman says, "You're afraid? Just brace yourself a little. It's a dog like any other." "Ah," he says, "It isn't a dog like any other." The dog did everything it could to prevent them from walking. Perron had to kick it to the side of the road in order to go on. Mme Perrault said: "Don't upset yourself by fighting with the dog." She takes him by the arm and she drags him. The dog is always under their feet but he doesn't bite them.

They had three or four arpents to go. Before arriving, the dog comes in front of Perron and puts his two paws on his shoulders; he couldn't go ahead. The woman was brave – me, I know it – she helped him. They succeeded in getting right to the house, but the dog doesn't take his paws from his shoulders. When they reach the door, in leaving the dog says, "Your wife is dead." The goodwife Perrault says, "You lie; she isn't dead." The woman wasn't dead, but she was near death.

This story I give you as I heard it told. It is Mother Perrault herself who told it.

THE WIZARD'S WHITE MAGIC

There were some men who passed for wizards – Alexis Dulac and big Jacquot, of Saint-François (Beauce). They both feared each other. Each claimed to have more skill than the other in giving charms and making magic.

One day Alexis was threshing with the flail in his barn. When big Jacquot passed, he knew of this. He says to himself, "We must see today which of us two is the stronger." He goes into the barn and says: "Today we are going to see which of us two is the most powerful. Can you make the water of the Chaudière River come into your barn?" It was almost a hundred and fifty feet to the river from the barn. Alexis replies, "I can't, nor can you either." On this big Jacquot says, "You're going to see if I can't." Suddenly there is thunder, flashes of lightning, and the water of the Chaudière starts to get ruffled, to boil up, and flow toward the barn. It takes only an instant for the water to reach the barn door. The water comes into the barn. When Alexis sees it in his threshing room, he climbs on the partition. Immediately the water reaches the partition. He climbs on the beam. When he was on the beam he looks outside the barn through the door; he sees that the water will soon be as high as the door. He says, "The cursed one is going to drown me in my barn." From the beam he takes a spring and dives into the threshing room. There isn't a drop of water. He just missed killing himself in the fall.

It was white magic. Dulac told this to his son; it's his son that I heard tell it, and also another son, Pierre Dulac.

4. LA COMPLAINTE DE CADIEUX
Joseph-Charles Taché

The legend of the death of Cadieux is one of the earliest and most widespread of the native French-Canadian tales, and his "complainte" is believed to be the first song composed in Canada about a Canadian incident. Cadieux is said to have died in 1709, and by 1800 his story was known to almost every voyageur. Many early travellers and fur-traders mention the legend, and at least thirteen different versions of the song have been collected.

Dr. Barbeau noted that George Nelson was the first to write of the story in his manuscript Journal of 1802, where he spoke of a canoe that had "a miraculous escape" and of "one unfortunate creature" who was found dead "in a hole he had himself dug out with a paddle." Then about 1820 John J. Bigsby heard the same tale incorporated in a song. There is some evidence that the story was based on a real incident, but it very early acquired such legendary details as the vision of the Virgin Mary that guided the canoe, and the verses written in blood on a sheet of birchbark.

One of the most complete accounts of the story and song appeared in Joseph-Charles Taché's Forestiers et voyageurs, first published as a book in 1884 and frequently reprinted. The following is a fairly literal translation.

I was speaking to you a moment ago about the wars with the Indians; now I'm going to tell you the story of a brave Canadian who played a great role in one of these wars.

64

Going up the great Ottawa River no one fails to stop at the Little Rock of the High Mountain in the middle of the Seven Falls portage, below Grand Calumet Island: there is the grave of Cadieux, of which everyone has heard.

Every time the company canoes pass the Little Rock an old voyageur tells the young men the story of Cadieux; the old voyageurs who have already heard it like to hear it again, when they don't retell it themselves. This time it was old Morache, an elderly guide, who unfolded to us the story of Cadieux's adventures.

Cadieux was a voyageur-interpreter married to an Algonquin woman; he usually spent the winter hunting and the summer dealing with the natives on behalf of the merchants. It was the time of the last Iroquois' expeditions: Cadieux had spent the hunting season at Seven Falls portage where he lived with some other families: it was then the month of May and Cadieux was waiting for the natives from the Island and the Courte-Oreille (Ottawas) who would be going down to Montreal with their furs at the same time as he.

The greatest peace reigned in the huts at Little Rock, when one fine day a young brave, who was roaming around the rapids and the lower portage, arrived all out of breath in the midst of the families scattered among the huts, and cried: "The Iroquois! The Iroquois!"

Apparently an Iroquois war party was at that moment only a league below the Seven Falls portage: they knew it was the time when the canoes went down the Grand River on their way from the hunting grounds, and they wished to attack.

There was only one way to escape: to try to run the rapids, a thing almost unheard of, for, as old Morache said, they are not thick and fast, the canoes that run the Seven Falls!

But that was not all, however: someone would have to stay to make a diversion, drawing the Iroquois into the woods, and stopping them from seeing what was happening once they began the portage. For those who know the Iroquois of that period will easily understand that without such a stratagem, the sight of the fresh tracks left by the families would lead them immediately to split into two bands, one going up and the other down the river in pursuit of the fugitives.

Cadieux, as the most capable and expert of all, assumed the dangerous but unselfish mission, taking with him a young Algonquin in whose courage and loyalty he had perfect confidence. Their end achieved, Cadieux and his companion planned to take the surest road to rejoin their people, who would send to meet them if there was too much delay.

They left the cabins: once their preparations were made, Cadieux and his young companion, armed with their guns, axes, and knives, and furnished with some provisions, left to cut off the Iroquois. It was agreed that the canoes would leave the shelter of the river and shoot the rapids as soon as they heard the sound of rifle shots from the direction of the portage.

An hour had not passed before a rifle shot rang out, followed soon by another, then by several. During the struggle, in the noise of the shots, the canoes, caught up in the terrible currents, bounded through the bubbles and foam, plunged and rose on the crest of the waves that carried them into their course. The skilled oarsmen, men and women, at both ends of each canoe, guided their movements, avoiding the sharp points of the rocks, and holding with their paddles those frail bark canoes in the most favourable stream of water shown by the state of the tops of the waves and the shape of the currents.

They had, on taking off, commended themselves to the good Ste Anne, and they prayed most sincerely all the time.

"I saw nothing in the Seven Falls," later said Cadieux's wife, who was a pious woman, "I saw nothing but a noble Lady in white who hovered over the canoes and showed us the way!"

The canoes were saved and arrived in a few days beyond reach of their enemies at Two Mountains Lake. But what were Cadieux and his Indian doing during this time, and what became of them? This is what happened, as was learned much later from some Iroquois and the people sent to meet the brave interpreter.

Cadieux had first let the Iroquois enter the portage. After choosing the most favourable spot for keeping out of sight of the river, he lay in ambush a short distance from the path, well hidden in the thick bushes; he had at the same time hidden his companion on some higher ground to give the impression of several parties as the fighting went on.

Cadieux let pass the Iroquois scouts, who scanned the edge of the path, and the first warrior canoe-bearers, until, the enemies having reached the spot where the young Algonquin was hidden, he heard the shot of the latter and the cry of a wounded enemy.

The Iroquois, thus suddenly attacked, jumped with surprise and stopped at once; but before the porters could even lay down their burdens, Cadieux fired a second shot into the midst of the train and struck down a second warrior.

Cadieux had probably arranged to meet his companion in a kind of small clearing a little removed from the portage, for it is towards this spot that both headed after successfully firing from the shelter of the bushes.

The advantage with which the two brave men attacked their many enemies did not keep the young Algonquin from falling under their blows. He did not rejoin Cadieux at the rendezvous; but he sold his life dearly.

For three days the Iroquois beat the forest to find the tracks of the families, not even imagining that they had been able to go down the rapids; for three days also they tracked the brave voyageur in the woods. Three days and three nights that were without sleep or rest for the unfortunate Cadieux! At the end of that time the invaders, despairing of finding the families and of beating their elusive adversary, convinced besides that they had lost the advantage of their foray, turned their canoes to go back down the Grand River.

Several days had passed since the families had left Little Rock; they learned that the Iroquois had gone back, and Cadieux had not yet arrived: three men set out then for the meeting place of the interpreter and his companion. The three voyageurs went back up the Ottawa right to the Portage of the Fort without finding any traces of what had happened; there they began to see signs of the Iroquois' passage, and above that signs that they recognized as showing that their friend had stayed in the vicinity.

When, arriving at the portage of the Seven Falls, they found a little shelter built of branches which seemed to have been abandoned, they resolved to push their search a little farther in case Cadieux and his companion had perhaps been obliged to go up the river to take refuge with the Island Indians.

Two days later, the thirteenth since Cadieux and the families separated, they retraced their steps after having consulted the Indians who met them, certain that their two friends were back at Two Mountains Lake or dead.

In passing again near the Little Rock, they saw, far away on the edge of the portage path, beside the little shelter that they had thought abandoned some days earlier, a wooden cross which they approached with respect mixed with a strange wonder.

The cross was planted at the head of a grave, scarcely hollowed out in the ground, and in this grave lay the still fresh corpse of Cadieux, half buried in green branches. The dead hands were crossed on his breast, on which lay a large sheet of birchbark covered with writing.

The voyageurs picked up this bark which could reveal to them the mystery of their friend's death and explain the extraordinary circumstances; one of them who could read, read the words confided to this wooden paper, and re-read them several times, facing the scarcely cold body of the brave Cadieux.

From what they saw and what was written on the bark, the voyageurs concluded that poor Cadieux, his mind spent by fatigue, lack of sleep, anxiety, and privation, had ended, as is almost always the case in such circumstances, by wandering blindly until he came back to the same place he had left; that once there he had lain without plans, according to the phrase of old Morache, for several days, sustained by fruits and a little hunting, without making a fire in his little shelter for fear of the Iroquois, getting weaker from day to day; that at the time they passed this spot two days earlier, he had recognized them after investigation, but that the burst of joy gave him such a shock that he lay without word or movement; that after they left, at last having lost hope, feeling himself near to death and gathering a little strength in these solemn moments, he had, after writing his last farewell to the world of the living, prepared his sepulchre, set his cross on his tomb, placed himself in his grave, and heaped up over him as best he could the branches with which his body was covered, to wait thus, in prayer, the death that he knew could not be long in coming.

Cadieux was a voyageur, poet, and warrior; what he had written on the bark was his death chant. Before lying down in this cold tomb by the Seven Falls portage, the imagination of one who had so lived with nature was exalted, and, as he was accustomed to compose voyageur songs, he had written his last song on this wooden sheet.

He addressed himself first, in this death chant, to those who gathered round him, announcing his approaching end and his regrets in leaving life; then he speaks of his sufferings, of the anxiety he feels for the families that he had brought together in his care, whom he calls friends. He speaks of his terrible fears at the sight of the smoke of a camp near his shelter, of his too great satisfaction in recognizing the French faces, of his powerlessness to call them and to dart forth toward them, of their departure without being aware of his presence, and of his desolation.

Cadieux sees a wolf and a crow coming to smell his sick body; by calling on the gaiety of the hunter and the pride of the forest warrior, he threatens one with his gun and tells the other to go feast on the corpses of the Iroquois he had killed.

He then charges the nightingale, companion of his sleepless nights, to carry his farewells to his wife and his children whom he loved so much; then, like the good Christian he is, he places himself in the hands of his Creator and recommends himself to the protection of Mary.

Some voyageurs claimed that Cadieux did not know how to write and that the fact of this song written on the bark could be, consequently, only the result of a miracle, but Cadieux, without being educated, knew how to write like all the interpreters of that period. Always this thing has been seen as it is told.

Here is that lament of Cadieux which he wrote on bark at the Little Rock of the Seven Falls, after placing himself in the grave hollowed out by his own hands:

> Little rock on the high mountain,
> I come here to end this campaign.
> Ah, sweet echoes, hear my sighs!
> Languishing, I am soon going to die.

Little birds, your sweet harmonies
When you sing draw me again toward life.
Ah, if I had wings like you
I would be happy within two days!

Alone in these woods where I am worried,
Thinking always of my dearest friends,
I ask "Alas! are they drowned?
Have the Iroquois killed them?"

One of those days when I went away,
On returning I saw smoke;
I said to myself, "Ah, great God, what is that?
Have the Iroquois taken my home?"

I went a little to the side
To see if it was an ambush;
Then I saw three French faces
Which filled my heart with great joy!

My knees folded, my feeble voice stopped,
I fell down. Alas! they prepared to go away:
I remained alone . . . No one to console me
When death comes with such great desolation.

A howling wolf comes near my cabin
To see if my fire no longer crackles.
I tell him: "Go away from here
For by my faith I see your coat."

A black crow flying at random
Comes to perch beside my roof.
I tell him: "Eater of human flesh,
Go to look for other food than me.

"Go back there, in the woods and swamp
You will find several Iroquois bodies;
You will find some flesh, also some bone;
Go farther away, leave me in peace!"

Nightingale, go tell my wife,
Tell my children, that I take my leave of them,
That I have kept my love and my faith,
And henceforth they must give me up.

It is here then that the world abandons me,
But I have aid from you, Saviour of men!
Very Holy Virgin, ah, do not abandon me.
Allow me to die between your arms!

The three Canadians wept as they read the brave Cadieux's death chant on the bark. They strengthened the wooden cross, filled up the grave holding the remains of this great man, raised a mound over the solitary tomb, and prayed for the peace of their friend's soul.

The bark on which Cadieux's lament was written was taken to the Lake post; the voyageurs set an appropriate air to this song, so typical of the rude life of the hunter and forest warrior, so surprising in its thoughts and so worthy of note because of the circumstances of its composition.

They were in the habit of keeping a copy of the lament as written on the bark fastened to a tree near Cadieux's grave at the Seven Falls portage. This was still done in my time, and it is in the same spot that I learned Cadieux's story, of which the voyageurs are so proud.

5. CHANSONS D'ACADIE

Although most French Canadians live in Quebec, there are also many in other provinces, notably the Maritimes and Ontario. The Acadians of the east coast are particularly distinctive: they trace their history back to Champlain's founding of Port Royal in 1604: a settlement famous for the nightly banquets of the Order of Good Cheer where the old folk songs were sung. During the next two and a half centuries Acadia changed rulers frequently as the English and French warred over their North American colonies. In 1755, on the brink of the Seven Years' War, the Acadians of the Annapolis Valley were expelled and dispersed among the English colonies along the Atlantic coast, some making their way down to Louisiana where they became known as Cajuns. However, many escaped deportation by fleeing to the woods and then taking refuge with other French settlers in areas that later became New Brunswick and Prince Edward Island. Later some of the Acadians who had been deported returned to the Maritimes, and to-day their descendants form a substantial part of the population of all three Maritime Provinces.

The Acadian folklore naturally has much in common with that of the Québecois, but it also has some individual characteristics. The three Acadian songs that follow are unusual, reflecting three different elements of French-Canadian folklore. The first, "*Où vas-tu, mon petit garçon?*" was one that Father P. Arsenault, the curé of Mont-Carmel, had learned from his mother and gave to Dr. Barbeau in 1924. It is a French version of the ancient ballad known in English as "*The False Knight upon the Road*" (Child 3) and, as it is unique in Canada, this suggests that the Acadians, hearing it from their Scottish neighbours, may have translated it into their own language.

The second, "*Le Vieux Sauvage*," is also unusual: it is a mock-tragic song probably composed by a *coureur de bois*, one of the unlicenced traders who ranged the woods in search of furs. To compete with the organized traders they adopted many of the habits of the Indians, wearing moccasins and fur caps, leggings, and buckskin coats, and often lived with the Indians throughout the winter, coming out only in summer to take their furs to Montreal. This song reflects those early backwoods days. A *voyageur* who has been separated from his comrade meets an old Indian who tells him that his friend has died in the woods and that the Indians gave him an honourable burial. The odd exclamations seem to be an attempt to suggest Indian speech.

The third, "*Le Sergent*," obviously dates from the period of the American Revolution. French Canadians chose to remain under British rule, for the Quebec Act of 1774 had guaranteed them religious freedom and French civil law; but a few discontented individuals did make their way south to join Washington's army and fight their traditional enemy. However, most French Canadians regarded such actions as foolish, and that attitude is reflected in this little song about a young fellow who, despite his father's warnings, decides to run off to Boston to fight the English. He gets banged up in the war and comes home to Papa, who says, "*I told you so!*"

OÙ VAS-TU, MON PETIT GARÇON?

Où vas — tu, mon p'tit gar —çon? Où vas — tu, mon p'tit gar —çon? Je m'en viens, tu t'en vas, nous pas —sons. —Je m'en vais droit à l'é —col', Ap —prendr' la pa —rol' de Dieu, Di —sait ça un en — fant de sept ans.

2.   – Qu'est-ce qu'est plus haut que les arbr's? (*Bis*)
      Je m'en viens, tu t'en vas, nous passons.
      – Le ciel est plus haut que l'arbr',
   Le soleil au firmament,
      Disait ça un enfant de sept ans.

3.   – Qu'est-c' qu'est plus creux que la mer? (*Bis*)
      – L'enfer est cent fois plus creux,
   L'enfer aux feux éternels,

4.   – Qu'est-c' qui pousse sur nos terr's? (*Bis*)
      – Les avoines et les blés d'or,
   Les châtaignes et les poiriers,

5.   – Que f'ras-tu quand tu s'ras grand? (*Bis*)
      – Je cultiverai les champs,
   Nourrirai femme et enfant,

WHERE ARE YOU GOING, MY LITTLE BOY?

1.   "Where are you going, my little boy?"
      I'm going, you're going, we're passing.
      "I'm going right to school
   To learn the word of God."
      Thus said the child seven years old.

2.   "What is higher than the trees?"
      I'm going, you're going, we're passing.
      "The sky is higher than the tree,
   The sun in the firmament."
      Thus said the child seven years old.

72

3. "What is deeper than the sea?"
    "Hell is a hundred times deeper,
    Hell with its eternal fires."

4. "What grows on our lands?
    "Oats and golden wheat,
    Chestnuts and pears."

5. "What will you do when you grow up?"
    "I will till the fields
    To feed my wife and child."

LE VIEUX SAUVAGE

REFRAIN
>   *Ah! Ah! tana, ouich'ténaga, Ouich'ka!*
>   *Ah! Ah! tana, ouich'ténaga, Ouich'ka!*

2. Avec sa vieill' couverte et son sac à tabac, *Ouich'ka!*
    Mon capitaine est more, est more et enterra, *Ouich'ka!*

3. Mon capitaine est more, est more et enterra, *Ouich'ka!*
    Sont quatre vieux sauvages qui port'nt les coins du drap, *Ouich'ka!*

4. Sont quatre vieux sauvages qui port'nt les coins du drap, *Ouich'ka!*
    Et quatre sauvagesses qui chant'nt le "Libera," *Ouich'ka!*

THE OLD INDIAN

There was an old Indian all painted black, *Ouich'ka!*
With his old blanket and his tobacco sack, *Ouich'ka!*

2. With his old blanket and his tobacco sack.
   My captain is dead, is dead and buried.

3. My captain is dead, is dead and buried.
   Four old Indians carry the corners of his pall.

4. Four old Indians carry the corners of his pall
   And four squaws chant the "Libera."

LE SERGENT

"Mon pa—pa si vous me bat — tez, oui, j'i — rai m'en—ga—ger A bord des Bos — to — nais bat — tre con — tre l'An—glais." A Bos—ton il s'en est al — lé: "How ma — ny men fi — red a— way?" "Vou—lez—vous m'en — ga — ger pour un ser—gent guer — rier?"

2. "Oui, nous t'engagerons, si tu veux fair' le bon garçon,
   Nous irons t'y mener à la têt' de l'armé'."
   Le sabre à son côté et le pistolet à la main,
   François marchait devant comme un vaillant sergent.

3. Dès la première volé', les mâchoir's lui ont fêlé's.
   François tomba en bas; on s'ecria: "Hourra!"
   Mais il s'est relevé: "How many men fired away?
   Il n'faut pas s'arrêter pour un sergent blessé."

4. François se lamenta à son cher et bon papa
   Qu'il avait été blessé par un coup d'grenadier.

- "Je n'té l'avais-t'y pas bien dit qu'tu périrais par le fusil!
A présent t'y voilà, ramass'-toi comm' tu pourras!"

THE SERGEANT

1. "Papa, if you beat me, I will go to enlist
    On the side of the Bostonians to fight the English."
    To Boston he went: "How many men fired away?"
    "Do you want to hire me as a warlike sergeant?"

2. "Yes, we'll hire you if you'll be a good boy.
    We're going to put you there at the head of the army."
    A sword at his side and a pistol in his hand
    François marched ahead like a brave sergeant.

3. At the first volley his jawbone was broken.
    François fell on his face; they shouted: "Hurray!"
    But he raised himself up: "How many men fired away?
    It's not necessary to stop for a wounded sergeant.

4. François wailed to his dear and good papa
    That he had been wounded by a shot from a grenadier.
    "Didn't I tell you that you'd die by the gun?
    Now there you are, pick yourself up as well as you can."

6. CHANSONS FRANCO-ONTARIEN
Germain Lemieux

The large French-Canadian population in northern Ontario has been extensively studied in recent years. Father Germain Lemieux has headed an important collecting project which has already produced a number of publications and a large folklore archive.

Father Lemieux was born in the Gaspé in 1914, joined the Jesuit Order in Montreal in 1935, and was ordained in 1947. He began collecting in the area around Sudbury in 1948, and within ten years had taped more than six hundred songs, thirty folktales, and several legends, and published two small brochures of folk songs and two of folktales. In 1959 when the University of Sudbury was established, he set up its Institute of Folklore and continued to publish songs and tales from his collection.

Most French-Canadian songs are versions of old French songs: Dr. Barbeau estimated that the purely Canadian repertoire represented only ten percent of the total. It is the one in ten composed in Canada that best reflects the life of the Canadiens, although the French songs they chose to preserve also throw light on their society.

"Le Vieux Sauvage" and "Le Sergent" from Chansons d'Acadie are two examples of new world songs; the following three from Father Lemieux's collection are also native Canadian. The first is an interesting example of the canoe songs which were so much a part of the early history of our country. Most paddling songs were old-world ballads with new refrains, but this is a fine expression of the voyageur's feeling for his canoe. The second is the lament of a pioneer farmer who leaves his farm to become a raftsman: the "cages" were piled-up rafts of logs on which the men lived as they piloted the timber down the river. The third is a humorous comparison of the habits of French Canadians with those of other nationalities.

MON CANOT

♩ = 102

1— As— sis sur mon ca—not d'é—cor— ce; As—sis à la

frai — che du temps; Oui, je bra — ve tous les ra — pi—

des, Je ne crains pas les bouil — lons blancs!

3— Mon ca — not est . . .

4 . . . Et là, je l'ver—se sur la pla — ge C'est ma

ca — ba — ne pour la nuit. Et là, je l'ver—se sur la

pla — ge C'est ma ca — ba — ne pour la nuit.

76

2. Je prends mon canot, je le lance
   A travers des rapid's, des bouillons blancs
   Et là, à grands sauts, il avance. ⎱ Bis
   Je ne crains mêm' pas l'océan. ⎰

3. Mon canot est fait d'écorce fine
   Que l'on pleume sur les bouleaux blancs.
   Les côt's ell's sont fait's de racine ⎱ Bis
   Et les avirons de bois blanc. ⎰

4. Et quand ça vient pour le portage,
   Je prends mon canot sur mon dos;
   Et là, je l'verse sur la plage ⎱ Bis
   C'est ma cabane pour la nuit. ⎰

5. J'ai traversé les flancs des côtes,
   Aussi le grand fleuve St-Laurent.
   J'ai connu les tribus sauvages ⎱ Bis
   Et leurs langages différents. ⎰

6. Un labourer aim' sa charrue,
   Un chasseur, son fusil et son chien,
   Un musicien aim' sa musique. ⎱ Bis
   Moi, mon canot, c'est tout mon bien. ⎰

MY CANOE

1. Seated in my bark canoe,
   Seated in the coolness of the day;
   Yes, I brave all the rapids,
   I do not fear the white foam!

2. I take my canoe and I launch it
   Across the rapids, the white foam,
   And then by great leaps it advances.
   I am not afraid even of the ocean.

3. My canoe is made of fine bark
   That they strip from the white birches.
   The sides are made of root
   And the paddles of white wood.

4. And when we reach the portage
    I take my canoe on my back;
    And there I turn it over on the shore,
    It is my home for the night.

5. I have travelled along the coasts,
    Also the great St. Lawrence river.
    I have known the Indian tribes
    And their different languages.

6. A farmer loves his plough,
    A hunter his dog and gun,
    A musician loves his music.
    As for me, my canoe is all my wealth.

LES CANAYENS SONT LA!

Yen a qui aim'nt la bonn' cui — si — ne, Des fêvr's au lard et des p'tits pois; Ou bien du lard aus — si des "bi — nes," Yen a qu'en mang'nt, d'autr's qu'en mang'nt pas. Des cor — ni — chons pis d'la sa — la — de, Yen a qu'en mang'nt à s'rendr' ma — la — des. Mais pour man — ger d'la soupe aux pois Les ca — na — yens sont tou — jours là! Ah! ah! les ca — na — yens sont tou — jours là!

2. Y a plusieurs manièr's de se battr'
    Pour l'italien, c'est l'poignardeau;
    L'américain, sur la tomate
    Fesse à coups d'pieds, à coups d'marteau.
    Mais l'irlandais, c'est une brique,
    Ça ne vaut pas même une chique;
    Quand il s'agît d'bûcher dans l'tas
    Les canayens sont un peu là!
    Ah! ah! les canayens sont un peu là!

3. Nos bons voisins, dans leur sagesse,
   Ont voté la Prohibition;
   Paraît qu' dans les jours d'allégresse,
   Il faut pas fair' rôder l'flacon!
   Mais nous, les canayens, moins bêtes,
   On a bien pensé qu' pour les fêtes
   De n'pas passer sans mouiller ça;
   Les canayens sont toujours là!
   Ah! ah! les canayens sont toujours là!

4. On voit des portraits sur *La Presse*
   Des gross's famill's du Canada;
   De douze enfants et mêm' de treize;
   Ça n'pouss' pas seul tout ce mond'-là!
   Il faut bien croire que nos mères
   N'ont pas eu peur de la misère!
   Ah! pour peupler le Canada
   Les canayens sont toujours là!
   Ah! ah! les canayens sont toujours là!

THE CANADIENS ARE ALWAYS READY!

1. There are some who love good food,
   Beans with pork, and small green peas;
   Or plenty of pork also with beans,
   There are some who eat it, others who don't.
   The spoiled gherkins in the salad,
   There are some who eat them and make themselves sick.
   But to eat pea soup
   The Canadiens are always ready!
   Ah! ah! the Canadiens are always ready!

2. There are several ways of fighting:
   For the Italian it's the dagger;
   The American, on the sauce,
   Uses kicks or blows of the hammer.
   But the Irishman uses a brick;
   That isn't worth a quid;
   When it comes to licking the crowd
   The Canadiens are never there!
   Ah! ah! the Canadiens are never there!

3. Our good neighbours in their wisdom
   Have voted for prohibition;
   It seems that in the lively days
   They didn't need to hang around the bottle!
   But we, the Canadiens, less stupid,
   We can't think of feasts
   Passing without wetting our whistles.
   The Canadiens are always there!
   Ah! ah! the Canadiens are always there!

4. We see pictures in *La Presse*
   Of the big Canadien families;
   Twelve children or even thirteen;
   No one can do that by oneself!
   We must believe that our mothers
   Had no fear of misery!
   Ah! to people Canada
   The Canadiens are always ready!
   Ah! ah! the Canadiens are always ready!

VIE PENIBLE DES CAGEUX

♩ = 76

Les ha — bi — tants de par chez nous, Dans leur jo — lie cam — pa — gne. Fe — ront bien mieux de lu'y res — ter A cul — ti — ver leurs far — mes. Fe — ront bien mieux de lu'y res — ter A cul — ti — ver leurs far — mes, Et au mo — ment d'la ma — la — die, Le prêtr' les ac — com — pa — gne!

2.   C'est dans l'état là où je suis,
      Sur le pas du voyage;
      Moi, j'ai quitté tous les plaisirs   (Bis)
      De ma jolie bergère.
      Mais le plaisir, c'est loin de moi,
      Et ma jeuness' se passe!

3.   C'est dans l'été, en descendant
      Sur ces cag's ennuyeuses,
      Lorsqu'on n'y voit qu'le ciel et l'eau,   (Bis)
      Les nuées sont nombreuses.
      On les regard' mais trop souvent,
      Ell's devienn'nt ennuyeuses!

THE HARD LIFE ON THE RAFTS

1.   The habitants who live near us
      In their pretty country
      Would be much better to stay there
      And cultivate their farms.
      Would be better to stay there
      And cultivate their farms,
      And in time of sickness
      The priest keeps them company.

2.   That's the state I'm in
      On the verge of a journey.
      I've left all the pleasures
      With my pretty shepherdess.
      But pleasure is far from me
      And my youth is passing.

3.   It's in the summer coming down
      On those tiresome rafts
      When one never sees the sky or the sea
      The clouds are numerous.
      I see them but with too much looking
      They become wearisome.

7. TALL TALES OF DALBEC
William Parker Greenough

Greenough, a nineteenth-century New England novelist who wrote under the pseudonym of G. de Montauban, made frequent trips into Quebec for both business and recreation. He knew the French Canadians well and in 1897 he published Canadian Folk-Life and Folk-Lore *in which he described their occupations, amusements, festivities, and songs, and related some of the tales he had heard from them.*

Many of these tales featured a fabulous hunter named Dalbec, and Greenough recounted several he had heard from a lumberman and guide named Nazaire. They are fantastic yarns based on exaggeration, akin to some of the "Jokes and Anecdotes" recounted in the Anglo-Canadian section.

DALBEC'S WONDERFUL SHOT

There was once a very famous hunter named Dalbec, who lived in the village of Ste Anne. He had been hunting all day and was returning home when he came to a little round lake, on the opposite side of which he saw a fox. Just as he raised his gun to fire, six ducks came sailing from under the bushes nearer to him. He hesitated at which to shoot, and decided to try his chances at both. Placing the barrel of his long gun between two trees, he bent it into a quarter of a circle, fired at the ducks, killed them all, killed the fox also, and the bullet came back and broke the leg of his dog that was standing by him.

DALBEC AND THE BEAR

Dalbec was in the woods making maple sugar, when he saw a bear coming round as if bent on mischief. Having no gun, Dalbec crawled under an empty hogshead (such as are often used to hold the sap as it is collected). The bear came smelling up, trying to find a way to get in. At the right moment Dalbec reached his hand through the bung-hole and seized him by the tail. The bear started off on a run down the hill, dragging the hogshead after him with Dalbec inside of it. They came to a lot of fallen timber, where the hogshead stuck, but Dalbec held on till the tail came out and the bear escaped.

DALBEC AND THE GEESE

He had been ploughing one day, and at night, just as he was going to put his horse in the barn, he heard a flock of wild geese in the air over his head. He went into the house and got his gun, but it was so dark he could seen nothing. Still hearing the noise, he fired in the direction from which it came. As no birds fell he concluded he had missed them, so he went into the house, ate his supper and went to bed. In the morning he was going for his horse again when just as he was stepping out of doors a goose fell at his feet. It was one of those he had shot at and it had been so high up it had been all night in falling.

DALBEC FLIES THROUGH THE AIR

It was the morning of the 'Toussaint' (All Saints' Day) that Dalbec had gone out early, shooting. He had expended all his ammunition and was returning home when he saw a flock of wild ducks swimming about among the timbers of a raft that had gone ashore at the mouth of the river. The water was cold, but Dalbec went into it up to his neck and waded round until he could reach under the logs and get hold of the legs of a duck. When he caught one he pulled it quickly under the water and fastened it to his belt. In this way he secured about a dozen. All of a sudden he felt a commotion, and before he knew what was happening he found himself raised into the air and carried off. A strong northeasterly gale was blowing and away he went up the St. Lawrence. Just as he passed the church at Ste Anne he heard the first bell of the mass sound, and he wished he had stayed at home instead of going shooting. At the rate at which he was going he had not much time to think; but presently he realized that something had got to be done. He reached down and twisted the neck of one of the ducks. That let him down a little and he twisted another. So he kept on until, when he had done with them all, he found himself dropped on the ground in front of the church at Sorel, and heard the second bell of the mass. He had been carried seventy-five miles up the river in just half an hour.

8. PARLOUR GAMES IN FRENCH CANADA
Maurice Tremblay

This account of the parlour games played in Ile Verte, a small island in the St. Lawrence River near the mouth of the Saguenay, throws considerable light on the social life of rural communities in French Canada. As Maurice Tremblay suggests, some of the games reflect various aspects of French-Canadian culture and different phases of history. Similar games were popular in other areas of rural Quebec, and some of the same patterns occur in games played by Anglo-Canadians.

The thirty-odd parlour games described below were collected at Ile Verte in 1948 during research work in social anthropology, undertaken on behalf of the National Museum of Canada. The list cannot be considered to include all the parlour games played on the island, as, owing to our greater interest in studying other aspects of the local culture, a systematic study could not be made of this particular trait. We are sure that this list can be added to when there is further opportunity for investigation, because the way of life on Ile Verte is particularly favourable to the practice and perpetuation of this type of recreation.

Notre-Dame de l'Ile Verte, situated 130 miles below Quebec, and three miles from the south shore of the St. Lawrence River, forms a small French-Canadian parish of thirty-eight families comprising 300 people, whose leisure pastimes have remained exclusively related to family life and gatherings of relatives, neighbours, and friends.

There is no commercial, or even organized recreation on the island. No cinema, no pool room, no parochial hall, no sport club, not even a restaurant. Nevertheless, leisure time is plentiful. As a matter of fact, livelihood is earned chiefly from the cultivation of small farms, and from wicker fish traps; and apart from seeding time which coincides with the heavy herring catch in the spring, during which time the inhabitants labour almost day and night, people do not work very hard on Ile Verte. Especially during the long winter months, except for a few odd jobs around the house, there is very little to do and, in the evening, people are ready for their favourite pastime – *la veillée*. The sons, who have been on coastal vessels plying the St. Lawrence during the navigation season, have returned home and join in these evening reunions to the great delight of the marriageable girls. People talk, play cards, sometimes dance, and often play parlour games. It was, in fact, at one of these reunions that most of the games, described below, were gathered.

These games are no doubt part of the common French-Canadian cultural heritage, although scientific proof cannot be advanced for lack of sufficiently complete documentary evidence. This branch of research in traditional games has as yet hardly been explored in French Canada. To our knowledge, there are only two scientific publications on the subject: the collection by Lambert and Barbeau which was published in the *Journal of American Folklore* in April, 1940 (vol. 53, pp. 163-181), and the excellent monograph by Madeleine Doyon, published in the third issue of the *Archives de Folklore*, 1948 (pp. 159-207), entitled "Jeux, jouets et divertissements de la Beauce."

Of the thirty-two games we have collected, twelve are to be found in one or the other of these publications, or in both. Moreover, the writer already knew at least ten more of these games, having become familiar with them in his native region of the Lower St. Lawrence.

In fact, many of these games, by their names at least, are representative of various aspects of French-Canadian culture and of different phases of its historical formation.

"Le Clairon du roi joli" ["The Bugle of the Handsome King"] tells of the kingdom of France, of the France before the Revolution to which the French Canadians have remained sentimentally attached.

"Arracher la souche" ["Pulling up the Stump"] recalls the epic of the French settlers who carved themselves a new land from the very heart of the Quebec forests, and the sustained effort of a prolific people to find new acres on which to establish fresh generations.

"Sauter le rapide" ["Shooting the Rapids"] reminds us of the renowned adventures of the French-Canadian coureurs de bois and voyageurs who travelled the wide-flung continental river systems from the Gulf of Mexico to Hudson Bay and from the Atlantic to the Rockies.

"Le jugement dernier" ["The Last Judgement"], "La demande de grâces à la Sainte-Vierge" ["Asking Favours from the Holy Virgin"], and "La Sainte-enfance" ["The Holy Child"] reflect the deep religious feeling which is one of the distinctive traits of French-Canadian culture.

"Charger le mouton" ["Loading the Sheep"] and "Tirer la vache" ["Hauling the Cow"] depict the vigorous rural traditions of French Canada. "Pet en gueule" ["Breaking Wind"], another example, comes from that strain of Rabelaisian humour, so much a part of the French spirit, which still lives in New France.

Nevertheless, while these games seem to be part of a common heritage, we have no doubt that a comparative study would show that some of them are variations which have developed in the small insular community where they were collected. For example, it is altogether possible that the game, "Plonger le loup marin" ["Diving like a Seal"] was of local derivation, as seals are especially numerous in the waters surrounding Ile Verte.

The games mentioned may be subdivided into two distinct but complementary groups: games of strength and skill, and games of hoax and mystification.

The interest of the first group for the players comes from the competitive element the games provide from the pleasure of defeating a contestant and giving a demonstration of one's strength or skill.

85

The second group consists of games of hoax and mystification and if these games are always played on the same occasions it is due to the fact that if peasant wisdom encourages ambition and appreciates real worth, it endeavours on the other hand to teach humility in success, a knowledge of one's own shortcomings, and the acceptance, with equanimity, of the vexations as well as of the joys of life.

A. GAMES OF STRENGTH AND SKILL

1. PULLING UP THE STUMP

The first player gets down on his hands and knees; the second sits on the shoulders of the first, facing toward his feet; he crosses his feet under the first, and, giving some jerks, he tries to make him raise his hands from the floor and to tip him backwards.

2. KISSING HIS THUMB

The player, hanging by his right arm from a pipe or beam, must raise his body so as to kiss his thumb.

3. DRINKING

A basin full of water containing a five-cent piece is placed on the floor; one player gets down on the floor in a prone position and, supporting himself on the tips of his toes and fingers, dips his head into the basin and brings out the coin with his mouth.

4. BREAKING THE THREAD

The player, lying full length on his back, must break, by raising his head, a thread that someone holds under his nose.

5. LOADING THE DEAD MAN

A player lying on the floor makes himself limp like a dead man; a second player tries to load him on his shoulder.

6. LOADING THE SHEEP

A player lying on the floor flounders about like a sheep while a second player tries to load him on his shoulder.

7. SMACK BOTTOM

Two players, each holding a towel in his right hand, sit on the floor, the feet of one between the legs of the other; while one rolls on his back,

86

the other slaps him on the buttocks with the towel, and so on in turn as quickly as possible until one of the players asks for mercy.

8. CUTTING THE SHEEP'S THROAT

A child sits down and scratches the ground with a stick. Someone asks him:

"What are you making?" – "A hole."
"Why?" – "To make a fire."
"Why make a fire?" – "To heat the water."
"Why heat the water?" – "To whet my stone."
"Why whet your stone?" – "To cut the sheep's throat."
"Chase it, then!"

The one who was seated gets up and runs after the questioners. The first one he catches sits down and answers the questions in his turn.

9. UPSETTING THE HATS

The player sits with his legs crossed on a broom that rests on two chairs facing each other; with another broom he tries to knock down four hats that are placed on the four posts of the two chairs.

10. DISLODGING THE KNIFE

The player sticks a knife in the wall level with his head. Then taking a broom, he measures on his sleeve the length of his arm to the armpit; he grasps the broom at this spot with his right hand. Holding the broom thus, he passes it between his legs from the back, holding it from the front with his left hand. He must then jump so as to dislodge the knife with the end of the broom.

11. THREADING A NEEDLE SITTING ON A BOTTLE

A bottle is laid on its side; while sitting on it with his feet crossed, the player must thread a needle.

12. DUELLING WITH A FORK

First the feet of the players are tied together; then their hands are tied together under their thighs while each holds a fork between his hands; each then tries to prick the buttocks of his opponent with his fork.

13. RAISING THE STIFF

One of two players lies on the ground, holding himself stiff, and the other, seizing him by the legs, must raise him and throw him over his shoulder.

14. DIVING LIKE A SEAL

The player, his hands crossed behind his back, must let himself fall on his chest and stomach without touching the floor with his chin.

15. JUMPING THE SWAYBACKED HORSE

A chair is placed in the middle of the room; a player, standing facing the chair, puts his hands on the seat; then a second player jumps over the shoulders of the first so as to land sitting on the chair; a third leaps on the shoulders of the first, and then as many others jump on the group as the first can support.

16. PULLING THE LEG

The two players lie side by side on their backs with the head of one by the feet of the other; they hold each other by the forearms and raise the left leg three times; the fourth time they catch the other's leg and each tries to overturn the other.

17. PULLING THE STICK

Two players, sitting facing each other on the floor with the soles of their feet together, hold a broom horizontally. Each pulls the broom toward him and the stronger lifts the other.

18. PULLING THE FOX

Two people who take part in the game go down on all fours facing each other; a long piece of cloth knotted at the ends goes around their necks; each tries to pull the other to his side.

19. TURNING THE BROOM

The player, seizing a broom by the large end and holding it against the ceiling, must turn around fifty times, keeping his eyes fixed on the end that rests on the ceiling. He then has to place the end of the broom at a previously indicated spot in the room.

B. GAMES OF HOAX AND MYSTIFICATION

20. HIDE THE CAP

All those playing shut themselves in a room while someone hides the cap; the winner is the one who finds it.

21. THE BUGLE OF THE HANDSOME KING

The players sit in a circle and pass an object from hand to hand while one person placed in the centre of the circle tries to discover where the object is. During the game they sing this song:

1. It passes, it passes, it is passed,
    The bugle of the handsome king.
    It passes, it passes, it is passed,
    The bugle of the handsome king.

2. I have it in my hand here,
    The bugle of the handsome king.
    I have it in my hand here,
    The bugle of the handsome king.

3. It has just left here,
    The bugle of the handsome king.
    It has just left here,
    The bugle of the handsome king.

22. ASKING FAVOURS FROM THE HOLY VIRGIN

A woman with a veil over her hair sits on a chair and plays the part of the Holy Virgin. Others bring to her one who wishes to ask a favour; the favour asked, she who plays the Holy Virgin makes the applicant come close to her and sprinkles him with water with which she had previously filled her mouth.

23. MAKING A BEAM BLEED

A knife is stuck in a beam and the person who wants to see the beam bleed is asked to fix his eyes on the knife; while he looks at it, a glass of water is poured on his head from behind.

24. THE LAST JUDGEMENT

A table is set in the middle of the room and covered with a large rug, one corner of which reaches the floor; another rug is placed facing the table with one corner extending under it. The player who takes the part of the judge sits on a chair placed on the table. The people to be judged are kept apart in another room; they are led in one by one. After being questioned, each is condemned to hell; a player hiding under the table, concealed by the rug covering the table, pulls the rug on which the condemned man is standing; he falls on his back.

25. LAUNCHING THE SHIP

One of the players lies on his back; a second lies on top of him, with his head at the other's feet, and also on his back. The first then puts his legs over the shoulders of the other, holding his legs between his arms, while a third pours a glass of water in his face.

26. WEIGHING THE BACON

A blanket is put over the head of the person to be weighed; while two others pretend to weigh him by raising him under the arms, a fourth puts a basin under the one being weighed and they let him fall into it.

27. BREAKING WIND

Two men lie down with the head of one by the feet of the other; one places his seat against the other who breaks wind if he can; they try it in turn.

28. NURSING THE SICK

The one playing the doctor is kept apart; when he is called they give him a spoon whose handle has previously been heated.

29. THE HOLY CHILD

A player's eyes are covered and someone draws a child on his forearm with a pen and folds the forearm over his other arm; when his eyes are uncovered he is surprised to find that he holds a child in his arms.

30. SHOOTING THE RAPIDS

Several people sit astride a long bench; the first grips the end of the bench while the others cross their hands over the eyes of the one in front of them; the game is supposed to consist for the first in not losing hold while the others pull him backwards, but actually the second has his hands covered with soot with which he smears the face of the first player without his knowledge.

31. HAULING THE COW

One of the players gets down on all fours with his hands and feet tied; the second player sits on the ground with his right leg between the arms and his left leg between the legs of the first; then he puts his head under the other's stomach so that his head sticks out; a third player tips them over on the side; it is then impossible for them to separate themselves in spite of all their efforts.

32. SEEING THE MOON

Someone covers the head of the curious one with a coat, taking care to place one of the sleeves over his eyes; then they pour a glass of water in his face through the sleeve.

9. THE EARLY DEVELOPMENT OF FRENCH-CANADIAN FOODWAYS

Jay A. Anderson

The study of the food and cooking customs of folk groups is becoming an increasingly important part of folklore. Food and drink have always played a significant role in rituals and they are the subject of many folk beliefs. In Canada we are conscious of the characteristic dishes of our various cultural groups, some of which have inspired books like Edna Staebler's Food That Really Schmecks: Mennonite Country Cooking. *The French-Canadian foodways are especially suitable for study as they have developed in this country for over three centuries.*

Of the dozen important regional cuisines that evolved among North America's folk cultures, the French Canadian is one of the most significant. Not only is it unique, with its unusual mixture of French and native American foods and techniques, but it also has been remarkably durable. While many other folk foodways have become nostalgic memories in the minds of grandmothers, centuries-old French-Canadian techniques for obtaining and processing foods are still being passed on from father to son, mother to daughter, in many parts of Quebec. To appreciate its uniqueness and durability, we must look closely at its history, stressing its origins in northwestern France, and the Canadian environment that moulded it.

Most of the French colonists came from the northwestern provinces bounded by the Seine and Loire rivers. In the first half of the seventeenth century some four thousand peasants were recruited from Normandy, Brittany, Maine, and Poitou. Government officials felt that an immigrant used to the cold rainy climate along the Channel coast would fare better along the Saint Lawrence River than, say, a farmer from Provence. Their expectations were fortunately realized – only one colonist out of four died before establishing himself.

Despite its comparatively cold, wet winters, the French northwest was a good dairy country, with little relief, moderate rains throughout the spring and summer, few milk-souring heat waves, and soil better suited to root crops and legumes, fruit trees, and hay than cereals. The inhabitants evolved a mixed system of agriculture, arboriculture, and animal husbandry, stimulated by their position close to the coastal European trade routes which constantly infused new techniques for procuring and processing food. By the late sixteenth century, the folk culture, shaped from above by the feudal system, was a complex and comparatively successful peasant economy. At its heart was a triennial rotation system by which the land surrounding each village or estate was divided into three large fields: one for a winter cereal like rye or buckwheat, one planted with the proverbial "oats, peas, beans, and barley corn" – all spring crops, and the third lying fallow. Every year these crops were rotated. Supplementing them were vegetables and fruits from kitchen gardens and orchards, fish and molluscs from nearby rivers or the coast, and game trapped on waste moorland or poached from estate forests.

Even with the natural fecundity of the region and the variety of potential food sources, the peasant diet was constantly threatened. Overpopulation, repressive feudal levies, and inflation in the price of a few essentials like wheat and salt combined to undermine the French peasants' standard of living in the seventeenth century. At the time when most colonization took place, their diet consisted of cereal grains, legumes, pork offal, salt or dried fish, vegetables and fruits from the household garden and orchard, and dairy products from the family's one or two cows. Cereals, legumes like field peas, and fruits were dried either in the open or in crude flax ovens. Fish and some pork were smoked, but the high price of salt made this process a luxury. Fruits and some cereals were made into beer or wine, cider being the cheapest and most popular wine. Autumn and winter humidity precluded the storage of root crops and vegetables. Cooking was done over an open fire in iron kettles or on grills, although some foods were baked in the seigneur's oven.

Meals were frequent: a breakfast of porridge with pancakes around dawn, followed by meals in the field at mid-morning, noon, and midafternoon, consisting of bread or pancakes, cider or ale, and possibly cheese. The heavy evening meal at dusk would include a soup or stew made from legumes, vegetables – usually cabbage or turnips – and some meat or fish. Cabbage soup was popular partly because of the widespread belief that it prevented hair from falling out, cured venereal diseases, and increased mothers' milk. Eels were considered a delicacy, and meat was worth its weight in salt – the peasant's gold. On Sundays or holidays, a feast might consist of roast pork or hare, or, if that were too luxurious, blood pudding or stewed pork chitterlings or lungs. What kept the peasants in calories were the buckwheat porridges and pea soups; what kept them in protein and therefore alive was the little milk they drank or ate as cheese. Fortunately "white meat," as dairy produce was called, was available and considered beneficial, especially for children.

Although they were poor, peasant farmers knew what the good life could be. Their seigneurs provided a constant example of how much good food was available to those with enough land. The bourgeois of Normandy and Maine had already developed gastronomy into an art, and many of the classic poultry and seafood recipes using the creams and ciders of the region were popular. Garden vegetables, fruits, and cheeses were also widely used by those who had the excess land and servants needed for intensive agriculture. Monastic seigneuries were often model farms and the monks gastronomes. The northwest in general and Normandy in particular had many independent farmers to whom the promise of more land would have been inviting. Most of those who sought to emigrate did so not only out of a desire for greater freedom from the feudal system but to improve their lot. Canada meant more and possibly better land, and land to those peasant farmers used to running self-sufficient homesteads was the provider of food, clothing, and shelter.

Fortunately, the natural environment along the St. Lawrence where most of the French colonists settled was in many ways similar to the one left behind in France. Except for the long, bitter winter, the climate was temperate with cool moist springs and summers. Soil along the river basin was well drained with mild acidity and moderate leaching; it would maintain its productivity if carefully tilled. The topography was on the whole flat with few hills of any consequence. Thus, with some exceptions, the same crops raised in the old country could be grown in the new. An early settler sent back this optimistic picture: "I inspected everything, the cultivated land which I found sown and filled with fine grain, the gardens full of all kinds of plants, such as cabbage, radishes, lettuce, purslain, sorrel, parsley, and other plants – squashes, cucumbers, melons, peas, beans, and other vegetables as fine as those found in France, together with the vines brought and planted here, already well advanced, in short everything increasing and growing visibly."

The new environment did differ in some respects. Winter was a major shock. Although forewarned, the colonists found the Quebec winter longer and colder than any they had experienced. However, they adapted to it with incredible rapidity, transforming the long four or five months of enforced semi-idleness into a season of indoor conviviality, highlighted by traditional religious and secular feasts. A second major difference was the extensive forest cover. What small forests there were in northwest France were jealously guarded by the seigneurs; peasant farmers were fortunate to be granted the right to gather deadwood for their fires. Thus, although the difficulty of clearing the hardwood maples along the St. Lawrence was arduous, the settlers looked upon the forests as an economic asset providing timber for fuel, tools, and utensils as well as the chief source of sweetening: maple syrup. The last major difference between the old and new world natural environments was the St. Lawrence itself. As the main means of communication and trade between the mother country, the small urban centres at Quebec, Trois Rivières, and Montréal, and the seigneurial settlements, the river profoundly influenced settlement patterns and the resultant economic life. Both the seigneurial estates themselves and their farms were laid out in parallelograms often twenty times as long as they were wide, giving river frontage to as many seigneurs and settlers as possible. This settlement pattern also had the added advantages of equitably sharing the cost of the road building and upkeep and of providing individual seigneuries and farms with a variety of sources to draw on for food. A man could often fish, farm, and hunt on his own property. The Quebec environment, in short, offered the potential foundation for a folk society and culture based on self-sufficient homesteads.

Most of the colonists who disembarked in this strange new world were peasants or tradesmen familiar with the problems of rural life. An important part of their "cultural baggage" consisted of the skills needed to secure from the land with their own labour the food, clothing, and shelter needed by their families. Many could plant and harvest cereals, legumes, and root crops, tend apple trees, breed poultry and stock, and even trap a rabbit or eel. Those skills they lacked and needed – fishing and hunting – they picked up from the few colonists who knew how – fishermen from Normandy and Brittany and the seigneurs themselves – or from the Indians. The latter not only passed on their fishing and hunting lore but also taught the settlers how to grow maize, pumpkins, and beans, and to make maple sugar. Since open-field plowing was initially impossible because of stumps, Indian methods and crops were valuable. By the end of the seventeenth century roughly thirty thousand acres on three hundred and fifty seigneuries had been cleared, and a small but successful peasant society and culture firmly established on the land.

Despite the differing backgrounds of the seigneurs – there were merchants, soldiers, priests, and gentlemen farmers – most of the seigneuries or land grants were similar. They varied in size from a few acres to thirty or more square miles, depending on the social rank of the seigneur. As already noted, these seigneuries and the independent farms within them were laid out in long narrow strips perpendicular to the river. In the colony's early decades, houses were built in a line by the main road running along the St. Lawrence. As river front land filled up, additional ranges of farms deeper inland were ceded. Each successive range was similar to the first, with houses strung out along secondary

94

roads bordering the end of each range. Fishing and forest rights were generally granted to these landlocked newcomers.

The absence of natural and cultural subdivisions within the St. Lawrence river valley makes it possible to reconstruct a typical seventeenth-century farm, its food supply, and cuisine. It would have contained a farm house and outbuildings, with a kitchen garden, orchard, fields of buckwheat, peas, beans, and hay, some pastures, and a stand of maples. Cows would graze in the pasture, with swine and poultry in pens nearer the house. The farm would rely primarily on these resources for food. However, a farmer would make use of his fishing and hunting privileges to obtain seasonal specialties. Mussels and small migratory birds were plentiful in the spring, berries in the summer, and wild turkeys in the fall. He would also make use of the grain mill, bake oven, and cider press of the seigneur who derived a tax from their operation. Later this arrangement proved too inconvenient and costly for the seigneurs and they allowed individuals to erect their own. Bake ovens either separated from the houses or combined with the fireplaces became a fixture on each farm. The more expensive cider presses and mills, however, were centralized and used in common by the farmers of a particular range. Some purchases were made at nearby village markets – salt and spices being most in demand – but there was little trade beyond this. The typical French-Canadian homestead was virtually self-sufficient.

The seventeenth-century cuisine, reflecting the traditional foodways brought over from France and the resources of the new Canadian environment, remained essentially unchanged for three centuries except for the acceptance of the potato and of new cooking methods when the enameled stove was introduced in the late nineteenth century. Even this transition from the open hearth to the range meant simply that old foods were cooked in newer, easier ways.

At the heart of any regional folk cuisine or foodway complex is what Max Sorre, the French cultural geographer, calls the "dietary regime" – a particular group's basic "ensemble of foods and their preparations that sustain it throughout the year."[1] Often a dietary regime is characterized by the major sources of calories and proteins, its "core diet."

During the pioneer period of French Canada when successive waves of colonists began filling in the seigneuries between Montreal and Quebec, the core diet consisted of buckwheat, peas, pork, fish, apples, and milk.

Buckwheat, a hardy cereal that had been introduced into France from Asia Minor in the sixteenth century, was extremely popular in the damp region from which the colonists came. It even thrived in the poor, rock-strewn soil of Brittany. Further, it could be made into a long yeasty loaf similar to that baked of better but less hardy wheats. The northwestern French peasant preferred this loaf to the flat unleavened cake, often made of oats or barley, popular in similar cold, moist regions along the

Atlantic coast of Europe. Buckwheat was also used in porridges similar to oatmeal or corn meal mush, and in pancakes. Probably far more buckwheat was simmered or grilled over the open hearth fire than was baked in an oven. Once the oven became a fixture in the Quebec home, loaf bread and dough recipes – tartes, tourtières, etc. – used up more buckwheat flour.

Field peas and other legumes grow well in moist climates with unexceptional soils. Thus they came into widespread use in western Europe both as fodder for stock and as cereal substitutes for humans. In many regions they began to replace cereal porridges during the seventeenth century because they were easier to grow and to keep. Dried peas or beans could be stored for years and then quickly turned into the flavoursome soups immortalized as "pease porridge hot, pease porridge cold." The whole yellow field pea and broad white bean became especially important in the cuisine of northwestern France. Their affinity for absorbing the flavour of either smoked or salted pork fat was realized early and most recipes for pea soup or baked beans call for pork. The popularity of yellow peas was recorded by an early trader who described how the dish was prepared in a voyageurs' camp: "The tin kettle in which they cooked their food would hold eight or ten gallons. It was hung over the fire, nearly full of water, then nine quarts of peas – one quart per man, the daily allowance – were put in; and when they were well bursted, two or three pounds of pork, cut into strips, for seasoning, were added, and allowed to boil or simmer till daylight when the cook added four biscuits, broken up, to the mess, and invited all hands to breakfast. The swelling of the peas and biscuit had now filled the kettle to the brim, so thick that a stick would stand upright in it . . . The men now squatted in a circle, the kettle in their midst, and each one plying his wooden spoon or ladle from the kettle to mouth, with almost electric speed, soon filled every cavity."[2] Although recipes prepared by the habitants' wives were more creative, using herbs and vegetables, the manner of eating from a communal kettle was the same.

The early staple meats were pork and game, especially venison and wild hare. In most European and American folk cuisines, pork came close to being a second staff of life, due to the pig's propensity for turning virtually anything edible, from acorns to scraps, into usable cuts of meat. The folk saying, "You can eat everything but the squeal," had validity in both France and Quebec, and recipes using pigs' blood, trotters, intestines, and even lungs were current. In Quebec, pigs were butchered after winter's arrival, in November or December, so spoilage was kept at a minimum. Some cuts were preserved by freezing, others later appeared on the table as salt pork or ham. Salting was the more expensive method of preservation, and a full salt box a high peasant priority. Smoking used salt in its initial curing process – dry salting or brining – but the quantity used was small. Once cured, the hams were hung in the chimney to smoke. They resembled dry or air-cured hams more than the pungent smoke-house products we are familiar with today. Fresh game supplemented pork frequently, with venison, hare, and turkey roasts being common in the early pioneer period. Later, these roasts were replaced by stews and pies. An old recipe calls for stuffing a hare with the meat from pigs' feet and then simmering it in cider. Gradually, however, wild game came to be less and less relied on. Farmers looked upon it more as a luxury than a necessity. In some areas, droves of small migrating birds were netted and made into stews to be eaten on special occasions. Hares remained so popular, however, that they were domesticated and regularly served up in stews, roasts, and pies.

Fish and molluscs were both imported and gathered locally. Breton and Norman fishermen had been taking herring and cod from the Grand Banks a century before colonization began. The massive catches were salted or cured along the Maritime coast before being shipped back to Europe. The fishermen welcomed a domestic Canadian market and diverted much herring and cod down the St. Lawrence as the population increased. Of course, the river itself and its numerous tributaries offered a closer and fresher supply, and many colonists picked up fishing skills from their knowledgeable fellows or from the Indians. They caught many varieties, two of the most popular being eels and sardines. The taste for these had been carried over from France where they were peasant delicacies. Eels were smoked or dried, "eaten green," or used as the basis for stews. A medieval recipe called for browning eel in butter, then simmering it with sweet herbs and cider. In Quebec, onions were added, creating the classic *matelotte d'anguilles* or sailor's eel stew. Mussels and oysters in the tidal reaches of the St. Lawrence were gathered every spring in enormous quantities and used in chowder. As in coastal France, molluscs and non-oily fish were simmered with cream, cider, salt pork, and onions in a copper kettle called a *chaudière* or *chaudron*. This dish was borrowed by the British colonists to the south where it became New England clam chowder. Without a lacing of hard cider, however, it loses its original distinctiveness.

Apples were raised in the northwest of France as early as the Roman occupation, but the fame of Normandy and its neighbours as a spectacular apple-producing region began in the mid-sixteenth century when Henry IV brought a number of new and exceptional varieties from Navarre. They thrived in the cool moist climate and quickly became popular among the rich, who used them for wine-making, and the poor, who used them as table fruit. Both peasant and bourgeois colonists experimented with different varieties in Quebec immediately after their arrival and after only half a century were growing many varieties in great quantities. Most were cider apples high in sugar and malic acid. Although some apples were eaten out of hand or cooked in tarts and pancakes, most went into the cider presses to be made into the Quebec version of *cider doux* (sweet cider) and later *calvados*. Because of the widespread suspicion of water, cider became the primary table beverage. Some colonists did try to raise grapes, remembering Cartier's description of a St. Lawrence island as the "island of Bacchus," but their efforts paled before the incredible apple harvests. Later, especially in the nineteenth century, wines were made of just about every wild fruit and flower imaginable, but these were never in regular use.

The last important food in the core diet was milk and its derivatives, cream and cheese, for the St. Lawrence river valley was potentially ideal dairy country. The cool moist summer produced good pastures and hence milk with little spoilage. Norman cattle, celebrated for the high cream content of their milk, were imported early and became the forerunners of the "Canadian" breed, a pureblood line of very good milk producers. Pierre Kalm, an early visitor to Quebec, wrote: "Milk enters into the preparation of almost all of the farmer's dishes . . . The French have a strong taste for milk and great quantities of it are consumed, especially by the young . . . Generally they boiled it, then threw into it chunks of bread and much (maple) sugar." [3] The concoction was served up in the evening in a huge bowl from which everyone in the family spooned out his share. Milk and buttermilk were drunk by themselves. Butter, on the other hand, was used only in sauces and doughs; not until much later did it replace pork fat as a spread for bread. This heavy use of dairy products rounded out an already excellent core diet. Compared with the peasants in the France they left behind, the habitants were well nourished.

This core diet was supplemented by wild berries: cherries, raspberries, and hawthorns, and garden vegetables, notably carrots, onions, cabbage, turnips, and later potatoes. Early recipes for cabbage, leek, cauliflower, and potato soup exist, all of which were made with cream or milk. The potato, which was introduced via the British colonists in New England, became almost as important as the yellow pea in the late eighteenth century. It was generally fried with onions and salt pork. Mashed potatoes were also an important ingredient in some home-baked bread. No precedent for this exists in France, but many varieties of potato bread are found in eastern Europe. About the same time the potato was introduced, tea and coffee came into demand in the cities among the bourgeoisie. Because of their high cost, they failed to catch on with the habitant until the nineteenth century. The poorer farmers made a coffee substitute from roasted barley or beans which they brewed with milk, and it is still drunk in some remote areas.

The daily menu, like the core diet, changed little from the earliest days. An early breakfast of pancakes, salt pork, bread, and cider continued until tea and coffee replaced the cider. On Sunday mornings, until very recently, stews made of meatballs similar to the Scandinavian variety flavoured with nutmeg and cloves were served. Breakfast was followed by a lunch at noon of pea soup, fried potatoes with perhaps an onion sauce, a garden vegetable like cauliflower, and spoons of maple sugar or molasses. In winter, when meat was more plentiful, boiled beef or a meat pie might also appear. A pâté made of jellied pigs' feet, fish, or cold ham would be more usual in the warmer seasons. At four o'clock, the remains of lunch would be eaten along with a salad of cucumbers or radishes sliced on a piece of bread with pork fat or butter. Finally, in the evening around eight or nine o'clock, the bowl of milk and bread mentioned before would be customary. Cider would be drunk at all the meals, including the last.

The introduction of the stove in the nineteenth century lightened the women's daily work load, but the core diet, and the menu described above, changed little. What did change was the attitude toward how food should be prepared. Gradually, a French-Canadian folk gastronomy evolved. Classic dishes, often associated with holidays, were invented and diffused. Tourtières, meat ball stews, swallow pies, various sausages, onion sauce, grattons, maple sugar pies and candies, and doughnuts are all examples. Long after folk society and culture vanish from Quebec, these culinary achievements will remain as a living record of great history.

III Anglo-Canadians

III Anglo-Canadians

In comparison with the extensive collecting and study of French-Canadian traditions that have been carried on over the past half century, research into Anglo-Canadian folklore is still in its infancy. The main centre for such study at present is Memorial University in St. John's, the only English-language university in Canada that has a folklore department. The hundreds of tiny outports around Newfoundland's winding coast have provided ideal conditions for creating and preserving folklore, and students who come from the outports have been able to gather much interesting material from their native communities. The massive collections they have built up have made the Memorial University of Newfoundland Folklore and Language Archive (MUNFLA) second in importance only to Laval's Archives de Folklore.

Elsewhere individuals have collected a good deal of regional folklore, and local histories and related studies have produced much incidental material. Anglo-Canadian collectors have been particularly interested in folk songs: they have collected and published far more songs than any other type of lore. There are some collections of superstitions and supernatural tales, mainly from Nova Scotia, and quite a few studies of regional dialects, particularly from Newfoundland. Very few Anglo-Canadian animal tales or tales of magic have been found, but jokes and anecdotes are widespread. These include the widely popular tall tales and ethnic jokes, of which the "Newfie" jokes are the most common Canadian form.

Many books and articles reflect the broad scope of folk culture now encompassed by the term folklife – architecture, costumes, cooking, crafts, arts, and customs. Many pioneer accounts help us to understand what life was like in our country before people lived in cities and worked in factories, and recent researchers have been studying our material folk culture. Attractive books describe Canadian houses, barns, log cabins, fences, churches, and lighthouses, as well as more specialized items like furniture, pottery, quilts, and hooked rugs.

But folklore is not simply a study of the past. Ethnic jokes and tall tales are being told today. Most people still retain some superstitions, traditional customs continue, and a whole new crop of belief legends is circulating among modern teenagers. The study of urban lore is just beginning in Canada, and changes in traditional life-styles remain to be documented.

1. THE QUEST OF THE BALLAD
W. Roy Mackenzie

Although the collecting of French-Canadian folk songs was already well advanced by the early twentieth century, the first major collector of English-Canadian songs, W. Roy Mackenzie (1883-1957), began his collecting in 1908. Not only was he the first "to carry the study of balladry in America out of the library and into the field," as MacEdward Leach put it, but he was also the first to recognize "the fact that these songs of Nova Scotia were not only important as songs, but even more as expressions of the lives of the people who sang them." His two books, The Quest of the Ballad *and* Ballads and Sea Songs from Nova Scotia, *were pioneer works and remain two of the finest contributions to folklore scholarship on this continent. In Herbert Halpert's words, "Before 1920 in America, only one remarkable book by a regional folklorist, W.R. Mackenzie's* The Quest of the Ballad, *shows any real interest in describing both cultural setting and informants, and in using setting and personality to show how and why folksongs are preserved." The whole of this book makes fascinating reading, and the following section illustrates its qualities.*

THE DISCOVERY OF BOB

One of the friends to whom I told the story of my quest was a doctor in Tatamagouche, a village about twelve miles from River John; and among his patients was an octogenarian named Bob Langille, who lived a couple of miles outside of the village with his two sisters, and they, also, were well stricken in years. Bob was unable to repay the doctor's services with coin of the realm, but on one or two occasions he had shown his gratitude to his benefactor by singing some old songs which he evidently regarded with a lover's jealousy and with a father's pride. So ran the report of the doctor, who agreed to convoy and to introduce me in proper form, since, as he very sagely observed, I should be in danger of expending much eloquence to little purpose if I should go unsponsored. Accordingly, thus stoutly attended, I set out one morning for the humble abode of the ancient trio.

We found our potential ballad-singer in the little door-yard behind the house, making feeble efforts to split a block of wood. He greeted my friend with the profoundest respect, acknowledged my introduction to him, and immediately disappeared within the house. We followed him as far as the kitchen to pay our respects to the two old sisters, who were enjoying the unseasonable comforts of a blazing wood fire.

After I had given a fairly complete account of my parentage, occupation, and place of abode in answer to the insistent demands of the sisters, . . . Bob loudly avowed that he would be the willing servant of any friend of the doctor's, the latter went on his way, and Bob and I retired to an inner room, an apartment almost bare of ornament or furniture, but happily separated by a partition from the torrid clime of the kitchen. Here we began to review the situation.

"It's seldom I sing me songs to anybody nowadays," said old Bob. "The time was when a man was thought somethin' of if he could set up fer a whole evenin' and sing the old English songs, but now a man's no good onless he kin sing these new-fangled Yankee songs with no sense nor no story to them."

It soon appeared that, as this prologue suggested, Bob was a Britisher of intense and blazing patriotism. "Once I sung a song fer a Yankee sailor about the *Chesapeake* and the *Shannon*," he announced. "It was a good song too, an' it told about the British beatin' the Yankees like they deserved." "He was a younger man than I was," he added gleefully, "an' he'd a' licked me fer it if they hadn't been too many Britishers around fer him."

It may seem strange that this flaming enthusiasm for the British flag should exist in a man who, as his name indicates, was of French origin, but the fact is that the same uncompromising loyalty towards an adopted rather than a parent land is manifested by all the people of Bob's age, race, and condition of life in that particular part of Canada. Much of our conversation that morning was about the Battle of Waterloo, and Bob became as excited over the topic as if he had just received news of the downfall of Napoleon . . .

My whole endeavour was to establish myself in the character of sympathetic and interested auditor, and in this I was so far successful that I could at length feel that there would be no offence in suggesting that a good old-fashioned song should be produced to enliven the occasion. Bob leaned forward, fixed his gaze earnestly upon a knot in the floor, and "studied" for a few moments; then, throwing back his head and closing his eyes, he began with a suddenness and a volume of sound that for the moment harrowed me with fear and wonder. It would not have seemed possible, without auricular evidence, that such a frail old body could be made the propelling power for such thunder-blasts of music. The voice was now cracked and hoarse, and perilously uncertain on the upper notes, but the evidence was clear on the point that old Bob had been in his day a mighty singer of ballads.

His manner of delivery was different from that of Little Ned and of many other singers whom I have heard more recently. They, as a rule, sang with a careful retardation on the last words of each stanza; but Bob proceeded from line to line, and from stanza to stanza, with the greatest rapidity and vehemence. On the last line of the song, however, he practiced the device which has been used by every ballad-singer I have ever listened to, that is, he sang the first part of the line in the regular way with eyes closed and head thrown back, then made a swift and sudden descent from the empyrean of music, opened his eyes, leaned forward, glared upon his audience, and pronounced the last few words in an emphatic conversational tone.

This, as it seems to me, is a most effective way of apprising the audience that the story is rounded out and brought to a victorious conclusion. It is – to introduce an easy and unstrained analogy – as if Pegasus had completed his flight, brought his rider safe to ground, and allowed him to spring lightly from his seat to converse with earth-treading mortals before beginning the next ascension. And the symbolic action employed for the production of this effect is frequently reenforced by an emphatic impact of the right hand upon the knee.

The first song had no title that Bob had ever heard. "Ye kin call it what ye like," he assured me when he saw my anxiety to know how it had been referred to in the days when it was a song worth knowing. One would not have to seek far for the implied title, but since from Bob's point of view the song was of great importance and the title negligible, I shall out of respect for his memory give the song in full:

'Twas of a beautiful damsel, as I have heard it told,
Her father died and left her five thousand pounds in gold.
She lived with her uncle, as you may plainly see,
And she loved a ploughboy on the banks of sweet Dundee.

Her uncle had a ploughboy. Young Mary loved him well,
And in her uncle's garden her tales of love would tell.
....
....

One morning very early, just at the break of day,
Her uncle came to Mary, and then to her did say,
"Arise, young lovely Mary, and come along with me,
For the young squire's waiting for you on the banks of sweet
    Dundee."

"A fig for all your squires, your dukes and lords besides,
For young William he appears to me like diamonds in my eyes."
"Hold on," said her uncle, "for revenged on you I'll be,
For I will banish William from the banks of sweet Dundee."

The press-gang came on William as he was all alone.
He boldly fought for liberty though there was ten to one.
The blood did flow in torrents, he fought so manfully.
He'd rather die for Mary on the banks of sweet Dundee.

One morning as young Mary was lamenting for her love,
She met the wealthy young squire down by her uncle's grove.
He put his arms around her. "Stand off, base man," said she,

....

He put his arms around her and strove to throw her down.
Two pistols and a sword she spied beneath his morning gown.
Young Mary took the pistols, the sword she handled free.
She fired and shot the squire on the banks of sweet Dundee.

Her uncle overheard the noise and hastened to the ground.
"Now since you've killed the squire I'll give you your death-
    wound."
"Keep off," then says young Mary. "Undaunted I shall be."
He closed his eyes no more to rise on the banks of sweet Dundee.

Young William he was sent for and speedily did return.
As soon as he arrived upon the shore young Mary ceased to mourn.
The banns were quickly published, their hands were joined so free.
She now enjoys her ploughboy on the banks of sweet Dundee.

The wall of reserve was now demolished, and behind the ruins appeared a fair garden of cantatory fervour, from which Bob continued,
without any urging from me, to send forth resounding peals of music.
Indeed, my chief trouble now was to persuade him to pause occasionally
and give me a song in such form that I could copy it out. He sang so
rapidly that no human being without the accomplishment of shorthand

could possibly follow his voice with pen and paper. Then, when he attempted to repeat the song without the music, he had to go pretty rapidly in order to maintain the continuity of his recitation; and ever and anon he would forget a line and suddenly burst into a loud roar of song, which meant that he was "backing up" to go through the whole stanza in the hope of catching the stubborn line off its guard . . .

But to return to the performance of Bob, in which, I think it may safely be assumed, the reader is more interested than in the discomforts of Bob's audience. There were other ballads of the same general nature as the one I have cited – brave tales of distressed but resourceful maidens and young men of humble birth and noble qualifications; and, interspersed among these, were some stirring tales of sea-fights with pirates or with the national foes of Britain. These sea-ballads were held in the greatest esteem by Bob, and the particular one that found supreme favour in his eyes was "The *Little Fighting Chance*." The reasons for this will be readily found if I present the ballad itself:

On the fourteenth of July once so clear was the sky.
We saw a sassy frigate come bearing down so nigh,
Come bearing down upon us as we sailed out of France.
The name that she was called was the *Little Fighting Chance*.

Chorus: So cheer up, my lively boys. Let it never be said
That the sons of old Britannia would ever be afraid.

If I had been a listener of the good old-fashioned sort I could not have sat gazing silently and impassively at the singer who was making this passionate appeal to my loyalty and manliness. This lack of the proper response in me put upon old Bob the constraint of piecing up my imperfections in himself, and, as he delivered the last word of the brave chorus, he opened his eyes, glared upon me with an access of patriotic fervour, and bellowed, "They never was afraid yit, me boy!" Then, having supplied the comment which he should have had merely to stimulate, he closed his eyes and proceeded with redoubled vigour:

We gave to them a gun and the battle had begun.
The cannon they did roar and the bullets they did fly.
It was broadside for broadside. We showed them gallant sport.
And to see the lofty yards and the topmasts rolling overboard.

We fought them four hours, the battle was so hot,
Till four of our foremost men lay dead upon the spot.
Sixteen were wounded, made twenty in all,
And down with the French lily, boys, the Frenchmen one and all.

O now, my brave boys, since the prize is our own,
What shall we do for jury-masts? for spars we have none.
So we tore in with a sweet and pleasant gale,
And early the next morning to the feet of our king sail.

So now, brave boys, since we have gotten safe to shore,
We'll make the ale-houses and the taverns for to roar.
Here's a health unto King George and all his gallant fleet!
We'll smother all the Yankee dogs that ever we do meet.

The reader of the uninspired lines might easily dismiss "The *Little Fighting Chance*" as an incoherent, half-rhymed, metreless attempt at poetic narrative. But I, who have heard it delivered with conviction by one who was in his own way a severe enough critic, cannot regard it so lightly; for I cannot forget how lovely and pleasant to Bob was the imagined relegation of French lilies, Yankee dogs, and all things offending the good King George, to one indiscriminate slaughter-bed.

The song which followed this is brief enough to present in full. Its interest lies in the fact that it shows a very neat combination of the two apparently irreconcilable topics which have been taken up separately in the two ballads just presented – the dauntless maid and the English victory at sea.

As we were a sailing down by the Spanish shore,
Our drums they did beat and the guns loudly roar.
We spied a lofty admiral ship come ploughing down the main,
Which caused us to h'ist our tops'ls again.

Come, boys, let us be hearty, come, boys, let us be true,
And after our enemy we quickly shall pursue.
Soon as we overtake them upon the ocean wide
With foresail set we'll give them a broadside.

They gave to us another as good as we sent.
For to sink each other was our whole intent.
At the very second broadside our captain he was slain.
Up steps a damsel his place for to maintain.

"O quarters, O quarters, my brave British boys."
"No quarters, no quarters," the damsel she replies.
"You have the best of quarters I can to you afford.
You must fight, strike or sink, my boys, or jump overboard."

Now since we gained the victory we'll drink a glass of wine.
Drink to your own true love and I'll drink to mine.

Here's a health unto the damsel, the damsel of fame,
So boldly she fought on the *Union* by name.

As Bob sang I made efforts to copy, or, when the motion was too swift
for me, I leaned back, closed my eyes in imitation of my entertainer, and
resigned myself to the pleasant task of learning some of the tunes. The
two old sisters hovered about, as Othello says of Desdemona,

But still the house affairs would call them thence,
Which ever as they could with haste dispatch
They'd come again and with a greedy ear
Devour up Bob's discourse.

If the song happened to have a refrain they would join in, and frequently
they would accompany him through a line or a stanza which had lodged
itself in their memories. And at all times they commented freely on the
stirring events which their brother was celebrating in stentorian song.

Finally it reached the hour of high noon, and as I had no desire to
forfeit the esteem of the two sisters, who were becoming more and more
impressed by my friendly and conciliatory manners, I cast false delicacy
to the winds and accepted their invitation to join the family at their
meal of boiled potatoes, mammoth slices of bread, and tea that had been
boiled until a spoon would stand upright in it. Bob laid aside his hat and
drew up to the board, but in him the spirit of poetry was not wholly
supplanted by gross desires for bread. "There was a man once," he announced, as he laid his folded hands upon his place, "that made up a
piece of poetry for a blessin' on his dinner, and I'll give it to ye:

Some hev meat and cannot eat,
And some would eat that hev no meat,
But we hev meat and we kin eat,
And so God bless the giver."

"Amen!" responded old Maggie fervently; and, ceasing to reflect upon
the cavalier treatment that verse receives during the process of oral
transmission, I addressed myself to the business in hand.

While we were partaking of the food thus consecrated, Bob and his
sisters were moved to discourse upon that period of their lives which had
been called up by the performance of the morning. Though they were
now living hard by the sea-coast, they had spent their earlier years in
New Annan, a Scotch settlement about twenty miles inland. Bob had
been a cobbler by trade. He had worked his bit of land in season, and,
when occasion called, had gone from house to house building and repairing shoes. His love of ballads was such an early growth that he could not
remember the time when he had not immediately appropriated and
tucked away in his capacious memory every new one that came in his

path; and since in his capacity of itinerant cobbler he had visited from time to time most of the homes in a singing community, he had had ample opportunity of acquiring new songs in exchange for old ones. "Ah, sir," cried old Kitty, moved by these reminiscences to a burst of enthusiasm for the splendour of the past, "it was nathin' but singin' an' dancin' in them days. Many's the time we would take hold of hands an' go through the fields to a dance singin' the old songs together."

After the family had moved down to Tatamagouche, which was about thirty years before I made their acquaintance, Bob had learned most of his sea-songs, and these, I suspect, had had the effect of crowding out some of the older ballads which he had learned in New Annan . . .

When we finally pushed our chairs back and proceeded to load our pipes, Maggie, the younger of the two sisters, announced that she had a song that she was going to sing for me "while Bob was gittin' rested up." I cheerfully bade her sing on, and she at once composed herself and began with a plangent vigour which showed that she had studied her brother's methods to some purpose. Her song was the "Gaspard Tragedy":

In Gaspard of late a young damsel did dwell.
For wit and for beauty few did her excel.
A young man did court her for to be his dear,
And he by his trade was a ship carpenter.

He said, "Dearest Mary, if you will agree,
And give your consent, dear, to marry me,
Your love it can cure me of sorrow and care,
Consent, then, to wed with a ship carpenter."

With blushes as charming as roses in June
She answered "Dear William, to wed I'm too young;
For young men are fickle, I see very plain.
If a maiden is kind her they quickly disdain."

"My charming sweet Mary, how can you say so?
Thy beauty is the heaven to which I would go.
And if there I find channel if I chance for to steer
I there will cast anchor and stay with my dear."

But yet 'twas in vain she strove to deny,
For he by his cunning soon made her comply,
And by base deceptions he did her betray.
In sin's hellish paths he led her astray.

110

Now when this young damsel with child she did prove
She soon sent her tidings to her faithless love,
Who swore by the heavens that he would prove true,
And said, "I will marry no damsel but you."

Things passed on a while. At length we do hear
His ship was a-sailing, for sea he must steer,
Which pained this poor damsel and wounded her heart,
To think with her true love she must part.

Cried she, "Dearest Will, ere you go to sea
Remember the vows you have made unto me.
If at home you don't tarry I never can rest.
O how can you leave me with sorrows oppressed?"

With tender expressions he to her did say,
"I'll marry my Mary ere I go to sea,
And if that to-morrow my love can ride down,
The ring I can buy our fond union to crown."

With tender embraces they parted that night
And promised to meet the next morning at light.
William said, "Mary, you must go with me
Before we are married our friends for to see."

He led her through groves and valleys so deep.
At length this poor damsel began for to weep,
Crying, "Willie, I fear you will lead me astray,
On purpose my innocent life to betray."

He said, "You've guessed right. All earth can't you save,
For the whole of last night I was digging your grave."
When poor Mary did hear him say so
The tears from her eyes like a fountain did flow.

"O pity my infant. O spare my poor life.
Let me live full of shame if I can't be your wife.
O take not my life lest my soul you betray,
And you to perdition be hurried away."

"There is no time disputing to stand,"
But instantly taking a knife in his hand
He pierced her fair breast, whence the blood it did flow,
And into the grave her fair body did throw.

He covered her body and quick hastened home,
Left nothing but the small birds her fate to moan.
On board ship he entered without more delay,
And set sail for Plymouth to plough the salt sea.

A young man named Stewart of courage so bold
One night happened late for to go in the hold,
Where a beautiful damsel to him did appear,
And she in her arms held an infant most dear.

Being merry with liquor he went to embrace,
Transported with joy at beholding her face;
When to his amazement she vanished away,
Which he told to the captain without more delay.

The captain soon summoned his jovial ship's crew,
And said, "My brave fellows, I'm afraid some of you
Have murdered some damsel ere you came away,
Whose injured ghost now haunts on the sea.

"Whoever you be, if the truth you deny,
When found out you'll be hanged on the gallows so high,
But he who confesses his life we'll not take,
But leave him upon the first island we make."

Then William immediately fell to his knees.
The blood in his veins quick with horror did freeze.
He cried, "Cruel murderer, what have I done?
God help me, I fear my poor soul is undone.

"Poor injured ghost, your full pardon I crave,
For soon I must follow you down to the grave."
No one else but this poor wretch beheld the sad sight,
And raving distracted he died that same night.

Now when her sad parents these tidings did hear,
Soon searched for the body of their daughter so dear,
In the town of Southampton in valley so deep,
Her body was found, which caused many to weep.

In Gaspard's green churchyard her ashes now lie,
And we hope that her soul is with God in the sky.
So let this sad tale be a warning to all
Who dare an innocent young maid to enthrall.

This time it was Bob's turn to act the part of bystander and to evince a sympathetic interest in the progress of events. He became more and more wrought up as the heroine's fortunes darkened, and his excitement grew overpowering as the singer described poor Mary's grief when the perfidious William prepared to execute his master-stroke of villainy:

> He led her through groves and valleys so deep.
> At length this poor damsel began for to weep,
> Crying, "Willie, I fear you will lead me astray,
> On purpose my innocent life to betray."

Then followed the cool and murderous response of William:

> He said, "You've guessed right. All earth can't you save,
> For the whole of last night I was digging your grave."

This was too much for human endurance. "The damn scoundrel!" roared Bob, "I wisht I hed him be the throat fer a minute or two!" Then, with a renewed sense of the pathos of the situation, "Ah, the pore gyurl! I can't keep the tears out o' me eyes when I think of her!" But his sister, swelling with importance over the applause she was evoking, had now got several lines beyond the point that had stimulated Bob's wrathful outburst.

I have written the song down as it fell from the lips of Maggie, but I have been enabled to do so because she sang it for me on a subsequent occasion after my wife and I had hit upon the scheme of copying songs line about in order to double the speed of the work. If I had to rely upon the results of this my first visit, the "Gaspard Tragedy" should go unrecorded so far as I am concerned. It impressed me then as being one of the most interesting songs I had heard that day, and I at once made the effort to copy it; but I might as well have tried to capture a wireless message. Old Maggie could make an easy and unhesitating passage through the ballad on the wings of song, but, divested of these wings, she became incapable of the slightest progress; nor could she, though with the best intentions, go slowly enough with her singing for me to get the words down.

But at this unhappy juncture Bob, who had been earnestly "studying" with his head in his hands, suddenly leaned back with his eyes tightly closed, and resolved himself into a tornado of song:

> Arise, arise, ye seven brethren,
>   And put on your armours bright.
> Arise and take care of your younger sister,
>   For your eldest went away last night.

Then was the oil of gladness straightway poured upon my troubled head, for this was an "English and Scottish popular ballad" at last. Old

Kitty and I settled our backs against the wall and drew on our pipes with a contentment which no elusive ship-carpenter could mar, while Bob, raging like one inspired, whirled onward through the reverberating stanzas.

'Twas on the road, 'twas away they rode,
   'Twas all by the light of the moon,.
Until he looked over his left shoulder
   And saw her seven brethren drawing nigh.

"Lie down, lie down, Lady Margret," he said,
   "And by my two steeds stand,
Until I fight thy seven brethren,
   And thy father, who's nigh at hand."

She stood and saw her seven brethren fall
   Without shedding a tear,
Until she saw her father fall
   Whom she loved so dear,

"Withhold thy hand, Lord William," she said,
   "For thy stroke it is wonderful sore.
For it's many's the true love I might have had,
   But a father I'll never have more."

She took her white pocket-handkerchief,
   That was made of the hollands fine,
And wiped her father's bloody bloody wound
   That run redder than the wine.

"Choose ye, choose ye, Lady Margret," he said,
   "Will you here abide?"
"O no, I must go wheresoever you go,
   For you've left me here no guide."

He mounted her on his milky white steed,
   And he on his dappled grey.
The bugle horn hung by his side,
   And slowly they rode away.

'Twas on the road, 'twas away they rode,
   'Twas all by the light of the moon,
Until they came to the Erint waters,
   That was raging like the main.

He lighted down to take a drink
    Of the spring that run so clear,
And down the stream run his good heart's blood.
    Sore she begun to fear.

"Lie down, lie down, Lord William," she said,
    "For you are a slain man.
 O no, it is your scarlet red cloak
    That's reflecting on the main."

'Twas on the road, 'twas away they rode,
    'Twas all by the light of the moon,
Until they came to his mother's chamber door,
    And there they lighted down.

"Arise, arise, dear mother," he says,
    "Arise and let us in,
For by all the powers that is above
    This night my love I've won."

"O mother, mother, make us a bed,
    And sheathe it with the hollands fine,
And lay Lady Margret by my side
    And sound sound sleep we'll take."

Lord William he died at the middle of the night,
    Lady Margret ere it was day,
And every true lovers that goes together
    I wish them more luck than they.

When Bob opened his eyes upon the last line of the ballad I was waiting with raised pencil to conduct him through a second and more prosaic recital; and when I left the abode of song late that afternoon, with my right arm hanging limp from the shoulder, my comfort was that I had, at least, discovered one gleaming nugget in the mine of base metals.

2. SUPERSTITIONS AND THE SUPERNATURAL IN NOVA SCOTIA

Mary L. Fraser

Where W. Roy Mackenzie was the pioneer in collecting Nova Scotia folk songs, a Catholic nun, Mary L. Fraser (1879-1957), was the first to make an extensive study of the province's popular beliefs, superstitions, customs, legends, and folktales. She published her collection in 1932 as Folklore of Nova Scotia. *While her interpretation of folklore now seems somewhat naïve, her material is genuine and reflects the mingling of Indian, Scottish, and French traditions characteristic of the region. The extracts that follow illustrate some of the most widespread beliefs and legends.*

FOLK CURES

The superstitious practices resorted to in order to obtain cures are many and varied. Among the Acadians, only certain men in the village were endowed with the power of performing the cures. These men could stop the flow of blood from a bad cut, or cure a toothache simply by passing their hand over the part affected. Again, if an individual afflicted with warts went to them for a cure, they would take a pea, tie it up in a rag and throw it into a well. With the pea went the wart.

In the sections of the country peopled by Highlanders, only the "seventh son" had the privilege of curing people by merely stroking the diseased member. These men, who were rare enough, were frequently sent for from long distances to give relief to some sufferer. (223)

In these districts, too, warts were disposed of in a variety of ways, all of which point to ancient pre-Christian beliefs with regard to the transference of disease from one person to another, and for which witches were once tried and condemned to death. For example, blood from the warts was put on a cloth which was then dropped in the path of a passerby. (2581) Or stones, to the number of warts, were put into a bag, which was then thrown over the right shoulder on to the road so that it might be picked up. The person picking it up got the warts. (2638)

More significant still of pagan descent was the practice of rubbing stolen meat on the warts and then burying it. When the meat decayed the warts disappeared. (2467) Another certain cure was to take a string with one more knot than the number of your warts and throw it after the first funeral that passed, saying "Take this with you and rot in the grave."(2438)

Yet another example of the transference of disease to old mother earth is found in this cure for a pain, which the teller saw tried: If when running you should take a pain, bend down, pick up a stone, spit on it, and put it back with the spit next the ground. The pain will disappear." (2104)

Sprains were cured by an old woman saying a rhyme over the injured member, or by placing around the sprain a string made from white spool thread knotted with seven knots. The person who is responsible for this bit of information asserted that she had actually had a sprained ankle cured in this way.

Toothache could be cured in a variety of ways. A person with a charm for it took a rusty nail into the woods, and drove it into a tree, saying at the same time: "May you be there all pains and aches." The suffering person was cured as soon as the nail was driven. (2379)

A preventive of toothache was to chew the wood of a tree that had been struck by lightning. A Christian element was introduced into the cure when a prayer was written on a piece of paper, which was put into the mouth over the aching tooth. (2382)

But it was generally a woman who had these charms, for witches were the lineal descendants of the Druidesses, who were remarkable for their magic. For example, a woman who had a charm would rub a sore throat with water and recite an incantation, and a cure would be effected . . .

GOOD AND BAD LUCK

What may be considered another survival of a belief in witches is the curious superstition that prevails with regard to meeting women. Here are some specimens: "On setting out on a trip, if you meet a woman it is bad luck; but if she is red-headed, it is worse – turn back. (3795) But if you meet a white horse and afterwards a red-headed woman, it is all right." Evidently the white horse is so potent in luck bringing that he can override the terrors of even a red-headed woman. (7099)

Again, miners are sure of an accident if a woman should go down into the mine. (3482) If they meet a woman first on going to work, they are afraid. Women have been deterred from visiting mines because of this superstition. Good luck for the whole year was brought to a house by a man coming as first visitor on New Year's Day. (3886) A woman would bring only bad luck. (3890) It was also regarded as good luck for a man to come to a house on May Day. On this occasion he was not allowed to leave until he had eaten something.

A black cat running across your path indicated bad luck; a hare doing likewise was worse; but a squirrel brought good luck. (3814, 3876) Once upon a time witches were supposed to have assumed the form of black cats and of hares. This superstition may be a survival of that belief . . .

There was a belief among Highlanders that everything had a tendency to grow during the increase of the moon. (7961) In fact, they considered that the harvest moon caused just as much ripening as the sun. This belief gradually extended to other things; consequently a farmer would never kill an animal for food when the moon was on the wane; he waited until the increase. (7695) A girl would not have her hair cut except when the moon was on the wane; otherwise it would grow too fast. To see the moon over your left shoulder was bad luck; to see it over the right was good luck. (5920, 5924) Any wish you made the first time you saw the new moon was sure to come true, provided you had something in your hand at the time you saw it, and that you made the Sign of the Cross.

Meeting a funeral was regarded as very bad luck for anybody, but especially for a wedding party. (5442) An old saying has it that:

> "Happy is the corpse that the rain falls on;
> Happy is the bride that the sun shines on." (4783, 5505)

To go in the same direction with the funeral was regarded as all right . . . (5450)

SECOND SIGHT

That some persons are endowed with the gift of Second Sight is a well-authenticated Celtic belief. The Gaelic name for it, *da-shealladh*, does not mean literally "The Second Sight," but "The Two Sights," the vision of the world of sense and that of the world of spirit . . .

Those who had the gift were sometimes very sensitive about it. They made no parade of it, but concealed it as much as possible. (This local information I have from a man who has been in close touch with several people endowed with Second Sight, and who got several of the stories which follow from them at first hand. On account of their sensitiveness, he asked me to suppress both his name and theirs, for some of the seers are yet living, and all of them have many relatives in the country.)

At Fraser's Mills, Antigonish Co., a man was going down a hill one day when he saw on the road at the foot of the hill a number of men carrying a dead man to the side of the road. He recognized all the men as his neighbours except the dead man, whom he had never seen before. All disappeared in a moment. This visionary then went away to the States but returned a number of years later to see the old place once more. During this visit he was coming down the same hill one day when he saw the same group of men carrying a dead man and placing him exactly where he saw him so many years before. This time it was the reality. A young man whom he had never seen before had just been killed at that spot. (D1825.7)

The story that follows I heard my father tell many a time. Apart from this one instance, he never saw anything preternatural in his life.

When he was a young man in his teens, he left his home in Antigonish County to seek his fortune in California. After several years, he had amassed a sum of money, which he was contemplating investing in a ranch stocked with a large number of cattle. On the night before the transaction was to have been completed, he was lying awake thinking it all over, and very anxious about its being the best thing for him to do, when into the moon-lit room walked a young woman whom he had never seen before. She was dressed in black, with a white ruffle about her neck. She stood at the foot of the bed, and in a warning voice repeated three times: "Do not buy these cattle or you'll be sorry for it; come home." She remained long enough to have her features indelibly imprinted on his memory; then she disappeared as mysteriously as she had come. He did not doubt for a moment but that the warning was supernatural. The next day he wrote to his brother, who was in Boston, asking that he meet him in Chicago, where an exhibition was in progress. Leaving the deal open, he set out for the east.

On his arrival in Chicago, his brother urged him to continue his journey home to see his aged mother, and he consented to do so. Now, his mother had always worried about the welfare of her absent boy, so when he got home she begged him to remain, and urged him to buy a fine farm that was for sale at Antigonish Harbour. To please her he went to see the farm, but had no intention of buying it. He was packing his trunk for California when his mother increased her pleadings and begged him, with tears, to remain at home. He could resist no further.

After he had bought the farm, he was conducted to the nearest neighbour's house to be introduced to the family. As he sat in the living room at nightfall one of the daughters of the family brought in a lighted lamp. The moment she entered, he rose to his feet, fixed his eyes upon her, and stared in speechless amazement. She was dressed in black with a white ruffle around her neck – in a word, she was the woman who had brought him home. She was totally unconscious of the wanderings of her spirit, was indignant at being stared at by this stranger, and left the room. Only two years later, when she was his promised wife, did he tell her the cause of his rudeness. (D1825.1.2)

There lived at the rear of a farm at Antigonish Harbour an old man who was remarkable for Second Sight. He was popularly known as "Mountain Rory." One morning the owner of the farm came into the house and said: "Mountain Rory had a strange story for me this morning. He told me that when he was coming over the mountain early today he saw a great many men working out there, some digging, some building a railway, and so on. Whoever lives to see it, there will be some kind of works set up out at the rear of this farm yet." This year (1928) the prediction is being verified. A company has bought up that land, with its fine gypsum deposits, and are at this writing building a railway out to the Harbour. (D1825.7)

A good many years ago a young man at Antigonish returned home from work one evening looking as pale as death. To his mother's anxious inquiries, he answered that he was sick from what he met on the road. He told her that a funeral passed him that he thought was his own, for he named all the people at it, the whole country-side, he himself being the only one missing. A week later he was drowned accidentally. Something went wrong with the water-wheel at the mill where he was working and he went down to fix it. Some one by accident turned on the water in the mill-race. Great sympathy was felt for his family, and everybody turned out for the funeral. It was remarked that everyone whom he had named as present at the phantom funeral was there. (D1825.7.1)

FORERUNNERS

Closely allied to Second Sight is the belief in forerunners, especially with regard to death. There is a persistent tradition that the spirits of the living rehearse the making of coffins, the funeral preparations, even the funeral processions. Those who have the Second Sight see these things, those who have not very often hear what is going on, although they cannot see them. Very few Nova Scotian Celts are brave enough to walk in the centre of a highway after nightfall, for fear of encountering any of these phantom funeral processions. That their fears are not un-founded may be seen from the tales that follow.

The grandfather of the man who told me this story used to go very often to see a relative of his who was dying. One night this relative seemed so near death that he remained until a very late hour. As he was returning home by the highway, walking in the middle of the road, for he was not a superstitious man, he was almost smothered by some terrible obstruction that he could not see. With difficulty he succeeded in getting off the road, and then he stood aside and listened. He could hear distinctly the sound of passing feet, then came the clatter of wagon wheels which he could even hear going over a stone on the road. He waited until what seemed a whole procession had gone by, then made for his home. As a slight snowfall was covering the ground, he determined to go the next morning to look for tracks. At daybreak he was again on the road, but not a track could he see. The sick man died the next day, and he was convinced that it was the phantom of his funeral procession that he had encountered. (D1827.1.2)

In pioneer days there were no undertakers, so coffins had to be made in the most convenient place in the neighbourhood. Many people heard in advance the assembling of the boards for the purpose, and the ghostly strokes of the hammer . . . .

Two young women were sitting up with a child who was dying. It was a beautiful fine night and in that country home everything was quiet. Suddenly the silence was broken by the sound of hammering and sawing in the workshop near by. They looked out; the door was closed, nobody was about. One of them looked into her grandfather's room, from which the sound of his deep regular breathing could be heard distinctly. "Isn't it strange," she said, "there is grandfather sleeping quietly, yet listen to his spirit working out there at the coffin that he'll make only tomorrow." They listened in silence to the uncanny sound. The lunch that was brought in to them could not tempt them. The baby died before morning, and the grandfather made the coffin the next morning as they knew he would. (D1827.1.2)

Some years ago, people who live on a certain hill at Barrachois, Cape Breton, used to watch a phantom train glide noiselessly around the headlands of the Bras d'Or, and come to a stop at a gate leading to one of the houses. One who saw it herself told me how at seven o'clock every evening for a whole month every family on the hill would go out of doors to see it. Every coach was lighted, but no people could be seen. At the hour of its approach, some people sometimes went down to the track to get a better look at it, but were disappointed at its not coming at all, although the watchers on the hill saw it as usual. At the end of the month, a man was killed by a train just at the gate to which the phantom train used to come. Nobody saw it afterwards. (E535.4)

Automobiles, which have run in such numbers over our roads for the past twenty-five years, had their forerunners half a century ago. One evening fifty-one years ago, a young man at Mull River, Inverness Co., was going on a message to a neighbour's house when he saw before him on the road a very terrifying object. It was large and black and had a red light in the middle of its back. A stream of light came from the front of it, so bright that he could see the shingles on the house to which he was going. It went up to the house, passed around it, and then came down the road so swiftly that he jumped aside to let it pass. Terrified, he made the sign of the cross, then looked to see the terrible *bochdan*. The bright

121

front lights had turned once more to red. He heard no sound. Not until twenty-five years later did he discover of what it was a forerunner. (Story told me by the man's sister.)

Trains, too, had their forerunners in several places. Years before a railway was built through Inverness Co. trains were seen and heard. One evening a man who lived a mile above Mabou River, when returning from feeding his cattle in the barn, heard the sound of a train passing where no one ever thought it would pass. He called his wife and children, and they all listened to the clatter of the "Judique Flier" as it made its way over the grassy slopes and wooded hills of this beautiful country-side. Contrary to all expectations, when the railway was built several years later, the route it took was through that particular part of the country . . . .

FAIRY LORE

The early settlers of Nova Scotia brought with them from the old lands a belief in the existence of fairies. The whole district which the town of Inverness now covers was formerly called the Shean (from the Gaelic *Sithean*, meaning the house of the fairies). In this district there was a small hill, shaped something like a large hay stack, where the old people used to see the "little people" in thousands. People in general would not walk about in that place at night; but when they did so, as soon as they approached the hill the little visitors vanished. A man who owned a farm at that place was so much troubled by noises of no natural descrip-tion that he sold his place in order to get rid of them. (F211)

An old pedlar used to go around the country with his wagonload of goods drawn by a rather miserable-looking grey horse. One night he put up at Mr. MacNeil's house near Castle Bay, and his horse was comfort-ably housed in the near-by stable. In the morning when Mr. MacNeil, who was up betimes, went to the stable, he was surprised to find the stranger's horse decorated with braided tail and mane. He expressed his surprise to the pedlar, who told him that this was a nightly occurrence, and he ascribed it to the fairies. No matter in what part of the country he was, or what precautions were taken to prevent intruders from enter-ing the stables, the same thing took place. When they gave the horse water in which a silver coin was placed, the plaits unravelled of them-selves. (F366.2.1)

Mr. Murphy told me of another prank played by the fairies on the farm adjoining his grandfather's lot at Low Point. A man from the old country went out reaping one day in a field of this farm, when, lo and behold! he perceived that all the stooks previously made had been turned upside down. "I didn't think we had any of the 'little people' in this part of the world," he declared in his astonishment. (F399.4)

The Acadians are quite familiar with these little creatures under the name of "lutin." In olden times they used to hear, about sunset, a noise in the air like the flapping of the wings of a flock of large birds. This was followed by the sound of the rolling of wheels, the laughter and singing of men and women, the ringing of bells, and the barking of dogs . . .

At night the "lutin" would come and make braids in the horses' manes and drive or ride those horses that were best and swiftest. The horses so treated did not suffer any ill effects of the rough usage to which they were subjected. (Mr. Henri Le Blanc, an Acadian, gave me this information. I have consulted several other Acadians in different sections of the country, and found them all of the same opinion with regard to the mischievous "lutin.") (F262.1, F399.4)

DONALD MacNORMAN AND THE FAIRY CHILD

In general, however, the fairy tales that are current in Nova Scotia are importations from the Celtic lands that have been handed down by oral tradition. A good specimen of these tales was obtained for me by a kind friend from Mr. Neil MacLellan of Broad Cove. He told it to her in Gaelic, and she translated it.

Many generations ago there lived in one of the glens of Scotland a kind old man of the name of Donald MacNorman, and his wife, Red Janet. Their home was in the upper part of the glen near a big rock. The glen was surrounded by high mountains. There was nothing to break the silence of their solitude except the murmur of a river as it flowed gently past their door, and the song of the birds as they sang sweetly in the grove above their house.

Many a time Donald would stand listening to the moaning of the wind on the craggy mountain tops – those mountains that had been buffeted by many a fierce gale for hundreds of years.

No stranger from land or sea but was welcome at Donald's house. His home and table were at the disposal of the traveller. This was a satisfaction to him, for he felt that he was rendering service to others.

As is the case with every other mortal, Donald's happiness was not complete. He had no heir who would hand down his name to future generations. But Donald had great faith in the fairies, and firmly believed the strange stories he had heard about them from his ancestors. No doubt his surroundings had something to do with confirming this faith. He felt that they might do for him what they had done for others, and his confidence in them was not in vain, for the fairies gave him to understand that the long-desired heir would one day in the near future come to gladden his home. At this news his happiness knew no bounds.

No robin on the branch, nor no nightingale in the glade, sang sweeter than he.

One fine evening on arriving home from his boats he was met by the nurse, who placed a beautiful child in his arms. There was great rejoicing. The whole neighbourhood assembled, and for days the glass went the rounds to do honour to the little stranger.

Everything went well for a time. There was not a cloud on Donald's horizon that little Norman did not dispel. But alas! the day was near at hand when Donald's brightest dreams and sweetest hopes were to be shattered. One dry, cold day in spring, when Donald and Janet were working in the fields, they left a little girl to take care of the child. After putting him to sleep in the cradle, the girl went out to play. When she came back, what was her surprise to find instead of the healthy child she had left in the cradle, a thin, miserable little infant.

Immediately the little girl ran to tell the parents. The news soon spread abroad, and great sympathy was felt for the grief-stricken father and mother. Search was made high and low for little Norman, but without success. Finally, in despair, Donald thought he would have a look at the stranger who replaced his beloved child. Standing over the cradle, he raised his hands in horror, saying: "May God be between us and you. I know this creature does not belong to this world." Janet said that she could not close an eye while the creature was under the roof. "If that is the case," said Donald, "you will be without sleep for many a day, for it does not seem to be in a hurry to leave." Then they began to wonder what they would do about the child. The only way they could solve the difficulty was to keep it and treat it kindly. The child seemed to respond to their treatment, for it seemed to be enjoying life.

At last Donald and his friends came to the conclusion that it was the fairy queen who had taken little Norman away and had put this child in his place. So Donald was advised to place the child on the big rock above the house, and leave it there all night. If the fairy queen should hear it cry, she would come for it and leave Norman in its place. So this was done. Donald hoped that if the fairy queen failed to come for it, the eagles might carry it off. Early next morning he went to the rock, but found that neither fairy queen nor eagle had come for the fairy child. The only thing to do was to bring it back home.

After this it became more intolerable than ever. It kept up a continual howl night and day; and like the lean kine of Egypt, the more it ate the thinner it got.

Then a lame tailor came to Donald's house to make him a suit of clothes. It was harvest time, and all were busy. After breakfast Janet went to the fields with her husband, and left the fairy child in the tailor's charge.

124

They had not gone a long time when the child raised itself on its elbow in the cradle and looked cautiously around. When it saw that they were alone in the house, it turned to the tailor and told him not to be afraid, for if he promised not to tell anybody, it would play for him the sweetest tune he had ever heard. Then it pulled a chanter from behind it, and began to play. The tailor was so entranced that he could not sew another stitch. He stuck the needle in the coat he was making, crossed his legs, and listened. But he was not long in this position when he saw twenty maidens dressed in green cloaks come in. Then music and dancing began in earnest. The tailor, with his eyes almost jumping out of his head, sat watching them. At last he jumped up, threw the coat away, and joined in the dance. During the dancing he made an attempt to swing one of the maidens, but to his astonishment he found that she was only a shadow. Once when turning around one of the maidens struck him such a blow that he saw stars. Raising his hand to ward off the blow, he found himself seated in his chair with his coat on his knees, just as he was before the music began. On looking around, he found that there was no one in the house but himself and the child lying quietly in the cradle as if nothing had happened. The harvesters came home, and the tailor was very happy when the coat was finished, for he did not wish to go through a like experience again.

Shortly after this, the "little one" began to get up and sit by the fireside when the others went to bed. It would spend hours rocking itself and singing sad songs. This used to annoy Donald, so one night he threatened to get up and punish the strange creature for disturbing their night's rest; but Janet begged him not to have anything to do with the child lest some misfortune might befall them.

Donald was getting ready to go to the forge one day when, to his great surprise, the fairy child asked him to get news from the blacksmith for him. The news that Donald brought was that the forge on the hillside was burned to the ground, anvil and all. At this the child got excited and screamed out: "My loss! My loss!" It took the chanter in its hand and began to play, at the same time leaping and running over the hills. When Donald, who was watching the performance, returned to the house to relate to Janet what he had seen and heard, lo and behold! he found in the cradle his own little Norman, lying quietly and smiling at him.

If there was sorrow at the loss of Norman, there was a hundred times more rejoicing at his recovery. A great feast was prepared, at which all the neighbours were invited, the lame tailor included. If there was joy at Norman's birth, there was still greater joy at his return from the land of the fairies. (F321.1.2.3, F261, F379.5*)

THE PHANTOM SHIP

If you have never heard of the Phantom Ship that appears periodically off the coast of Port Hood, you cannot have been long in Cape Breton, for the appearance of this phantom is so well authenticated that the whole countryside knows about it, and many have seen it. The last time the ship was seen before this writing was in November, 1929. A truthworthy witness of the prodigy tells the story.

"The evening was calm. The short-lived November sun had trailed a path of glory across the broad bosom of the Gulf of St. Lawrence, and had gone down in splendour beneath the waters. The long beam from the revolving light on Port Hood Island grew gradually in brilliance as darkness settled down over the sea. The whiteness of the houses on the islands became as indistinct as the greyness of the barns, and soon only a dark outline against the sky marked where the islands stood. Lights twinkled here and there along the shore. The honk of a passing automobile alone broke the stillness, as night enveloped the little town in quiet peace. I retired to rest with the breeze from the sea fanning my face.

"I wakened suddenly. The wind had risen and I was uncomfortably cold. I arose to close the window – when, lo! out on the Gulf was a full-rigged ship burning furiously. I stood amazed. Stories I had heard of the phantom ship flashed across my mind. As I watched, I saw the flaming sails drop from the ropes, and then the ropes themselves part from the fiery spars. Soon the masts, too, went down in a shower of sparks, and the lonely fire-filled hull drifted into the night and disappeared.

"How long I had watched I know not; but a clock somewhere in the house struck midnight as, chilled to the bone, I turned from the window, my mind filled with questions." (E535.3)

3. CELTIC TALES FROM CAPE BRETON
MacEdward Leach

In English-speaking Canada most collectors have concentrated on folk songs, with the result that we have many fine folk-song books but very few of folktales. In contrast to the rich fairy-tale collections of French Canada, the British reports are scanty, and come mainly from the Maritime Provinces. The Scottish Gaels have preserved more of the ancient tales than other settlers from Britain, and some of the best examples were collected by the noted American folklorist, MacEdward Leach (1892-1967).

126

In his introduction to the tales, Dr. Leach notes:

> *Cape Breton was settled by a superior people, a people who came from a rich cultural background of story, poetry, and song. The beauty, the imaginative power, the dramatic quality, the richness of detail of the old Celtic lore is unsurpassed in western Europe ... Often on the periphery of a culture the most archaic elements are found. It is conceivable that older stories and songs might be found in Cape Breton than in Scotland or Ireland. With this in mind I went to Cape Breton in 1950 expressly to search out evidence. I secured in Gaelic and English a large store of material: songs, beliefs, stories. Very little of it is a part of living culture; rather it is recalled from the past by the very old. The significant part is that these "fragments" show how widespread must have been Celtic story material and song material in the formative years of modern culture.*

Dr. Leach noted twelve tales altogether, some of them fragmentary. The following are three of the most complete.

CORNU AND HIS SONS

Told in Gaelic by Ronald Smith, age ca. 75, of Inverness.

Cornu lived at the king's palace with his three sons. The king also had three sons. One day the king's sons got in a fight with Cornu's sons, and one of the king's sons was killed. That evening the king said to Cornu, "All three of your boys came home tonight, but only two of mine returned. For this reason, I am going to have you and your three sons put to death, unless you go to the king who owns it and bring back to me the famous mare."

Cornu and his sons set out at once. On the way they stopped at a grist mill and asked the owner how they could get into the palace. He suggested that they get into grain bags and so be smuggled into the palace. Each of them crawled into a bag, and the porters unsuspectingly carried them into the palace. That night they slipped out and began to put the bridle on the mare, but she neighed loudly, and they had to hide again in the bags. The king, hearing the neigh, called to his soldiers to look at the horse. The soldiers could find nothing amiss. After they had departed, Cornu and his sons crawled forth again and again essayed to put the bridle on the mare, but again she neighed and again the king sent out the soldiers, but they found nothing since Cornu and his sons had got safely back in the bags. They tried it a third time and this time the king himself went, and he discovered the intruders.

When they stood before him, the king said to Cornu, "Have you ever been closer to death than you are at this moment? If you have and can prove it by a story, I will let one of your sons go free." "Yes," said Cornu, "I have been closer to death. Once I was milking cows when twelve great cats came, and one of them began to purr very loudly, and I asked him what he'd take for the purr, and he said one cow. I agreed, and then all the cats began to swallow all the cows, and I climbed to the top of a tree, but the tree began to bend, and the cats were about to devour me when a man came and shot the cats." The king agreed that Cornu had proved his point and released one of the boys.

Then the king said, "If you have been closer to death a second time than you are now and can prove it with a story, I'll release a second son." "Well," said Cornu, "I used to sail, and one day as I was sailing along the shore, I saw a giant in a cave about to kill a girl. I shouted at him, but he refused to let her alone. He killed her and then turned on me. He had only one good eye. I told him I'd cure his eye, and he agreed to let me try. I mixed up some hot medicine and poured it into his eye, and it blinded him. The giant tried to catch me, but he could not because he was blind, and I hid among the goats in the cave. Then the giant told his son to open the gate and let the goats out. He stood in the doorway feeling each goat as it went out. There was a little goat at the end of the line; I took it on my back and slipped out between the giant's legs. When I got outside, I called, 'Catch me if you can.' The giant answered, 'Since you are so clever, take this ring.' Then he threw the ring to me. 'Have you the ring on your finger?' 'Yes,' I answered. Then the giant shouted, 'Ring come here, come close.' The ring began to drag me toward the giant, but I escaped by cutting off my finger." The king agreed that Cornu had fulfilled the condition, and so he set the second son free.

Then the king said, "If you have been closer to death a third time than you are now, I'll release your third son." Whereupon Cornu told the third story. "One time I was at the seashore when a beautiful ship came in. I went on board, and it sailed away to a house in the ocean. There was a woman there raising a poker to a child. When I asked her what she was doing, she replied that she was going to kill the child for the dinner of the giant who lived there. I told her to hide the child and so she did. I went up the stairs and lay down among the dead men there. The giant came home and made a great feast of the dead men and then went to sleep. Then I killed the giant and saved that baby. And that baby was you." When the king heard this he released the man and all his sons.

THE MAGIC GIFTS

Told in Gaelic by Hector Campbell, age ca. 70, of Judique.

Once upon a time a man cut his hay and made it into a stack. Then the wind came and blew the stack away. When the man saw this he went to the God of the Winds and told him that he would have to pay for the hay he had destroyed. "That is only fair," said the God of the Winds, and he gave the man a duck. "Now," he said, "whenever you want money, just squeeze the duck and a gold piece will drop out." The man took the duck and departed. On the way home he stopped for a night at an inn. There he told the keeper about the duck. In the morning the duck was gone. He was told that it had flown away during the night.

Back home the man thought again about the hay; thinking that he had not been paid for it, he set out a second time for the home of the God of the Winds. When he explained about the loss of the duck, the God of the Winds said, "Yes, your hay is not paid for; here is a mill; just turn the handle when you want money, and the mill will grind out gold." The man stopped at the same inn, and the same thing happened, for when he awoke in the morning, the mill was gone.

He then made a third trip to the God of the Winds. When he told the God of the Winds about the loss of the mill, the God of the Winds asked him where he had stayed the night. When he told him, the God of the Winds said, "Those people have stolen the duck and the mill. So you take this sod, and when they ask you what you do with it, tell them that you say, 'Wrap me up, wrap me up.'" So the man took the sod and departed. That night he stopped at the inn. And when they asked him about the sod, he said, "I say to it, 'Wrap me up, wrap me up.'" After he was sound asleep, the people at the inn stole the sod and, thinking it would produce gold like the duck and mill, said to it, "Wrap me up, wrap me up." Instantly the sod began to wrap up everything in the place, the furniture, the wagons, the sheep and cattle, even the people themselves. Whereupon they cried out and woke the man, who, after they had restored his duck and mill, rescued them from the sod. Taking the duck and mill he went home.

THE MARVELOUS PIPER

Told in English by Mrs. Dave Patterson, Benacadie Pond, age ca. 75.

This is a true story; it happened to my grandfather. Now his father was a poor man, and when his wife died, leaving him with one son, he married a widow who was well-off, and she had two sons. She was mean to his son; she made him eat in the kitchen and made him set there and not come into the parlour with the rest. Her sons played the pipes fine. She brought them two sets of pipes, and she paid a lot for them, and all his son had was a little old chanter. He couldn't play very well. One day he was out in the hills herding the cows and trying to play on his little chanter when who should he see but one of the little fairy men, and this one said to him, "Do you want to play as well as your brothers?" And he said he did. "Well," said the little man, "put your fingers in my mouth, don't be afraid." He put his fingers in the little man's mouth, and then he picked up the chanter and played such marvelous music that he charmed the fishes out of the water and the little birds from their nests and milk from maidens' breasts. When he went home, he did not say anything about it, but sat in the kitchen as usual. The next day a man came there to hire one of the brothers to play the pipes on his steamer to entertain the people. He had heard that these two boys were good pipers. He asked them to play so he could choose. When they had finished, he said to his wife, "Who is that fellow I see out there in the kitchen?"

"Oh, he's just the boy that tends the cows," she replied.

"Well, I see he has a chanter," said the man. "Let's hear him play."

"Oh, you won't want to hear him. He can't play. All he makes is noises on his wretched chanter."

"Let me hear him anyway," insisted the man. So the boy was called in and given the pipes, and he played so wonderfully that even the step-mother had to admit that he was better than her own sons. And he got the job, and became the piper on the steamer. One day when the steamer was eighteen miles off shore, it began to leak. The captain did not know what to do. Then the boy said to him, "If you warm my fingers, I'll play distress music so loud that they will hear it on shore." So they warmed his fingers, and he went up on the upper deck, and he played distress music so loud that they heard him on shore and sent out another boat and rescued all the passengers. After that the boy came ashore and settled in this valley, and all his sons were great pipers after him because they learned from him. And that is why this valley is called Piper's Glen.

4. NEWFOUNDLAND RIDDLES
Elisabeth B. Greenleaf

When Elisabeth Bristol Greenleaf went to Newfoundland in 1920 to teach at a Grenfell Mission School at Sally's Cove, she was fascinated by the rich folk culture she found around her. Nine years later she returned with a trained musician, Grace Yarrow Mansfield, and together they produced Ballads and Sea Songs from Newfound-

130

land, *the first extensive collection from the island and still one of the best.*

Mrs. Greenleaf's interest in Newfoundland folklore was not restricted to songs: she also collected riddles, as she tells us in this article. She found them to be much more common among the inhabitants of the outports than among people in less isolated communities, and the result was one of the finest regional collections of riddles reported in North America.

> "I'll tell you a merry riddle
> To while the time away."

We have all heard riddles and doubtless know a few that we can say ourselves, but it was a surprise to me to find myself in a village where everyone knew a great many riddles, and for pastime invented new ones from events of daily life.

This was in the island of Newfoundland, far north on the west coast, where the sun sank over the blue waters of the Gulf of St. Lawrence. The village, Sally's Cove, was twelve miles from a steamship port of call, and some fifty miles from the railroad, so the ruddy British folk were thrown upon their own resources for entertainment, and they certainly entertained thoroughly and well their American Grenfell summer volunteer school-teacher.

One boy would ask this riddle:

> *Brown I am, and much admired,*
> *Many horses have I tired.*
> *Tire a horse and weary a man,*
> *Tell me this riddle if you can.*   – A saddle. (1564)

I might come back with this familiar one:

> *Little Nan Etticoat, in a white petticoat*
> *And a red nose;*
> *The longer she stands,*
> *The shorter she grows.*   – A candle. (611)

These, of course, are good old traditional British riddles, whose origin is lost in antiquity. But Aunt Fanny Jane Endicott came in one day from working in the garden and propounded this riddle:

> *Green, slender and strong,*
> *Ten bring it along.*

131

The answer is the green stalks of rhubarb she was carrying in to the house in her ten capable fingers. I could not match that out of my day's experience, for people who read a great deal seem to lose this fresh, poetic approach of folk close to nature and not much dependent on the printed page.

In Sally's Cove, I heard the riddles in the long evenings, or while on a "cruise" in the berry patches. (Even a simple walk takes on a nautical name in sea-going Newfoundland.) Soon I heard them even in school.

The children were shy and spoke very badly, I thought, running their words together in a jumble, placing the sentence accent wrongly, and so forth, so I used the last period every day to practise singing and recitations, soon finding that they especially liked to tell riddles. Each pupil had to stand up and repeat his riddle until the class understood him and I was satisfied with his diction. The answers had to be given distinctly and in order, too. Interest in the riddle would keep them trying even to the twentieth repetition. My American ear was slow in comprehending their Newfoundland accent, which, in this village, was a modification of the speech of Devon and Dorset in England.

The period was always fun and reached a climax, I thought, when small, six-year-old Lillian of the blond hair and loyal, passionate heart broke through her binding shyness to ask, in the tiniest, humming-bird voice, "What stands on one leg and smokes?" When the answer had been guessed – a kerosene lamp – the children told me it was a new riddle to them, Lillian had made it up herself.

On another trip to Newfoundland, I tried another method for securing riddles. Dr. Martha Beckwith of the Vassar College Folk Lore Foundation had suggested that in a strange place, where you did not have time to get acquainted with the people, you could offer the children a penny for each different riddle they could tell you. I was accompanied by a musician and we were engaged in recording the lovely folk-songs sung in Newfoundland. However, one beautiful morning in Fogo on the east coast, our work was interrupted because all the young men and boys were rushing down to the steamship wharf and hiring out to unload coal from a freighter which was heading into the harbour. All their winter coal is brought to Fogo in two trips by freightship from North Sydney, Nova Scotia, and it is a pretty important thing to get that coal unloaded before ice or storm prevent.

Watching that jolly crowd of young people on the wharf, we were suddenly impelled to try Dr. Beckwith's suggestion, so we offered, "A penny for every riddle we haven't heard." With a whoop and a rush they were upon us. The quiet harbour resounded with riddles and we were pursued to the edge of the dock and had to back up against a big spile. Moreover we found that a "penny" was indeed an English penny, worth two cents, United States. My assistant had not been in the island long enough to understand their strange and rapid pronunciation, so she held the purse and paid out the great coppers while I wrote the names of the children and the riddles they told. Again and again we had to stop and get more change and the riddling was still going on when the coal ship was moored alongside. The Norwegian captain was curious and joined the group. He could not understand the spoken English, but he could look over my shoulder and read the words as I wrote them and then he, too, could laugh and enjoy the fun.

In these jolly ways the following collection of Newfoundland riddles was made, and I hope you will find them jolly and interesting reading. They should carry you back in spirit to the days of Good Queen Bess in Merrie England, when the folk were freshly in love with their new and expressive language.

The riddles differ in origin, form, content, age, social class, and spirit, and in other respects. It is a fascinating exercise in imagination to try to picture the life of the composers. You must always keep in mind that folk-riddles are intended to be spoken, not to be read. If the lines do not rhyme in reading, you may fairly assume that the words are pronounced differently in Newfoundland, and probably do rhyme in speech. I will indicate some of the pronunciations.

For convenience, I have grouped the riddles in several classifications. Of course, the folk never classify them.

ABOUT THE BIBLE, OR IN RELIGIOUS SPIRIT

1. *The garden was laid with a fair pretty maid,*
   Red as a rose in the morn.
   She was a wife the first day of her life.
   She died but never was born.   – Eve.

2. *There's a tree in the valley,*
   Fifty two branches round.
   Each one bears seven
   Which the Lord sent from heaven.   – The year. (1038)

3. *What was born, lived, and never had a name?*   – Lot's wife.

4. *There was a man of Adam's race,*
   He had a certain dwelling place:
   'Twas all compact and covered o'er,
   And no man dwelt there since, nor e'er before.   – Jonah.

5. *I never was, but am always to be,*
   None ever saw me, nor ever will see,
       And yet I am the confidence of all
       Who live and breathe on this terrestrial ball. – Tomorrow. (97)

ABOUT EVERYDAY LIFE

1. *Four legs up and four legs down,*
   Soft in the middle and hard all aroun'.   – Bed. (69a)

2. *The old woman she pit it and pat it;*
   The old man doffed breeches and got at it.   – Bed. (1742b)

3. *Formed long ago, yet made to-day,*
       Employed while others sleep;
       What few would like to give away,
       And fewer still to keep.   – Bed. (1596a)

4. *What's got a tongue and cannot talk?*   – Shoe. (296)

5. *What's got an eye and cannot see?*   – Needle. (282)

6. *Hairy in and hairy out,*
   Hairy in a hairy's mout'.   – Mouse in cat's mouth. (1419)

7. *Long legs, crooked thighs,*
   Bald head and no eyes.   – A pair of tongs. (80)

8. *As I was going up a gravelly knap',*
   I saw a little boy with a little red cap,
       A stick in his hand, a stone in his belly;
       Riddle me this and I'll give you a penny.
   (knap' means hill.)   – Cherry or gooseberry. (635b,636)

9. *As I was going up the road* (pronounced rud)
       I met my sister Ann.
   I cut her throat and sucked her blood
       And let her body stan'.   – Bottle of rum. (805t)

10. *As I was going up to London Bridge,*
        I met my brother John.
    I chopped off his head and drank his blood
        And let his body stan'.   – Bottle of wine. (805j)

11. A houseful, a roomful,
        Couldn't catch a cupful.   – Smoke. (1643)

12. 'Round the house and 'round the house
        And into the corner it goes.   – Broom (695)

13. A rich man puts it in his pocket;
        A poor man heaves it away.   – Snot from the nose. (1724)

14. Round as a marble, deep as a cup,
        All the king's army couldn't lift it up.   – Well. (1315)

15. A row of white horses upon a red hill,
        Here they goes, here they goes, here they stops still.
                                                            – The teeth. (503)

16. Round as a hoop, deep as a pail;
        Never sings out 'till it's caught by the tail.   – A bell. (1316)

17. Over gravel I did travel,
        On white oak I did stand,
        I bought a mare that never foaled,
        And held a bridle in my hand.   – Man aboard schooner. (414)

18. I've got a goose and she is a prize.
        Whoever buys her will be wise.
            She's got legs and walks on none,
            Seeks her fortune far from home.   – A sailing ship. (372)

19. Flour from England, fruit from Spain,
        Mixed together in a shower of rain,
            Put in a bag, tied with a string,
            Tell me this riddle, I'll give you a ring. – A plum pudding. (1096)

20. What is that which belongs to you
        But others use it more than you do?   – Your name. (1582)

21. Long and slinky, like a trout,
        When it bawls, its guts come out.   – A gun. (1266)

22. What stands on one leg with its heart in its head?
                                                            – Cabbage. (32)

23. *What's got four legs and can't walk?*   – A chair. (306)

24. *What goes up the hill and down the hill,*
And spite of all, yet standeth still?   – The road. (122)

25. *Humpty Dumpty on the wall,*
Humpty Dumpty had a great fall.
    All the king's horses and all the king's men
    Couldn't put Humpty Dumpty together again.   – An egg. (738)

26. *Crinkety crank, under the bank,*
Ten drawing four.   – Milking a cow. (976)

27. *Riddle me, riddle me, right-y-o,*
Me mother give me some seed to sow;
The seed was black, the ground was white;
Riddle me, riddle me, right-y-o.   – Writing in ink. (1063)

28. *What drinks his own blood and eats his own flesh?*
     –A burning lamp. (774)

29. *What has four legs and smokes a pipe?*   – A stove. (320)

30. *What's six brothers running after each other*
    and never catching up?   – A wheel with six spokes. (997)

31. *Four step-standers,*
Four down-hangers,
    Two lookers,
    Two crookers,
And a swing-em-out.   – A cow. (1477)

32. *Four brothers under one hat.*   – A table. (993)

33. *Old Mother Twitch she had but one eye,*
And a long tail which she let fly,
    And every time she goes over a gap,
    She leaves a bit of her tail in the trap.
     – Needle and thread. (533)

34. *Five after one!*   – Fingers hunting a louse in the hair. (972)

35. *Riddle me, riddle me, what is that,*
Over the head and under the hat?   – The hair. (1436)

36. *Long, slick and slender,*
    Tickles where 'tis tender.   – A horsewhip. (1464)

37. *Brown I am and much admired,*
    Many horses have I tired;
    *   Tire a horse and weary a man;*
    *   Tell me this riddle if you can.*   – A saddle. (1564)

38. *Ten drag,*
    Wooly bag
    Over calf hill.   – Putting on a woolen stocking. (1200b)

39. *What goes 'round the house and leaves but one track?*
                                      – A wheelbarrow. (174)

40. *I haven't got it and I don't want it, but if I had it,*
    I wouldn't sell it for a thousand pounds.
                    – A bald head (or a baby, say the bachelors). (1593)

ABOUT NATURE

1. *I went into the woods and got it;*
    I sat down to look for it;
    The more I looked for it, the less I liked it;
    Not being able to find it, I came home with it.
                                      – Thorn in foot. (1635)

2. *In the woods I done it,*
    I sat down and viewed it;
    Against my will to keep it still
    Right straight home I brought it.
                – A man cut his foot while working in the woods. (1640)

3. *What goes over the water and under the water*
    And never touches the water?   – An egg inside a duck. (169)

4. *What's the strongest thing in the world?*   – A h'emmet (an ant).

5. *What is it that floats on the water as light as a feather,*
    And a thousand men couldn't lift it?   – A bubble. (1661)

6. *What lives in winter, dies in summer,*
    And grows with its roots upward?   – An icicle. (1057)

7. *Green as grass, but 'twasn't grass,*
   Red as blood, but 'twasn't blood,
   Black as coal, but 'twasn't coal.
   'Long comes a pretty love
   Whipped it in the grinding hole. — A blackberry. (1373)

8. *In yonder valley there runs a deer*
   With golden horns and silver hair.
       It's neither fish, flesh, feather, nor bone;
       In yonder valley it runs alone. — The sun. (392b)

9. *Cut me up in pieces and bury me alive,*
   The young ones will live and the old ones will die.

                          — Potatoes. (95)

10. *As I was going through a field of wheat,*
    I picked up something good to eat;
        'Twas neither fish, flesh, feather, nor bone,
        I let it stay till it ran alone. — A bird's egg. (1237)

INVOLVING PLAYS ON WORDS

1. *As I was going over Westminister Bridge,*
       I met a Westminister scholar.
   He took off his hat and drew off his gloves
       And what was the name of this scholar? — Andrew.

2. *When it's started, 'twas done;*
   When it's half done, 'twas done;
   When it's finished, 'twasn't done.

                         — A girl named Dunn who got married.
           (Says Rege Roberts: "She should have married a Finnish.")

3. *As I was going over the captain's bridge*
   I saw a ship a-sailing.
   What was the captain's name?
   I told you once, I told you twice,
   What was the captain's name? — The captain's name was Watt.

4. *Twenty sick (six) sheep went up the gap;*
   One died, how many came back? — Nineteen. (N.C. 119)

5. *A black sheep and a white sheep,*
   A horny sheep and one not;
   A long-tailed sheep and a short-tailed sheep;
   How many sheep have I got?   – Two.

6. *A man rode up a hill,*
   But yet he walked.   – Yet was his dog. (N.C. 206)

7. *What went to the North Pole and stopped there,*
   And came back because it couldn't go there?   – A watch. (130)

8. *A horse has what a man has not;*
   The Americans had it and lost it.   – A mane (The ship *Maine*).

9. *Down in the dark valley I saw a great light,*
   All bridled, all saddled, all ready to fight;
   Brass was his arrow and steel was his bow;
   Three times I have told you and still you don't know.
                    – Awl or all. (N.C. 198)

10. *Londonderry, Kirk and Kerry,*
    Spell me that without a K.   – T-H-A-T.

11. *Two h'Os, two h'Ns, a h'L and a D,*
    Put that together and spell it to me.   – London.

12. *'Tis in mountains, not in hills,* (pronounced cels)
    'Tis in meadows, not in fields,
    'Tis in me, and not in you,
    'Tis in men and women too.   – The letter M.

COMPOSED IN SALLY'S COVE

1. The girls get the water from the brook. They take two buckets and a large wooden hoop, fill the pails at the brook, set them down just far enough apart so as to be able to lay the hoop inside the handles. Then when they pick up the buckets by the handles, the hoop holds the full pails away from their skirts, so they don't get water on them. Moreover, the hoop seems to take some of the weight from the arms.

   Thru a narrow path of wood I went.
   Between two waters I came back.   – Fetching water on a hoop.

2. *Jim's is in under,*
    Joe's is on top;
    Our little dory
    Goes over the lop (waves).

This is one of my favourites. It pictures two young men sawing boards for their dory. They are working a pit-saw; that is, a platform is erected; one man stands on top sawing through the log lengthwise. The other end of the saw is worked by another man standing underneath the platform, getting saw-dust in his eyes. What labour, compared even to a water-power saw-mill! But the boys had no money, yet they had lumber and time, so they made themselves their dory.

3. *As I was going over the mesh,* (marsh)
    I saw a poor thing eating moss;
    I couldn't bear to see poor thing eating moss
    So I took moss hold and hauled moss all out.
                    – A fox-trap, the jaws of which were concealed in moss.

4. *As I was going over the world, triggum, traggum,*
    I met a bum, biggum, baggum;
    I ran home and fetched tom, tiggum, taggum,
    And brought bum, biggum, baggum,
    Out of the world, triggum, traggum.
        – John Charles Roberts was going through the woods, and saw a
        deer, so he ran home and got his gun, shot the deer, and brought it
        home.

5. *Green, slender, and strong,*
    Ten bring it along.
    – Picking rhubarb.
                                            – Mrs. Daniel Endicott

6. *As I was coming down the road*
    I saw two wings chase four wings,
    Till four-legs broke up the fight.
        – A bird was chasing a dragon-fly, when an ox came along the
        road and let the dragon-fly escape.   – Daniel Endicott.

ABOUT DEATH AND LIFE

This group of riddles is the most difficult to understand. I believe they are of great antiquity, coming perhaps from an age when talking in riddles was one of the characteristics of magicians or priests, way back almost in the age of myths. For instance, this *cup* seems to remind me of the cup of the Holy Grail. The riddles about murders speak of the time when the will of a noble or chief might be the sole law, and it was essential to present the case in a way to arouse his interest, just as Nathan presented his case to David. This is guess-work. I do not know.

1. *As I was going over London Bridge,*
   I saw a house;
   In that house there were a pantry,
   In that pantry there were a shelf,
   On that shelf there were a cup,
   In that cup there were
      Something what you can't do without.   *– Blood.(1156)*

2. *In the woods there is a pond,*
   In the pond there is a boat,
   In that boat there is a cup,
   In the cup there is
      Something everyone shall taste of.   *– Death. (1157)*

3. *Riddle me, riddle me right,*
   Where was I last Saturday night?
   The winds did blow, the trees did shake,
   I saw a hole the fox did make.

      – A man dug a grave for his sweetheart, but she was up in a tree nearby and saw him. (AT 955C:N.C.105)

4. *Love I sit, love I stand,*
   Love I hold fast in my hand;.
      I can see love, but love can't see me,
      Tell me that riddle and I'll marry thee (or *hung I'll be*).
      – On East Coast: A girl had a crackie (little dog) named Love. He died and she made a chair of his bones and asked the riddle of her sweetheart.
      – On West Coast: A man murdered his sweetheart, made a rocking chair of her bones, and would be hung if it were known. (N.C. 104)

CONUNDRUMS

In addition to the riddles, the Newfoundlanders often ask conundrums. I have gathered together just a few to show how they enjoy playing around with words.

1. *What is a little pig doing when he is eating?* – He's making a hog of himself.
2. *Why does a lamp smoke?* – Because it can't chew.
3. *What's the first thing you do when you go to bed?*
    – Squat the feathers. (Make a hollow in the feather bed.)
4. *What has the key on the inside and the lock on the outside?*
    – A piano.
5. *What goes up when the rain comes down?* – An umbrella. (N.C. 95)
6. *Why is Fogo like a match?* – It has a Brimstone Head.
7. *What kind of tree do you hold in your hand?* – A palm.
8. *What do you do to a rooster to keep him from crowing on Sunday morning?* – Get him stuffed on Saturday night.
9. *Do you know what NOTHING means?* – A legless stocking without any foot.

5. NEWFIE JOKES
Gerald Thomas

The tendency to ridicule any group that differs from the norm is very deep-rooted in human psychology and joke cycles directed at various minorities have formed a large part of North American urban lore. These are sometimes referred to as "ethnic jokes," although that is a misnomer as those ridiculed are not always an ethnic group: they may be "hillbillies," "Aggies," "Okies," or, in Canada, "Newfies."

Many of the cycles have been directed against immigrants: the Pat and Mike or fool Irishman jokes came quite early, but in more recent times the type has become identified as the Polack joke, although most of the "Polack jokes" are also told about other groups. Earlier, of course, they were known as fool, numskull, or moron jokes.

In Canada the same jokes have been applied to the Ukrainians ("Ukies"), French-Canadians ("Frogs"), Pakistanis ("Pakis"), and perhaps most extensively to the Newfoundlanders ("Newfies"). As the nicknames indicate, the jokes are closely related to "blasons populaires": the slurs or taunts by which people of one group characterize those of another. However, the jokes are not entirely exoteric: both Ukrainians and Newfoundlanders tell the jokes on themselves. Bob Tulk, a Newfoundlander, has published a series of small paper-bound booklets entitled Newfie Jokes *which have had an amazing sale in Newfoundland as well as on the mainland – the first, which is said to have sold 100,000 copies a year for five years, bears the introduction: "This book was published not for the purpose of making fun of New-*

foundlanders, but to show that most of us can take a joke as well as give one."

These cycles usually include some jokes based on the language peculiarities of the group in addition to more general jokes deriding its supposed stupidity and objectionable habits. The language jokes are more closely identified with one particular group, while the derogatory jokes shift readily from one group to another. In the following examples numbers 70 to 74 play upon Newfoundland pronunciations. Most of the rest have parallels in other joke cycles. They were all collected by Gerald Thomas in 1968, and came largely from Newfoundlanders.

The great vogue for "Newfie" jokes in Newfoundland came during 1965, with occasional recurrences of favour since, one of which was in the early months of 1968. This collection was made between September and December 1968 as a project in a graduate class in American Folklore at Memorial University. Some of the informants were students in my French classes; the rest were colleagues in the Departments of Romance Languages and Linguistics.

Only a very small number of characteristics are the subject of humorous attack in the "Newfie" joke. As typified by this collection, the Newfoundlander is primarily a numskull figure. Jokes from older European tradition are told side by side with the numerically greater, and frequently shorter, North American ethnic jokes. The poverty of the Newfoundlander is mocked, as is his dirtiness and, to a slight degree, his alleged laziness. In this collection are more jokes poking fun at the Newfoundlander as a numskull than all the jokes mocking his poverty, dirtiness, and laziness combined. So while superficially it may appear that the "Newfie" joke is but the old Polack joke writ new, there are indications that the Newfoundlander has acquired a stereotype which he shares with the French Canadian, that of the Canadian numskull. It is a stereotype not only in the eyes of the non-Newfoundlander, but, surprisingly, also in the eyes of many Newfoundlanders.

An interesting and socially significant question is why do certain groups acquire the characteristics with which they are labelled? Why are Newfoundlanders considered stupid, Polacks dirty, or Scots and Jews avaricious? If such humour related to ethnic groups alone, it might be possible to seek the cause of mockery in social, economic, and educational factors. It would be possible to argue that the characteristics of stupidity, poverty, dirtiness, and laziness attributed to the Newfoundlander derived from his confrontation in the post-Confederation era with the sophisticated urban societies of Toronto and Montreal, to which cities many Newfoundlanders flocked after the island became Canada's tenth province in 1949.

Twenty-five years after Confederation, Newfoundland still lags behind the rest of Canada in many ways; for a variety of reasons, there is a continued emigration to the mainland. The island ranks lowest among all Canadian provinces in terms of the proportion of its school enrolment which reaches university level. Per capita personal income is also the lowest among the provinces, and Newfoundland's unemployment level has been described as critical. Lack of education entails a lack of economic security, which in turn condemns the uneducated to a generally demeaning way of life. Newfoundland, even today, is more socially backward than many other parts of Canada; it is still possible to hear people claim with pride that the Newfoundlander's way of life has hardly changed in over two hundred years. There is enough truth in such an assertion for folklorists and sociologists to view the island as a researcher's paradise.

There is a joke (not included in this collection) which describes the problems faced by a Newfoundlander when he changes from an axe to a power-saw to cut his daily tally of wood. He manages to keep up to the level of pre-power-saw production, but finds it particularly tiring. He complains about the new tool, and is frightened out of his life when the vendor presses the starting button. This rather gross example may explain something of the Newfoundlander's reputation as a numskull. His poverty is a readily observable feature by mainland standards and not in itself particularly humorous. But since the whole body of ethnic jokes includes not only the humour of stupidity but also that of poverty, dirtiness, and laziness, it is perhaps inevitable that such related characteristics also be applied to the new butt. It would seen that once one stereotype has been established, related types of humour tend to follow it.

The "Newfie" joke is, of course, far older than Confederation, although it is to Confederation that it owes its present widespread popularity. Before the Newfoundlander had easy access to the Canadian mainland, he told the same jokes later to be told about him east of Toronto. Newfoundland is a divided island, divided between "Townie" and "Bayman"; in many people's minds, this division is more accurately stated as St. John's opposed to the rest of the island. At one level, this division is expressed in political and economic jealousies between St. John's and the various other regions of Newfoundland; at another, in the insults to be found scribbled as bathroom graffiti at Memorial University. The "Townie" tells "Newfie" jokes about the "Bayman" or "Outporter," and one Bayman may tell the same joke about another. Townies seem to have the quasi-monopoly of the formulaic-type joke; the longer and more traditional humorous narratives have not been demonstrably ousted from the Bayman's repertoire.

A brief addendum gives essential biographical information on my informants and lists the jokes supplied by each. [See pp. 302-303]

STUPIDITY

(Many of the following fall under the motif section J1730-1749: Absurd ignorance.)

1. A Newfie walked up to an Air Canada official in Montreal and asked: "How long does it take to fly to Newfoundland?" The busy attendant replied, "Just a moment, sir." The Newfie said, "Thanks" and walked on.
2. A Newfie was on a flight from Montreal to Newfoundland when the pilot announced that No. 1 engine was out and the flight would take a half hour longer. A second time the pilot announced that No. 2 engine was out and the flight would be delayed one hour. Then again the pilot said that No. 3 engine was out and the flight would be delayed one and a half hours. The impatient Newfie shouted, "Damn it, if this keeps up we'll be here all day."
3. Did you hear the latest Newfie joke? It's about the boundary dispute between Labrador and Quebec. The Newfies are throwing dynamite across the border. The Quebec people are lighting it and throwing it back.
4. Two Newfoundland fishermen went out in their dory. They came to a berth they did not normally use, and dropped their lines. In next to no time the boat was full, a day's work in a few hours. The one said to the other: "This is some berth. We'll have to mark the spot so that we do as well next time." "That's right," says the other, "pass me the knife." He cuts a notch on the gunnel, at the spot where his line had been. "That's no good," says the other, "You'll have to find another way." "Why's that then?" "Well, boy, we may not be using the same boat tomorrow." (AT 1278; J1922.1; E5.6.1)
5. There were two Newfies working in a ditch in Toronto and the temperature and humidity were close to 100. They were sweating like hell and one questioned why the foreman was allowed to sit in the shade of the trees while they worked. So Joe went over and enquired this of the foreman. The foreman held his hand out in front of a tree and asked the Newfie to strike it. As the Newfie swung, the hand was pulled back and the Newfie hit the tree. The foreman replied, "That's why." When Joe arrived back in the ditch, his partner Bob asked why. Joe raised his hand before his own face and asked Bob to hit it. As Bob swung, the hand was drawn back and

Joe was belted in the face. Joe replied, "That's why." (J2131[a]; E3.7)

6. A new carpenter was helping an experienced Newfoundland carpenter with a house. The new man says to the old, "The heads is on these here nails the wrong end." But the experienced carpenter says, "No, me lad, them there nails is for the other side of the house." (J2259*[k]; E4.4)

7. Two mental patients were trying to escape from the hospital and one said to the other, "I'll flash the light down to the ground and you slide down on the beam." The other replied, "Do you think I'm foolish? When I get half down you'll turn off the light." (J2259*[mb])

8. The doctor sent two mental patients to clean up a room. When he checked on it he found one upside down from the ceiling. "What are you doing up there?" asked the doctor. "I'm a light bulb," was the reply. The doctor felt this was too much so he told the patient to follow him. When he looked back he saw the second patient coming. "Why are you coming?" asked the Doc. Second replied, "You're not getting me to work in the dark." (J2259*; E3.6)

9. Well, there were two hunters, you see, a Newfie and a Canadian. They hadn't had any luck, when they came across a girl. Eyeing her up and down the Canadian said, "Are you game?" "Yes," she replied, and the Newfie shot her. (J2259*[p]; E5.7.2)

10. Did you know how a Newfie ties his shoelace? He puts one foot up on a chair and ties the shoe on the other foot. (J2259*[zb]; E7.3)

11. How does a Newfoundlander scratch his elbow? First scratches the palm of his hand and then puts his elbow in the palm of his hand. (J2259* [z])

12. How does a Newfie fan himself? (Informant holds his hand in front of his face, then shakes his head violently.) (E7.5)

13. Why do Newfies have round shoulders and flat heads? When you ask them a question they shrug their shoulders, and when you tell them the answer they slap their forehead and say, "Jesus!" (E9.2.)

14. A Newfoundlander walked up to a man in Ottawa with a bag under his arm and said to the man, "If you can tell me how many chickens I've got in this bag, I'll give you both of them." (J2666.4*; E14.1)

15. Two men went looking for a job one day. One fellow went into the employment office and got a job. When he came out the other fellow asked him if they had asked difficult questions. "No, boy," the other fellow replied, "he asked me if I was blind in one eye, what would I be, and I said half blind. Then he asked me if I was blind in two eyes, what would I be. I answered, totally blind, of course. That's all there is to it." The other fellow went in and the first

question he asked was, "If you had one ear gone, what would you be?" He replied, "Half blind." The second question was, "If you had two ears gone, what would you be?" He replied, "Totally blind." "But how can that be?" the agent asked. "Well, it's like this," the fellow replied. "If my two ears are gone then my cap will fall down over my eyes and I won't be able to see, will I?" (J2721; E1.5)

16. There were two Newfoundland brothers, Pat and George, who always shared things. They had two boats, so Pat took one and George took the other. They had also two nets, so Pat took one and George took the other. They also had two horses, but they didn't know how they could tell them apart. So Pat said that he would cut his horse's tail and then they would be able to tell them apart. But this would only work until the horse's tail grew out again. So they thought and thought about what they were going to do. Finally George said to Pat, "I'll tell you what we'll do; why don't you take the white one and I'll take the black one." (J2722)

17. Then there was the Torontonian who had a brain operation. It was not entirely successful and he was, according to the doctors, doomed to idiocy for the rest of his days. The patient escaped from the Ontario Hospital where he was confined and a prolonged search failed to find him. Two years later, the surgeon who had performed the operation met the patient in the street. He questioned the patient on a number of things and then asked where he had been for the two years. "Oh," said the patient, "I've been doing quite well. I was teaching school in Newfoundland." (X691.4.1*[a]; E1.6)

18. Why does it take five Newfoundlanders to pop popcorn? One to hold the pot and four to move the stove. (*This and following jokes would fall under motifs J2700-2749: The easy problem made hard.*)

19. How many Newfs does it take to paint a barn? One hundred. One to hold the brush and the other ninety-nine to move the barn back and forth. (E7.6.7)

20. Why did the Newfie move his house two inches? He was trying to tighten his clothes-line! (E7.1)

21. How many Newfies does it take to replace a light bulb? Three. One to hold the bulb and two to turn the ladder around. (E7.6.5)

22. Why don't they allow Newfoundlanders to have coffee breaks on the Mainland? Because it takes too long to retrain them. (E3.9)

23. Do you know how a Newfie counts his catch? One fish, two fish, another fish, another fish . . .

24. Did you hear about the Newfie who went ice-fishing and caught 150 pounds of ice? (E5.6.1)

25. There was once a Newfoundlander walking down a street in Toronto with a pair of water skis on his back. A man approached him

and asked why he was carrying them, as he had seen him the previous day doing the same thing. The Newfie looked discouraged and told the man he had bought the skis a couple of months ago and was going around ever since looking for a lake with a hill in it. (E5.5)

26. What's the definition of gross ignorance? 144 Newfoundlanders. (E1.3)

27. How can you tell a bottle of Coke in Newfoundland from a bottle of Coke on the mainland? On the bottom of the (Newfoundland) bottle is written "Open other end." (E8.4)

28. A Toronto woman called a firm which was renowned for its landscaping and interior decorating. A man from the company soon arrived and the lady showed him around the house. Every time she asked what colours he would recommend for a particular room, he used to go to the window, raise it, and call out, "Green sides up!" before answering her. This happened several times and the woman's curiosity got the best of her. "Is this some kind of ritual?" she asked. "No," he replied, "it's simply that I've got two Newfies next door laying sod." (E3.4)

29. A gentleman wishing to have a brain transplant first talked it over with his doctor. The doctor informed him that a German brain would cost him $800, a Swedish brain $1000, and a Newfoundland brain $100,000. He then asked the doctor why a Newfoundland brain would cost so much. The doctor replied, "It was never used before." (X691.3*; E1.5)

30. A Newfie went into a restaurant in Niagara Falls and ordered a large pizza. "Would you like it cut in four pieces or eight?" asked the waitress. "Better cut it in four," said he. "I don't think I can eat eight."

31. A man from Newfoundland signed his welfare cheque in Toronto Xxx. The officer asked him what were the two small x's. The Newfie replies: "Aw me, man, them's for me B.A. from Memorial."

32. What is a dope ring? Six Newfoundlanders holding hands. (E1.7.2)

THE CLASSIC MORON, OR THE LITERAL FOOL

33. Did you hear about the Newfie girl who traded in her menstrual cycle for a Honda? (*This and others in this section would fall under motif J2259*[p]: Fool's action based on a pun.* F2.30.4)

34. Did you hear about the Newfoundlander who thought her typewriter was pregnant because it skipped a period? (F1.11.3)

35. Did you hear about the Newfie girl who was half-way to Norway before she found out that a nineteen-inch Viking was a TV set? (F1.11.3)

148

36. Did you hear about the Newfie who spend four days in Sears looking for wheels for a miscarriage? (F2.30.2)
37. Did you hear about the Newfie who drank a bottle of hand lotion to stop a little chap inside? (F2.30.5)
38. Did you hear about the Newfie who took a roll of toilet paper to a crap game? (F2.29.1)
39. Did you hear about the Newfie who put iodine on his pay cheque because he got a cut in pay? (F2.21)
40. Did you hear about the Newfie who turned off the lights in his car because he had stripped the gears? (F2.30.1)
41. Did you hear about the Newfie who backed off the bus because he heard someone was going to grab his seat? (F2.22)
42. Did you hear about the Newfie who thought a mushroom was a place to neck? (F1.6)
43. Then there was the Newfie who studied all night for the urine test. (F2.3)
44. Did you hear about the Newfoundlander who took his pregnant wife to the supermarket because he heard about their free delivery? (F2.30.3.)
45. Did you hear about the Newfie who thought "no kidding" meant birth control? (F1.11.2)
46. Did you hear about the Newfie who wore a Union suit because his wife was having labour pains? (F2.10)
47. Did you hear about the Newfie who sat home crying because her husband was out shooting craps and she didn't know how to cook it? (J2259*[pd])
48. Did you hear about the Newfoundlander who picked his nose apart to see what made it run? (J2259*[pe]; F2.17)
49. Did you hear about the Newfie who looked in a lumber yard for a draft board? (2259*[pq]; F2.26)
50. Why were the two Newfies drowned in Conception Bay? They were trying to build a concrete basement on their boat. (F2.5)
51. What happened to the Newfie who bought two snow tires? They melted! (F3.4)
52. Did you hear about the Newfie who wouldn't go out with his wife because he found out she was married?

SEX

53. A young married couple from Newfoundland were beginning to get worried about the size of the family they would have in a short time if things continued the way they were going. They had two children already and were only married not quite two years. Upon advice from a friend he went to visit a doctor who told him that he could

easily arrange something for him. The doctor gave him some birth-control pills and instructed the way that they should be taken, taking for granted he knew they were for his wife. A short period later he came back to the doctor in quite a rage. He rudely told the doctor that he had tricked him, for he had taken the pills the way the doctor told him they should be taken and his wife was pregnant again. (Cf. H2.3)

54. A Newfie walked up to the Doc and asked to be castrated. The Doc asked him was he sure, so he insisted. He awoke in a double room and asked his mate what operation did he have, and his room-mate replied that he had been circumcised. Newfie said, "Damn it, that's the word I was looking for."

55. Did you hear about the Newfie who lost his girl friend because he couldn't remember where he had laid her? (H4.4)

56. Did you hear about the Newfie who was so lazy that he married a pregnant woman? (H2.4)

57. Why wasn't Jesus Christ born in Newfoundland? He couldn't find three wise men or a virgin! (H1.4.3)

58. What is the definition of a Newfie virgin? A girl who can outrun all her relatives. (H1.4.4)

APPETITE

59. How do you get a Newfoundlander out of the back garden? Put the garbage in the front. (C5.7)

60. What's the most dangerous job in Newfoundland? Riding shot-gun on a garbage truck. (C5.1)

61. Why does a Newfoundlander colour his garbage can orange and black? To make himself believe he's eating at the A & W. (C5.6)

DIRTINESS

62. If there are four houses around a cesspool, which one is the New-fie's? The one with the diving-board. (G6.15)

63. What do you have when you have a swimming pool full of Newfies? A Bay of Pigs. (G4.1)

64. Do you know the definition of air pollution? The Newfoundland Parachute Brigade. (G6.11)

65. How do you get a Newfoundlander out of a bathtub? Put some water in it. (G1.6.1)

66. How do you break a Newfoundlander's finger? Punch him in the nose. (G3.2)

67. Where do you hide a nickel on a Newfoundlander? Under a bar of soap. (G1.9)

68. A Newfoundlander went into a bar in Toronto with a pig under his arm. "Where did you pick that up?" asked the barman, and the pig replied, "Out in the alley." (G4.4)

69. There was a skunk trapped in a building. They sent an American in to get it out, and after a while he came running out, holding his nose. Then they sent a Newfie in. After a while the skunk came running out, holding his nose. (X691.5.1*; G4.5)

THE NEWFOUNDLAND WAY OF LIFE

70. There was this social worker in the outports. She came to one house, knocked at the door, and a young girl answered. "Could I speak to your father?" said the social worker. "Oh, no," says the girl, "fat'er ain't home, 'e's in jail." "Do you have a mother I can talk to?" "Oh, no, mot'er's in t'e lunatic." "Well, do you have any brothers I can talk to?" "Oh, yes, der's t'ree, Tom, Dick and 'Arry." "Could I speak to Tom?" "Oh, no, Tom took after fat'er, 'e's in jail." "Well, what about Dick? Is Dick here?" "Oh, no, 'e took after mot'er, 'e's in t'e lunatic." "Well, what about Harry?" "Oh, you can't talk to 'Arry! 'e's at Harvard." "What! Harvard! What's he studying?" "Oh, my dear, 'e ain't studying – dey's studyin' 'e!"

71. A man had just returned from Toronto to his parents' home around the Bay and of course he was anxious to display his new "culture." When the meal was over, he produced a basket of oranges he'd brought with him, and offered it to his friends. His mother watched open-mouthed and finally said in utter amazement and scorn, "'Ark o' George, callin' 'is oranges 'fruit'!"

72. Two Newfies went to Toronto and were staying for the first time in a high-class hotel. One decided to go to the dining-room for breakfast the next morning. When he returned, the other asked him what he had had. The first replied, "I can't remember, but it begins with an N." "Was it a norange?" The first said, "No." The second said, "Well, it must have been a napple." The first again said "No." The second says, "Ah, I knows, it was a negg."

73. Two Newfoundlanders were attending a hockey game at the Montreal Forum. The letters CH were written on the ice, meaning Canadiens-Habitants, the name of the Montreal team. "Look, George," says one, "What's dat CH doin' out dere?" "Ah ye fool," said the other, "Dat's Centre Hice."

74. What do Newfoundland Baymen say for "Sock it to me?" – "Whip it to I."

75. How do you measure the Newfoundland population in Toronto? Count the basement apartments in Italian houses and multiply by ten.

76. What is a Newfie's set of luggage? Two shopping bags.
77. There was once a Newfoundlander in Toronto who got homesick. He went to the railway depot to buy a ticket for the journey home. The ticket cost $48 but the poor Newfie only had $47.95. Desperate, he went out on the street to bum a nickel. The first man along was a very distinguished-looking businessman. The Newfie approached him and asked him for a nickel, saying he needed it to get back to Newfoundland. The businessman reached down into his pocket and retrieved a quarter, giving it to the Newfie and telling him to take a few more of his Newfie friends with him.

As a final comment on the anti-Newfie joke:
78. Do you know how to save a Newfoundlander from drowning? No? Good! (L5.7.)

To set against this large body of Newfie jokes, it is only fair to give the Newfie the last word.
79. What's black and blue and lies on the floor? A mainlander who's just told a Newfie joke!
80. Newfie fishermen were fishing in what were, at that time, Canadian waters (this is pre-1949). A Canadian patrol boat come up, and the skipper shouts out, "Don't you stupid Newfs know you're fishing in Canadian waters?" "Oh, yes," replied one the Newfies, "but we're only catching Newfoundland fish." "How do you figure that out?" asks the Canadian. "Well, all the fish with the big mouths are Canadian, so we throw them back in."

No collection of Newfie jokes would be complete if it ignored Joey Smallwood, the benevolent despot who dragged the island into Confederation in 1949.
81. Mr. Smallwood and his wife were flying over Newfoundland in a plane. Mr. Smallwood began to talk about the poor, unfortunate people down below. Mrs. Smallwood said, "Why don't you give one of them a twenty-dollar bill and make them happy?" "I'll do better than that, I'll give two people a ten-dollar bill and make more people happy." "You can do better than that; give out four five-dollar bills and make four people happy." "I can make still more people happy if I give out twenty one-dollar bills." A little boy in the next seat said, "You can still do better than that because if you would jump out of the plane, then you would make everyone happy."
82. Joey was visiting the mental hospital and everyone removed his hat, all but one. Joey decided to question him. "Do you know that I'm Joey Smallwood and you should remove your hat?" The pa-

tient replied, "That's O.K., I was Winston Churchill when I came here."

83. Joey Smallwood was belting along the Trans-Canada in his limousine on the way to his ranch on Roaches Line. A policeman flagged him down for speeding. Joey pulled down the window and when the police saw who it was, he said, "Oh, my God!" "Yes," said Joey, "and don't you forget it!"

6. A MUMMERS' PLAY FROM NEWFOUNDLAND
Barney Moss

In Canada no form of folk drama has been very deep-rooted or widespread. Early settlers in Newfoundland and the Maritimes brought with them some of the old-world Christmas dramas and performed them during the eighteenth and nineteenth centuries, but the folk play had almost died out by 1900. However, the disguising and home-visiting elements of the mumming tradition continued in various parts of eastern Canada down to recent times. Mumming, also known as mummering or janneying, was widely practised in the outports of Newfoundland, and a related custom known as belsnickling was common in some parts of Nova Scotia originally settled by Germans.

A few of the plays performed in Newfoundland were printed in St. John's newspapers: Barney Moss contributed the one that follows to The Newfoundlander *in 1950. It is typical of the mummers' plays that were performed throughout the British Isles until fairly recent times, and retains many of the speeches found in English texts.*

The folk play always features a contest between a hero and his enemy, and includes a doctor who restores the fallen to life. It was originally a solstice ritual symbolizing the victory of the life-giving forces over the malignant powers of winter, sterility, and death. The pattern is ancient and universal but the names of the characters change with the country and the time. In England the hero was usually called St. George and his enemy the Turkish Knight, while Father Christmas introduced the play. The characters often ended with a song which varied with the locality.

Other forms of the folk drama about death and rebirth include the plough play performed in January, the pace-eggers' play for Easter, the soul-cakers' play for All Souls' Day (Hallowe'en), and the sword dances which were linked to various festivals. Thomas Hardy, who had seen the countrymen of his native Dorset perform a mummers' play, gives a vivid description of one in The Return of the Native.

"This is an account of the mumming play that was used on X Mass times in the early days by the first settlers in Newfoundland. They used to start out St. Stephen's Day and visit from house to house. They would keep it up for twelve days, everyone clad in war equipment that was required to do battle in those days. It's a great play, well worth resurrecting for the benefit of future generations. I have seen the old fellows at Christmas time acting it, all dressed in uniform. There's no play today can come up to the old-fashioned mumming play, because at X Mass times everyone is into it." (*Note: In all cases Mr. Moss spells Christmas in the old form of "X Mass." The normal spelling has been substituted in the play.*)

BEELZEBUB

Here comes I, Beelzebub, and on my shoulder carries my club
And in my hand a threepenny pan; ain't I a smart jolly old man.
If you don't believe what I do say, step in Father Christmas and clear the
    way.

FATHER CHRISTMAS

Here comes I, old Father Christmas, all in my merry bloom.
Come, gentlemen and ladies, come, give me little room;
Room, room, brave gallant, room; give me room to rhyme
And I will give you some revels to pass away old Christmas time.
Old activity, new activity, the like was never seen,
I pray you now Dim Dorthy step in.

DIM DORTHY

Here come I, Dim Dorthy, with a fair face and a fat commarity,
Although my commarity is but small, I'm the biggest bully of them all.
If you don't believe what I do say, step in Sir Guy and clear the way.

SIR GUY

Here comes I, Sir Guy, a man of mighty strength,
Who slew down Duncow, eighty feet in length;
Is there anyone here holds King George a spleen,
I'm resolved to conquer, it's for King George I'll die.
If you don't believe what I do say, step in King George and clear the way.

KING GEORGE

Here comes I, King George a man of courage bold,
And with my glittering sword I won ten crowns of gold,
I fought the fiery dragon till I brought him to great slaughter,
And by those bloody means I won the Queen of Egypt's daughter.
Close in a closet I was kept, then upon a table rack,
And after that upon a rock of stone,
'Twas there I sat and made my grievous moan.

154

Then the Turkish Knight put his foot on land to fight;
To fight I would even if I was slain, till every drop of blood would quiver
in his veins.
If you don't believe what I do say, step in, Valiant Soldier, and clear the
way.

VALIANT SOLDIER
Here comes I, the Valiant Soldier bold, Slasher is my name,
Sword and buckler by my side in hopes to win the game;
My head is made of iron, my ribs are made of steel,
I means to fight the Turkish Knight and slay him in the field.

KING GEORGE
Hark, I hear a footstep.

VALIANT SOLDIER
That may be the Grand Turk.

GRAND TURK ENTERS
Here comes I, the Grand Turk, out of prison for to fight,
To fight King George, that man by name, if I had him what dreadful
work I make;
I would cut him and slay him as small as dust,
And send his body to the devil for a Christmas pie crust.

KING GEORGE
Stop! Stop! Don't speak so hot,
There's a man in this room thou knowest not.
I'll cut thee and slay thee and when that is done,
I will fight the bravest champion that's under the sun.

GRAND TURK
Why, King George, did I ever do you any harm?

KING GEORGE
Yes! Therefore you deserve to be stabbed.

GRAND TURK
Stab for stab, I will punch you to the ground,
Where I mean to lay your body down.
(*The battle is set in array between King George and the Grand Turk.
King George slays the Grand Turk, his body lying dead on the ground.
King George, sorry for his brother champion, calls for a doctor.*)
Doctor, doctor, come with speed,
And help me in my time of need;
The time of need I never saw before
Till I saw my brother champion lying dead upon the floor.
Is there a doctor to be found?

DOCTOR

Yes, there's a doctor here at hand
Who can cure your brother champion
Of his deadly wound and make him stand.

KING GEORGE

What can you cure, noble doctor?

DOCTOR

I can cure all things: Itch, stitch, the 'pox, the palsy and the gout,
And if the divil is in him I can root him out.

KING GEORGE

How far have you travelled, noble sir?

DOCTOR

I've travelled from England through France and Spain,
And always back to old England again.
I have a little bottle in the waistband of my breeches pocket
Called ice, some tice; some gold for lice; some the wig of a weasel;
The wool of a frog and eighteen inches last September's fog.
Hold it over a slow turf-fire in a wooden saucepan.
Mixed with a hen's tooth and a cat's feather;
Three drops to his temple and one to his heart,
Rise up, brother, and play your part.
(*The dead Turk is brought to life by the doctor's medicine. The Grand Turk cries out.*)
Terrible! Terrible! The like was never seen,
A man knocked out of seven senses into a hundred and nineteen;
Not be [by] bucks nor it [yet] by bears, one of the divil's whirligigs
blowed me up in the air.
If you don't believe what I do say, step in Turkish Knight and clear the
way.

TURKISH KNIGHT

Here comes I, the Turkish Knight,
All from the Turkish land to fight,
To fight King George or the Valiant Soldier bold, Slasher is his name;
Show me the man before me will stand,
I'll cut him down with my courageous hand.

VALIANT SOLDIER

I'm the man before you will stand
And that you soon shall know.
And if you do your worst or best
I'll give you blow for blow.

156

TURKISH KNIGHT

I don't mind your words as figs,
Neither your blows or bumps,
If you cut me off my legs,
I'll fight you on my stumps.
(*The battle is on between the Turkish Knight and the Valiant Soldier.
The Turk, wounded, falls to the ground.*)

VALIANT SOLDIER

O see, O see, what I have done,
I have cut him down like the fallen sun;
Ten thousand more such men I'll fight,
For to maintain King George's rights.

TURKISH KNIGHT

O stop, O stop your hand, there's one thing more I crave,
If you spare me my sweet life I'll be your English slave.

VALIANT SOLDIER

Arise, arise you Turkish dog, and to your country make your way,
And tell unto your Turkish fleet what a champion old England bears
    today.
Step in Oliver Cromwell and clear the way.

OLIVER CROMWELL

Here comes I, Oliver Cromwell, as you may suppose,
I conquered many nations with my copper nose;
I made the French to tremble, the Spanish to shake,
I fought the jolly Dutchmen until I made their hearts ache.
If you don't believe what I do say, step in the captain of the play.

THE CAPTAIN AND HIS WIFE APPEAR

Here comes I, the captain of the play
And to my men I lead the way.
And I stood on the pewter rock of fame,
And on the champion bear the blame.
I'm not like some of those Turkish dogs
That go out after night and disturb the people and make a noise.
Step in the wren and clear the way.

THE WREN

The wren, the wren, the king of all birds,
St. Stephen's Day I was caught in the firs;
Although I am little my honour is great,
Rise up, Skipper, and give us a treat;
If you got no rum give us some cake,

If you fills the plate of the small,
It will not agree with those boys at all,
But if you fills it of the best,
We hope in Heaven your soul will rest.

(*Song follows, sung by the crowd.*)
Ye midwives and widows, come now pay attention
To those few lines I'm now going to mention.
Of a maid in distraction who is now going to wander,
She relied upon George for the loss of her lover.

(*Chorus, after each verse*)
Broken-hearted I'll wander,
For the loss of my lover,
My bonnie light-horseman
Was slain in the war.

Three years and six months since I left England's shore,
My bonnie light-horseman will I ever see more.
She mounted on horseback, so gallant and brave,
Amongst the whole regiment respected he was.

If I had the wings of an eagle as swift as the dove I would fly
I would cross the salt sea where my true love do lie,
And with my fond lips I would bear on his grave,
And kiss his pale cheeks so colder than clay.

7. LARRY GORMAN AND THE CANTE FABLE
Edward D. Ives

The most famous of Canada's folk composers is Larry Gorman, known all through the northeastern lumberwoods as "The Man Who Made the Songs." "Larry is the most appealing and most important figure in eastern woods minstrelsy from the 1870s into the present century," writes W.M. Doerflinger. "His songs are still being sung by old-time woodsmen from northern New Brunswick to the Androscoggin River in Maine, and in Larry's own day the news that he was working in a camp was enough to make shantyboys for miles around decide they wanted to join the same crew."

In addition to the songs he composed, many reminiscences about him circulate in the Maritimes. Of particular interest are several which fall into the pattern of the cante fable. This was originally a story told partly in song, but in recent times the form has broken down into a humorous anecdote with a verse for its clincher. The following samples show why Larry's quick wit and caustic tongue caused him to be both admired and feared. The most common of all, the humorous graces, are local adaptations of a fairly widespread joke form. They are all found in the book entitled Larry Gorman: The Man Who Made the Songs.

1. THE FROLIC (p. 20)

One time John Plestid of Arlington was holding a "work frolic"; everyone worked around the place during the day, and then in the evening there was a party and dance. The party had not gone on for very long before Plestid discovered that he was running out of drink, and it was just at this time that Larry Gorman and a friend arrived. Since they had not worked, they were not entitled to take part in the festivities; but many of the people there implored Plestid to give Larry something to drink so that he would not write a song about them. He acquiesced, and Larry felt called on to offer a toast:

> Here's to you, Mr. Plestid,
> You give us liquor while it lasted;
> We hope next time you have a frolic
> You won't run short of alcoholic.

2. MATT AND THE ANCHOR (p. 37)

Larry also went fishing with . . . Matt Howard. Early one season Matt lost an anchor; his wife, when he told her, said that she would pray every day to the Blessed Virgin Mary for its return. Months later, he and Larry hauled in their nets and, sure enough, there was the anchor, corroded but still recognizable. We can imagine the transports of joy and thanksgiving at home when Matt reported his luck to his wife, because sometime later someone asked Larry how the day's fishing had gone and he replied,

> 'Tis to the Virgin we must pray
> And every day must thank her;
> Matt went out to fish today
> And caught his little anchor.

3. MICHAEL McELROY (pp. 39-40)

Down in Miminegash there was a fellow by the name of Michael McElroy, a fisherman who also ran a lobster-packing factory. It was evidently a good-sized establishment including, besides the factory itself, a kitchen, a dining room, and the big "ram-pasture," sleeping quarters for the hands . . .

Larry disliked the ram-pasture, and when he woke up one morning and saw someone he didn't know sleeping on the floor (all the bunks were full), he is supposed to have fired this one off extempore:

> A stranger to the pasture came
> And slept upon the floor;
> He certainly made a great mistake
> For there are fleas galore.

No one person ever seems to have suffered more abuse at Larry's hands than this McElroy. It is claimed that he did Larry out of some wages, but whether the injury was real or imagined, Larry was angry and went after McElroy with every weapon at his command. He jabbed at him with quips, sniped at him with little verses, and gave him broadside after broadside from the heavy artillery of his *ad hominem*, his most fearful weapon. He even made use of a secret weapon: his hitherto unknown ability to cartoon. He drew pictures of McElroy and his family and gave them all long tails. One picture which made the rounds showed on one side fat, healthy fishermen coming to work for McElroy and on the other side the same men leaving him, all skin and bones and some on crutches. Clearly, Larry did not feel that McElroy spread a good table, and Larry liked to eat. He showed his disapproval in a more characteristic way one time when McElroy had some buyers from England down at the factory and brought them in to dinner. Everyone ate at one long wooden trestle table, and as they were preparing to sit down McElroy (why I'll never know!) asked Larry to say grace. Larry looked down at his plate and said,

> Oh Lord above, look down on us
> And see how we are forgotten
> And send us meat that is fit to eat
> Because, by Christ, this is rotten.

4. MORE EXAMPLES OF THE "GRACE BEFORE MEAT" (pp. 143, 144, 146)

(a) He went to the home of John McCollister of Miminegash, who had two young daughters who were getting supper . . . and they were

160

having porridge and just then a team drove in with two young men, so immediately they changed the table set-up and got a different supper for the young men and when they sat down to eat, they asked Gorman to say grace and immediately he replied:

> Oh Lord be praised, I am amazed
> How things can be amended,
> With cake and tea and such glee,
> When porridge was intended.

(b) Some officials made an unexpected visit to a camp. The Cook made a quick change of menu for dinner. Larry Gorman, aware of the change, on coming to his seat at the table remarked:

> Lord be praised! I am amazed!
> How quick things can be mended!
> Tarts and pies for us P.I.'s
> When codfish was intended.

(d) Back on P.E.I. one of Larry's neighbours stole sheep from one Mac-Millan; but he could not catch the old ram. Larry was at the neighbour's house for a meal one day, and was asked to say grace. Larry complied:

> Lord bless the meat that we do eat,
> Ham and I together;
> God send him speed that he will need
> To catch MacMillan's wether.

(e) On one occasion Larry had dinner at the home of the Sentners, who were distinguished in this fishing village because they were not fishermen but farmers. Larry evidently expected to eat rather well there, but he was served fish instead of the meat he had hoped for. Later on a friend asked him how he had fared, and he replied,

> Lord be praised, I am amazed
> How Sentners got their riches;
> They sold their meat to buy some fish,
> The dirty sons of bitches!

(f) Another time Larry went to dinner at the house of James Alfred Rix . . . and Rix's wife also made the mistake of feeding the poet fish. He looked at his plate and said,

> Oh herring, oh herring, what brought you here?
> You swam the seas for many a year.
> They brought you here for lobster bait
> And not for us poor devils to eat.

5. LARRY AND MRS. TEAZLE (pp. 57-58)

One time Larry was going up along the Nor'west on his way into the woods. He stopped at a house to see if he couldn't get put up for the night. The woman said no she couldn't put him up at all. "Well," Larry wanted to know, "would you give me something to eat?" She thought a long time about that before she finally said yes, she'd feed him, and she gave him a bite in the kitchen. They talked a little and in the course of things she asked him his name. And he told her. "Oh," she said, "will you do something for me?"

"What's that?" asked Gorman.

"Well, my husband died not long ago and I haven't got a verse for his tombstone."

"Oh," said Larry, "I could make one all right. What was his name?"

"Teazle," she said.

So Larry began:

"Mr. Teazle died of late,
Just arrived at Heaven's gate – "

"Oh that's fine, fine," said Mrs. Teazle.

"Well," said Larry, "that's all I'm going to make now, but if you'll put me up for the night I'll finish it in the morning before I leave."

So she put him up for the night. And the next morning she gave him breakfast. She didn't say anything about the verse during breakfast, but just as he got ready to leave she mentioned it to him.

"Oh, yes," he said. "I'll finish it up now. Let's see, How did I start it?

Mr. Teazle died of late – "

"Yes?"

"Just arrived at Heaven's gate – "

"Yes, yes?"

"Along came Satan just like a weasel
And down to Hell he dragged old Teazle."

Then Larry left.

6. THE MAN WHO MAKES THE SONGS (p. 145)

Once when Larry came out of the woods wearing a winter's growth of beard he went to a boarding house he knew to get a room. The landlady let him in, but she went on at some length to say that one person who

162

would never be permitted to set foot in her boarding house again was that Larry Gorman. Larry agreed with her, saying that all that fellow would do would be to make a nasty song about her. Later on, a friend, who recognized him in spite of the beard, asked him how he had gotten on with the woman. Larry replied,

> She treated me very kindly,
> But her eyes stuck out like prongs,
> Abusing Larry Gorman,
> The man who makes the songs.

8. JOKES AND ANECDOTES

Although myths and fairy tales are rather rare among Anglo-Canadians, they tell hundreds of jokes and anecdotes, the third major type of folktales. These fall largely into two main categories: numskull stories, and tales of lying, and below are three representative samples from different parts of Canada.

PAT AND MIKE JOKES FROM NOVA SCOTIA
Arthur Huff Fauset

These jokes, which Arthur Huff Fauset collected largely from Blacks in Nova Scotia during 1929, are typical of the "fool Irishmen" yarns which used to be very common in North America, particularly during the nineteenth century, when Irish immigration was at its height. Later many of the same jokes were told of Ukrainians and Newfoundlanders: see the section on "Newfie Jokes."

1. TAKE ONE FROM THE BOTTOM

One time Pat and Mike tried to reach the moon. So they piled some boxes on top of one another. They got so far and they didn't have no more boxes. So Mike said, "Take one from the bottom." So afterwards Pat said, "Are you hurt, Mike?" Mike said, "No, but I'm speechless." (AT 1250A; J2133.6.1)

2. WHY THEY WERE COLD

There were two Irishmen, Pat and Mike, traveling out one day. Night came on, and there was no house nearby. So Pat told Mike, "We got to sleep somewhere." Mike said, "I was just thinking about it." On and on they walked, and finally they decided to sleep in the fields. So they went to a field, and went to sleep. It was the spring of the year and quite cold. So Pat woke up and said, "Mike, I can't sleep, it's too cold." Mike said, "Neither can I." So they decided to get up and walk so they wouldn't freeze. Pretty soon they came to a gate. Mike turned to Pat and said, "No wonder we were cold. The gate was open." (J1819)

3. FAST TRAVELING

Pat was shingling a roof. He turned around to look at the priest coming up the road. He lost his balance and fell. So the priest said to him, "Did you hurt yourself?" He said, "No." The priest said, "The Lord must have been with you then." Pat said, "He must have been going some, because I come down there pretty fast." [Cf. "Goin' Some," p.188]

4. THE RIDDLE TEST

There was an Irishman out looking for a government job. So he went up to one fellow an' he said, "Look a here, I've been voting for you all me life. I ought to get a job of you." So the man said, "I guess we've got something for you to do, but before I give you the job you have to answer three questions. Now you go home and consider the questions, then come back tomorrow with the answers. And if you answer them correctly you get the job." Pat said, "Go on with your questions." The man said, "The first is, the weight of the moon. The second is, how many stars in the sky. And the last is, what I'll be thinking on when you come." So the next morning the Irishman come back. He found the old fellow in. He said, "Well, Pat, I guess you thought of what I told you. Now let's hear your answers. The first question, was 'How much does the moon weigh?' Well, how much?" The Irishman said, "One hundred weight." – "One hundred weight? Why, how do you make that out?" Pat said, "Well, the moon has four quarters and four quarters make a hundred, don't they?" The man said, "I guess you're right. Well, now, answer the second question. How many stars are in the sky?" The Irishman said, "Seven billion, eight thousand million, four hundred and fifty-two thousand." The man said, "How now, how do you make that?" "Well," said the Irishman, "if you don't believe me, you can go count them yourself." "That's right, that's right," said the old fellow. "We'll let that pass. But how about the last question. What am I thinking?" "Well, you think that I'm Pat, but I'm his brother Mike!" – It wasn't Pat. He had sent his brother Mike to answer the questions. (AT 922; H524.1, H691.1, H702.)

5. THREE DREAMS

It seems there was an Irishman, an Englishman, and a Scotchman. They made a plot, all the money they could get hold of was a penny. They considered what they was going to do with the penny to get something to eat for the three of them. So they sat down, thought awhile, said, "We'll get a penny token (small loaf of bread)." Scotchman wanted to divide it up. Englishman said, "No, too small, won't be enough for three of us. We'll hide the bread and go to sleep, and whoever dreams the truest dream will have the penny token." So they went and had their sleep and when they woke every fellow had their dream to tell. The Englishman said that he saw a bell that would cover Scotland over. The Scotchman said that he saw a pot that would cover over Ireland. Said, "Paddy, what did you dream?" Said, "Dreamt I got up in the night and eat the penny token." So when they went to look, he had. (AT 1626, K444)

6. DEAF AND DUMB

Pat and Mike, they were traveling along the road and they come to a farm house. So Mike says to Pat, "Pat, you'll have to make believe you're deaf and dumb, so we can get somethin' to eat." So they went to the door. Mike said, "Madam, will you please give my brother and me something to eat, he's deaf and dumb." The lady says, "Why sure. It's too bad your brother is deaf and dumb." Pat spoke up and say, "Bejabers, madam, it is that."

7. ALL DRESSED UP AND NO PLACE TO GO

Mike died and Pat and his wife went over and seen him whilst he was laying in his coffin. All of a sudden, Pat give a great big roar of laughter. His wife asked him the reason why he was laughing. He hesitated a few minutes, then his reply was, "Mike all dressed up and no place to go."

8. LET ME SPIT ON MY HANDS

They was traveling along. Wanted some water, came to a well. Pat was holding the other man by his legs. "Let me spit on my hands," says Pat. He let go to spit on his hands to get a new hold. And the other fellow went down head-first into the well. (AT 1250; J2133.5)

9. FENCE UP AGAIN

Two Irishmen bought a farm. There was a line between land up to a stone wall. Row who was to own it. They chucked down the wall. Each went to a lawyer. One fellow could read, one couldn't. The lawyer gave them a note to another lawyer. The fellow who could read opened the note and read, "Two fools, you skin one, and I'll skin the other." – "Faith, my skin is thin enough now without being skinned again, we'll put the fence up again." (X319)

10. FIREFLIES

An Irishman came to England. He went to a hotel to sleep. It was very hot and the mosquitoes came biting him, and he had to scratch a lot. Pat said, "My goodness, I don't know what to do." So Mike said, "Blow out the light and put up the window." Pat did this, and five minutes later a lot of fireflies came in. Pat said, "Oh, Mike, there's the darn things and they've brought their lanterns with them." (J1759.3)

11. LOOK OUT!

Pat and Mike were coming through a tunnel. The conductor came round and hollered, "All look out, coming through a tunnel!" Pat put his head out and got it bumped. He said, "Bejabbers, I thought you said all of us should look out." (J2460.1)

12. COLT AND WHEELBARROW

Pat stole a horse and wagon, policeman came after him. "Where did you get the horse?" – "Had it ever since it was a little colt." – "Where did you get the wagon?" – "Had it ever since it was a little wheelbarrow."

13. THE MOTHER OF GOD

Pat was an awful drunkard. The priest was always getting after him. One day he saw him drunk and he said to himself, "The rascal, he hasn't been to church for six months, an' he's always soused up." So he went up to Pat an' says to him, "Say, Pat, when you goin' to stop gettin' drunk, an' coming back to church?" Pat pulled out his watch an' said, "I'm goin' to pawn this, Father, an' pay off an IOU. Then after I do that I will change an' become a good man." The priest said, "Why don't you go in church and pray to the Blessed Virgin, maybe she'll send you the money." Pat said, "That ain't bad. All right, I'll do it, Father." So he went in church an' he prayed to the Blessed Virgin for ten dollars. He prayed so hard the priest thought he really meant it. So he got up on a balcony and dropped down a five-dollar gold piece. "There, now," he said, "maybe that'll cure Pat." But a few hours later a boy came up to the priest an' said, "Father, Father, shure an' Pat is coming' up the road beastly drunk." The priest said, "The rascal, gone an' took my five dollars an' got drunk off'n it. I'll fix him." So he got a big sheet an' wrapped it around him. Then he hid behind a thorn hedge. Just as Pat come up, he jumped out an' said, "Hello!" Pat looked at him an' said, "An' who are you, begorra?" The priest said, "I'm God." Pat said, "Begorra, I've been lookin' for you all day. Your mother owes me five dollars." (X459)

14. JUG A RUM

Irishman lived out in the wood. He was a great fellow for his drink. He had to go by a big pond, with a jug of rum. Heard, "Jug a rum, jug a rum." – "It's none of yer damn business, whether it's rum or not, I paid for it." – "Jug a rum, jug a rum." He took the jug and threw it.

Another Saturday night, the keg fell out of his hand and rolled away, saying, "Gooty goot, gooty goot," the sound it made running out. "Ah, faith, I know yer good, but I can't get to you."

15. BRINGING A LION HOME

Pat bet Mike five dollars he'd bring a lion home. So he goes out to the woods an' meets a lion. He drops his gun an' starts to run. He runs home, chased by the lion. When he gets to the house he yells, "Open the door, Pat, I'm bringin' home a lion." (X584.1)

16. FOUND ANOTHER

Time Pat joined a vessel. Lovely evening, stars all shinin' bright. Captain says to Pat, "Pat, you see that star right dead ahead." Pat says to the Captain, "Begor! Yes, sir, I do." – "Pat, steer the vessel right dead for that star." Pat says, "Sure I will, sir." So bimeby Pat dozed off at the wheel. When he came to himself the vessel was off her course. Captain came on deck, says, "Pat, I thought I told you to steer for that star dead ahead." Pat says, "Divil take you, Captain, I lost that star, but I found another one."

ONTARIO YARNS FROM JOE THIBADEAU
Edith Fowke

In Ontario it has proved much easier to collect folk songs than folktales from English-speaking informants, but one singer, Joe Thibadeau, also proved to be a fine story-teller. He was seventy-nine when I met him in 1964, and he willingly sang dozens of songs for me, as well as telling humorous yarns which were nearly all tall tales.

Despite his French name, Joe said his father was Scottish, born in St. John, New Brunswick, and his mother was from New York state. His father died, his mother married again, and Joe and his nine

brothers had to get out to work. He went to work in the lumber camps
when he was thirteen, spent quite a few years in the Lake of the Woods
and Rainy River district, and then settled in Bobcaygeon, a pretty
little town some thirty miles northwest of Peterborough. He was a
licenced guide for twenty-five years, and his tales of the days when he
worked for Paul Bunyan entertained hundreds of tourists.

1. BUNYAN'S BLUE OX

Well, he was quite a man, Paul Bunyan, and he had an ox he called the
Blue Ox. So the river where he was and where I happened to be, this Blue
Ox he had him tied up there to a tree. "Well," he says, "that river's
pretty crooked, isn't it, Joe?" and I said, "Yes, it's very crooked."
"Well," he said, "I better straighten it out, eh?" I said, "O.K., you go
ahead and straighten it out." So he gets a big loggin' chain and he
hitches it around a tree on the bend of the river, and he says to the Blue
Ox, he says, "Come on, Buck, get goin'!" And he drew out nine miles of
bends with one pull. And that Blue Ox sunk to his knees right in solid
rock! (AT 1960A; X1237.2.6*; X1733.4*[b])

2. BUNYAN'S TRICK

Paul says to me, one time, he says, "We can make a little bit of money
now quite easy," and I says, "Yeah? How do we do it?" "Well," he says,
"You know where Boyd's big island is on Pigeon Lake. Well," he says,
"we'll move that big island 'way down into Gannon's Narrows, and we'll
block the channel, and," he says, "then they'll have to pay us twice that
much to get it back." I says, "All right," so he says, "What you got to do,
catch a lot of those mud turtles – those big snapping mud turtles." So I
got about a thousand of them and took them up to old Paul, and he
placed them in channels, you know, right all around the island. And they
love bananas, mud turtles, so we got a long pole and we kind of hung
some bananas on the end of this pole and held them out like that, and
they come up and come up and come up to get the bananas, and we knew
the way we wanted it to go, you know – south, and they just went right
after those bananas, and accordance they did, they were hitched to the
big island and they had to move it, and they walked right away to Gannon's Narrows with it. Well, we got five thousand dollars for that.
(X1086.1*).

3. THE BIG FISH

Well, this big fish, he was a real big one, and I snubbed him to an
island on the lake, a small island. I tied the line there and I said, "O.K.,
play all you want to." And he just took three or four r'ars and he

straightened that tree right out like a piece of wood, and away he went with the island and everything. We never seen or heard tell of him since that day. (X1303)

4. THE BIG MOOSE

Well, this big moose, I wanted to get him, and I set down and I straddled the track, and I started pulling back on the track, and I pulled the moose right up to me and killed him. (X1759*)

5. THE WOLVES

Ralph went out a-huntin' with me, oh a lot of times. We hunt in the fall of the year for deer, so this time he said, "Well, I guess we'll go after wolves this time." So we went out and I heerd a pack of wolves comin' and I said to Ralph, I said, "They're comin' this way." "Yes," he says, "and they look very suspicious to me." Well, when one wolf you shoot him the rest'll turn around and eat him when they smell the blood. So I shot one and Ralph shot the other, and they all crowded in and come up, and they eat the two that we shot, yeah, eat 'em right up! So we keep shootin', and then I said, "There's no more, that's the last one." We had no more shells for the gun, and another one run out and we couldn't shoot him because we had no more shells. So I says, "What're we goin' to do?" He said, "There's nothing we can do." So the last one he got away. And that was fifteen wolves that we killed, and they kept eatin' 'em and eatin' 'em till there was only the only the one left – and we had no shells left. Do you remember that, Ralph? (X1216.1[bb])

[Ralph, Joe's nephew, was listening to the stories.]

6. DEER FOR DINNER

Near where I lived by old 'Caygeon, we were cuttin' oats with the old-time – what they call cradles – you mow them like a scythe, and Ralph was cradlin' those oats and I was rakin' em up behind him and bindin' 'em – I knew how to bind them in sheaves, you know. So we heerd a pair of dogs comin' and I said, "That sounds like wolves to me." "Yes," he says, "I guess it is, it must be wolves." So they were after a deer, and oh, it was a hot day right in the summer, and they brought this deer along and he jumped over the fence and got stuck in a snowdrift, and he run up with the cradle and cut his throat. And we had lots of fresh meat there for dinner. (X1605)

7. THE WOLVES AND THE BEAVERS

'Nother time I was goin' from one camp to the other. It was a moonlight night, a beautiful night, and I had about two miles to go so I struck out. This moonlight night showed me the light – beautiful! I got about half way and the wolves took after me. Well, I said, "I'm done!" I looked around and looked around, and I seen a tree there, and I shinnied up the tree and I set on a limb. And they howled and howled around the foot of that tree. Oh, I thought they were goin' to come up and get me, but a wolf can't climb a tree. So I took it easy, and I got so cold I said, "I'll have to do something." And the old leader of the wolves, he come out, left the pack and he come out under the tree, and he seen me up there. He howled a few times, and then they give that lonely wolf call, and the rest of them all come back again. And he led them away on to a big meadow, and they dug out a beaver house – the beaver, you know, they build houses. Well, he got them to work and opened it up, and do you know what they were doing? They were gettin' the beaver to come and chew the tree down to get me. Yeah! I just sat there and kept quiet, and they came and they chewed and chewed at the tree till down went the tree. But I was gone. And I made it back to my camp. But I was scared! (X1216.1[ab])

Oh, yes, I've had quite a time in my day. Heerd some awful stories, and I've heerd the wolves howl at night and howl all night in the lumber camps, you know . . .

8.   THE GHOST

My brother and me was up to Kinmount one time, and there was a lot of old buildings along the road, you know, that was never in use, so I said, "We'll go into this old building and we'll stay there for the night," I says. "It's gettin' pretty late and we gotta sleep some place." So we went in and we lay down in the corner and in the night I heerd a noise . . . clump . . . clump . . . clump, and I shook him and I says, "Lou, wake up!" And he says, "What's the matter?" "Do you hear that?" I says. "This is a haunted house, and I'm tellin' you, boy, there's someone in here right now. You'd better wake up and set up and take a watch and see what we can do." He said, "All right." So we got up and it walked across the floor upstairs . . . clump . . . clump . . . clump . . . Come to the head of the stairs, and my two eyes just stuck out like that. Clump- . . . clump . . . down the steps, down the steps and right into the kitchen where we were sleepin' in the corner. "Well," I says, "There's got to be something done," and I could see the white right in front of my eyes, and I jumped and just grabbed it, and threw it away out through the window. And do you know what it was? A sheep! It wasn't a ghost at all. (AT 1318; J1782)

170

TALL TALES AND OTHER YARNS FROM CALGARY
Herbert Halpert

Herbert Halpert, the American folklorist who later initiated folklore studies at Memorial University in St. John's, Newfoundland, collected the following tales during World War II when he was an American army lieutenant stationed in Calgary for seven months. They include some stories about famous Alberta characters, a number of international tall tales that became localized in Alberta, and a few more general folktales that are quite widespread.

Western Canada was one of the last frontiers in North America. As the open cattle range became crowded and was fenced in, the cowmen slowly drifted their herds north from the southwestern states to Wyoming and Montana. Some of them continued north up the old Fort Benton trail and so across the Canadian border into southern and western Alberta. For similar reasons farmers from Minnesota and other midwestern states unable to find land to their liking also made their way northwest to mix with settlers from eastern Canada as well as with the English and Scottish who had come directly from the old country.

Today this is still a country of rich variety. Cattle and horse ranching, wheat farms, coal mining, all centre around the small but very metropolitan city of Calgary. From Calgary in the rolling foothills it is just eighty miles west by trail to Banff and thence to Lake Louise – both world-famous resorts in the bare grandeur of the Canadian Rockies which rise sharply west to the Great Divide.

The Canadian Pacific Railroad came through the West in 1885. Tourists have been coming here since that time. Before those days, English "remittance men," usually ne'er-do-well younger sons pensioned off "to leave their country for their country's good," settled around this area. Buffalo, deer, and game birds were plentiful. Once the Indians were dealt with, by comparison with other areas the worst was over, for here the pioneers were favoured with winters milder than in the states to the east or immediately to the south.

Around Calgary one finds the reservations of many of the Plains Indian tribes: the Stoneys, Bloods, and Blackfeet. Today, good hunting, a congenial climate, and the casual friendly ease of the West still make living pleasant for the visitor. The famous annual Calgary Stampede, with some nostalgia and a little self-consciously, tries to recapture the "golden days" of this vivid frontier.

How recently this was frontier would be amazing to a Californian, but even more so to an Easterner. To be a member of the "Southern Alberta

171

Pioneers and Old-Timers'. Association" one has to have been here only before 1890. Farther south the date is a few years earlier. At the Old-Timers' meetings you find the pioneers are still plentiful and sturdy. Of course, when you start to collect pioneer lore, you are told the usual sorrowful tale: you should have been here ten or twenty years ago when so-and-so was alive. However, the folklorist knows enough to discount this, and informants are not too difficult to find. As a matter of fact, some of the best informants are not "pioneers" but people who came shortly after the turn of the century.[1]

. . . In the seven months in which I was stationed near Calgary and on one or two later visits I secured the bulk of this collection. About a dozen tales came from a Banff guide whom I met during a visit to Lake Louise, and a few come from Granum in the south of the province and Grande Prairie in the north.

All the stories given here were dictated to me. It should be noted that story-tellers in this Province are much more literate than those in many sections of the United States. This literacy sometimes is a handicap to the folklorist for such narrators often become stiffly self-conscious when they are dictating. This accounts somewhat for the uncolloquial "book-ish" quality of language in several of the stories.

Calgary is on a plateau over three thousand feet high and the altitude and dry air have a tingle, a kind of feverish excitement. The atmosphere has a deceptive clarity which makes the mountains look fifty miles closer than they are. In mid-winter the warm chinook winds come over the mountain passes melting the deepest snow and raising the temperature from well below freezing to a spring temperature in an amazingly short time. Sober descriptions of the effects of the "chinook" strike the newcomer as the wildest flights of imagination.[2]

It is the climate, with its sudden extremes of temperature, which forms the theme of many of the tall stories told in the area. Along with them one gets exaggerated hunting and fishing tales, and jests about the tenderfeet, tourists, and Englishmen. Regional pride is high. Calgary laughs at Edmonton to the north, but it joins with the rest of Western Canada in expressing through mockery the widely felt irritation at the eastern provinces.

As might be expected most of the folk tales found were carried in from elsewhere, but the majority of them have been thoroughly changed to fit local conditions. Some new ones have been made on the old models.

We find Paul Bunyan here adapted to a treeless country just as he has been in the southwestern oilfields. There is some possibility that the little we have about him dates from the "pre-literary epoch" of the legend, for it is reported as told in fragments and not in a connected narrative . . .

Of much more importance is a newly discovered folk hero, Dave McDougall, son of the famous early missionary, George M. McDougall. Dave has secured an immortality far different from his father's by the outrageous yarns he told about himself. He followed the pattern, common to the many Munchausens in the United States, of adapting and claiming as his own experiences far more yarns than he actually composed. Like John Darling in New York State, he infuriated many serious-minded Alberta citizens by his insistence that he spoke nothing but the truth.[3] Dave, a resident of Calgary in his later years, is reputed to have been a very prolific storyteller, but only a baker's dozen of his stories seem to be current. Among them are some which Dave's wife, an ideal helpmate for a yarn spinner, not only vouched for, but even blew up further. Dave's historically better-known older brother, John, who was both a missionary and an author,[4] was, if tradition may be relied on, an even more outrageous example of the Munchausen breed. Unfortunately I could get no more than a hint of the kind of stories he told, although many people around Calgary remembered both of the brothers[5] and after some hesitation spoke of them freely.

Before presenting the stories some information on when they were told and how they were learned is instructive. I asked Alex R. McTavish, aged fifty-two, whose father was the first blacksmith in Calgary, where he had heard the stories he had told me. Mr. McTavish has put a number of tall stories into verse, originally for the entertainment of his son who was overseas in the RCAF. He has continued his versifying for his own amusement, and several of his pieces have been published in newspapers. He said: "Heard them from here and there and all over. I've always been interested in old-timers, my father's friends – lived with them all my life. My father was a pioneer, and my uncles. It was mostly some particular character that told these stories. He probably invented some of the old-time characters."

"When were they told?" I asked. "Oh, sitting around the house in the evening – at branding time – sometime when people got together. More particularly when some greenhorn or tenderfoot – an eastern visitor – was present. These stories would never be told directly to the greenhorn, but would be told in his presence, and very often verified by one or more bystanders, and sometimes enlarged upon by a suggestion from a friend, or verified as to the exact position. They would tell it as a matter of course – just part of the daily conversation. Not as though it were anything out of the ordinary course of events – just a common bit of gossip. Naturally, if he had any brains at all, he would savvy that they were having fun at his expense."

I met fifty-eight-year-old Andrew Wright, better known as "Scotty," at Lake Louise last summer and got a number of excellent stories from him. He told me: "I come out to Canada 1904, from Scotland and I come out to the park New Year's Day 1905. I was a ranger in the park 1915-1928. I was guiding for two years, and I've been with the park engineers."

I asked Scotty, who, like most guides, is a fine yarn spinner, how he had learned his stock of tales, and was surprised to find how conscious the process is. Guides realize that storytelling is part of their stock in trade, and go to school in winter by having informal sessions in which they exchange yarns with their colleagues.

"The way I heard most of them stories: different local boys out with parties they each have their own stories. You have to entertain your guests when you're out – sittin' around the campfire nights. We usually have our *own* parties in the wintertime, and we set and tell stories. You've got to memorize them. I lived so much alone it comes easy. That's how it is with tourists. You have to tell them lots of things. Out in the hills when we hear news, we call it 'moccasin telegraph.' Someone come, give you somethin' to think about for a few days."

He remarked of Dave McDougall whom he had known at Banff: "McDougall he was one of the 'riginal old-timers. When he come to Morley – that's about thirty miles east of Banff – they come by prairie schooner." And he commented, after relating one of Dave's stories, "They knew he told so many outrageous stories. They just encouraged him."

Alex McTavish gave me further information about the McDougalls. "They lived in Morley. John lived in Calgary. He preached to the Indians in Morley. John was the brother of Dave – he (John) was the missionary. They were among the first white men to come to the western country. Their father, George McDougall, was a missionary in the West too. Came in the '60s, I guess.[6]

"Dave was a trader – he traded with the Indians, and also ran cattle, and he became a very successful business man.[7] Owned an oil well, built buildings – became quite wealthy, although he lost most of it before he died. After he retired he moved to Calgary. I'd met him in Morley when I was a lad. After that he lived on 4th Avenue – back of us.

"They were known as great storytellers – and, of course, John has written several books, about his travels in the West. They were good men – never drank, never smoked, never swore. They just romanced. They were here in this country in the early days, and I suppose wanted to impress the people with the things they had done."

Two points that Mr. McTavish stressed were that both McDougalls "told the stories for truth," and that members of the present generation of the family, especially the daughters, get very irate at the stories and deny that they were told. They do not seem to realize that the McDougalls now hold a position in folk legend that no denials will affect.

A very dignified elderly lady, who preferred that I omit her name, confirmed and amplified Mr. McTavish's observations. To identify her stories I have listed her as "Mrs. B.S." She told me with vigorous humour:

"They said the three biggest liars in Alberta were Dave McDougall; John McDougall was the other two.[8] John was the minister. Bob Edwards poked fun at John McDougall for his storytelling in the *Eye Opener*, with a pretended speech by John telling of his swimming across the Saskatchewan River with two ancient Indians on his back.[9]

"Dave used to tell us some whoppers. The family are living and don't believe he told these. I *know*! I've heard him tell them. He died just a few years ago. He was beginning to get a little batty toward the end. He'd come in to see me at Banff, and he'd tell me the same stories over and over again. This was in his later days. He was getting to be an old man. Mrs. McDougall backed him up in everything he told. It's an amazing thing to me how they *believed* these things. He told them so often, I think he believed them.

"On the whole I would agree with Mr. McTavish's viewpoint on these stories, those by McDougall and others. Some people called them damn lies, but they weren't really lies because a lie is a falsehood to deceive people. These were more romancing, a form of humour. They were called tall stories. I think they're really part of the humour of the country. Humour is naturally a little rough and uncouth in a new country."

Mr. McTavish gives us a good explanation of how and why these stories change as they are passed on.

"Each man that tells a story adds a bit on his own, or forgets to tell a bit, therefore gives the story a little different twist. Maybe he's of a little different turn of mind from the last fellow that told it to him. If it was told exactly the same way every time, it might not be true; but each man told it as he saw it. If it was a cut-and-dried affair, the story would always be the same – make it less interesting."

Interesting they are! With no further ado, let us turn to the stories themselves.

[The first thirteen stories are all about Dave McDougall.]

1.   THE LESSON
Told by Alex R. McTavish

Here's a story Dave told me one day over the back fence. Well the Indians were great fellows to race in the old days. They came along with their carts and their ponies, and Dave was coming with his carts – he was coming out for supplies – and met the Indians, and nothing would do but they'd stop and race. Dave didn't have much use for racing; it was a frivolous sport. But he said, "All right, I'll race you." He said to himself, "I'll teach these Indians a lesson." He had a fast horse that was hitched to one of these carts, and he went and got this fast horse out, and then he bet all his outfit, his string of carts and horses against the Indians' outfit, that he could beat their fastest horse. So he raced them and he beat them and won their whole outfits – then he gave it all back to the squaws so the squaws wouldn't be stripped of their trappings. He'd taught them a lesson.

2.   THE SECTION HOUSE
Told by Andrew Wright

Someone wanted to tell him about his ignorance. He had made his first trip to New York, him and his wife. The way local people in this vicinity would explain that, they knew this McDougall – you would almost say they hated to meet him – they knew he'd peddle a lot of lies about a place like New York. So when he started off on one of his big stories about the city, one gentleman in the party said, "When you got to the city of New York and got off at the station, I understand you inquired where the section house was!" – That's just the natural thing in the prairie where they don't have a station. They have a section foreman that gives you information.

3.   LONG TRIP
Told by Andrew Wright

About this McDougall. That one comin' from the Calgary Stampede was in the smokin' car – 1912 Stampede. A bunch of the boys was talkin' about the different ridin' events. This McDougall said, "Them boys can't ride like I used to ride in the old days." Well, he said, "When I was a young boy on the prairie, I used to ride fifty miles a day, day in and day out, week in and week out." Someone asked, "Well, where the hell was you goin'?"

4.   GOOD CLIMBING
Told by Mrs. B.S.

One day the boys came in tired after climbing Sulphur Mountain. And Dave said they weren't very good stuff. "When I was a young lad I'd run up Stoney Squaw in the morning for exercise, and climb up Rundle in the afternoon."

5. MANY BUFFALO
Told by Mrs. B.S.

He told me when he came to this country, the prairie was filled with buffalo. You could get out and walk for miles on the buffalo. You had to get out and pull the buffalo calves from between the spokes of the wheels to drive.[10] (X1238.1*)

6. BUFFALO MOVERS
Told by Andrew Wright

Well, he said, "When I was livin' with my wife in my young married days, years ago, when there was lots of buffalo on the prairie, we lived in a nice log cabin with spring water just outside the door. My wife asked me to get a pail of water. When I went outside and looked around, I found the cabin was half a mile from the water. It seemed that the buffalo rubbin' theirself on the corner of the building through the night had moved the cabin half a mile from the water hole." (X1238.1*)

7. ONE MORE
Told by Alex R. McTavish

Dave was getting food for the family and naturally in the western country there's always a shortage of ammunition. He was down pretty near to his last shell, and so he lay on the edge of the lake and waited till he got the geese in line. He got about a dozen in line and let drive. He was telling this story to his friends in the dining room and his wife was in the kitchen. He said, "I got fourteen with one shot." And his wife called from the kitchen, "Fifteen, Dave, fifteen! Don't you remember we found one in the grass the next morning?" (X907.1;X1122.2)

8. REMARKABLE CATCH
Told by Mrs. B.S.

Dave was sitting here, and he says, "You go up to Gull Lake?" I says, "Yes." He says, "Lots of big fish in that lake. Get any whitefish?" I said, "No, just pike left." Then he said, "I was going up to Edmonton one night and I had to camp overnight at Gull Lake. I went out to throw in my line. First thing I knew I had a fish – jack fish." He says, "I pulled it in and it weighed forty-seven pounds. And when we cut it open, there were six whitefish in it. They weighed seven pounds each. When we ate them – the whitefish – they were just like they'd come out of fresh water." (X1154.1)
– He was telling me the truth – he believed it.

177

9. FOOLING THE FISH
Told by Andrew Wright

He told this, must be twenty-five years ago, in Banff. He said, "While traveling on snowshoes over Lake Minnewanka ice which was three feet thick at that time, there was no snow in several places on the lake. Crossin' them places, I could hear a tremendous thump on the ice – which made me curious. Lookin' through the ice I see several large fish bumping their noses on the bottom of the ice. I was wearin' long German stockin's with red tassels on them. Then I realized the fish was takin' them for bait."

10. MIXED WEATHER
Told by Mrs. B.S.

He told me he was skating down the Bow, and he was chased by a pack of wolves. He took off his cap and threw it back, and the wolves stopped and fought over that. Then they gained on him, and he threw his scarf – and he kept on throwing things till he hadn't anything he could get along without. And finally the wolves were gaining on him and he thought that his end had come. Just then he turned a bend in the river – and there was a man there hoeing potatoes. And he came out with his hoe and killed one of the wolves, and he escaped. – This man hoeing potatoes while he was skating![11] (X1605)

11. THE INDIANS AND THE CHINOOK
Told by Mrs. B.S.

I never heard Dave tell this but they tell it. Dave said there was an Indian and his wife driving in from Morley – and a chinook was chasing them. And when they arrived in Calgary, the Indian had had a sunstroke, but his wife, sitting in the back, was frozen.[12] (X1606.1)

12. LEFT HANGING
Told by Mrs. B.S.

They were driving up to Edmonton, and there was very, very deep snow. They had to camp north of Calgary for the night. They were driving up from Morley. They tied the horses to some evergreens there, and pitched their tent. Through the night a chinook struck them. In the morning they couldn't find their horses. Then they heard a funny noise in the trees, and they looked up, and the horses were hanging in the trees – the snow had all melted. That's what a chinook will do.[13] (X1606; X1653.1)

178

13. OUTRACING THE CHINOOK
Told by Alex R. McTavish

Dave McDougall lived at Morley, which is about fifty miles west of Calgary, on the Bow River. He started to town with a team and bobsleigh. He was traveling east. A foot of snow was on the ground when he left his home. On the road he was overtaken by a chinook. (Chinooks always come from the west.) It was a particularly warm chinook, and, fearing that he wouldn't get to town before the snow melted, he whipped up the horses to a gallop. The snow melted so fast that the front runners were on snow but the back runners were in the mud. Try as he might he could not go fast enough to get the back runners out of the mud and up on to the snow.[14] (X1606.1)

– It is doubtful if he ever told it. They just hung it on him.

14. PAUL BUNYAN
Told by M.B. Graham

When Paul Bunyan built the Rocky Mountains,[15] it was the winter of the blue snow when the geese flew backwards. He hauled the rocks from Winnipeg with a big blue ox. He had a steam shovel; every time it took a scoop, it gouged out a hole the size of Lake Louise. (X1025)

They made flapjacks on a large griddle. The griddle was so large that the KP, he'd have to skate up and down the griddle with greased feet – butter his feet – to get it greased. (X1031.4.1)

He had an engine that was so large that every time the wheels made one revolution, it was payday. (X1025) – I heard 'em from different fellows around here. That was quite a few years ago – twenty years ago, I guess. I've heard 'em told in southern Alberta – Calgary. It's broken up in many pieces. I've heard just snatches. I just put it together. That railroad train I heard separately. I just worked it in.[16]

15. LARGE ENGINE
Told by M.B. Graham

While workin' for the CPR – they have the largest engines operating, that is, in the mountains through this sector, the Great Divide, I was tellin' him about the large engines we had on the CPR. He says, "That's nothin'! I worked for the Jerusalem Central. We had an engine so large that every time the wheels made one revolution, it was pay day – thirty days."[17] (X1025)

16. FROZEN HOT SPRINGS
Told by Andrew Wright

A tourist inquiring how cold the winter was in Banff, we told him it was so cold last winter that the ice froze in the Upper Hot Springs

179

Swimming Pool. One boy's feet went through the ice, and he got his foot scalded.[18] (X1620)

– Oh, we've lots of stories like that.

17. GREEN
Told by Andrew Wright

A tourist inquired from a local guide how come the water at Lake Louise was so green.[19] He replied, "A tourist fell in last summer."

18. HOW TO COOK A MARMOT
Told by Andrew Wright

A tourist went out on a pack trip for a month. After he'd been on the trail two weeks he thought he knew all about the game. Next time he thought he'd go on the trip himself and save money. One day going over a summit, he saw a large marmot . . . . – it's one of the last animals in the mountains that you'd care to eat; they're so greasy. – He inquired from the cook if he was hungry how he would cook one. The cook said, "Well, you have to kill it first. Then pack it along till you come to a nice cold spring. Put it in a large pot; then boil it for two hours, then strain the water off and refill the pot with cold water. Then boil it again for another two hours. When it's well done, catch it by the hind leg, throw it in the bush, and cut yourself some bacon."[20]

19. KILLED BY A BEAR
Told by Andrew Wright

When I was a ranger in Rocky Mountain Park in Banff, I was transferred to a new district. There was a stream of water coming out of a pass in the mountains that I was very interested in knowin' where it came from. I decided one day to travel to the top of the pass. I'd taken along lunch and my fishing tackle with me. On arriving at the top of this pass I saw a beautiful stream down in the valley below with a bunch of poplar trees growing near the river. I then decided on going down to try fishing in the stream.

While walkin' through the poplar trees near the river, I heard a noise to one side of me. Then I noticed a grizzly bear makin' for me. I then climbed up the first tree that I come to. The bear walks round the tree and growled. He then stood on his hind legs and tried to shake me off the tree. When that didn't work, he growled and left.

Thinkin' he had gone for good, ten minutes later I climbed down the tree, when to my surprise I see him walkin' on his hind legs towards me with a beaver in each arm. I then climbed up the tree again. When he got to the base of the tree, he put the beaver down, then growled at

180

them. Then the beaver really went to work. My how them chips did fly out of that tree! Then I realized the situation was bad. Presently the tree swayed and down I come along with the tree.

When someone in the party asked me, "What happened?" – You hesitate there till the question's asked –

The bear eat me up![21] (AT2202; Z13.2)

[Compare Joe Thibadeau's tale "The Wolves and the Beaver," p. 169.]

20. TAKING NO CHANCES
Told by Dr. B.J. Charles

This Englishman was here visiting a cousin of his, and in the morning he got up and he thought he'd like to walk from Calgary to the Rocky Mountains – they looked so close. (They're about eighty miles away.) He started at nine o'clock and landed home at five o'clock very much played out. When he told his cousin what he had done, his cousin told him "You must never do that again because you can't judge distance here – the air is so rare."

The next day they were going for a little walk together and they came to a little stream. The native Calgarian was going to step over it, but the visiting cousin took a look at it and started to take off his clothes. On being asked what he was doing, he said, "I'm not going to take a chance on stepping over. It may be a lot wider than it looks due to the rarefied air."[22] (J2214.12.1)

21. THE BEAR AND THE CHINOOK
Told by Mr. T.J. Taylor, aged seventy-eight

A man was walking to Calgary from Banff. And a bear took after him. And a chinook wind started to blow. The man made it all right. The man kept ahead of him – he was on snowshoes – and the bear couldn't travel because the snow was melting so quick he was traveling on water.[23] (X1606)

22. STRONG WIND
Told by Alex R. McTavish

The wind at Macleod – it blows all the time. The wind blew so strong that it blew a cow up against the barn. She starved to death before she got down.[24] (X1611.1)

23. WIND IN A HOLE
Told by Alex R. McTavish

Well, this fellow was walking in the mountains and he heard a noise – a peculiar noise of terrific wind – and he went to investigate. He discovered a large hole in the ground about ten feet across, and this wind was coming out of this hole. And while he stood there watching, a full grown buffalo blew right out of this hole. Then he lost his nerve, you see, and he wouldn't go back to the same place again. (X1611.1)

24. DRY SPELL
Told by M.B. Graham

During the dry spell in southeastern Alberta I had occasion to call on one of the old homesteaders. At the time I was driving a "Model T." There was a scarcity of water in the district. The car boiled, and I asked the homesteader for a little water. And he said they paid six bits a barrel for water – pretty hard to spare; but although it was pretty hot – no shade – I could stick around and cool off. It was only 108°, no trees, just bald-headed prairie. He says first to me, he says, "What are you doing?" I told him I was writing life insurance. "Well," he says, "You'll do no business around here. We've been dried out so bad." He says, "You see that old dog over there? The sun dried him up so bad he couldn't walk. I had to put him in the wheelbarrow in order to wheel him around to bark at the cows. That's all they saved was the bark." (X1643)

He said he had eleven seven-year-old bullfrogs that couldn't swim a stroke. He said he had a bunch of old sows up in the pasture. "When I penned them for the winter, I had to soak 'em four days in the irrigation ditch before they'd hold slop." [25] (X1643.1)

He says, "You see those sparrows up there in the telephone wires shootin' dust?" (X1643) – I came here in 1919. It's only fun; they're all from the district.

25. WHY THEY HOP
Told by Alex R. McTavish

There's a real lead in stories about the dry years in this country – in the early '80s. There's been many stories told about them. It didn't rain for so long that the ground began to crack. And these were not ordinary cracks, but they kept getting wider until the whole country was just a network of cracks leaving little islands with large crevices between. It's said that the rabbits used to walk like ordinary animals, but in order to get from one island to another they had to hop and therefore acquired the habit of hopping. Some people say that that's where the grasshoppers learned to hop – from jumping from one island to another. Prairie animals such as the antelope became very expert at it. In fact everything that travelled had to hop. Even the old-timers, who were very few in those days, did their share of hopping. Naturally they acquired a hopping gait too, but this gait did not stay with them after normal weather conditions sealed up the cracks. But there are some of the real old-timers

182

from the prairie region that still have a suspicious loping gait. (A2441.1.0.1)

26. MUDDY ROAD
Told by Mrs. B.S.

They used to call Toronto "Muddy York." Seems a man sank in this mud. Some friends tried to pull him out, and he said, "Well, wait until I take my feet out of the stirrups." His horse was gone altogether.[26] (X1655.1) – That's an old story down there; I heard it when I was a girl.

27. HOT WEATHER
Told by Mrs. B.S.

This was in Chicago. It was a hot day – they went down to the lake shore. One man said he'd never experienced heat like this. This old Southerner said this wasn't hot at all. That down South where he came from he saw a dog chasing a cat – and they were both walking![27] (X1633)

28. SOUNDS FREEZING
Told by Derek Chapman, aged twenty-two

(I read Ruttle's story, No. 34, to Derek at the riding stable shortly after Mr. Ruttle, the proprietor, had gone out. Then Derek said, "That's like the old one everyone knows.")
A farmer one cold morning in winter went to his back door to holler for his pigs. It was so cold out that as he yelled his words froze in the air. His pigs didn't come home until his words thawed out in the spring – then the pigs heard it.[28] (AT 1889F; X1623.2)

29. FROZEN WORDS
Told by Charles K. Underwood

The foreman came out to give orders on the ranch – it was at the old Bar U. It was 75 degrees below zero. It was so cold, d'you see, that the words froze in his mouth – and so he broke them off and handed them around so the men could get their orders for the day.[29] (X1623.2)

30. FROZEN IN PRINT
Told by George Ruttle

We used to have it pretty cold in Manitoba. We'd holler at the horses, and the breath would freeze and their name would be printed across their rump. (X1623)

31. PART BOILING, PART FROZEN
Told by George Ruttle

We often used to be boiling vegetables, and it would be so cold the side next the door would be all frozen over, the other side would be boiling.[30] (X1620)

32. FROZEN ON HOT FURNACE
Told by Mrs. B.S.

About the cold in Edmonton? We were visiting at the home of one of the leading citizens who declared he froze his case of beer sitting on top of the hot furnace – the furnace was going. But a lady here beat this one – she said it was so cold in her house that she froze her tongue in bed. (X1620)

– Calgary people love to get a joke on Edmonton.

33. FROZEN WOOD
Told by Alex R. McTavish

This fellow started from Calgary to go to Edmonton. It was a very, very cold spell – in fact the coldest spell they'd ever seen in the country. When he was on his way for a couple of hours he had to build a fire, and he couldn't see anything but green willows. To his amazement the willows were frozen so hard that they broke up and burned just like matchwood. (X1620) – I don't know where I heard it.

34. SPLIT DOG: GREAT BIRD
Told by George Ruttle

– Heard it in Ontario, I guess, Kent County – western Ontario. Oh, about fifty years. I'm pretty near seventy. That was old Tommy Robinson's story.

He said he went out deer hunting one day and his dog started up a deer and the dog took after it; and before it went far, it ran against a sapling tree and split in two. He said he picked the dog up and slapped it together and, watching the deer at the same time, he got two legs up and two legs down. He said when the dog started after the deer, when he got tired of running on the two legs he'd flip over and run on the other two.[31]

But he couldn't catch the deer, and he'd followed him so long he got lost in the woods. He was three days without anything to eat he said, and the only thing he saw was a hummingbird he said. Took a shot at it with his rifle – put a hole through it he could put his two fists through – knocked over a bushel of feathers out of it. (AT 1889L; X1215.11)

35. RIDING A FISH
Told by Charles K. Underwood

Miss Lou Neilson – she's a woman about fifty-five; she lives in Salt Lake City, Utah, now. She used to keep the picture show and hotel in Cardston. She was a great fisherman – one of the best fishermen in Alberta. She came home one time soaking wet at Waterton Lakes – that's the Peace Park – with no canoe. So a friend said, "Lou, where's your canoe? What happened?" "I lost the biggest fish I ever caught in my life. It weighed at least a hundred pounds. I was about three hundred yards from shore when I got this bite on my trolling line. As the huge fish neared the surface, it suddenly flipped its tail, upsetting the canoe, throwing me into the water. Luckily I held on to the trolling line, and when the fish rose again I slipped the line through his mouth, and straddling the huge monster rode him back to shore." Lou was then asked by the bystander why she hadn't brought the fish home. She replied, "Would you have killed the fish that saved your life?"[32] (X1303)

36. FISH ON DRY LAND
Told by Andrew Wright

Jerry Brown told this at a place called Bankhead, a coal-mining place close to Banff. Well, he said he went through a farmer's field to go fishing on the river. He said, "You talk about catching big fish." – We'd been talking about fish stories; he'd go one better. – He said, "My tackle was the finest money could buy. I'd only been fishin' a few minutes when I hooked on to a big one." He said, "I battled with it for two hours." He said, "When I finally got it out on the shore, while I was admiring it, it revived and chased me across the plowed field." He said, "That was my last fishing trip." (X1303)

37. CONVIVIAL SNAKE
Told by Alex R. McTavish

A man was fishing and he noticed, swimming in front of him, a little water snake with a frog in his mouth. The bright idea came to him that he could use the frog as bait, so he caught the snake and took the frog away. He felt so sorry about depriving the snake of his meal that he took out his liquor flask and dropped a few drops in the snake's mouth before he let him go. Well, he went fishing and used the frog successfully, and he didn't notice the snake coming back until it was knocking against his leg. And he looked down and there was the snake – with another frog.[33] (X1321)

38. MOSQUITOES AND POT
Told by Mrs. B.S.

This is just a story some minister told me about how bad the mosquitoes were one place. He had this pot hanging outside someplace and he heard a "click, click" and there were mosquitoes hammering on the pot. Their bill went right through, so he clinched them on the other side, you see? – thought he had them. But they just flew away with the pot.[34] (AT 1960M ;X1286.1)

He was a Scotchman; I don't know where he heard it. – Of course ministers are great fellows for yarns.

39. MOSQUITOES ON SNOWSHOES
Told by Art Ross

That's just a saying around here – that mosquitoes around Calgary hang around so late in the fall and they're so big, they run around with snowshoes on. (X1286.1)

40. MOSQUITOES FOR HORSES
Told by James Vert, of Granum, Alberta

Down at Namaka, Alberta, the mosquitoes were so big down there they used to hitch 'em up and plow with 'em. – I was down there that time. It was easy to harness them. (X1286.1)

41. STRONG TEAM
Told by Alex R. McTavish

Every part of the country has its strong team that it brags about, but in our country (Alberta) we *had* a strong team. It got stuck in a mud hole with a loaded wagon. The driver knew that there wasn't much to fear because he had all kinds of faith in his team, so he laid on the bud (the whip) and started to cuss. The outfit started to move all right, but when he looked down he was amazed to see that he was dragging the whole mud hole along with him.[35] (X1655)

42. LONG TEAM
Told by M. B. Graham

An old friend of mine, Slim Morehouse, hauled wheat from his farm to Vulcan, Alberta, with thirty-six horses on one hitch. This hitch was entered on several occasions in the Calgary Stampede – in the parade. Slim and I and a few of the boys were having refreshments. A fellow, after hearing of Slim's prowess, says, "Aw, that's nothing. I come from Texas. I drove a string of mules so long that the wheelers – the wheel team – were up to their knees in manure."

186

43. THE TASKS
Told by Andrew Wright

While sittin' in the beer parlour one evenin' the bartender was drinkin' in our company but was never known to buy a drink. He asked me to tell a story. I told this story:

A man died one time and went to the Pearly Gates. He was met by St. Peter to whom he told he'd led a clean life on earth and wished to enter Heaven. St. Peter said, "No, I'm goin' to give you several tests. The first one is, take this dipper and go down to earth and drain the Great Lakes dry."

After twenty thousand years he returned and told St. Peter the lakes were dry as a bone and he wished to enter. St. Peter said, "No, I've another test for you." And he gave him a pick and shovel and told him to go down to earth and level off the Rocky Mountains.

After twenty thousand years he returned and wished to be admitted into Heaven. St. Peter said, "I've one more test for you," and asked me[36] if I'd ever been in Banff. I said, "Yes." He also asked me if I'd ever been in the King Edward Beer Parlor. I answered, "Yes." He then told me to go down and sit in the beer parlor till the bartender bought me a drink, and he'd let me into Heaven. – He bought us a drink right away.[37]

44. MEAN FARMER
Told by Andrew Wright

Percy Williams, he's a painter in Banff, he said, "Never work for an Ontario farmer." He said, "I did one time. First morning he got me up at three o'clock. Told me it was gettin' late. Better have a light breakfast and go to work. He gave me a glass of water and a lantern. Along about eleven o'clock we were plowin' in the fields. He tried to encourage me by sayin' we would have a hot lunch – which turned out to be mustard sandwiches. So that one day's experience with an Ontario farmer was enough for me." (W152.12.1; W152.12.2)

45. MOOSE HUNT
Told by Bert Allen, aged twenty-one

A Scotchman just come out from Scotland – he was a neighbour to this Englishman. And he wanted to go hunting, so the Englishman said he'd take him moose hunting. So the Scotchman thought that was all right. When they got out there, the Scotchman got a look at the moose, and when he saw it, he exclaimed, "If thot's a moose, what do yer rats look like?" (J1759.1)

– My brother told that. It was an old yarn he heard Down East. It was told by an Englishman fighting with a Scotchman.

46. GOING SOME
Told by Miss Barbara Smart of Grande Prairie, Alberta

It's like the story told about the man caught in the tornado whose house was lifted right up and set down again. The local parson came and said, "My man, you are very fortunate, the Lord must have been with you." To which the man replied, "Well, sir, if He was, He was sure going some." [38]

– This is one of my Dad's favorite yarns.

47. NO, WE HAVEN'T
Told by Andrew Wright

This is about Pat and Mike on a deer hunt. While going up a ravine in search of game, Pat, who was in the lead, figured he was the boss of the hunting party. Mike noticed two ears of an animal on the skyline ahead of them. He drew Pat's attention to this. He said to Pat, "There's a deer." Pat informed Mike that he was going to do all the shooting, that Mike had nothing to do with it. Pat, taking careful aim, shot at the part of the head that was showing – it disappeared after he shot it. Mike said, "Pat, we've shot a deer." Pat bawled him out and said, "Mike, you've got nothing to do with this; *I* shot the deer." On arriving at the spot, Pat found he'd shot a mule. He turned to Mike and said, in a very meek way, "We've shot a mule." Mike said, "No, *we* haven't, *you've* shot a mule."

– They used to tell a lot of stories about Pat and Mike, but they've sort of died out. [39]

48. OBSTINATE WIFE
Told by Charles K. Underwood

A man was living with his wife and she was a terrible gossip: talk, talk, talk. And so he got sick of this – and one day they were walking alongside the river and she was constantly talking, and he said if she didn't stop he'd throw her in the river. They started another argument about the colour of a horse: whether it was white or black. She said it was white and he said it was black. He said she was wrong; and she said she was right. He said, "Wrong!" She said, "Right!" So he picked her up and threw her in the river.

She was drowning and hollered for help. He says, "If you'll admit that I'm right, I'll pull you out!" She said, "No, I'm right," and sunk for the first time. Going down for the second time she still said she was right. Third time the water'd gotten into her mouth and she couldn't speak, d'you see? And he said, "It's your last chance to be saved, old lady, am I right or wrong? If you're right make the sign of a pair of scissors." (Gesture of scissors with forefinger and middle finger.) And as she was

188

going down, the last thing he could see was her hand makin' the sign of a pair of scissors.[40] (AT 1365B; T255.1)

– I heard it in 1898, in Yarmouth, Norfolkshire, England. It used to be a keen delight of mine to hear these old yarns. That's an old story.

49. ONE FOR YOU
Told by Derek Chapman

There were two young boys in the graveyard. They were counting their marbles squatting on the ground in their usual style. One boy holding all the marbles was counting 'em out to the other fellow. And this is the way it went: "Now there's one for you and one for me," and he kept on saying, "One for you and one for me" – kept on saying it two, three times until accidentally one of the marbles dropped over the fence. So his line went this way then: "One for you and one for me, and the one over the fence is yours."

Now this continued until a farmer passing by happened to hear them saying this. He got out of his car and put his ear to the fence, and he listened, and this is what he heard in a very strange way: "One for you and one for me, and the one over the fence is yours." In very much excitement he quickly got into his tin lizzie and went straight to the preacher's house. In very much excitement he tells the preacher to come quick. "There's Satan and Jesus counting the people. Now he says, 'One for you and one for me and the one over the fence is yours.' I don't know who I belong to, but I'm mighty scared!" (AT 1791; X424)

– That's the only clean joke I know. It's my own original joke. I never heard it; I made it up myself. One time, I was passing by the graveyard with two or three other fellows and we actually saw two young boys counting their marbles in the shrubs surrounding the cemetery. In kidding one of the boys, we told him that we could hear Satan and Jesus in the graveyard and we made it up – you know. Can't say as I have heard anything like it. Lots of people know it though, because we published it in the paper: *The Calgary Herald* – where they have that column of jokes, "Prairie Wool." That was a long time – two years ago. It's a good clean joke that can be told anywhere. You won't hear that one anywhere else because us three fellows put it together ourselves.[41]

HOW DAVE McDOUGALL HUNTED WILD GEESE
By K. D. Johnson

This yarn, which is an elaborate form of No. 7 above, appeared in the Alberta Folklore Quarterly *of September, 1945, Vol. 1, No. 3. Mr. Johnson noted: "This story was told me by Corporal Chalmers after his return to Calgary from duty on the Stony Indian Reserve in 1897."*

A Mounted Policeman patrolling the Stony Indian Reserve at Morley called at Dave McDougall's house one day about noon. They invited him in to stay for dinner, the main dish being two roasted wild geese.

The meal over, they were having their after dinner smoke, when the policeman inquired: "Do you get many wild geese here, Mr. McDougall?"

"No," Dave answered, "very few. It was just my luck I got these. The road, you see, has been in such bad shape lately that we could not drive forty miles to Calgary for supplies, and we were running short of grub. Well, a couple of days ago I thought I'd go to the barnyard and kill a couple of chickens. I just got out into the yard when I heard a flock of geese honking. Looking around the end of the barn I saw a flock of about twenty geese circling over the coulee. Finally I saw them settle down in a little slough surrounded by high bullrushes, about three hundred yards from the house. 'Here,' I thought, 'is a good chance to get some good meat,' so I went back to the house for my gun, a single-barrel muzzle-loading shotgun with a steel ramrod. I put some powder in the gun and rammed it down with some paper, but when I looked for the shot I found my shot pouch was empty. My chance of getting some geese appeared to evaporate into thin air. Then an idea came into my head. Wrapping some paper around the end of the ramrod so it would fit tightly I shoved it down the gun barrel on top of the powder. I slipped a gun-cap on the nipple and I went out the back door. The geese were still there in the slough. Sneaking down the coulee out of sight of the geese I stalked them carefully until within about a hundred yards of the slough. Then I got down on hands and knees and crawled up into the bullrushes at the edge of the slough. The geese were sitting close together in the middle of it, most of them with their heads under their wings having a siesta. I yanked the gun to my shoulder and yelled 'Shoo!' As the geese all popped up their heads I pulled the trigger, waded out into the slough and, believe it or not, picked up *eleven* dead geese."

"Ah! but David," Mrs. McDougall reminded him, "ye forgot the one that fell behind the barn. That made the even dozen ye shot with that ramrod." (AT 1890F; X907.1,X1122.2)

9. THE BALDOON MYSTERY
Neil T. McDonald

The romantic ghosts that haunt English castles are rare in Canada, but we have had our share of poltergeists – the "noisy spirits" that cause unexplained physical disturbances such as fires, lights, broken objects, or showers of stones. Usually such phenomena occur in houses where there is an emotionally disturbed adolescent, and they are usually short-lived. In Canada there have been several striking cases, of which the three-year haunting of a Highland Scotch family at Baldoon, Ontario, is the most remarkable.

Apparently many strange events happened on the farm of John T. McDonald between 1828 and 1831. Some forty years later, Neil T. McDonald, John's younger son, collected statements from twenty-six people in the community who had knowledge of these events, and published them about 1871 in a 62-page booklet as The Belledoon Mysteries – an O'er True Story. *Two of the twenty-six statements, by M.L. Burnham and Allen M. McDonald, are given below.*

STATEMENT OF ALLEN M. McDONALD

This is what I heard my father, John McDonald, say he was an eye witness to. He was at McDonald's where these strange things happened and he saw a stone come in through the window and strike a man by the name of Neil Campbell in the breast. Mr. Campbell, being an unbeliever in such mysteries, said in a bragging manner, "Send us another ball, old fellow, and I will catch it." No sooner said than another stone came through the window and struck him in the breast with such force that it stunned him. He was glad to say that that was enough, and stood, apparently breathless, and pale as a corpse, and he was satisfied that there was no fun in catching balls in this manner, and like many others, went home convinced that it was no humbug. Next he saw a stone, about the size of a hen's egg, and muddy out of the river, come in through the window, and roll on the floor. He picked it up and in a moment, another stone came, as above. Next he was there when one of the buildings was burning and saw on another building near the one that was burning a large black dog sitting there and watching the fire, when all at once he disappeared, and no one could tell how he went. Next a large stone came down the fire-place with such force that it bounded up to the ceiling and dropped on the unbeliever's head. He said it hurt him enough to convince him that there was more truth than poetry in what he had heard, and like many others who went, who did not believe in witchcraft, went home convinced that the handcuffs were off the old fellow, and this was the devil's work.

He next saw the McDonald house set on fire fifty times in one day and helped to put it out every time. Not a spark of fire was to be seen about the house, only when the fire broke out and then about fifty men were ready to put it out instantly. Next he saw an iron tea kettle rise off the fire-place and fly across the room full of boiling water and never spill a

191

drop, and the lid of the kettle blew off and struck the window casing with such force that it left a mark of the lid a fourth of an inch deep, which could be seen for thirty-five years after it happened. I have seen it myself hundreds of times. Again I saw an auger, which was hanging on a nail, blow across the room, and strike the bedpost with such force that it coiled around the post and the print of the auger could be seen for years after. The next is what John T. McDonald told my father about how he found out who it was that was troubling him. A preacher by the name of McDorman told McDonald that he would go with him; he would take him to a man by the name of Troyer, who had a daughter who could solve any mystery a person desired her to.

McDonald and the elder went to see her, and on the way he said he never heard such fearful noises as he did then. They had to go over what is called the "Longwoods Road," which is twenty-five miles long. Right in the heart of the woods there was a noise like people driving cattle, and noises like fighting, and cries of "Murder, Murder, Murder, help, help, help," and the night being fearfully dark, he said he never had such a fright in all his life. It seemed more like a week than a night, and the hair of his head stood straight up, and he thought several times he would with fear fall off his horse – for people in those days travelled on horseback – and the largest part of that night's journey was on an Indian trail. McDonald said that the elder was singing as happy as could be and he told McDonald to pay no attention to the noise, for he said it was the parties who were troubling him for they knew where and for what he was going and they wanted to frighten him back, so that they would not be exposed. He encouraged McDonald the best he could for the elder had the courage of a lion and feared neither the devil or any of his imps, and I believe if there were such courageous ministers on the walls of Zion, there would not be as many wicked people in the world.

When they arrived at Dr. Troyer's, they found his daughter at home and told her what they had come for and she told them she could give them the desired information after looking through a stone, which her uncle had found in a field while ploughing, as she did not like to look into it as it always frightened her, so that she always had a spell of sickness. McDonald begged of her to look into it and tell him who the parties were, and the cause of his trouble, and with this he would be satisfied. The doctor finally persuaded her to look into the stone, and on doing so the first question she asked was, "Did you buy a piece of land previous to this trouble?" Mr. McDonald answered yes. She then described the members of a certain family and asked if this family did not live by this land that he had bought. He answered yes. "Did this family want to buy it of you?" "Yes." "And you would not sell it to them?" "No, for I didn't buy it to sell, I bought it to keep for the family." She then told Mr. McDonald everything that had happened and told him that one of his buildings had burned two hours previous, and they being eighty miles from home set down the time and found on going home that she had told to a minute. She then asked him if there was not a stray goose, with a black head and part of one wing black, with his geese. He studied for a moment and said that he remembered seeing a goose of that description, but he thought it was one of his own. She said, "No, that is the old woman of the family mentioned, and she was the old witch. She turned herself into a goose and she was the one that brought up the balls from the river bottom that were marked and thrown into the river."

She then told him that if that goose was there when he got home to put some silver in his gun and shoot it, and if he hit it, it would disappear and he could not tell how, but the next day to go to this family's house, and he would find the old woman wounded by the silver he had shot her with the day before. He done so and found her wounded in the arm. He asked her a few questions in reference to the trouble, but she would give him no answer, for she knew that they were exposed. McDonald then went home and was troubled no more, but the old woman never had a moment of peace until she died. If she sat down she would jump up and say that she was sitting on a hot grid-iron. She suffered for her bad deeds in various ways. McDonald had nothing left but his land, as his stock had all died and his buildings all burned. In reference to his character, I can truthfully say that I knew John T. McDonald for more than thirty-five years, and I never heard anything amiss with him or his family. He was in good standing in the Baptist church for many years to my knowledge.

STATEMENT OF M.L. BURNHAM.

In the years of 1829 and 1830, being then about sixteen years of age, I was living with my father on St. Clair river and attending school in Wallaceburg, passing the home of John T. McDonald twice each week, and frequently stopping during these strange occurrences to satisfy my own curiosity. John T. McDonald was one of the many settlers that came over with Alexander Selkirk in the year 1804, some of whom settled near Wallaceburg and along Bear Creek, and nothing happened to mar their peace and quietness until about November, 1828, when McDonald's trouble commenced.

John lived with his father until he was married, when he removed to his own house about one-fourth of a mile from his father's frame house, which is now standing on the banks of the Channel Ecarte. About this time bullets commenced coming through the windows breaking a small hole in the glass and rolling on the floor, but hurting no one, although, as can be readily surmised, they were at times terribly scared. This continued up to the time the house was burned. But a short time after the house burned, the barn was also consumed. They were both set on fire by strange influences and apparently without the aid of any person; fire would start up in different places at the same time, and when this was extinguished, it would start up in other places, and so on until January 1830, when the buildings were burned to the ground. John then moved his family to his father's house but no sooner there than the balls commenced coming through the windows until all the glass was broken, even to that over the doors; and there was a corner cupboard with glass doors, and balls came out of the cupboard breaking the glass doors. They picked up these balls, marked them, put them in a leather shot bag, tying a string around the mouth of the bag, hanging it upon the chimney, and these same balls would immediately come back through the window. They then threw these balls in the Channel Ecarte where the water was very deep and in a short time these same balls would come back through the windows.

About this time the old man's barn was burned with all its contents, and being in the winter, it left the stock without feed. The matter now became exceedingly troublesome, as the family had to watch all night for fear of being burned in their beds as the house was set on fire a great many times, both in night and day, but with the aid of friends they managed to save the house. At this time a large number of people came to see how the matter was carried on, and without exception, it was said to be the strangest thing they had ever seen. Nearly all laid it to some supernatural power, and none undertook to account for it in any other way.

At this time everything in and about the house seemed under the influence, nothing in the house could be kept in place; the shovel and tongs would run about the floor as would other things about the house. The cooking was done by a large fire-place, and it was extremely difficult to keep anything upon the fire. The old Dutch oven would empty itself, making it extremely hard to get enough material cooked to satisfy their hunger.

One thing seemed strange: throughout the whole proceedings no member of the family sustained any bodily harm, although missiles would come into a room where there was congregated twelve or thirteen persons. The only object of the persecutors seemed to be to worry the people and destroy their property. They had a house and two barns burned and nearly all their stock died. If any of the stock had young, they died, if a hen laid an egg, the hen would die, and the same uncertainty seemed to hover about everything. All the conventional preventatives such as placing a horseshoe over the door, etc., was tried without avail. The idea that inanimate things can move around and through hard substances without any visible person to propel them, is difficult to solve, nevertheless it is true as they have been seen by the writer and other living witnesses, and the strongest disbelievers have had to say it was something they could not account for.

About the first of March, 1830, McDonald heard through the writer's father that there was a doctor living in the township of Walsingham who understood some of the workings of such things, and McDonald thought he had better go and see him as he was a very worthy man. The country at that time was almost wholly unsettled and he had to go through what was known as the long woods a distance of thirty miles without a house. While riding along he was beset with clubs and stones, as if his errand was known by the evil one. He told the doctor his troubles, who told him that he would go and find if possible the cause of it. They started, and strange to say, they experienced no trouble on the way home. When they arrived at home, the doctor took a small stone out of his pocket and looked at it and said: "Oh, I see, I see, this is a new way they have of making people suffer." He then said: "Mr. McDonald, they will not disturb you tonight." This was Friday evening, and the doctor came up to my father's, S.H. Burnham, on the St. Clair, as Mr. Burnham was an old neighbour of the doctor's in the township of Walsingham. The doctor stayed at father's until Monday and said they would do nothing then, but they might try once more, and while the family was gone to the church on the Sabbath, the house was left alone, as there had been no trouble since Friday, but when they returned the table was turned upside down and all the dishes in the bottom and the Bible open on top of them. Nothing further has to our knowledge happened to disturb the families who have since rented the farm.

The doctor told father what was being done and who was doing it, and said if they did anything more, they would be punished with death. My father then wanted to know what had caused the trouble and the doctor said it was about land. Be it understood that the doctor had never been in this part of the country before nor had he ever known any of the members of the McDonald family, nor that such a family existed, until McDonald told him of the trouble he had been having and which had been caused by the interference of some person or persons unknown to him and of whom the doctor soon told him. I mention the facts about the doctor to show that he had no knowledge of the affair before going there. This matter can only be ascribed to some supernatural agency. We read in the Bible that there were witches in the time of Solomon, and that they were troublesome, for at one time Saul ordered that all witches and wizards throughout the kingdom should be put to death. The mystery connected with this affair is not in the cause, but the question is this: How can these things be carried on and no person seen engaged in any way, at any time, or in any place?

What I have written about this matter is true, for I was present at a great many of these performances, and actually saw them carried on without being able to give any reason for them. They were carried on day and night, to the great discomfort of the family and those with them. Many strangers came to spend the night and witness these things which were worse at night and required more watchers to keep things in their place and attend to the fires that were being set about the barns and house. The barns were finally burned, and some of the visitors were so frightened at what they had seen that they were glad to get away from the place. I have described but one hundredth part of the acts that were performed there, but enough has been said to convince the most skeptical of all the unbelievers of the Bible that there is something about it that cannot be accounted for or throw any more light on the matter than the information which we get from the Holy Bible.

Now, anyone having any scruples or doubts about the matter can get any desired information from the writer concerning it; or if they wish to ask any questions concerning the characters of the families concerned, the writer knew them before the affair commenced and since, and never knew or heard that they were guilty of any crime, but were always much respected. One of the family was a magistrate, and most of them belonged to a church and do to this day. I will now close my account of the affair, as there are other witnesses beside me.

10. SONGS OF THE GREAT LAKES
Ivan H. Walton

The two largest groups of native Canadian folk songs are those composed by men who worked on the sea or in the woods. Louise Manny's Songs of Miramichi *and my* Lumbering Songs from the Northern Woods *feature songs of the lumbermen of New Brunswick and Ontario, and most of the Nova Scotia and Newfoundland collections contain songs of the sailors, sealers, whalers, and fishermen of the east coast. However, very few songs of the Great Lakes have found their way into print, although Great Lakes sailors did compose a great many songs during the nineteenth century, and nearly a hundred had some run in tradition. The most important collector in this area was Ivan Henry Walton (1893-1968), an authority on Michigan marine lore who spent his summers collecting from old-time sailors along the shores of the Great Lakes on both sides of the Canadian-American border, and then painstakingly researched the background of each song.*

Like the Maritime sea songs, those from the Great Lakes fall into two main groups: ones that describe particular voyages, and ones that describe shipwrecks. Just as the shantyboys composed a song for every lumbercamp and for every man killed in the woods or on the rivers, so the sailors apparently composed a song for every voyage and for every ship that was lost. The following small sampling from Dr. Walton's unpublished collection gives a vivid picture of life – and death – on the Great Lakes ships during the peak period of the 1880s and 1890s. They are all songs he collected from Canadian sailors. Unfortunately the tunes are not available, but most of the Great Lakes songs went to well known tunes. For example, "The Schooner John Bentely" went to the popular "Down Derry Down" tune used for the better known Great Lakes song, "Red Iron Ore," and "The Jennie P. King" probably went to the tune of "The Cruise of the Bigler." As Bob Reid told Dr. Walton, "I just use any tune that fits."

IT'S ME FOR THE INLAND LAKES

The following song was obtained from Captain Walkingshaw of Port Colborne, Ontario, in the summer of 1933. He said he had learned it from Lakes sailors, but could not recall when or where. The mention of superior living conditions and wages and the easier discipline on the Lakes vessels probably explains why many "shellbacks" from the Atlantic came to the Lakes.

If ever I follow the ships again
To gather my spuds and cakes,
I'll not be workin' a deep-sea hack,
It's me for the inland Lakes.

You get a berth that's really a berth;
An' the jaw that the skipper takes –
No end I swear – it's a wonderful life,
It's me for the inland Lakes.

The runs are short, the vessels good,
Ah! real men are the mates;
They're men, and they can handle a ship,
It's me for the rolling Lakes.

Late gales may blow an' seas run high,
An' the lees full of country Jakes;
But quarters are warm an' the grub is great,
It's me for the inland Lakes.

THE SEAMEN'S UNION

The following is a fragment of a Canadian seamen's union song which was obtained from Henry McConnell of Picton, Ontario, in the summer of 1938. He did not know the occasion, author, or air.

> We are a band of seamen, a jolly, jolly crew,
> As ever sailed the ocean or wore the jackets blue.
> We plow the deep dark waters without a thought of fear;
> We sing and sport in every port, and drive away dull care.
>
> We are a band of seamen with a password and a sign;
> The shamrock, rose, and thistle around our banner twine.
> The maple leaf is our embrace, Victoria is our Queen;
> Not hers the blame, our Union's name the Orange and the Green.
>
> Here's a health to every captain who ships a union crew;
> Here's a health to the girls with flowing curls that like the boys in
>   blue.

ON GRAVELY BAY

The following account of the vicissitudes of a young landsman temporarily working on a harbour dredge making improvements in the harbour at Port Colborne, formerly Gravely Bay, at the Lake Erie end of the Welland Canal, was obtained in Orly, 1933, from E.J. Buzzard, of Erieau, Ontario. "I began sailing on windjammers in 1867 at the age of fifteen, and sailed for twenty seasons and then got married. My wife thought I'd make more money in the hotel business, and I guess she was right – but I had more fun sailing." He learned the song from some of his early shipmates.

> I was a handsome nice young man, I hailed from Cleveland town;
> And for daily occupation I teamed for Johnny Brown.
> An' all day long I'd sport and play, my joy I ne'er begrudged
> 'Till I was sent to Gravely Bay to work upon a drudge.
>
> I had not been in Gravely Bay scarce one day, two, or three
> Before a very fair young girl fell into love with me,
> Sayin' "Mike, my man, give me your hand, from you I'll never
>   budge;
> With you I'll stay in Gravely Bay and work upon the drudge."
>
> Her mother standing at her door said, "Please don't make such
>   noise,
> And another thing, you're far too young to trust among those boys;

And that young man that holds your hand, if I can rightly judge,
Has just the eye that'll make you sigh before you leave the drudge."

"Now mother dear don't be severe," my darling then did say.
"Never eyes so fair nor such black hair was ever in Gravely Bay!"
I took her to my bosom then; the world did me begrudge,
And for many a·day she got my pay while working on the drudge.

But as the weeks did pass along, and the channel lengthened too,
A doubt oft came into my mind if she was really true,
And sad to relate, it is my fate, of women I'm no judge,
She loved not me, but all the men who worked upon the drudge!

"SCRUBBER" MURPHY

It seems to have been the universal belief among officers on sailing vessels on both salt and fresh water, a belief probably well founded in experience, that crewmen during their watch on deck must be kept busy, and many of the extant sailor songs refer to the scrubbing, swabbing down the decks, painting, rust chipping, and mending of the ship's gear that occupied their time when they were not engaged in the work of navigating the vessel. Mr. Iver Rolsing, former schooner captain and, in 1933, U.S. Inspector of Hulls at Buffalo, explained at the time that such work not only kept the vessel in good condition, but it kept the men from fighting among themselves and from getting into mischief. Only during the "dog watches" from four to six and from six to eight in the early evening when the whole crew were on deck and the watches "dogged" or changed tours of duty, were the sailors permitted to sit around and sing or otherwise enjoy themselves. The accompanying song is a good-natured exaggerated description of this type of work.

Extended inquiry among ex-lakesmen failed to identify "Scrubber" Murphy, but many knew of the song. It probably dates from the 1890s when bulk-carrying steam-powered vessels began seriously to cut in on the grain and ore traffic which the sailing vessels had formerly had almost to themselves. Mr. Rolsing stated that about 1905 a sailor known as "Blinky" Morgan made several trips with him and he would, under proper inducement, sing a song about a schooner captain, "Scrubber" Murphy, who had obtained his title from the persistence with which he kept his crew scrubbing down the decks. On one occasion his schooner rammed her jib-boom into the upper works of the steamer *Boston* causing considerable damage to both vessels, but, according to the song, the schooner captain was disturbed only because his crew were interrupted in their scrubbing.

In a crowded tavern one Saturday evening in Goderich, in the summer of 1934, when the writer mentioned the song to a noisy group of local sailors, Malcolm Graham, one of the group, at once began singing it and was joined by several others. At the end of the second stanza, however, he suddenly stopped and demanded a thousand dollars before he would continue or permit anyone else to do so. A few days later his price was reduced to a cigar, and he dictated the following version. He could not recall where he had learned it other than that he'd often heard other sailors sing it.

> Scrubber Murphy was the captain of the steamer called *Mohawk*,
> And Scrubber is the scrubber about whom all sailors talk;
> From painting and from scrubbing he'd the scrubber's title got,
> Given to him by the sailors of the gallant ship *Mohawk*.
>
> It was the spring of nineteen five Old Scrubber took command,
> And the orders that he first gave us was, "By your suge stand!
> Into your suge dip your brooms and at her lads you go,
> For I'm bound to have the *Mohawk* scrubbed before I go below."
>
> The crew all being well drilled men and knowing what to do
> Into the suge dipped their brooms and scrubbed the bulwarks
>   through.
> "On to her deck," Old Scrubber cried, and without more ado
> Those brave lads scrubbed the upper works while streams of water
>   flew.
>
> For ten long hours they scrubbed her down before the scrub was
>   o'er;
> Then "Rory," says he, "go scrap the mast and then we'll scrub some
>   more."
> Brave Rory for the mast did dash and never did let up
> Till Scrubber cried, "Come my lad and scrub the brindle pup."
>
> "Now the scrubbing is all done," says he, "we'll start the paint,"
> And hearty sailors that they were, they all began to faint.
> "Daniel," says he, "now go below and get the black and drab,
> And with the deck hands on her sides you may begin to dab."
>
> "Rory in the pilot house you go and shine the brass,
> And Alec go along with him, I want you to work fast.
> Reuben, on the upper deck you go and paint the green,
> And Donald you stand by the wheel, I want you to be seen."

Then away for Chicago this noble ship set sail,
But soon across her iron deck the scrubbing hose did trail:
"Start up your pumps," Old Scrubber cried, "and let her have some
    spray,
For I'm bound to have her scrubbed again before we cross the Bay."

When out upon Lake Michigan the weather it got thick,
Old Scrubber by the whistle stood and blew the signals quick.
"Angus," says he, "you stand by me and keep a sharp look-out,
And see that Reuben at the wheel don't turn the ship about."

At length a vessel's horn we heard a-blowin' three short blasts,
A signal that before the wind she was sailing free and fast.
The *Mohawk* crossed the schooner's bow and tore off her jib-boom;
They struck, and up the lads below came running from their room.

Then came the cry, "We're sinking fast!" from on the schooner's
    deck;
Old Scrubber turned the *Mohawk* round to try to save the wreck.
From ship to ship a line was paid, all hands were in great glee;
The schooner and her crew were saved and towed to Milwaukee.

And when we reached Chicago port, that city of great fame,
The orders that Old Scrubber got was, "Get a load of grain."
At Halstead street there is a bridge, and I'm sorry to relate
That it was beneath this very bridge we almost met our fate.

As toward this tall and lofty bridge we slowly made the crook,
Our mast got caught and down it came and nearly killed the cook
Who in his bunk lay dreaming of what next he would dish up
To the sailors of the *Mohawk* and Old Scrubber's brindle pup.

When the wreckage was all cleared away, it was the break of morn
An' we to an elevator went and got a load of corn.
Then out upon the windy lake we gaily sailed away
On our down trip to Buffalo where all good sailors stay.

Now round the port of Buffalo it is but common talk
How Scrubber Murphy scrubbed and scrubbed the steamer called
    Mohawk.
Now come you jolly sailor lads, an' our pay we will drink up,
And to hell with Scrubber Murphy and his God-damned brindle
    pup!

THE SCHOONER *JOHN BENTELY*

The schooner *John Bentely*, 525 net tons, was an ungainly three-masted canaller built in 1873 at the mouth of the Napanee River at Deseronto near the east end of Lake Ontario, for Captain W.B. Hall of Toronto. Her lines were such as to give her maximum carrying capacity through the Welland Canal. She was flat-bottomed, and, like most of the canallers, bluff-ended and therefore hard to steer. She foundered in Georgian Bay in her thirteenth year.

In the trip narrated in the following song, the schooner cleared Toronto harbour and sailed eighty miles southeast across Lake Ontario to Charlotte at the mouth of the Genesee River (present harbour of the city of Rochester, N.Y.). The vessel evidently leaked badly and required much pumping, and the forecastle where the sailors were quartered was, as was customary, not particularly sanitary or comfortable. At Charlotte they loaded coal for an Upper Lakes destination and set out for Port Dalhousie at the entrance to the old Welland canal. Before the schooner could enter the locks, the head sails had to be taken in and the jib-boom unshipped and brought inboard or topped up to the foremast. The 27-mile canal between Lake Ontario and Lake Erie had 27 lift locks to overcome the 327-foot difference in elevation, and negotiating them and towing through the levels between them was a long, slow process. The *Bentely* spent the entire night at it and arrived at Gravely Bay (Port Colborne on Lake Erie) the following morning.

The song was obtained in August, 1933, from genial seventy-five-year-old Captain Jeremiah Cavanaugh of Port Dalhousie who had spent most of his life on the Lakes. He stated that he was a member of the *Bentely's* crew on the trip concerned and "made up" the song at the time – "over fifty years ago." He added that "whenever men forward (crewmen as distinct from officers) would gather ashore and at once make for a saloon and have a drink or two, someone would call for a song, and then each man had to sing a song, clog (dance), tell a good story, or buy a round of drinks. I always had to sing 'The *Bentely*'."

> Come shipmates and listen, a story I'll tell
> About a flash packet, you all know her well
> She is a flash packet, a packet of fame,
> She hails from Toronto, and *Bentely's* her name.
>
> Chorus: *Derry down, down, down, derry down.*
>
> The dimensions of this packet now to you I'll tell:
> She was built by the yard and cut off by the mile;

She's round stem and bluff forward, no deadrise at all;
And she's owned in Toronto by Alderman Hall.

I shipped in this packet at the Northern docks,
I took a streetcar from Church Street to Brock;
And from there I steered straight for the ship
With a satchel in one hand, in the other a grip.

But on the way down I got blazing drunk;
I lost the old satchel and busted my trunk,
I tripped and I tumbled, and down I did fall,
And I cursed the old *Bentely*, the sidewalks and all.

At last to the ship I chanced for to stray,
And the captain came forward saying "We'll get under weigh;
We're bound for Charlotte, going there to load coal,"
And down the rough Lake the old *Bentely* did roll.

I was tired and weary, oh yes I was sick
From hearing the pumps go "clackety-click."
My bones they were sore from lying in my bunk,
And the rotten old bed-clothes were nothing but junk.

Then we left old Charlotte for the Welland canal,
And forget that last trip? oh no I never shall!
And then on our port bow Port Dalhousie did loom,
All hands gathered forward to top the jib-boom.

We towed into the harbour, our jib-boom topped high,
And all of the people they started to cry:
"Oh, where did you get it? Where did it come from?"
Or "Where in the devil does that raft belong?"

And when we got ready to go in the lock
The Sammies all gathered like geese in a flock,
And sure Grogan was there, and he shinned up a fender
Saying "Captain, you know me, I'm an old lock tender."

There lives in Toronto an ugly old thief,
He's called "Burk the butcher, who sells the tough beef."
It gives us the toothache and causes much pain –
We'll murder the old villain when we go there again.

We worked at canalling that entire night,
And in order to work we had to keep tight;

But on the next morning the captain did say;
"At last we've arrived in Gravely Bay."

THE *JENNIE P. KING*

Extended search has not revealed any barque-rigged "timber drogher" bearing the name *Jennie P. King*. The vessel is said to have been named for a well-known sailors' friend who in the 1870s had a number of establishments in various Lower Lake ports, and in the next decade transferred her activities to West Superior, Wisconsin. The vessel concerned could be identified, according to reports, not only by her name boards, but also by her carved figurehead, a woman's leg extended under the bowsprit, which was supposed to have been modeled by the original Jennie.

The details of life aboard a "timber drogher" given in the song seem to be authentic. The term "drogher," or its corrupted form "drover," seems to be of Caribbean origin, and on the Lakes was applied, with a slight derogatory implication, to canal-size timber carriers with timber ports in their sterns. They were mostly two-masted "canallers," built to the maximum dimensions that could pass through the old Welland Canal locks. They were bluff-bowed, had nearly rectangular hulls, were clumsy sailors, and hailed mostly from lower Lake Ontario. They usually had two pairs of sternports on either side of the stern post that could be opened to admit timbers. The top pair opened flush with the deck, and the other pair opened into the hold. Before the upright "donkey engines" came into use, these vessels at times carried a team of horses or mules on the bow deck for the purpose of working the capstan or other tackle used in loading the heavy water-soaked timbers.

Large quantities of squared timber, especially walnut, were shipped from the Toledo area in the 1860s and 1870s to Tonawanda, on the western end of the old Erie Canal, as well as to the head of Lake Ontario, for trans-shipment to the Atlantic and Europe. The line "To ride the halyards down" refers to the sailors' practice of going aloft to the crosstrees and swinging out on the halyard so that their weight would assist the other sailors on the deck in hoisting the heavy sails. The motley crew aboard seems to have been characteristic of the slow-going, clumsy timber carriers. The larger and more seaworthy grain and ore carriers got the pick of the experienced seamen who came to the Lakes by way of the Canal and the St. Lawrence, and the "droghers" got second choice.

The composer would get a good laugh from his audience when he mentioned their beating the schooner *Dispatch*, for the only vessel a drogher could outsail was another of the type which was still more clumsy. The horses referred to in the fifth stanza were those carried on the forward deck to work the capstan when the timbers were being loaded.

The song is incomplete. The remainder probably narrated the vessel's journey to her destination. At the unloading dock other workmen would take over, and the sailors would look for another berth or "site."

Norman "Beachie" McIvor of Goderich, Ontario, recited the first two stanzas aboard his harbour sightseeing boat in the summer of 1933, but had no notion of when in his sailor career he had learned them. The second stanza and the chorus and last two lines were, a few weeks later, obtained from Bronte, Ontario, lighthouse keeper Walter "Doc" Thomas and his former shipmate "Billy" Churchill as they prompted and corrected each other in "Doc's" waterfront bachelor shack. Later that summer, William Head of Picton, who had sailed the Lakes twenty years and fished them thirty more, supplied the rest. He attributed the song to "a sailor named Billy Clark who would make up songs while on a trip and sing them in harbour saloons for free drinks."

Now sit you down beside me and I'll sing you a little song,
And if I do not please you, I'll not detain you long.
I shipped in Tonawanda some timber for to bring
From Toledo at a dollar a day on the barque the *Jennie P. King*.

Hurray, boys, hurray! Come let us join and sing;
We'll drink a health to old Ned Irving and the crew of the *Jennie P. King*.

The crew jumped in the riggin', and up aloft did run
To see the halyards down, to see them it was fun.
Each man worked with a will, and soon we spread our wings,
And beat the schooner *Dispatch*, on the barque the *Jennie P. King*.

Upon this timber drogher we had a curious crew:
We had Uncle Sam's sea fighters, and Garibaldi's too,
An Irishman from nowhere who could dance and sing,
And shellbacks from the ocean on the barque the *Jennie P. King*.

And on this timber drogher were Canadians too, I think,
And Dutch from Tonawanda who like their lager drink.
We had men from other countries who liked to take a fling –
A jolly crew we had on the barque the *Jennie P. King*.

The lad who tended the horses he jabbered all the day,
And whether man or monkey no one could ever say.

Our cook came from the Erie, we thought her just the thing;
She fed the crew and officers too on the barque the *Jennie P. King*.

* * * * *

Now we're well down Lake Erie, Point Abino we clear,
Our bowsprit points to Buffalo, Toledo's in our rear . . .

A TRIP ON THE SCHOONER *KOLFAGE*

The schooner *Kolfage* was a small lumber hooker of 93 net tons built in Port Burwell, Ontario, on Lake Erie in 1869. In the middle 1890s, the period of the trip narrated in the following song, she was owned and sailed by Captain John "Minister" McDonald of Goderich, Ontario – so named because of his florid language – and was still in the lumber trade. Her shallow draft enabled her to enter harbours and rivers denied larger vessels.

John "Red" McDonald, sailor son of the "Minister," was a member of the crew on the trip concerned, and supplied the following stanzas in the summer of 1934. He said that at Chatham, about twenty miles up the Thames River from Lake St. Clair, they loaded supplies for a Georgian Bay lumber camp, and when they were about ready to start towing back down the river, two men, Jack MacCosh and Herb Pettigrew, signed on for the round trip. "They wasn't no real sailors, just two men the Old Man picked up to help out. They got enough of sailing on the up trip and wanted to get off. The Old Man cussed they out plenty and wouldn't give them no pay. Then he said to them, 'If you'll make me a good song, you can go.' They went away and came back next day with this one." "Red" then added significantly, "The Old Man would damn near give away his schooner for a good song. He give them each a dollar extra and tacked the song up in the cabin where it still was when he sold her."

Robert "Bob" Reid of Red Bay on the Lake side of the Peninsula stated, when visited later in the same summer, that when he purchased the *Kolfage* from Captain McDonald the song was still on her cabin wall. He also recited it entire. When asked about the tune, he replied, "I just use any tune that fits."

According to the song, they had a fresh following wind across Lake St. Clair on their up-bound trip, and raced a steamer into the "Cut," the dredged channel through the St. Clair Flats, and neither being willing to give way for the other, the schooner struck the steamboat a glancing blow on her bow, and evidently sent her aground. Before the two crews came to blows, a fresh breeze sent the schooner on up the river to Sarnia where they were windbound in the Bay under Point Edward. Next day they towed out into Lake Huron and promptly had another race. The

"Lake Ontario clippers" were slow, blunt-nosed canallers which they easily outdistanced. After waiting out a blow at Southampton, they continued on their way around the head of the Bruce Peninsula into Georgian Bay to their destination. There the sailors had to help unload the provisions and then load the rough sawed lumber and some heavy "twenty-four foot plank," which was not entirely to their liking.

We shipped aboard the *Kolfage* at Chatham, County Kent,
The fourth day of October, for Johnson's Harbour bent,
Commanded by McDonald, who always fast time makes,
Aboard the schooner *Kolfage*, Columbia of the Lakes.

The tug *Vick* took our line at twelve o'clock at night,
And down the Thames we towed mid moonbeams' somber light;
But when on Lake St. Clair the wind came dead ahead,
We put the big hook out, and all went off to bed.

Next morning we hoisted sail in a fresh wind from the east,
The *Kolfage* plowed the Lake through billows white as yeast.
We headed for the Cut with all her sails unfurled,
And with bending masts we smashed the record of the world.

A steamer hove alongside and we ran her neck and neck
Straight into the Cut, our speed we would not check!
We struck her starboard bow to keep us off the bank,
And our fenders scrubbed her side as we fetched up with a yank.

Angry words flew thick, their speed they had to check,
We damn near had a fight, every man was on the deck.
We cursed them high and low; they threatened to come aboard,
But the wind hauled to the south, and up the River we roared.

When Sarnia we reached late afternoon that day,
The wind again contrary, we anchored in the Bay.
We towed out in the morning about a mile or so
With the *Catarac* and *Vienna* from Lake Ontario.

All three then stripped for action, a race it was to be,
The Lake Ontario clippers claimed the supremacy –
With all our canvas set, we ran north like a steer,
And when that night came on they were far off in our rear.

Next day we reached Southampton and anchored off the shore
Just inside of the harbour while outside the seas did roar,

And there the schooner *Fulton* inside the harbour we found
In a waterlogged condition and also hard aground.

At dawn we heaved our anchor and hoisted sail once more
For northward up the Lake, just off the rocky shore.
We sailed along the Cape before a sou'west breeze,
And ran into a bay among lumber piles and trees.

We took on all our canvas and tied up to the dock.
And twenty men came down along the ridge of rock.
We then got out our dinner, for we were feeling lank,
And then got introduced to some twenty-four foot plank!

But before we started the plank, oat bags we had to tote,
And twenty barrels of flour from the bosom of the boat.
We hoisted up the flour till our fingers began to swell,
But we'd gladly hoist the flour if the planks had been in hell!

Now the vessel is all loaded, and we are on the shore,
And vow that planks and lumber we'll handle nevermore!
The *Kolfage* rounds the bend and disappears from view –
It's goodbye to Cap McDonald, here's our best regards to you.

THE LOSS OF THE SCHOONER *ANTELOPE*

A number of Great Lakes vessels have borne the name *Antelope* after
one of the most fleet and graceful of all wild animals, but the official
records of none correspond very closely with the information given in
the following song. A schooner of 350 tons, which may well be the one
concerned, was built in Buffalo in 1855, but her fate is unrecorded offi-
cially. Mr. John S. Parsons, ex-sailor and ship chandler of Oswego, New
York, for over half a century, stated in the summer of 1933 that the
schooner of the song was a "canaller" of approximately the size given
above, and was owned and sailed at the time of her loss in the early
1880s by Captain George Budd, also of Oswego, and his brother John
was mate.

The second, fourth, fifth, first half of the sixth, and last two stanzas of
the song below were obtained in the summer of 1933 from Edward
"Ned" Navin of Cobourg, Ontario, who sailed eight seasons in Lake
Ontario timber vessels in the 1880s and learned the song at that time.
Israel LaRoche of Wolfe Island at the east end of Lake Ontario, who
began his long sailing career in the middle 1870s and early learned the

song, added the first stanza. Ben Peckham, a former Oswego sailor, added the third and some lines to the seventh stanza. He said that his father, Thomas Peckham, a member of the *Antelope*'s crew at the time of the wreck, was the only man saved and it was he who wrote the song. Mr. Parsons added the last half of the sixth stanza, changed a number of lines in others, and supplied the air. He also confirmed Ben Peckham's statement about the senior Peckham.

Another version was published in the *Picton Times*, April 12, 1934, by Henry McConnell, and a third in C.H.J. Snider's "Schooner Days," CMXIII, in the *Toronto Evening Telegram* for August 20, 1949.

You all may bless your happy lot who dwell safe on the shore,
Free from the tempests and the blasts that round us sailors roar.
It's little you know of the hardships, nor do you understand
The stormy nights we do endure off the shores of Michigan.

On the sixteenth of November from Chicago we set sail;
Kind Providence did favour us with a sweet and pleasant gale.
With our canvas spread all to the wind and our hearts as light as air,
We left Chicago far behind, our colours flying fair.

Besides our captain and our mate there were eight of us on board;
Two lads shipped in Chicago, their names I never heard.
They were two gay and lively lads, from Ireland they came;
Their friends may weep, they're in the deep, they'll ne'er see them again.

On the seventeenth in the morning an angry storm did rise,
And fearful billows loud did roar, and dismal grew the skies.
We reeled her down, made all things snug, and then contrived a plan
To save the life of the *Antelope* off the shores of Michigan.

On the eighteenth in the morning – and what I say is true –
The ice upon our rigging froze, and the cold winds fiercely blew,
And no one thought in a few short hours that very afternoon
Some would be froze and some be drowned – the *Antelope* was doomed!

The cold increased, the tempest raged, the huge seas loud did roar –
With our canvas gone, both anchors out, we were drifting toward the shore.
Our captain said to his brother John, "I think I see the land,
But only One can save us now from the shores of Michigan."

We drifted with each pounding sea, and then we struck stern on:
Our mainm'st at the deck was broke, our yawl-boat it was gone.
The huge seas raked her fore and aft, and then she swung broadside,
And three men overboard were swept into that raging tide.

Our captain tried to swim ashore our precious lives to save,
But by his brave and manly act he was lost beneath the waves,
And only one of that gallant crew was in life once more to stand,
And for miles and miles the *Antelope* lined the shores of Michigan.

THE FOUNDERING OF THE *ASIA*

The Canadian wooden propellor *Asia*, 450 gross tons, cleared Collingwood, Ontario, on September 13, 1882, with a crew of twenty-four,
thirty woodsmen and supplies bound for a lumber camp near French
River, an oversized number of passengers, and much freight. She called
at Owen Sound and took on additional passengers and freight for Manitoulin Island and Sault Ste. Marie. When she departed northward across
Georgian Bay late that evening into a freshening wind and rough seas,
those on board filled all the cabins and many had only deck space. Barrels and boxes were piled on the hurricane deck and eight horses were
stabled on the main deck.

The wind and seas increased to dangerous proportions the next morning, and about noon when Captain J.N. Savage was trying to make the
lee of Lonely Island still some miles away, the vessel foundered with all
on board except two passengers who managed to regain their lifeboat
even after several capsizings. They drifted to an island where they were
picked up by an Indian canoeman and taken to Parry Sound where they
made known the fate of the vessel and those who sailed on her three days
earlier.

A song narrating the tragedy of the *Asia* soon appeared among Lakes
sailors. The accompanying version was obtained in the summer of 1934
from Mrs. Robert Reid of Red Bay, Ontario. She had sailed as cook on
Lake Huron lumber schooners for eight seasons in the 1880s and early
1890s, and learned the song aboard ship. Norman "Beachie" MacIvor
and John "Red" MacDonald, both of Goderich, Ontario, sang the song
using much the same lines. Volume VI of Mr. David Williams' scrap-
book, "Marine History of the Great Lakes," now in the Collingwood
Great Lakes Museum, has an expanded and rearranged version of the
song.

Loud roared the dreadful thunder, and stormy was the day
When the *Asia* left Owen Sound to cross the Georgian Bay.

210

One hundred souls she had on board, likewise a costly store,
But on that trip the gallant ship sank to rise no more.

The captain's name was John Savage, the mate I did not know,
MacDougall was the purser brave, lost in that fearful blow.
Three and thirty shantyboys, all hearty, strong, and brave,
Were bound to the French River camp, they met a watery grave.

Likewise young Billie Christie and his newly wedded bride
Were bound to Manitoulin where their parents did reside.
Now in the deep they all do sleep, their earthly trials are o'er;
Their friends will ne'er see them again along the Georgian shore.

Of all the souls she had on board two only are alive:
Miss Morrison and Tinkiss are all that did survive.
Miss Morrison and Tinkiss, their names I can't forget,
Were saved in a lifeboat which four times did upset.

Around each family circle, how sad the news to hear!
The foundering of the *Asia*, still sounding in each ear!

THE LOSS OF THE *MAGGIE HUNTER*

The schooner *Maggie Hunter* was an early Welland Canal-size vessel
well known on Lake Ontario in the 1870s, and had for some years before
her tragic end been in the general carrying trade on the Lakes. According to John S. Parsons, sailor, ship chandler, and historian of Oswego,
N.Y., the *Hunter* sailed out of the local harbour one late autumn
evening in the early 1880s into a gathering northwest storm and was
never seen again. She had on board eight men and a cargo of coal for
Toronto 140 miles westward up the Lake. The body of Captain Frank
Nixon and some wreckage came ashore near Fair Haven about fifteen
miles west of Oswego, and it was assumed that the vessel foundered in
that vicinity. Captain Nixon, according to Mr. Parsons, had the reputation of being a skilled and daring sailor. Nelson Hodgins of Picton who
recalled most of the following song, stated that on the evening the
Hunter was lost, vessels going into Oswego harbour met her towing out
and advised Captain Nixon not to attempt the crossing, but he, anxious
to get to Toronto before the harbour froze, continued on his way to his
death and that of his crew.

The version below was supplied in the summer of 1933 by William
Head of Picton who had sailed in Lakes windjammers for twenty-five
years and fished Lake Ontario for thirty more.

Sad and sorrowful is the tale to you I will relate:
It's about the loss of the *Maggie Hunter*, her crew, and their sad
    fate.
They sank beneath the stormy deep, in life to rise no more,
When a raging hurricane did sweep Ontario's rocky shore.

They left Oswego on their lee, the white seas high did roll;
They were bound for Toronto city with three hundred ton of coal.
There never was a jollier crew sailed over Lakes or seas,
As their flowing canvas they put on and set her to the breeze.

They sang their songs so merrily as dashed the foaming spray,
And little did they think that day they soon would pass away,
Little did that gallant crew think they were doomed to die,
And before the dawn of another day beneath Ontario lie.

Outside of the Oswego pier it blew a lively gale,
And by order of their captain they shortened their snow-white sail.
Of all the captains on the Lakes Frank Nixon was their chief
As he sailed out that fateful day with his canvas closely reefed.

Daniel Sharp he was her mate, from Port Credit he did hail;
He was as good a seaman, boys, as ever there set sail.
The Newman brothers were before-the-mast, good sailors both and
    true,
Together with four other men, made up the *Hunter*'s crew.

Dusk came on and darkness too; it was a dreadful night,
And the ill-fated *Maggie Hunter* soon was lost to sight.
They soon were lost to sight, brave crew! and will be seen no more;
They lie beneath the stormy waves far from their friends and shore.

A boom, a hatch, a broken spar, and the captain's pallid face,
Of this sturdy craft and gallant crew were found the only trace.
Off the city of Fair Haven it is supposed she lay,
But that will never be made known until the Judgement Day.

Now all you men who follow the land and there a living make,
It's little do you know or think of the dangers on the Lakes;
But after this when storms arise, think of the night it blew,
And the *Maggie Hunter* last was seen and her brave and gallant
    crew.

11. SQUARE DANCE CALLS
J.D. Robins

The national dances of many of our various cultural groups are still performed in Canada and are encouraged by the Canadian Folk Arts Council. However, the dance that is most truly Canadian is the square dance: it is popular with both English and French, and from the east to the west coasts. As in the United States, it began with the early pioneers: those who remembered the English country dances took on the role of callers to direct their less experienced neighbours in the steps. Later the patterns became more formalized, and today square dancing is a popular pastime with many city folk.

In his youth Dr. John D. Robins (1884-1952) worked in the lumberwoods of northern Ontario where he heard many traditional songs and stories, and throughout his life he holidayed in Ontario's lake country. Below he gives some traditional square dance calls that he noted in Goulais Bay at the south-eastern tip of Lake Superior in the summer of 1945. He also lists some of the popular tunes known by two local fiddlers. The fiddle was the most common instrument used to accompany square dancing in pioneer times.

Following the Ontario calls and tune titles are two short samples of calls used in western Canada.

ONTARIO DANCE CALLS
As called by Ronald MacDonald, Goulais River, August, 1945.

FIRST CHANGE

Address your partners, corners address.
Join your hands and away to the west.
Break and promenade back.

Head two couples go forward and back.
Forward again and go right and left through.
Right and left back.
Same two couples change and swing.
Change 'em back, and promenade half.
Back and swing to place.

Allemand left, right hand to partner,
And grand right and left.
Meet your own and promenade.

(Repeat for second couples.)

First couple lead out to the right.
Chase your lady around those two,
Half way round and the gent comes through.
Chase your gent around those two,
Half way round and the lady comes through.
Swing when you meet, and the two couples swing.
Lead out to the next and the same old thing.

*(Couple repeats above performance with all three other couples until
they reach their own place in the set again. Then all go allemand left.*
*Then second couple leads out and repeats performance, and so on
until all couples have made the rounds. Figure ends with promenade
all.)*

BREAKDOWN

All couples go allemand left, right to your partner,
And grand chain right and left, all the way round,
And swing your partners when you get home.

Pass your partner, balance all to the corner lady.
Turn and swing behind you.
Promenade with the lady ahead of you.
Pass her by and balance all to the next lady ahead.
Turn and swing behind you.

*(And so on until partners are reached again. Figure ends with
allemand left, swing, and promenade home.)*

FIRST CHANGE

Tune: "The Girl I Left Behind Me"

First couple lead out to the right
And be so nice and kindly.
Pass right through, balance back to back,
And swing the girl behind you.

Then pass right back, balance back to back,
And be so nice and kindly,
And when you're through just turn around
And swing the girl behind you.

Take your lady and lead to the next . . .

(Repeat performance until all places are reached, and other three couples repeat same figure. Figure ends with usual allemand left and promenade.)

SECOND CHANGE

Tune: "Little Brown Jug"

First couple lead out to the right,
Right hands across and circle half.
Left hands back and circle.

Right hand to your opposite lady,
Left to your partner, and half promenade.
Right and left through and lead to next couple . . .

(Repeat above performance with two remaining couples. Other couples all repeat performance, and figure ends with usual allemand left and promenade home.)

BREAKDOWN

Tune: "Sailor's Hornpipe" or "Soldier's Joy"

First couple out to the right
And gent take the lady by the wrist,
And around that lady with a grapevine twist.

Down the centre with a whoa back gee,
And around that gent now, don't you see,
And circle four in the middle of the floor.

Lead up four and balance six.
Around that lady with a grapevine twist.
Down the centre with a whoa back gee,
And around that gent now, don't you see.
And circle six and don't get mixed.

Lead up six and balance eight.
Around that lady with a grapevine twist.
Back to the centre with a whoa back gee,
And around that gent now, don't you see,
And circle eight when you come straight.

Allemand left to your partners
And grand chain right and left.
Meet your partners, promenade home.

(Next couple then lead out and repeat above performance, and so on until remaining three couples have completed figure. Figure ends with usual swing and promenade.)

FIDDLE TUNES PLAYED IN GOULAIS BAY

Dr. Robins made up the following lists from information he gathered from Jim Robinson and Ken MacDonald in Goulais Bay in August, 1945. He noted: "The first list I got from Jim Robinson. Ken added the items in the second list. He certainly knows most of Jim's tunes, too, possibly all of them. Jim has forgotten some that I used to hear him play forty or more years ago. Jim was eighty-one on August 16, 1945."

1. Rory O'More
Sailor's Hornpipe
Money Musk
Devil's Dream
Irish Washerwoman
Wilson's Clog
Beautiful Nell
Life on the Ocean Wave
Arkansas Traveller
The Flowers of Edinboro
Colin Cooper (Highland Fling)
Comin' through the Rye
Miss McLeod's Reel
Jim Blake
Hundred Pipers
Soldier's Joy
Opera Reel (given by Jim as Upper Reel)
Virginia Reel
The Two Sisters

2. Paddy on the Turnpike Road
Rickett's Hornpipe
The Night I was Married
Smash the Window
Mason's Apron
Wagner (Breakdown)
Stage Reel (Very popular among the Indians, who call it Whitefish on the Rapids)
Clean Pea Straw
Tatter Jack Welch
Cabhair feigh (Deer Antlers)
    – a Grant Clan tune
Macdonald's Reel
Drowsy Molly

WESTERN CALLS

This is a sample of "calling off" for a four-handed reel, as given at the Alberta Old-Timers' Ball at Edmonton, Alberta. It was quoted in The Mail and Empire, *February 6, 1928, from the* Edmonton Journal.

Balance your pardners, one and all,
And grand right and left around the hall.
Promenade around in a single file,
Lady in the lead in the Injun style.
Ladies bow low and the gents bow under,
Couple up tight and swing like thunder.

Lady round the gent, and the gent goes so,
And the lady round the gent, and the gent don't go.
Leave the lady and home you go,
Opposite the gent with a do-si-do.
Jump right up and never come down,
And swing that calico round and round.

In a radio talk, "Tales of the Old Times," given on December 28, 1932, E. A. Corbett, then Director of the Extension Department of the University of Alberta and later head of the Canadian Association for Adult Education, commented:
  "Once at a half-breed dance at Lac la Biche, the caller off used some extraordinary verses. One only I can remember:

Now swing the one that looks so neat;
Now swing the one with them big feet.
Now swing the one with the funny bone;
Now swing the one you call your own.
Jump right up and never come down
And swing that calico round and round."

12. FOLKWAYS

The vast field designated as "folklife" is the most fully covered of all aspects of Canadian folklore. There are hundreds of first-hand accounts of the folkways and customs of our early settlers, the best known being those of the two famous Strickland sisters: Susanna Moodie's Roughing It in the Bush *and Catharine Parr Traill's* The Backwoods of Canada.

The first two items, about building a log house and making maple sugar, are typical of many such accounts in pioneer journals. They come from a century-old narrative by John Cunningham Geikie (1824-1906). Although his book sounds like a first-hand account, Dr. Geikie notes: "The narrative is that of a family, not my own, nor am I intended where the first personal pronoun is used. But I can vouch for every detail as literally correct."

Another very important area of folklife deals with men who work on the sea and in the woods. As noted earlier, the lumbermen and the fishermen created the greatest number of our native Canadian folk songs, and these give vivid pictures of the hardships and tragedies characteristic of their occupations. Parallel prose accounts occur in many first-hand narratives and novels of pioneer life.

In Up to Date, or The Life of a Lumberman, the author's first sentence is: "The name I have been known by since I came to Canada is George S. Thompson; what my right name is I am not quite sure." He says he was born in India about 1846, the son of a British officer who later went to fight with the Confederate Army in the American Civil War and was killed there. The boy returned to England to try to find his family but failed, and in 1869 he sailed from Liverpool to Quebec. On the ship he met George S. Thompson, a youth who was supposed to go to work for a brother he had not seen since infancy. He offered to exchange papers with the author who accepted and henceforth was known as Thompson. He went to Minden in Haliburton County, Ontario, where he was welcomed by his "brother" and worked for him for a year. Then he decided to go into the bush to learn the lumbering business. The following section of his book describes his first winter in the woods. In the rest of the book he gives a very detailed description of lumbering in various parts of Ontario in the 1870s and 1880s, illustrating it with his own sketches and many photographs. Although his account of his own life is rather melodramatic, what he writes about the life and work of the lumbermen is obviously based on first-hand experience and observation.

The story of the cattle round-up comes from "The Reminiscences of H2 Jack" by John O. McHugh, a manuscript written in longhand, 1959-1960. Mr. McHugh was born in Calgary in 1895, the seventh child of Felix Alexander McHugh who owned a ranch between the Bow and Oldman rivers, some fifty miles down the Bow from the North West Mounted Police fort. Felix McHugh (1851-1913) built the first building in Calgary in 1884 and also took part in railway construction. He bought the first cattle that were shipped over the Canadian Pacific Railway from Ottawa to Maple Creek and drove them overland to his H2 ranch in 1883. At his death he was worth three-quarters of a million dollars.

BUILDING OUR LOG HOUSE
Cunningham Geikie

The look of the house which was to be our dwelling was novel enough to me, with my old ideas about houses still in my head. It was built a little back from the river, far enough to give room for a garden when we had time to make one; and the trees had been cut down from the water's edge to some distance behind the house to make things a little more cheery, and also to prevent the risk of any of them falling on our establishment in a high wind. The house itself had, in fact, been built of the logs procured by felling these patriarchs of the forest, every one of which had, as usual on Canadian farms, been cut down . . . Building the house must have been very heavy work, for it was made of great logs, the whole thickness of the trees, piled one on another, a story and a half high. The neighbours had made what they call a 'bee' to help 'raise' it – that is, they had come without expecting wages, but with the understanding that each would get back from us, when he wanted it, as many days' labour as he had given. They manage a difficult business like that of getting up the outside of a log-house more easily than one would think. First, the logs are cut into the proper lengths for the sides and ends; then they are notched at the end to make them keep together; then an equal number are put at the four sides to be ready, and the first stage is over. The next step is to get four laid in the proper positions on the ground, and then to get up the rest, layer by layer, on the top of each other, till the whole are in their places. It is a terrible strain on the men, for there is nothing but sheer strength to help them, except that they put poles from the top of the last log raised, to the ground, and then, with hand-spokes, force another up the slope to its destined position. I have known many men terribly wrenched by the handspoke of some other one slipping and letting the whole weight of one end come upon the person next him. The logs at the front and back were all fully twenty feet long, and some of them eighteen inches thick, so that you may judge their weight. After the square frame had been thus piled up, windows and a door were cut with axes, a board at the sides of each keeping the ends of the logs in their places. You may wonder how this could be done, but backwoodsmen are so skilful with the axe that it was done very neatly. The sashes for the windows and the planking for different parts of the house were got from a saw-mill some distance off, across the river, and my brother put in the glass. Of course there were a great many chinks between the logs, but these were filled up, as well as possible, with billets and chips of wood, the whole being finally coated and made air-tight with mortar. Thus the logs looked as if built up with lime, the great black trunks of the trees alternating with the gray belts between. The frame of the roof was made of round poles, flattened on the top, on which boards were put, and these again were covered with shingles – a kind of wooden slate made of split pine, which answers very well. The angles at the ends were filled up with logs fitted to the length, and fixed in their places by wooden pins driven through the roof-pole at each corner. On the whole house there were no nails used at all, except on the roof. Wooden pins, and an auger to make holes, made everything fast. Inside, it was an extraordinary place. The floor was paved with pine slabs, the outer planks cut from logs, with the round side down, and fixed by wooden pins to sleepers made of thin young trees, cut the right lengths. Overhead, a number of similar round poles, about the thickness of a man's leg, supported the floor of the upper storey, which was to be my sisters' bedroom. They had planks, however, instead of board, in honour of their sex, perhaps. They had to climb to this paradise by an extraordinary ladder, made with the never failing axe and auger of green, round wood. I used always to think of Robinson Crusoe getting into his fortification when I saw them going up.

The chimney was a wonderful affair. It was large enough to let you walk up most of the way, and could hold I can't tell how many logs, four or five feet long, for a fire. It was built of mud, and when whitewashed looked very well – at least we came to like it; it was so clean and cheerful in the wintertime. But we had to pull it down some years after, and get one built of bricks, as it was always getting out of repair. A partition was put up across the middle and then divided again, and this made two bedrooms for my brothers, and left us our solitary room which was to serve for kitchen, dining-room, and drawing-room, the outer door opening into it. As to paint, it was out of the question, but we had lime for whitewash, and what with it and some newspapers which my brothers pasted up in their bed-rooms, and a few pictures we brought from home, we thought we were quite stylish. There was no house any better, at any rate, in the neighbourhood, and, I suppose, we judged by that.

MAKING MAPLE SUGAR

With the first opening of spring, and while yet the snow lay thick in the fields and the woods, the season of maple sugar-making commenced. It seemed extraordinary to me for a long time that sugar should be got in quantities from a great forest tree, the modest sugar-cane having been always in my mind the only source of it – except, indeed, the sugar-beet, by the growth of which Napoleon tried to make France furnish her own sugar, instead of having to buy English colonial sugar from any of the European ports. But a great quantity is made, in Canada and the United States, from the maple, both for sale and home use, a vast amount being eaten by the native-born Canadians as a sweetmeat, just as we eat candy; and very little else is known in many parts of the backwoods for household purposes. The best days for sugar-making are the bright ones, after frosty nights, the sap running then most freely. The first thing we had to do with our "bush," which is the name given to the maples preserved for sugar-making, was to see that each tree was provided with a trough, which we made out of pine or some other soft wood, by cutting a log into lengths of perhaps two feet, then splitting each in two, and hollowing the flat side so that it would hold about a bucketful of sap. We next took narrow pieces of wood about a foot long, and made spouts of them with a gouge, after which we made a cut in each tree with the axe, three or four inches long and an inch deep, in a slanting direction, adding another straight cut at the lower end of it with the gouge, that there might be no leaking, and sinking a hole for a spout, where they met; the gouge that cut the spouts making the hole into which they were thrust. Below these spouts the troughs were set to collect the sap, which was carried as often as they were nearly full to another, of enormous dimensions, close to the fire. These colossal troughs are simply huge trunks of trees hollowed out for the purpose; ours would have held fifty barrels. The emptying into this was made every morning and evening until a large quantity had been gathered, and then the boiling began in large 'kettles,' as they are called, made for the purpose, and suspended over the blazing fire from a stout pole, resting on two forked branches thrust into the earth at each side. The sap once in the kettles has a hard time of it: the fires are kept up in royal brightness for days together, not being allowed to die out even during the night.

It was a very pleasant time with us, though it was hard work, and what with the white snow, the great solemn trees, the wild figures dancing hither and thither, and our loud merriment, it was very striking when the evenings had set in. One of the kettles was chosen for "sugaring off," and had especially assiduous watching. Not a moment's rest could its unfortunate contents get from the incessant boiling we kept up; fresh sap being added as often as it seemed to be getting too dry. In its rage, the sap would every now and then make desperate efforts to boil over; but we were on the watch for this also, and as soon as it manifested any intention of the kind, we rubbed round the inside of the kettle with a piece of pork-fat, beyond the limits of which it would no more pass than if it had been inside some magic circle. My sisters were as busy as we at every part of the process, and their poor dresses showed abundant and lasting memorials of their labours, in the rents made in them by the bushes. What we were all like, from head to foot, after a time, may be more easily conceived than described. Our smudged faces, and sugary, sloppy clothes, made us all laugh at one another.

As the sap grew thicker with the incessant boiling, another element was added to our amusement in the stickiness of everything we handled;

if we leaned against a log at hand we were fast bound; and the pots, pans, ladles, buckets, axe-handles, troughs – everything we touched, indeed, seemed to part from us only with regret. We were fortunate in having no young children amongst us, as they would, of course, have been in the thick of the fray, and have become half-crystallized before all was over. The "clearing off" was managed by pouring in beaten eggs when the sap was beginning to get thick. This served to bring all the impurities at once to the top, so that we could readily skim them off. Several ingenious ways had been told us of knowing when the process was complete. One was by boring small holes in a flat piece of wood, and blowing on it after dipping it into the syrup; the sugar going through the holes in long bubbles, if it were boiled enough. Another plan was to put a little on the snow, when, if it got stiff, it was time to pour all out. Everything that would hold it was then, forthwith, put into requisition, after having been well greased to keep the sugar from sticking, and, presently, we had cakes, loaves, lumps, blocks, every shape, in fact, of rich brown-coloured sugar of our own making. Some, which we wanted to crystallize, was put into a barrel, and stirred while cooling, which effectually answered the purpose. Small holes bored in the bottom made the sugar thus obtained whiter than the rest, by allowing the molasses mingled with it to drain off. We kept some sap for vinegar, which we made by simply boiling three or four pailfuls until reduced to one, and corking this up in a keg for a time . . .

The sugaring-off day was rather a festivity with us, as we followed the custom of a good many of our neighbours, and invited some young folks to come to a carnival on the warm sugar, which is very nice, though I should not care to eat as much at a time as some of our visitors did. The quantity of sap which a single tree yields is astonishing. I think some gave not less than fifty gallons, and the loss of it seemed to do them good rather than harm. The older and stronger the trees the better the sap, and the more abundant – a peculiarity which it would be well for each of us to be able to have said of his own life as it advanced. The Indians must have been acquainted with the property of the maple for ages; stone sugar-making utensils, of their manufacture, comprising stone troughs and long stone spouts, hollowed out and pointed for sticking into the trees, having often been found in some districts. The few who still survive keep up the habits of their ancestors in this, as in other respects, numbers of them offering sugar which they have made, for barter, each spring.

A WINTER IN A LUMBERCAMP
George S. Thompson

. . . Next day I engaged with Norman Barnhart, bush superintendent for Mossom Boyd, the lumber king of the Trent River, to go up to one of the shanties in the capacity of shanty clerk. My wages were to be, I think, twenty dollars a month, board, lodging and tobacco free. The shanty I was assigned to was located in the township of Harburn, fifteen miles north of Haliburton. Mr. Boyd had acquired the right to cut and remove the pine timber from the English Land Company, and the season I went up was about the first cutting done in that township. My shanty had a crew of about fifty men; the foreman and the majority of the crew were French-Canadians; the crew were civil, obliging and a hard-working lot. They treated me very kindly, and I soon got to be a great favourite with them, and soon I was right at home in the bush.

My duties consisted in keeping the men's time, and charging up to the men such articles as they required, and looking after the supplies, plant, etc., received, consumed, or sent away from my shanty. I also had to keep strict account of the number of pieces of timber and sawlogs made and hauled to the stream each day.

Our crew that winter made both square timber and sawlogs. The two gangs of timber makers – five men in each gang, went through the bush ahead of the sawlog makers, and selected and cut down the trees suitable for square timber. A timber gang would make about six pieces of timber per day, on an average, equal to about 400 cubic feet. A gang of sawlog cutters in those days consisted of five men – three to chop the trees down and cut and top the tree square with their axes when felled, and the other two men to saw the tree into lengths required for sawlogs, usually in 12 to 16 feet sections. Five logs to the tree was a good average, to get from the trees, and 75 logs was a good average day's work for the gang of five men to cut. In those days nothing less than 14 inch diameter at top end would pass for a sawlog, and it had to be straight and sound at that. Three knots or more in a log made a cull of it; even butt logs with a hollow or the least bit of shake had to be cut off and left in the woods to rot. It is needless to say that such a system caused a great waste of wood, for the extent of territory a crew would run over in one season was enormous – only about one-third of the standing trees would make such a class of logs, and therefore the balance were left untouched, probably to be soon afterwards burnt, for the chips left by the timber makers, and the tops of the trees that had been felled, along with brush heaps piled up in making places for railways or skidways and roads which were opened in order to have the timber and logs hauled to the stream, left the bush full of inflammable material. The least spark of fire the next summer set the bush in a blaze. In this way millions of dollars worth of pine and other wood have been destroyed. Of course in those days pine trees were cheap, the supply apparently inexhaustible. But times have changed since then. All see now that a few years more will practically exterminate the pine forest of Canada. No such waste goes on now. Instead of chopping the trees down they are sawed, so the butt is already squared when the tree falls . . . The tree when felled is now sawn up into sections; crooks, rots, spunks, shakes and knots – everything now goes into the sawlogs, to be dissected on its arrival at the mill. Nothing is left in the bush – even small trees six inches in diameter are now cut down, which I think is wrong . . .

I have already stated how twenty out of our crew of fifty men were employed; about fifteen more are kept cutting trails or roads, so that the horses and oxen could get to the timber and logs and haul them to the stream or railways. The sawlogs if any distance from the stream would in most cases have to be piled up on skidways or rollways, so that no time would be lost when the sleighing came in collecting a load and hauling to the stream. The square timber had to be collected together in much the same way. The balance of our crew were teamsters and loaders, with the exception of the cook and his helper, or "devil," as he is usually called.

The size of our shanty was about forty feet square. The walls were made of large pine logs, notched and dovetailed together, and were six logs high. On top of the walls from end to end were two enormous stringers or beams to hold up the roof which was also made of pine logs formed of halves of trees hollowed out, called scoops, and the greatest expense in building a shanty is making the scoops or roof. The walls of the shanty and the roof were stuffed with moss on the inside, and the walls on the outside plastered with mud. A large opening, about eight feet square, was left in the centre of the roof and a wooden tapered chimney, about six feet high, built up to carry off the smoke from the fire place or camboose, which was built of sand and stone in the centre of the shanty. The opening in the roof, or the chimney, let in lots of daylight, so no windows were required, and at night the huge fire supplied all the light necessary. Sometimes a floor of logs was put in, but just as often none. One door, about five feet square, and the shanty was ready for the bunks or sleeping berths of the men, which was built of poles around one side and end. The other side and end was occupied by the foreman, clerk, and cook, and there was an unwritten law which strictly prohibited any of the crew occupying or taking up the foreman's side of the shanty. A stable built in the same rough way to hold about ten pair of horses, and a small storehouse and granary completed the set of buildings. The cost of the lot would be about three hundred dollars, for the crew would often put them up and have them completed in the space of three days . . .

The great objection to one of these old camboose shanties is that it takes an enormous quantity of wood to supply sufficient heat to keep them warm in the winter. Half a cord would only make an average fire, and the chances are one will be half blinded with smoke the greater part of the time. So great a nuisance is this that it is said the smoky odour on one's clothes can be detected by any one with a good "smeller" nearly half a mile distant. When the fire gets low during the cold winter night the large opening in the roof lets in the cold and the crew sometimes are half frozen to death.

The cookery outfit of a camboose shanty, in the early days, consisted of half a dozen bake kettles for baking bread, and one for baking beans in ashes, which is done by covering the kettles with hot ashes. Often in taking off the cover or lids a few pounds of ashes or sand would get into the beans, but a good cook claims that the ashes saves pepper and helps digestion. In addition to the half dozen kettles, there are two large pots and a tea boiler; that, with a butcher knife and a fork, completes the cooking utensils. The clerk gives out to each man a tin plate and dish, but the crew have to furnish their own knives and forks – that is if any of them could not get along without them. Most of them, however, do worry along with a jack knife.

One blanket was allowed to each man, and two men usually slept together. The men turn in with all their clothes on – socks as well – and the only use a shantyman has for a coat in the bush is to make a pillow of it for his bed. If a man attempts to wear a coat in the bush the foreman will soon tell him to take it off and ask him if he cannot work hard enough to keep himself warm.

In those early days the food supplies to the men consisted of bread, pork, and beans. The men could have tea if they paid one dollar per month for it. My first winter in the shanty I fared well, for game was plentiful, and I used to kill enough to supply the foreman and myself, and often sufficient to give all the crew a feast. On Sundays some of the crew would catch some fish, which helped to give us a variety.

Sunday is cleaning up day, the men doing their washing and mending on that day – that is the few that would go to that trouble. Quite a number would never change their under-clothes or shirts until the clothes were wore out, and as to washing their feet, such a thing never came into their minds, for the old heads among them knew their feet would get washed often enough in the spring when river driving commenced, and wading in the cold water in the rapids often up to their waist, and sometimes their shoulders. This would soon wash all the dirt off them. Lost socks would often be discovered that way in the spring, the dirt on the men's feet being so thick they would forget having put the socks on months before, and the first wading in the water in the spring would often bring the lost socks to light, much to the astonishment of the wearer. An old cotton bag usually did service as a towel for

225

all the crew. Seldom was there ever a looking-glass, and the entire furniture of a lumber shanty consisted of the grindstone.

The hours per day the men worked in the bush or on the river all depends on how little sleep the foreman can worry along with. Before clocks were introduced into lumber shanties, I have seen the foreman mistake the bright moonlight for coming daylight, and wake the crew up and take breakfast, only to discover later that it was probably about the middle of the night, and it is a common occurrence for the men to walk three or four miles through the bush to their work, and then have to build a fire to keep them from freezing or being eaten up by the wolves until daylight came, so that they could see to work; and it's strictly against rules to come to the shanty before dark night. A clock in a shanty is worse than useless as far as the crew are concerned, for the foreman usually has the clock about two hours too fast, so the crew seldom pay any attention to it. Dinner time is any time one gets hungry. The shantymen now a days fare much better as regards food and lodging than we did in the early days – but the hours of work are just as long . . .

I well remember the first Xmas evening I spent in a lumber shanty. Our foreman sat up with the crew and told us fairy and ghost stories. The crew were very superstitious (most French Canadians are) and for that matter I am myself. That Xmas evening there was a fearful gale blowing, and towards midnight when our foreman was in the middle of one of his blood-curdling and hair-lifting stories, the crew all gathered around him with their eyes fairly bulging out, crash, bang! down came right amongst us a big pine limb which the wind had broken from a huge pine tree that stood some distance from our shanty; the wind carried the limb and dropped it down our camboose chimney, and it made a fearful crash when it struck our pots and kettles. A more frightened crew I never saw, and I guess we all thought the devil had us. After we recovered a little from our fright the foreman said it was sent as a warning to some one who was neglecting his religious duties, and he looked straight at me when he said it. I retorted by saying that I thought it had been sent to stop him telling such infernal lies. After a hearty laugh we all retired to our beds for the night . . .

I was sorry when our shanty closed in the spring. Any of our crew who were not engaged for the "run" were paid off. Quite a number of the men go up to the bush about the first of September when timber-making, log-cutting, skidding, road-making and also stream improvements, such as dams, piers, etc., can all be done cheapest, and to best advantage. This work takes up all the time until sufficient depth of snow comes (about ten inches) to commence to haul the timber and sawlogs to the streams. Very little timber is made or logs cut after Xmas, the snow usually being too deep for the men to do such work to advantage. Anyhow the hauling of the timber and logs generally takes up all the time of the foreman and the crew until about the middle of the month of March; then preparations have to be made for the drives – for the streams clear themselves of ice mostly in the month of April, and then the real hard work of the raftsmen or river-drivers commences, for the timber and logs must be got down the same stream by the spring freshets, or if the flood of water is allowed to run off and get ahead of the drive then the timber and logs will have to remain in the stream until the next spring. That is what lumbermen call "sticking" or "hanging up" a drive, and it is a great loss to the owner as well as being thought a disgrace to the foreman and crew who worked on it, and a foreman who sticks more than one drive soon loses his reputation and gets reduced to the ranks . . .

The objective point for the square timber is Quebec, and the sawlogs on the Ottawa river to the owner's sawmill at Ottawa and other points on that river. Sawlogs on the Trent River go to Fenelon Falls, Bobcaygeon, Peterborough, and Trenton; on the Georgian Bay, they mostly go to Waubaushene, Midland, Little Current, and many are sawn up at the mills at the mouth of Spanish, French, and other rivers tributary to the Georgian Bay. Since the Americans have came over to Canada enormous numbers of sawlogs are towed across Lake Huron to Bay City and other points in Michigan. The river driving and rafting takes up all the spring and summer months, and when a man engages for the "run" he is obliged to stay until the timber reaches its destination. In the early days, and even yet on the Ottawa River the men had to sign a agreement similar to the one the sailors sign when joining a ship, only the one the shantyman signs is more like a chattel mortgage on his life for one year . . .

Those among our crew who were engaged for the run, when our shanty broke up that spring were sent to the depot or headquarter shanty, where they could be best employed until navigation opened. The depot shanty is where all the provisions and all the supplies are forwarded to from the nearest railroad point, and from there are distributed as required to the other shanties on the limit. It is where the bush superintendent, chief clerk, bush rangers, and log scalers make their headquarters, and where all men leaving are settled with and paid off . . .

After our shanty broke up, my books were inspected by the chief clerk, everything checked off, and the cost of our shanty ascertained. Against this was credited our output of timber and sawlogs by which the bush superintendent could tell if our winter's work was satisfactory or not. If the cost was found to be too much (or above the usual average cost) the chances were that the foreman would be discharged. The superintendent was well pleased with my work and the way I had performed my duties, and I was re-engaged to stay on one of the drives in the same capacity. We had about a month's time in which to make preparations for the drives, such as building boats and scows, capstan, and cribs or

227

floats on which to carry our provisions across the lakes and down the rivers, and to put the tents on for the men to sleep in; and also to make pike poles and levies as well as tools used by the men in rafting and river-driving . . .

Towards the last of the month of April of that first season of mine in the bush, the men were divided into four crews of about fifty each, and a foreman and assistant foreman was placed in charge of each crew, and the bush superintendent controlled the lot. We were all put out under canvas, the canvas being old – discarded military tents. The snow was still on the ground, in some places nearly three feet deep; each man was allowed one regulation blanket, but the men used to make a good bed out of balsam boughs taken from the trees, which are plentiful in all parts of Canada. When the boughs are broken up fine and nicely laid on the ground about six inches deep, they make one of the finest mattresses possible. In fact it is all the mattress a shantyman would get either in the shanty or on the river, and even today the old time shantymen will use nothing else in their beds at home. The Indians always use balsam brush under their blankets, and one good feature about it is no one will ever catch cold who uses them for a bed; the perfume of the balsam bough is strong but not at all objectionable.

The first work to be done on a river is to break all the dumps and get the logs and timber afloat. Breaking the dumps is a very dangerous piece of business. Often thousands of pieces of sawlogs will be in one intricate mass, piled up mountains high on the bank of some stream or lake where the mountain is too steep to get down with the sleighs. The men commence to work at their dumps as soon as the stream is clear of ice, and of course the logs at the base of the dump have to be rolled in first to allow the other ones to follow. Often after a few logs have been rolled into the stream the whole lot may be set in motion and they will come down with a great crash; the men then have to be very nimble and "skin out" of the way as best they can, often taking a dive in the water to escape. The water in the spring is mixed up with masses of ice, and a dip into it at such a time is anything but pleasant, but is preferable to having a few dozen sawlogs roll over one's body . . .

Often the breaking of the dumps and getting the logs afloat takes up several weeks, and it is a vexatious delay but one which cannot be avoided. Our drive that first spring was much delayed in that way. The trouble is that all the time that kind of work lasts, the spring freshet is running away. To hold as much of the freshet back as possible until the water can be used to best advantage, dams are built. Wherever possible a reservoir is made of a lake or even a beaver meadow. When the stoplogs are taken out of the dam the rush of water, if the dam is full, is great, and the flood sends the logs tumbling over the rapids, and the noise they make as they are driven and pounded against the rocks in the rapids and tumbling over the falls often reminded me of the thunder of cannon when heard in the distance.

Occasionally a stick of timber or logs running too thick together will cause a jam in the rapids – often in dangerous and difficult places, perhaps where the banks of the stream, the sides of which are solid rock mountains high and as straight up as the side of a house. Then the best men, "jam crackers" or white-water men, as the boys call them, go on to "break the jam" or pick out the key log or stick that is holding the rest. Often the key stick or log will have to be cut with an axe, and probably when half cut through the pressure of the mass of logs behind it cracks the stick and in a second the whole is a seething twisting curling mass of logs up-ending and turning in every shape, and going at a terrific speed. It is in such places where a river-driver's nerve and agility finds play as well as his cool, level head; he has often to spring as quickly as a squirrel in picking his way over the swiftly moving mass – often jumping ten or fifteen feet from one moving stick or log to another before he gets a chance to make his way ashore – that is, if he is fortunate enough to get ashore. Often they get caught or struck by a log and badly injured; or get thrown in the madly foaming rapids, when a desperate battle for life commences, his comrades witnessing the terrible struggle and often utterly impossible to help him. The sight is a thrilling one, and frequently ends fatally. Once on the Gull River I witnessed such a sight; my crew of nearly one hundred men lined the banks and rushed out on the logs on the side jams as they saw a poor fellow trying to swim as he was being tossed and thrown about like a cork. In this case the river was wide, and the mad current kept him in the middle of the stream, out of reach of us all. On he went until he came to the brink of a straight falls of nearly thirty feet; swiftly he approached and over he went and was lost to view for a few seconds, when he bobbed up again we could see he had been badly hurt and was much exhausted, but bravely again he tried to steady himself to go over the next cataract, a couple of hundred yards below, and as he went over the last ten-foot falls, we seen him throw up his arms and that was the last we seen of him alive. I instantly had the dam closed at the head of the rapids and the water lowered, and then we commenced our dismal search. We found his mangled body fully three-quarters of a mile below where he had been thrown in by being struck by a piece of timber in a moving jam on which he was working just above the first falls. The poor fellow was only about twenty-four years of age. He was always venturesome and such scenes are of frequent occurrence; sometimes a rope is fastened around a man's body and held by others on shore, when he is working on the "key stick," chopping it in two; then if the jam breaks suddenly his comrades pull him ashore with ropes. It is only in extremely risky cases that a rope is used, because it is seldom that less than half a dozen men can do anything towards breaking a jam, and sometimes it takes all the crew several days, if a bad one. The un-written law among river-drivers is when a bad jam forms in a dangerous place the foreman is first to inspect it, then when he has decided where to commence the attack he signals what men he wishes to go and assist him. The men all gather on the bank, but none offer to go on the jam until the foreman calls, for too many men on a jam is always a source of danger, the jam being liable to go without an instant's warning; any unnecessary men would only impede others in their run to shore. The foreman is also best judge of who is the most capable men in such a case; but a foreman, to have or retain the respect of the crew, must always be first to the front in a dangerous place, and it is rarely any man refuses to follow his lead; and when out on the jam the first thing they do is to take a glance to spot the safest apparent looking way for making their run ashore in case of the jam taking a sudden start, for in that case it is every one for himself.

We had two stretches of about three miles each of very bad river that spring; there was not sufficient improvements done on the stream to allow a quick run of the enormous quantity of timber and logs that we had in our drive, so the spring flood got away from us, and we had to leave behind fully one half of our drive, which was a very serious loss to the firm, for logs especially are apt to get badly damaged by worms and decaying sap-wood when "hung up" dry in the streams; if left afloat in deep water, no danger that way is sustained, but logs or timber hung up means a year longer before realizing on them, and piles up the interest account fast.

The crew I was with were paid off, myself with the rest, and I was glad of it, for the mosquitoes and black flies were very bad – no rest night or day could be got – for at night the mosquitoes get in their work and so do another insect which go by the name of "shantyman's pet"; the shanty-man's shirts and blankets are their favourite breeding place, and any-where over a shantyman's person is their hunting grounds. They are built somewhat on the principle of a potato bug, and an old male one is almost as large . . .

THE CATTLE ROUND-UP, 1906
John O. McHugh

The H2 ranch's cattle round-up in the fall of 1906 was just before the severe winter that hit everyone so hard. Most cattle outfits lost at least fifty per cent of the herds and a good many ranches lost more. But that fall we had no idea of the weather that was in store for us.

Most of the H2 cattle ranged between fifteen and twenty miles of the home ranch; the ranch was flanked on the north by the Bow River and

230

just a few miles east of the buildings the river took a big bend to the north, so this took in a lot of north-east grazing as well as straight east, south, and west. In describing the range I must not forget to tell you about the two Arrowwood Creeks that run from the south-west to the north-east, where they empty into the Bow River. These creeks are about five miles apart depending on where you cross them, as the distance between them varies as they run across the prairie. They have cut out ravines which vary in width and depth depending upon the contours of the country they pass through. They are identified as East Arrowwood and West Arrowwood. They are located in a south-easterly direction from the H2 Ranch and the most of the cattle herds watered on these streams when out on the range. In the late summer the grass near these watering places was very short on account of so much grazing, and the cattle after watering would hang around for a couple of hours, and then drift back to where the grass was plentiful. Sometimes going two or three miles back, you could see them strung out for a mile or so following one another on well-worn paths. Possibly while riding around the range you might also see patches of buffalo brush that grew to a height of from two to three feet. Near one of these patches you might see one cow all alone and wonder why she had not gone out to graze with the others. Then, when riding through the buffalo brush you would see about a dozen young calves pop up and then you would know what the cow was doing there alone. She was baby-sitting with the young calves while their mothers were out shopping. The young calves found it too tiring to go back to the good grazing with their mothers, and the mothers, after filling up on good grass, would string back again to where they left their calves. Then it would be the calves' turn to get a bellyful of nice fresh milk from their mothers.

To watch the wanderings of the different herds of cattle and the timing of the various functions of the day was a study in itself. As the young cowboy began to notice these things, he gradually gained experience in the handling of stock and therefore became more valuable to his employer. Many puzzling questions would arise and if he had sufficient experience he could generally figure out the answer.

On these close round-ups we used the chuck wagon, an ordinary wagon with a two to three decker box on it. The tailgate of the box was removed and in its place was fitted what we called a chuck-box. This box was approximately four feet high and about three feet deep and was all fitted out like a pantry, having shelves and divisions and drawers, etc. The box would open by pulling down the side facing the rear. The side pulled down had a leg in the centre and was hinged to the box. When pulled down, the hinges would hold it in place at the bottom of the box, and the one leg would drop out on a hinge and would reach the ground to form a table for the cook. We also had a curtain that dropped down over the end of the box to keep out the dust.

The cook tent was pitched so that the door was right up against the table. The tin stove was set in place, the stove pipes put up, and a fire kindled with wood. After it got going good the cook would look around for some "buffalo chips" or some old and dried cow droppings and put them on the fire. They would burn slowly and keep a nice fire sufficient for cooking. He would then start his meal, boil spuds with their jackets on, put on a pot of pork and beans, fry some steaks, boil some dried apples or prunes, and make some tea or coffee. At the proper time he would call out: "Come and get it before I throw it out!"

The cook would have all the food on the stove and as each cowpuncher filed in he would pick up a cup, spoon, knife, fork, and plate near the door. Then he would make the rounds of the pots, piling up grub on his plate and filling his cup with tea or coffee. When loaded up, he would go over to a corner of the tent, sit on a bed roll, place his plate on his knees, his cup on the ground, and eat. When he was finished he would take the eating things out, scrape off his plate, and put them in a big wash-up pan which was waiting to receive them. I have followed one man through the routine so that you would have an idea of camp life. If you multiply this by ten or twelve which would generally complete the crew of cowboys on the round-up, you would have the picture. Add a little confusion which occurred at times, especially when the cowboys would be extra hungry and try to rush things a little . . .

After dinner the jingler would corral the cavey (that means the man who was herding or guarding the extra saddle horses would put them in the corral). This consisted of a long rope about every ten feet. This long rope would be placed on the ground in a circle, leaving a space open to act as a gate entrance. The guy ropes would be fastened to the ground by means of stakes. There would be a number of willow stakes, about three and one half feet long, with forked ends. These forked ends would be put under the guy rope near the circular rope, and the stake would be placed standing up, thus raising the long circular rope. As each stake was put in place the long rope would form a circle, and we would have a round rope corral. Although there was only one rope as a fence the horses usually stayed inside, and if any tried to escape there would be men standing around to stop them.

It was something to see the different stunts and evasive tactics the older horses would think up to prevent their being chosen for a ride. Some would put their heads down near the ground and keep them there so you could not rope them. Others would keep their heads up but when you threw the loop at them they would dodge just enough so the rope would miss, and then they would look at you, and you could imagine what they were thinking. So you would pull your rope in, build another

232

loop, and throw again. If you missed three times in succession you lost your reputation, and another man would step in and try. Sometimes you would stand around with your bridle in hand while other men would be getting their horses and saddling up and you would begin to hatch up a little grudge against the horse that caused you to lose your roping reputation. But when you finally got him, you would lose all antagonism as you would realize you had a good servant and a faithful pal for the afternoon ride and he was entitled to his little joke on you. When you threw on your saddle and mounted, you would go off together the best of pals.

Each cowboy would have a string of from six to twelve horses and as he would only ride one horse at a time, the others would be turned loose to graze. When the captain of the round-up wanted the horses of the cavey put in the rope corral, he would just say, "Jingle the cavey." The man that herded and watched them at night was called the Night Hawk. The twenty-four hours of the day was divided between the Jingler and the Night Hawk into two shifts of twelve hours each. This left three men around camp all the time and when a move was to be made, it was up to these three men – the cook, the Jingler, and the Night Hawk. They had to catch the wagon horses, harness them, strike camp and move; then set up camp in its new location. There would be two tents, one for the cooking and sleeping and one tent for sleeping only. The three camp attendants would sleep in the cook tent, and the cowboys that rode circle would sleep in the other tent. When the night guard on the herd that was already rounded up would be changed every two hours, they would not disturb the two camp attendants. At this time the Night Hawk would be on duty with his cavey.

For bedding we would use a ground sheet, or bed sheet as we called them. This was a canvas sheet just over twice as long as the blankets and about six inches wider than the width of the blankets. It had a row of snaps and rings on the side. To make up one of these beds you would first spread out the sheet, spread your blankets on one half, and pull the other half over and snap the sides. To roll them you would start at the end, which would be the open end, and you would have a neat bed roll, wrapped securely in a canvas sheet and tied with a small rope. You could then throw it in the wagon box for a move or leave it in the tent to sit on.

The first chore in the morning after getting dressed was to roll up your bed which was spread out on the ground for sleeping. Then you went to the rope corral and got your mount for the morning circle. A great many of these horses used for the morning circle were green at the job, what we called colts. They were just freshly broken and it was a matter of schooling for them on the morning circle. We would go out around the outlying bunches of cattle and start them in to a central assembly point, and it was not necessary to have a well trained horse for this purpose. Many of these horses put on a bucking exhibition for a starter, but you would generally tell before you mounted him what you could expect, because when you saddled him up, he would get a hump in his back and would keep it there until he uncorked. After that he would straighten out and act fairly decently for the rest of the ride, although you had to watch him and be on the alert for any further demonstrations.

The round-up captain instructed the men as to the circles they would take. There was what he would call the inside circle which would be to go to the cattle that were grazing out to about five miles and bring them into the central point. In this case we figured on making a cut (which means separating the cattle according to brand) on a good-sized flat on the West Arrowwood Creek. They would drive easily towards the water where after they had a drink they would be held in a herd. The outside circle would cover almost to a ten-mile limit, and any cattle found on the outside circle would also be started into the central bunch. Now you should be able to get the picture of cattle stringing along from all directions into a centre. The bulls of each bunch would generally be in the lead and would be bellowing as they came, stopping now and again to paw the ground and roar their defiance to all comers . . .

When all the outer circle riders got in with their drives of cattle, they were all held together in one herd, eighteen hundred to two thousand head. It was just about noon so we had dinner and changed horses again. This time we took the old and well-trained horses to work and cut the herd. To work a herd of this size took a good many hours and we set to as soon as possible. There were a number of riders assigned to holding the herd and a number appointed to ride into the herd and cut out the H2 cattle. If you were riding a good cutting horse it simplified matters. You would ride into the herd and on spotting an H2 you would put your horse on it and once the horse knew the one you wanted he would never leave it until it was out of the bunch. He would follow it and work it to the edge of the herd on the side where he was cutting out and starting another herd of cut-outs. When the animal was out of the herd it would generally break back to try and re-enter, but the horse would run him clear. The critter would then see the other bunch and go over to join them.

Often in a large herd a holder and a cutter would change jobs so that the cutting horse would have work that wasn't quite so strenuous, and after about half an hour they would change back again. And so the work went on until the herd was worked and the cutting all finished. Then the herd would be started off to one side, two cowboys on either side forming a funnel or bottleneck where all the herd would pass a few at a time to be checked over for any H2's that might have been missed. The cut herd

234

would be kept under guard both day and night until an opportune time arrived to start them back to the ranch.

I have outlined a day's busy procedure on a round-up, and it should give you an idea of how interesting and fascinating the cowboy's life was when the country was all open. This was before the homesteader came in and fenced it up. If there was sufficient time before dark, the camp attendants would strike camp for a quick, short move. The Night Hawk would generally drive the chuck wagon, having four horses to pull it. He would start off with a whoop and crack the whip, and he and the cook with all the camp equipment in the wagon would go galloping across the prairie to the next camp site with the Jingler whooping it up behind the cavey and trying to keep up to the chuck wagon. It was really something to see this mad dash – four horses pulling a wagon, all on the high lope and the galloping cavey behind. From the time they arrived at the new camp site it would take about forty-five minutes to make camp and have the next meal cooking on the stove. As soon as they stopped they would unhitch the chuck-wagon horses, unharness them, and turn them loose, climb in the wagon, throw out the cook tent, let down the cook's table, put up the cook tent, set the stove in place, put the pipes up, and light a fire. While the cook was preparing the next meal the Jingler and Night Hawk would finish staking out the rest of the guys of the cook tent and putting in a few stakes along the side canvas. When the circle riders arrived it would be up to them to pitch the other tent, stake it down, throw the bed rolls out of the wagon, put them in the tents, and put up the rope corral. Everyone moved at a fast clip when there was anything to be done.

THE TWO BIT CAYUSE

Original author unknown. Brought up through the years in the memory of John O. McHugh

I've twisted bronchos off and on
Ever since I hit the trail
And I think I know a cayuse
From his nostrils to his tail.

But 'twas down on the old Bow River
In the year of nineteen-one
When I was twisting bronchos
For F.A. McHugh and Sons.

Now there they had a buckskin cayuse
He wasn't worth two bits to keep.
He had a black strip down his back
And wool just like a sheep.

He wasn't much to saddle
And it darned near killed the boss
To have to pay ten dollars
To break that two bit hoss.

But when I crawled upon him
He took naturally to air
And every time he went aloft
He tried to leave me there.

Until at last he went so high
The lights of Gleichen shone
And there we parted company
And he came down alone.

Well the boss drug me in the bunk shack
And said "Twister don't you croak
For you've got a ten spot coming when
That two bit hoss is broke."

I ain't got no millionaire relation
Awaiting me down east
But I ain't going to ride no aeroplane
Or electric flying beast.

But I'll sell my chaps and saddle,
Let my long shank spurs rust,
For now and then you'll find a horse
That yours truly cannot bust.

13. AUTOGRAPH VERSES FROM SASKATCHEWAN
Edith Fowke

Children's lore has not been extensively explored in Canada, although it is the easiest form of folklore to collect. Still, a number of people have noted various skipping, ball bouncing, and counting out rhymes and singing games. So far non-singing games and autograph verses have been largely neglected.

Because of the dearth of English-Canadian folklore from Saskatch-ewan, I have chosen to represent children's lore by the following verses culled from autograph books filled by friends in Lumsden and Regina between 1927 and 1933. Most of them appear in similar collections from other regions, and many are still turning up in the books of modern-day children.

REMEMBER ME

1. I oughta smile
   I oughta laugh
   But in this book
   I autograph.

2. What shall I write?
   What shall it be?
   Just two words
   Remember me.

3. If scribbling in books
   Remembrance ensures,
   With the greatest of pleasure
   I'll scribble in yours.

4. Remember me when far far off
   Where woodchucks die with the whooping cough.

5. On this clean page
   On this clean spot
   I'll write the words
   Forget-me-not.

6. Your album
   Is a garden plot
   In which I plant
   Forget-me-not.

7. When you are washing in the tub
   Think of me before you rub.
   If the water is too hot
   Cool it but forget-me-not.

8.   A word there is in every tongue,
     A word to memory dear,
     In English 'tis "Forget-me-not,"
     In French 'tis "Souvenir."

9.   If you see a monkey in a tree
     Pull his tail and think of me.

10. When you glance through this book
     As you often will
     Think of the silly guy
     Who wrote up hill. [*lines written on a slant*]

11. Forget you? No, I never can
     As long as I can whistle.
     I may as well forget to scream
     When I sit on a thistle.

12. In the woodbox of your memory
     May I always be a chip.

GOOD WISHES

13. I wish you health, I wish you wealth,
     I wish you joy in store,
     I wish you heaven after death,
     What could I wish you more?

14. May she to whom this book belongs
     Few sorrows know, if any,
     Her gloomy hours be short and few
     And her happy days be many.

15. Take the word Pluck
     Subtract the letter P
     And what is left
     I wish to thee.

16. May you never feel the colour of this page [*blue*].

17. Rosy is this page
     Tho' marred by me
     But rosier still
     May your future be. [*written on a pink page*]

238

18. May Dame Fortune always smile on you
    But never her daughter Misfortune.

19. May you have just enough clouds in your life
    To make a glorious sunset.

20. May your life be like arithmetic –
    Friends added, joys multiplied,
    Sorrows subtracted, and enemies divided.

21. In the equation of your life
    May sorrow be the unknown quantity.

22. May your life be like a footprint,
    Leave a mark but not a stain.

23. May the crosses of your life
    Be entwined with roses. [*lines written to form a cross*]

24. May a mousie never leave your flour barrel with a tear-drop in her
    eye.

FRIENDSHIP

25. Find new friends
    But keep the old,
    One is silver
    The other gold.

26. Friends are like melons.
    Do you want to know why?
    If you want to find a good one
    A hundred you must try.

27. Choose not your friends by outward show
    For feathers float while pearls lie low.

28. Friends are like ivy on a wall,
    Together they stand and together they fall.

29. A friend is one who knows all about you
    And loves you just the same.

30. I wish I were a bunny
    With a little tail of fluff,
    I'd jump upon your bureau
    And be your powder puff.

31. In your little Ford of friendship
    Regard me as a rattle.

32. Leaves may wither
    Flowers may die
    Friends may forget
    But never will I.

33. I am just like an empty purse,
    There is no change in me.

34. When rocks and hills divide us
    And you no more I see
    Just take your old tin lizzie
    And come and visit me.

35. As down the river of life I glide
    In my little bark canoe
    I hope we will have a lovely ride
    And only have room for me and you.

```
                                 N       E
                                 O       S
                                         E
                         E       L       N
         U               H       E       I
36.      O               T       B       H
         Y      F        Y       L       C
         E      O        L       A
         V      Y        P       A       T
         O      A        M       R       O
         L      W        I       O       N
                         S       N
         I      E                N       S
                S        T       T       I
         G      E        U       E
         N      N        B       T       S
         I      I                K       I
         Y      H        A       C
         A      C        E       I       S
         S               T       T       H
                                         T
```

240

ADVICE

37. Keep your face towards the sunshine
    And the shadows will fall behind you.

38. Never

    And never

    But always

39. Don't take life too seriously,
    You won't come out alive anyway.

40. Be happy while you're livin'
    You're a long time dead.

41. Any poor old fish
    Can drift along and dream
    But it takes a regular live one
    To swim against the stream.

42. When you are up to your neck in hot water
    Be like the kettle and sing.

43. Always be like a piano – upright,
    grand, and square.

44. When you come to the end of your rope
    Tie a knot and hang on.

45. ook up
    augh
    ove
    ift.

46. Why stay in and study
    An ancient history date
    When you can make a modern one
    At a quarter after eight.

47. Don't worry, kid.
    Just remember the mighty oak
    Was once a little nut like you.

48. Men's love is like Scotch snuff –
    Take a pinch and that's enough.
    Profit by this sage advice –
    When you fall in love think twice.

CURIOUS COMMENT

1. You may talk of the very mild weather,
    You may speak of the birds how they sing,
    But when a man sits on the point of a tack
    It's a sign of an early spring.

2. He who sits on a thistle
    Shall surely rise.

3. For beauty I know I'm no star,
    There are others more handsome by far,
    But my face I don't mind it,
    You see, I'm behind it.
    It's you guys out in front get the jar.

4. Y Y U R
    Y Y U B
    I C U R
    Y Y 4 me.

5. This world that we're living in
    Is mighty hard to beat.
    We get a thorn with every rose
    But ain't the roses sweet?

6. The more you study,   The less you study,
    The more you know;   The less you know;
    The more you know,   The less you know,
    The more you forget;   The less you forget;
    The more you forget,   The less you forget,
    The less you know,   The more you know,
    So why study?   SO WHY STUDY?

7. When the world looks sorter black
    'N' you feel inclined to cuss,
    It's satisfaction just to think
    The blame thing might be wuss.

242

8. Two in a hammock
   Attempted to kiss
   When all of a sudden
   They landed like ˙sıɥʇ

9. Adam made love to Eve,
   Punch made love to Judy,
   But the funniest thing I ever did see
   Was a flea making love to a cootie.

10. By hook or by crook
    I'll be last in your book.

11. By pen or by quill
    I'll be darned if you will.

12. Just to outdo another
    I'll write on the cover.

14. WESTERN VERNACULAR
John D. Higinbotham

In recent years scholars have been studying the amalgam that is our language and tracing the development of Canadianisms. M. H. Scargill notes:

> *It is in its vocabulary that Canadian English is most distinctive; and it is in its varied names that Canadian English is most appealing . . . Although, as is the case with American English, the greater part of the vocabulary is shared with British English because it is derived from that source, hundreds of words of various origins have made their way into the Canadian language either directly or through the United States. New names for new conditions of life, for new flora and fauna, for new peoples, new politics, new weather, all have joined the vocabulary of the new world to that of the old in Canadian English and given it a vitality and variety that few other languages know.*

Regional studies of dialects and place names in Canada are numerous; the largest number deal with Newfoundland, and others with eastern Canada. Because the west has not been surveyed as exten-

sively, the following article by John David Higinbotham is of particular interest. Mr. Higinbotham (1864-1961), a pioneer Lethbridge druggist who lived in southern Alberta during the 1880s, gives a remarkably comprehensive survey of the language of western Canada during its early period of settlement.

There is something particularly picturesque and expressive, if not entirely elegant and refined, about the vernacular of the West. To the "pilgrim," "stranger," or "tenderfoot," the phraseology is frequently "Greek" and almost invariably bewildering. "Use and wont," as Carlyle has said, "everywhere lead us by the nose" and had he resided in the West, he would unquestionably have added by the ears also, for ere long the strange expressions lose their grossness, vulgarity, and novelty to the newcomer and slowly but surely he finds himself unconsciously using them and eventually incorporating them permanently into his vocabulary.

"Westerners as a rule speak the purest of English," writes a Briton, an editor of more than average ability, "but in their conversation many words are used which are not found in Worcester or Webster." This is not saying, however, that they will not be, for already many native-born Western words have not only found their way Eastward, where they are now used colloquially, but even into the modern dictionaries. The Westerner, however, does not await the dictum of the lexicographer, but generally uses the words first to hand and best suitable for clothing his ideas or giving force to his expressions . . . .

When I first hung out my pharmacy shingle in the West in 1881, I was a thorough "tenderfoot." A cowboy – named from his gambling proclivities "Seven-up Davis" alias "Four-Jack Bob" – wearing a buckskin shirt and pair of chaps (leather overalls), with his sombrero on the back of his head, walked into my dispensary. After eyeing the rows of, to him, mysterious-looking bottles and then me, he said: "Say, young man, are you the doc that runs this pisin-slinging outfit?" I replied that I acted in that capacity.

"Well then," said he, "can you save it today?" I told him that I did not understand what he meant.

"Look-a-there now, none of yer joshing; can't you save a life?" I answered that I would endeavour to do my utmost, but desired to know who was dying. His huge frame shook with laughter at my ignorance of Hesperian vernacular, and then said: "What! No Rocky Mountain Dew, no Old Alky, or to give you the straight tip, seein' you're a pilgrim, none of the Old Creatur, eh? I raised a cache yesterday," he went on, "but blew it all in last night, and now I am feeling dead tough, hat two sizes too small, and head aching as if I'd been busting a broncho, for there's none left to straighten up on; so loosen up, now, young feller, and give me a pick-me-up."

I returned shortly with a tonic-potion which as suddenly disappeared as if he had run the "joker" up his sleeve. After thanking me in his rough manner, he threw a one dollar bill on the prescription desk and was making his exit when I called him back for his change, remarking that half of it was more than sufficient. Remonstrance was in vain, for his reply, as he closed the door, was: "Corral your dust, young man, four bits ain't enough for such a way-up lay-out."

Where but in the West would one hear of a person being "so cross-eyed that when he wept the tears ran down his back." What a vision instantly appears when one hears them say, "Too dead to be buried was that old cayuse," or what malediction in "Them coal miners have hearts so *small* that you could pack them into the kernel of a mustard seed, and so *hard* that they'd punch a hole in the buzz-saw of a mosquito."

Hippocrates and Longfellow both gave it as their opinion that art was long and time fleeting; the western philosopher's version of it is: "We're a short time living and a long time dead." . . .

What could be more forcible than the expression used by a cowboy after he had performed a magic feat in harness repairing: "Hold, sir? Yes, till hell freezes over!" Or more descriptive than: "He was running that fast that you could have played a game of draw poker on his shirt-tail." Descriptive also: "That pony is not as large as a bar of soap after a hard day's washing."

The cattle rustler who invented the "spade brand" (a spade or shovel heated to redness and applied over a horse or cattle brand for the purpose of obliterating it) is said to have died so suddenly of "diptheria" that he hadn't time to get his boots off; he "danced on air," or was, in other words, lynched.

An untameable animal is sometimes described as being "wild and woolly and hard to curry and never to be combed below the knees."

An Indian, on account of his insatiable appetite "has no meal time 'cept all the time, when he has material to work upon."

As saloons, "joints," and "hangouts," at time euphemistically described as "parlours," have always been numerous factors in almost every Western town, drinking terms are consequently many and varied. A thirsty habitué of one of these resorts described his feeling in the following: "I've a head like a bee-hive, and I'm dry as a bit of salt codfish inside a bed of hot ashes." The bartender, at the request of one who has deposited the necessary amount of "dust," politely says: "Name yer pizen, gentlemen." Another "whisky slinger's" call, "Come, fellers, get yer feet into the trough," is a somewhat coarser phrase . . .

If the language in ordinary use in the Old West was descriptive, poetic, and fanciful, none the less so were its extraordinary nicknames. There is no doubt that many an alias was assumed in order to conceal a dubious past, and perhaps to avoid answering in court for crimes committed which might merit the wearing of inconveniently heavy "government jewellery" (ball and chain).

Doubtless many of these appellations were given in contempt, derision, or sportive familiarity, or from one or more of the following sources:

On account of general appearance or complexion as: Black Steve, Bear-paw Jack, Bleary-eyed Bill, Cat-eyed Dick, Flopping Bill, Sawed-Off, Short and Dirty, and Tanglefoot Ben.

Card-game names: Four-Jack Bob (a muleskinner who lost a string of mules by betting on four jacks, or knaves), Keno Bill, Poker Brown, Monte Joe, and Seven-up Davis.

Characteristic idiosyncrasies, history, or occupation: Adobe Jack, Calamity Jim, Clinker Charlie (this personage mistook a clinker for gold-bearing quartz), Dog-eating Jack, Johnny-come-lately, Coyote Frank, Liver-eating Johnson, Rattlesnake Jim, Sand-bag Tom, Sourdough Bill, Steam-boat George, Yeast-powder Bill, Whisky Brown, and the Man-who-has-a-dress-suit.

Habitat: Alberta Jim, Belly-Butte Jim, Canada Bill, Cut-blank John, Mississip, Montana Joe, Irish, Old Cheyenne, and Sweet-grass Billy.

Religion: Dogan Bill, Jew Jake, Mormon Bill, and Parson Tom.

Ranch Life: Billy-the-buster, Broncho Jack, Bull-whacking Ben, Buzzard Head Andy, Diamond R Brown (from cattle brand), and Six-line Jack.

The following are some of the peculiar place-names found in the West: Bear Gulch, Bull's Head, Dead Man's Coulee, Eyebrow Hills, Freeze Out, Ghost Pound Creek, Hill of the Murdered Scout, Medicine Hat (or The Hat), Moose Jaw (or The place-where-the-white-man-mended-his-cart-with-a-moose-jaw-bone), Pile of Bones Creek, The River that Turns, Robber's Roost, Scratching Hills (used by the buffalo when "moulting"), Seven Persons Creek, Skunk Bluff, Stand Off, Slide Out, Whoop-up, Whisky Gap, and Writing-on-Stone . . .

The following is a guide to some of the common phrases encountered in southern Alberta during the 1880s:

"Arbitrators" is a somewhat descriptive name applied by the gambling fraternity to dice. The six-shooter, six-gun (usually shortened into "gun") and shooting-iron are also known as "arbitrators" but much more frequently as "equalizers." Among stockmen a hard winter is also called an "equalizer." A certain pugilist of more than local fame is reported to have insulted a Western cowboy of rather diminutive stature. The latter observed that the Lord had created big and little men but that Colonel Colt had made "equalizers," one of which the puncher quickly produced and elevated. A glance down its gleaming barrel brought from the bully a hasty apology and checked effectually further insolence.

"Ari-stock-rats," sometimes "moccasin aristocracy," is a term used to designate the half breeds (or Métis, which they prefer being called).

"Away up" or "way up in the red" is the *magnum bonum* of life and no doubt had its origin among gamblers, red chips in the game of poker usually denoting high stakes. The above expression is also used as descriptive of an exhilarant state of being, such a person is also said to be feeling "pretty lucky"; one in the opposite condition of health is "a little off his feed." A complaining petulant person goes about "beefing,""belly-aching," or "grousing." . . .

A person in dire straits is "down to bed-rock" or "hard-pan"; "away-in-the-hole" and "out-at-the-seat" are also indicative of poverty, while any predicament with but one outlet is spoken of as a "ground-hog case."

A "broncho-buster" is a man who breaks in range horses to the saddle; he is also known as a "buccaroo." An untrained native horse is a "broncho" and the short quick jumps he makes when first saddled are called "bucks" or "buck-jumps." A man "bucks" when he deliberately refuses to obey. "He came to the last hurdle and then he bucked" is a ranch simile illustrative of rebellion after being driven to desperation. Male Indians, likewise constables in the Mounted Police, are denominated "bucks."

In the early days freight had to be brought into the country by bull and mule trains; the drivers employed on the former were "bull-whackers," on the latter they were designated "mule-skinners." The whole train, consisting of five or six "strings" of twenty bulls yoked to three "prairie-schooners" or canvas-topped wagons, is superintended by a "wagon-boss." When any obstruction is encountered, such as a river or steep hill, one wagon is frequently unlimbered and left until called for; this operation is termed "dropping trail."

"Bad medicine," "chaffy," "snide," "jim-crow," and "pizen" are applied to anything worthless on the Eastern slope of the Rockies while "cultus" – a Chinook Indian word – is most frequently employed with like significance upon the B.C. side. The first of these words is strictly of Indian origin and refers to the divinings of their "medicine man." Telegraph- wires are "bad medicine" to the red men, on account, it is supposed, of the havoc played by the electric current among some of the "braves" who were too inquisitive and meddlesome.

Eight "bits" make a dollar, a bit in silver amounting to 12½ cents. Money is known under a variety of appelations, some of which are rarely used. Here are a few:

The "beans," "chips," "checks," "dope," "dust," "flimsey," "lead," "meaks-kim" (Blackfoot), "needful," the "queer" (counterfeit), "rocks," "root," "scads," "stamps," "shinnias" (Cree), "otter-skins," and "the velvet." "Dig-up" is the Western equivalent for "raise the wind" in the east, and a person in affluent circumstances is "well heeled" or "well hooked-up."

A dance, entertainment, or spree is known as a "blow-out," and when a man squanders his "pile" upon anything he "blows himself."

A detached low mountain is a "butte," a steeply rising hill with a flat or rounded front is a "bluff," a narrow ridge of land is known as a "hog's-back," and the precipitous escarpments of clay bordering on a river are "cut-banks." The dry bed of a stream when deep is a "gulch" or "coulee," its inclined sides distinguishing it from a canyon the sides of which are perpendicular.

Anything hidden, especially if in the ground, is "cached." To "raise a cache" is to come upon or discover a quantity of liquor that has been concealed. A "cayuse" is an Indian pony, also called a "shaganappi" (literally, common or ordinary); this word is, however, usually applied to raw-hide.

Western clergymen or missionaries are "church-agents," "devil-dodgers", "gospel- grinders," "gospel-pounders," "hymn-howlers," and "sky-pilots." The churches are "gospel-mills" from the pulpits of which they dispense "soul-grub" to the people.

When a person dies he is said to have "crossed the great divide," "gone to the sand- hills" (Indian), "passed in his checks," or "moved over the range." The clergyman is then called in to give him a good "send-off." The usual result of a "lynching-bee" is that one has taken the "hemp-line route to the great hereafter."

A fenced enclosure in which cattle or horses are temporarily confined for branding or other purposes is a "corral." This word is also used as a verb meaning to capture, surround, or detain.

The "drop," "dead nuts," and "dead immortal cinche" express a certainty, the inevitable, so also "dead open and shut" and "shut like a jackknife," but when you hear a "mule-skinner" say that his leaders "jackknifed" on him he merely conveys the information that the mules at the head of his string swung around until they faced him.

In the commissariat department grub is a general term for everything eatable. Under this head we have:

"Sour-dough," "dope" (butter), "dough-gods" (dumplings), "flap-jacks" (pancakes), "tin-cow" (condensed milk), "rattle-snake" (bacon), "sow-belly" (pork), "tent-pegs" (beef-steak cut into strips for camp use, especially if frozen), "baked-wind-pills" (Boston baked beans), "mountain oysters" (calves fries).

248

If a meal is longer in preparation than is considered necessary the cook is apt to be reminded that "we can't live on scenery for supper." When the "lay-out" is complete the cook calls: "grub-pile!" "wire in!" "grab-a-root!" or "come-a-runnin', you hungry hunters!" "Now, all you primeolifers, food's ready" is a somewhat more high-falutin' invitation.

Smugglers of contraband whisky from the United States into the Territories during the prohibition regime were "wine merchants," "importers," and "keg angels." A man was regarded as something akin to an angel if he was able to evade the vigilance of the Mounted Police.

Under the general term liquor we have "old alky" (alcohol), "red-eye," "blue-joint," "benzine," "bug-juice," "rot-gut," "tangle-foot," "life-saver," "pizen," "old creatur," "ozone," and "coffin-varnish" for whisky and "four percent" for a milder variety of beer.

A person "tears the bone out" when he exhibits great activity and when a "midnight rustler" (thief) "snakes" off his comrade's "plunder" (effects) and gets into a "fix" and in consequence has to "jump-the-ranch" he usually rides so fast that he "just hits the ground in high places." If, however, his pursuers "camp-on-his-trail" and things look "corky" for him he will likely "stand them off" with his rifle, but if they get "the drop" on him he will "weaken" and "loosen-up" his ill-gotten gains. If he refused to do this he would be "trail-branded till Kingdom come" (killed at the roadside).

Many of the words used by the cowboys in describing their outfit are, or were, originally from the Spanish. The leather leggings or breeches worn by them are "chaps" (chaparejos), their broad-brimmed hat with a leather hat-band is a "sombrero," the foot covers attached to the stir-rups and which frequently have long trailing ends are "tabaderos," their braided rope made of raw-hide or horse-hair is a "lariat" or "lasso."

A "hackamore" is a raw-hide or horse-hair halter, and a "macartie" is a rope of the same materials usually connected with the hackamore by means of a "theodore," or throat-latch.

A "latigo" is a long leather thong about an inch and a half wide used for tying the "cinche" and which takes the place of the buckle and strap of an ordinary English girth. The "vastos" is the outer skirt of a Mexican or stock saddle including the lining, a leather covering for the same is a "macheers," and the saddle-bags are "catenas." Again, in stockmen's language an orphaned or unbranded calf is a "dogy" or "maverick," a stupid animal is a "buzzard-head," a lean or bony one is a "crow-bait" or "harness-rack," an inferior one a "scrub." Newly imported and consequently unacclimatized cattle are "pilgrims," also applied to those unable to "rustle" or hunt for food.

An animal is "hog-tied" when thrown and all four feet tied together, "dewlapped" when the flesh of the brisket is cut leaving pendant pieces for purposes of recognition, and "wattled" when a similar operation is performed upon the jaw.

A collection of horses or cattle is a "band" or "bunch," and to separate one or more from the number is to "cut-out"; the latter word when applied to work of any description signifies planned or arranged. With reference to the above a cowboy who while upon "night-herd" had been contemplating the starry heavens remarked to his companion without the least intention of being irreverent: "I tell you, if God went to name those stars, He'd have His work cut out, wouldn't He?"

When a "band" becomes "rattled" (panic stricken) and they travel rapidly in the direction of the Rockies they are said to have "rolled their tails for the mountains." By hard riding on the part of the punchers a stampede is frequently "headed-off" or "milled." The latter is accomplished by turning the leaders and causing them to move in a circle until they run themselves down or tie themselves up. They are then "rounded-up" and driven back to their "range" or "stamping-grounds."

A ranchman's overalls are made of "Montana broadcloth," otherwise known as "duck." His waterproof coat is a "slicker," his riding whip a "quirt." In Western parlance courage is "sand," while credit is "jaw-bone," sometimes abbreviated into "jaw." To tease a person is to "josh" them; to carry anything is to "pack" it; feathers are "goose-hair"; a restaurant is a "hash-joint"; a "gunny-sack" or "war-pack" describes any receptacle from a canvas bag to a portmanteau; to drag anything is to "snake" it (this word also means to steal). When a "road-agent" or highwayman "holds you up" (compels you to throw up your hands), if he relieves you of your all you are "set plumb afoot." This term also applies in a painfully literal sense when you are "forty miles from nowhere" on the prairie and your horse draws his picket-pin and decamps for his range.

When one is obliged to undergo any humiliation he "chews dirt" or "gets the lash"; when married he is "hitched" or "hobbled"; if active he is said to "hump" himself and when he exhibits continuity in any field of labour he "stays-with-it" or "freezes-to-it."

In a certain town in southern Alberta a chief topic of conversation amongst local politicians was as to whether or not "shackers" would be permitted to vote at an election, a "shacker" being a person who occupies a temporary residence commonly known as a shanty or "shack." A house partly or wholly excavated in the side of a hill or mound is a "dugout."

A miner is "grub-staked" when a merchant or other furnishes him with supplies for his maintenance while prospecting for minerals. If he "strikes-it-rich" the confiding trader is usually rewarded by a share in the "claim." If, however, it does not "pan out" (materialize) he is "out-of-luck" or "in the hole."

That itinerant and ubiquitous personage known in the East as the tramp has a counterpart in the West under the cognomen of "grub-rider." The latter is equipped with a horse and has the happy faculty of arriving at a ranch just about meal time. He usually remains until informed that the proprietor would greatly prefer his room to his company. We have met the son of an English earl engaged in this enobling (?) profession.

Our prevailing warm westerly wind is a "chinook," coming as it does from the direction of the Chinook or Flathead Indian country.

"Outfit" is the great and universal word for any emergency; "lay-out" and "truck" have likewise a multitudinous variety of applications. It used to be said that in the West a person conversing need never be solicitous about running short of a word so long as "outfit" was in his vocabulary.

15. MONSTERS OF THE WEST: THE SASQUATCH AND THE OGOPOGO
M. Carole Henderson

This article surveys a type of modern folklore current in western Canada which has been much in the news in recent years. M. Carole Henderson, a native of British Columbia, is particularly interested in studying the relationship of folklore to Canadian culture. Here she discusses B.C.'s two famous monsters and advances some reasons why legends about monsters circulate more in western Canada than in eastern Canada.

Monsters of one form or another seem to have titillated the human imagination for untold years. Throughout recorded history, people have included super- or sub-human beings, giants, ogres, dragons, fanciful beasts of many descriptions, and frightening figures in widely variant forms among their cultural traditions. That all such people fervently believed in the literal truth of these monsters certainly is open to dispute, but the fact that they told stories about such creatures definitely is not. As Harvey Cox wrote about mankind's propensity for fantasy:

> . . . there is certainly [no culture] that lacks its share of wild and improbable stories. Fairies, goblins, giants, and elves – or their equivalent – inhabit the imagination of every race.[1]

It is, therefore, not at all unexpected that Canadians should have monster traditions, as indeed they have had and still do. The "loup-garou," or werewolf, was a rather common figure in French-Canadian folklore; the Bogey-man in many forms has been and still is used to control Canadian children; some people in Newfoundland still believe in fairies of evil temperament; and the native peoples once entertained various levels of belief in monsters such as Sedna, the hag the Inuit thought lived under the sea, and D'Sonoqua, the cannibal woman of the Pacific North Coast.

What is most surprising about current monster lore in Canada is the nature and locations of the most prominent beast traditions. Today, the most popular Canadian monsters are not those that pervaded the folklore of Canada's earliest and eastern settlers from Europe. Rather, they are the Sasquatch and the Ogopogo which, while having a venerable ancestry in Indian tradition, have acquired peculiar significance for the non-native populace of Canada, especially in the west.

Sasquatch, a wild ape-man of the woods, and Ogopogo, a lake serpent, are most commonly associated with British Columbia. There have, however, been accounts of them, or like forms, elsewhere in Canada and in the United States, as well as abroad. Sasquatch in particular is known in Washington, Oregon, and California where he is commonly referred to as "Bigfoot." Internationally, he appears as the Yeti or famous Abominable Snowman of the Himalayas, and under various names elsewhere. North American accounts of and international parallels to the Sasquatch are given in various sources.[2]

Ogopogo, by contrast, is more exclusively identified with Lake Okanagan in south-central British Columbia, though he or she (the sex of the monster is, as yet, undetermined) has definite relatives both at home and abroad. The Canadian relations include Cadborosaurus, or "Caddie" for short, a sea serpent first reported on October 11, 1933, in Cadboro Bay on the south-east coast of Vancouver Island. The most important international parallel of Ogopogo is, of course, "Nessie," the Great Orm of Loch Ness.[3]

The following discussion concerns the nature of the Sasquatch and the Ogopogo and their history in Canadian cultural tradition. It also considers the possible interpretations of belief in them and explains why these particular monster traditions appear in western Canada though not in eastern Canada. One obvious explanation, and one supported by a number of people, especially those who have reported seeing the monsters, is that these creatures really exist in the west. Many books such as *Sasquatch* by Don Hunter and Rene Dahinden; John Green's three works *On the Track of the Sasquatch, The Year of the Sasquatch,* and *The Sasquatch File*; R. P. MacLean's *Ogopogo: His Story*; and innumerable newspaper and popular magazine accounts give arguments in favour of the actual existence of the monsters. No attempt is made here to validate this explanation; rather, emphasis is given to the folklore nature of these beasts and their role as legendary figures in human culture.

More than three hundred eye-witness reports of Sasquatch/Bigfoot from Canada and the United States, as well as many other accounts, make it possible to create a composite description of the creature. Accordingly, Sasquatch (whose name is an Anglicization of a Coast Salish word meaning roughly "wild man of the woods") is between six and eleven feet, though most commonly seven or eight feet tall. Typically, he is covered in reddish brown or auburn hair, though other hair colours from black to silvery-white have been reported. On his head, this hair grows five to six inches in length and hangs in a "bang" over the forehead. Female Sasquatches (less frequently reported on than the males) have hairy breasts except immediately around the nipples. Other sexual characteristics are seldom remarked upon. The Sasquatch has broad shoulders (up to four feet), a barrel-chest, and no obvious neck, resulting in his hunched appearance. His face is monkey- or ape-like with a backward sloping forehead, a flattened nose, and a slit-like, lipless mouth. Often he is said to have a cone-shaped head and a very prominent big toe. His footprints are between twelve and twenty-two inches, though most commonly fourteen to eighteen inches, long and usually seven inches wide. The Sasquatch has seldom been known to show any aggressive behaviour and has most frequently been described as fleeing or standing immobile, staring expressionless, with his arms by his sides.

David Thompson gave the earliest recorded account of a reputed Sasquatch in a journal kept during his journey across the Rockies near the present-day site of Jasper, Alberta. In his entry for January 5 to 8, 1811, Thompson remarks on the belief current among the natives accompanying him in "the Mammoth" (a huge man-like creature said to inhabit the mountains) and on the party's subsequent discovery of huge tracks considered by the Indians and some of Thompson's men to be those of a young mammoth.[4]

Earlier accounts doubtless would exist had they been collected when extant, for Sasquatch-like beings have been a part of the native folklore of the Americas for centuries. Bacil Kirtley discusses the role of such creatures in the folklore of the North American native peoples in an article, "Unknown Hominids and the New World Legends," in *Western Folklore*. In Canada, the Cree told of the Weeketow, the Saulteux of the Windigo, and the Pacific North Coast peoples of wild woods creatures in various forms. In *Klee Wyck*, her account of travels among the Pacific Coast natives, Emily Carr gives a sensitive portrayal of one common form, D'Sonoqua, the cannibal woman who lured children into the woods and stole them away. Representative of Sasquatch stories obtained more recently from Coast Indians is the following account which Wayne Suttle collected from Julius Charles, a Lummi Indian, and published in an article "On the Cultural Track of the Sasquatch":

> The [Straits language term for the Sasquatch] is a great tall animal or whatever it was that lived in the mountains. It was like a man but shaggy like a bear, like a big monkey seven feet tall. They went away when the whites came. (The Indians never killed any; it was a pretty wise animal, or whatever you call it.) If you saw one it made you kind of crazy. They throw their power toward you.
>
> Over 40 years ago some fellow across the line [in Canada] went hunting deer early one morning when snow was on the ground. He saw one and followed it to the edge of a lake where it disappeared. He went home and got kind of crazy. His wife put him to sleep by the fire (they were living in a kind of smokehouse) and while she was out getting wood he rolled into the fire and died. (He was a half-breed named Arthur – lived up toward the Fraser.)

The Coast Indians considered the wilderness in which they lived to be inhabited by many strange creatures, most of which can be identified as animals of nature. Others, unknown to Europeans, have typically, though perhaps unjustifiably, been classified as mythical supernatural beings. It cannot be proven that the Indians themselves saw these creatures as mythical, but anthropologists and other scholars have generally considered them such, much to the dismay of Sasquatch buffs like Rene Dahinden and John Green who cite the Indian stories and belief as evidence for the actual existence of the Sasquatch.

Other than the native accounts, stories of Sasquatches began appearing in the late nineteenth century. The first major account, and the only well-documented story ever of a capture of a supposed Sasquatch, appeared in a Victoria newspaper, *The Daily Colonist*, on Friday, July 4, 1884. Apparently, the crew of a train travelling between Lytton and Yale, B.C., pursued and captured a gorilla-type creature standing about 4 feet, 7 inches tall and weighing about 127 pounds, whom they dubbed "Jacko." He had long, coarse black hair on his head, and resembled a man except for having short glossy black hair all over. His forearm was much longer than a man's and he possessed extraordinary strength demonstrated by his ability to take a fresh branch and tear it in two as no man could do. Jacko's ultimate fate is unknown though he was to be taken to London and exhibited.

There were reports soon after of sightings of similar creatures both in the Fraser Canyon area of the mainland and on Vancouver Island. Accounts of the Sasquatch surfaced sporadically from the 1920s to the 1950s. In the 1920s, J. W. Burns, a school teacher on the Chehalis Indian Reserve near Harrison Hot Springs, popularized the term "Sasquatch" by writing frequent articles about the creature, which were often based on Indian stories and which achieved wide circulation in newspapers and magazines throughout North America. As a result, Harrison Hot Springs adopted the Sasquatch image for advertising purposes, and for some years sponsored a local celebration called "Sasquatch Days."

Another unique Sasquatch story is set in British Columbia in the first half of this century, although it was not collected until thirty-four years after it supposedly occurred. In 1924, Alfred Ostman, a construction worker, spent his vacation looking for a lost gold mine near the head of Toba Inlet in the Coast Mountains. After several days of hiking, camping, and prospecting, during which his camp was disturbed several times, he was awakened one night by something picking him up. He was carried for some hours into the "camp" of a Sasquatch family, consisting of an adult male, adult female, a young girl, and a boy, where he remained captive for six days. He was unharmed by the Sasquatch, who seemingly left him to his own devices, enabling him to observe them at close quarters. He noted that they never ate meat nor did any cooking while he was with them; they spent a considerable portion, but not all, of their waking hours looking for roots and other foodstuffs; and they communicated with one another through sounds and signs. Finally, he managed to escape when a disturbance resulted from the elder male Sasquatch's swallowing a can of snuff. Ostman ran away, was not, to his knowledge, followed, and eventually came upon a logging camp where he was treated hospitably. He told the loggers of his prospecting activities, but nothing about having been captured by a Sasquatch. In 1958 he related his full story to John Green who published it in *On the Track of the Sasquatch*.

Much Sasquatch-lore surfaced in the mid-1950s as a result of the vastly increased publicity the creature received at that time. In 1957, Harrison Hot Springs decided to sponsor a "Sasquatch hunt" as its 1958 British Columbia Centennial project. Though the plan never reached fruition, it achieved its primary purposes of gaining publicity for the region and arousing interest in the Sasquatch. Many people formerly reluctant to discuss their encounters with or stories about the Sasquatch came forward, and soon John Green, editor of the weekly newspaper in nearby Agassiz, amassed a considerable collection of such material, much of which he has published in his books on the subject.

Many of these accounts are similar to the following ones from the Randall V. Mills Memorial Archive of Northwest Folklore at the University of Oregon in Eugene:

SCARED TO DEATH

I talked with a gal from British Columbia who allegedly made a sighting that is interesting in the respect we are talking about

255

because she was out camping at the time with her husband near a lake they, ah, had been there a short time when, ah, she decided to go out into a clear cut area and gather some firewood . . . . She was bent over gathering this firewood and she saw this thing watching her. Now, um, she of course got pretty frightened, went back to camp, was too frightened, she said, to tell her husband because her husband might, ah, disbelieve her or her husband . . . might, ah, just, she didn't want to tell for fear that, for fear of the way he might react, he being a queer, so she kept it to herself as much as she could, but she couldn't sleep that night, she felt very uneasy, she felt as though the hair were standing straight up on her head, finally she broke and told her husband and her husband says, "My God, why didn't you tell me sooner? I felt the same way. I felt strange. I felt as though something bothered me about this place" and they packed up immediately and left. (Collected by Paul Axtell from Jack E. Sullivan of Canby, Oregon in December, 1973.)

A similar story is set on the mountains behind Vancouver:

A BRITISH COLUMBIA BIGFOOT

COLLECTOR: I've been trying to explain what the Sasquatch is for X, she's from New York. Do you know any good stories?

INFORMANT: Hey, that's strange, I'd just been thinking about this truckdriver that picked me up when I was hitching up from L.A. last month. We stopped for lunch along the way and he told me the time he saw the thing himself. He called it Bigfoot though, not Sasquatch.

X: What'd he say about it?

INFORMANT: Well, first he started talking about 'Nam [Viet Nam] and how when he'd been there he'd kept getting this scary feeling every once and awhile where the hairs on the back of his neck would stick out and he'd get shivery all over. He came back and was living with his grandparents up in Vancouver, B.C. One night they got in a fight and he left . . . do you know Vancouver at all?

COLLECTOR: A little, I've been there a couple times.

INFORMANT: Well, there's a road that goes up behind Grouse Mountain and he drove part way up and parked there. He was sitting there when he felt that scary sensation on his neck again. He got so nervous that he drove right off. He went back the next night, just as it was getting dark and he got the same scary feeling. This time he stayed and he said that he was sitting there looking out over the low hills with the moon rising when all of a sudden a huge two-footed animal lumbered across the nearby horizon. It was too big to be a bear and it walked on its hind legs until it went out of sight. (Collected by Helen Rockey from an informant anonymous by request on June 16, 1974.)

Construction crews or lumbercamp gangs have sometimes reported encounters with the Sasquatch. The following is a retold version of one such report from Big Horn Dam, about twenty miles west of Nordegg, Alberta, on August 23, 1969:

There is the old report . . . getting old now, of the workers there were about 15 men or a larger number of men building this dam, and they were looking up on top of this hill and they saw this creature up there watching them and, ah, they thought it was unusual. It looked like a man anyway, but it seemed to be bigger and had hair and so forth. It sat down and they estimated its height because they compared its height when it was sitting with the height of a tree I think or rock and later they went up and they had men looking up there comparing the height of a man to the rock or tree and they estimated his height was fifteen feet. Now that's a good bit big for any man walking on two feet, perhaps they didn't make their estimation right, but one can certainly deduct that it was big. (Collected by Paul Axtell from Jack E. Sullivan, December 1973.)

A more precise "eye-witness" account in Green's *Year of the Sasquatch* gives more specific details, e.g., there were five men altogether watching; the creature was visible for almost an hour, ten minutes of which it sat; its height was estimated by comparing its size and a man's height to trees in the background. The difference between these two versions of the same event – one told from immediate experience and the other second-hand – is a good example of how belief tales and superstitions often become generalized through passage in the oral tradition.

Many other tales tell of Sasquatch frightening people, very occasionally coming into settled territory or disturbing work camps, being sighted in the headlights of cars, and so forth. Since the mid-1950s Sasquatch reports have increased significantly both in the United States and Canada. Interestingly enough, in British Columbia, the Sasquatch himself is seen more often than are his footprints, whereas in the west coast American states the reverse is true.

Despite media portrayals of Bigfoot beliefs and sightings during frontier times, the Sasquatch was not really "discovered" by Americans, in the sense that the general populace became widely aware of the creature, until 1958. Since then, sightings, hunts, footprint casts, innumera-

257

ble newspaper and magazine accounts, and even films (three supposedly of the creature itself and one Hollywood-type "monster" documentary) have become widely known in both Canada and the United States. Professional anthropologists, folklorists, zoologists, and other scholars as well as interested laymen of various backgrounds have devoted considerable attention to the Sasquatch, yet it remains a mystery, though one which now intrigues many people, and which, as a result, is exploited for publicity and profit.

Today the Ogopogo is in a similar position. There are regular sightings of the creature at the same time as it has become symbolic of the Okanagan region, is used in much advertising, and is commemorated in souvenirs, statues, and even an official B.C. Government Department of Recreation and Conservation marker at Squally Point on the west side of Okanagan Lake reading:

> OGOPOGO'S HOME: Before the unimaginative, practical white man came, the fearsome lake monster, N'ha-a-itk, was well known to the primitive superstitious Indians. His home was believed to be a cave at Squally Point, and small animals were carried in the canoes to appease the serpent. Ogopogo is seen each year – but now by white men!

Despite the many sightings, there are relatively few descriptive details, making even a composite picture rather vague. Essentially, Ogopogo is said to be serpentine, dark (often grey-black or deep green) in colour, large (up to sixty feet long), and very strong. It moves – often very quickly – in undulations so that it is most frequently identified by humps appearing above water. It has a head like that of either a sheep or a horse and is, despite earlier categorization as a carnivore, supposedly at least partly vegetarian.

The earliest known records of Ogopogo are the pictographs (drawings on rocks) near Lake Okanagan done before the arrival of the white man. The Okanagan Valley Indians had many stories about and names for this lake demon, monster, or sacred creature which they dreaded. They avoided the Squally Point region, and lived in terror of a storm anywhere on the lake, for they thought that the beast would vent its legendary fury by lashing the waves with its tail, then would rise from the lake and kill them. Travel on the lake therefore commonly necessitated special ceremonies and protective markings on the canoes.

When the first white settlers arrived in the Okanagan Valley in the latter half of the nineteenth century, some of them displayed considerable fear of the lake creature. Men patrolled the lakeshore near Kelowna with guns to protect their homes and families, and some supposedly even tried to catch the beast with makeshift monster fish-lines made of light cable ending in iron hooks baited with fresh meat.

Numerous sightings – both from pioneer days and more recent times – are recounted in Dorothy Hewlett Gellatly's *A Bit of Okanagan History* and R.P. MacLean's pamphlet *Ogopogo: His Story*. In her article on Ogopogo in the *B.C. Motorist* (November-December 1973), Mary Moon gives several oral accounts of sightings including a detailed description of a 1949 incident involving one Leslie Kerry, his wife, and guests. Mr. Kerry was about to take his guests out on the lake in his motorboat when he saw Ogopogo about a hundred feet away, lying on the water with "some thirty snakelike feet visible." The creature's body was shiny, between eight and twelve inches around, and dark olive green "like the back of a trout." There were no fins, but Ogopogo's tail was forked like that of a sockeye salmon, and bobbing up and down. Since no head was visible, Mr. Kerry presumed that the creature was feeding on the lake weeds. Kerry had his guest, a Mr. W. F. Watson, quietly row the boat closer. Watson stopped shortly, however, fearing that the children with them would be frightened or attacked. Everyone there thought that they were seeing the Ogopogo whose sinuous body was showing "about three undulations, apparently separated from each other by a space in which that part of the undulation would have been underwater. The length of each of the undulations that could be seen would have been about five feet." The party watched for five to ten minutes as the whole thing submerged slightly and came back up. Then Kerry called his wife on shore who took a close look, then went to get the binoculars and to call the neighbours. In all, the Ogopogo was visible for some fifteen minutes.

Other accounts have appeared with considerable regularity in British Columbian newspapers. For instance, on July 7, 1954, the *Vancouver Sun* reported that Ogopogo had been sighted by fifteen people at a resort at Peachland. The resort owner, A. M. Moore, who had seen the creature before, said that there were four flat humps visible and that Ogopogo was at least fifty feet long. The lake monster disappeared when a plane flew overhead.

Perhaps the most interesting feature of these stories is that Ogopogo has gradually been transformed from the vicious monster known to the Indians and early settlers into a frightening but beneficent Okanagan mascot. Even the adoption of the name "Ogopogo" reveals this change. Derived from a parody of a popular English music-hall song about a funny and fanciful creature, Ogopogo gradually became accepted as the appropriate name for the local denizen in the late 1920s.

Today, the creature is regarded as the symbol of the region, and of major events held there like the annual Kelowna Regatta. Some people maintain that the Ogopogo is merely a publicity stunt to attract tourists and promote the regatta, and, without a doubt, it is used in this manner. For instance, annually at regatta time, offerings are made to the beast with great ceremony and publicity, so that the weather will be fair for the celebrations. There are, however, many people who are firm in their belief in the creature. Some have formed the Ogopogo Serendipity Society; others harbour their belief silently; and still others strive to validate the lake monster. For example, J. G. Ridland argued that it might be the progeny of a fertile prehistoric egg preserved by a cataclysmic change in temperature in the cold (1°C) bottom water of Lake Okanagan, then propelled by a seismic disturbance to warmer, shallower water suitable to hatch it.[5]

There are many similarities among the recent international eye-witness accounts of the Sasquatch and the Ogopogo. Both also have parallels in the recorded folk traditions of many nations, and fall within the motif categories in Stith Thompson's *Motif Index of Folk Literature*.[6] The tales about these monsters are usually told in one of two ways: either as true stories of personal or second-hand experience, or as tall tales of fabulous beings. This distinction is, essentially, made on the basis of belief since the former stories involve at least some literal belief in the monsters while the latter are grounded in fantasy. This duality of tales probably dates back to the native peoples, as Suttles argues in his paper "On the Cultural Track of the Sasquatch."

Most accounts of the monsters are short, relatively simple, and largely unpatterned. They generally take the form of personal anecdotes or reminiscences, seldom verging on the more definitely structured forms of folktales or becoming sufficiently widespread and standardized to be classified as belief legends. Where there is no belief among the community of tellers or listeners, the stories assume many of the characteristics of tall tales.

The most obvious uses of these monster traditions – publicity and tourism – have already been mentioned. Some people also use the stories to entertain themselves or others, to frighten children into good behaviour, and to delineate special groups of monster hunters and other enthusiasts. Canadian tellers and their audiences commonly associate these stories and the monsters themselves with particular geographic regions, primarily British Columbia. While environmental factors are insufficient to explain the existence and nature of the monster tales, they have certainly had a strong formative influence on these stories. Natural features often play a significant role in the tales themselves: for example, the forested mountains in the Sasquatch stories or lake conditions in the Ogopogo tales. More significantly, at least some of these monster accounts undoubtedly arise from natural conditions. It is not at all difficult to imagine beasts of manifold forms lurking in the thickly forested, frequently mist-covered Coast Range mountains of British Columbia. Also, a very deep lake, bottomless according to some accounts, and given to unpredictable squalls, is food for the inventive mind. Both locales, then, are somewhat fear-inspiring, for they are, to some degree, unknown, largely uncontrolled, and given to changeable conditions. To provide himself with immediately satisfying explanations for such natural phenomena, and to make tangible his fear, "Man tends to conceive the conceivable," as John Napier remarked in *Bigfoot*.[7]

The monsters are clearly vestiges of the retreating wilderness. Stories about them indicate the persistence of the garrison mentality which, according to many scholars, was engrained in Canada's early settlers. This mentality results from the isolation of pockets of civilization amidst the wilderness and the zealous protection of these pockets, or garrisons, from the dangerous, frightening wilderness. The Sasquatch and Ogopogo are, then, symbolic of this danger and fear. Stories in which they are not terribly fearsome such as most of the more recent Ogopogo accounts indicate man's gradual conquest of the wilderness and of his fears associated with it. There are decidedly fewer stories of harmless, non-frightening Sasquatch than similar stories of Ogopogo in part because the Coast Mountains are largely uninhabited, unexplored, and therefore unknown, whereas the Okanagan region is well-populated and thoroughly civilized.

These monster traditions are an integral part of the cultural identity in the regions to which they pertain. In fact, they are among the very few traditions recognized by the Anglo-Canadian majority group in British Columbia which, like most Anglo-Saxon groups, has failed to identify with or through its own folk traditions. It is typical of western Anglo-Canadians to utilize the traditions of the native peoples for cultural expression. Stories about the Sasquatch and Ogopogo illustrate this pseudo-Indianism of the west and indicate the exploitation of native peoples' traditions by western Canadians for the development and maintenance of their distinctiveness.

This last point partly explains the currency of monster traditions in the west, but not in the east of Canada. Eastern Canadians have not relied as much upon native peoples' traditions for the creation and expression of their local cultural identity since, unlike western Canadians, they have had their own shared traditions to use for such purposes. Except among certain minority cultural groups, community-oriented and based traditions, like *Märchen*, legends, and ballads, are difficult to find in western Canada, though not so in the east. The settlement pattern of the country was largely responsible for this situation, for eastern Canada was settled early, by relatively homogeneous groups of people who lived together in villages while western Canada was settled during the industrial era, largely by individuals of diverse ethnic backgrounds. The social and cultural circumstances in the west, then, fostered the creation and preservation of individual traditions like anecdotes, tall tales, and reminiscences – categories to which the monster tales usually belong.

One other reason for the prevalence of monster stories in British Columbia is the fact that wildernesses, and mountainous forested wildernesses in particular, are the legendary milieu of such creatures. These wildernesses exist in few places any more; British Columbia is certainly one of them.

British Columbians, and some other Westerners, maintain and popularize their monsters partly because these creatures are something distinctive which Easterners do not have. The beasts represent the mystery, strength, and untamed nature of large parts of the Canadian west, especially British Columbia. As this area moves fully into the twentieth century, becomes thoroughly "civilized" and populated, the monsters may vanish. Then again, they may persist because they may really be there, or because mankind naturally believes that they are there – somewhere.

16. URBAN TALES
Susan Smith

MIGRATORY LEGENDS

One of the most flourishing types of folklore in modern society is the migratory "belief legend," sometimes known as the "urban tale." As Linda Degh notes, "Legends do not seem to wither under the impact of urban life. On the contrary, they appear to be the hardiest of folk narrative forms, not only in adjusting easily to modern conditions, but by generating new types based on the most up-to-date issues of contemporary life."

Such legends are particularly rife among teen-agers, who sometimes call them "scary stories." These tales, which are always sworn to be true, are told at social get-togethers such as pyjama parties, pub gatherings, nights at summer camps, canoe trips, or camp reunions. Usually some evidence is cited to establish the event as truth, and many are carefully localized. However, the most common legends are at least continent-wide. Linda Degh says that the type usually exists in a "fragmentary, incomplete form" and has a "tendency to be more communal than any other folklore genre in its composition and performance."

Susan Smith collected the following Ontario versions of some of the most common belief legends in 1973 from teen-agers who lived in Toronto or its suburbs and who had heard them in summer camps. "The Hook," "The Boyfriend's Death," and "The Babysitter" are all widely known today; the other tales are less common, although "The Disappearing Hitchhiker" is a classic, and it and "The Cadaver's Arm" are older than most of the rest. The last, "Bloody Fingers," is a sample of the comical or pun endings sometimes imposed on apparently scary tales. Others known in Canada as well as the United States include "The Vindow Viper," "Stop the Coffin," and "The Rapping from the Coffin."

THE HOOK
Told by Brian Smith, 14, Willowdale, 1973.

There was this couple sitting in a car at Lover's Lane near Midland, Ontario. They turned on the radio in time to hear a flash that a mentally insane person had broken out of the Penetang Hospital for the Mentally Insane and that people should be on the look-out for him because he was dangerous. He could be recognized by the hook on his right hand.

The couple talked about this for a little while and the girl asked the guy to take her home because she was a little scared. The guy said that there was nothing to worry about because the man would never be around there where they were. Still the girl insisted on going home. Her boyfriend was annoyed and the car screeched off to take her home. After seeing his girl to the door he started walking back to his car and suddenly saw this hook on the door handle of the passenger side of the car.

(Brian heard it at Camp Shawanaga two or three years earlier.)

THE BOYFRIEND'S DEATH
Told by John Briggs, 14, Willowdale, 1973.

A guy and his girlfriend are on the way to a party when their car starts to give them some trouble. At that same time they catch a news flash on the radio warning all people in the area that a lunatic killer has escaped from a local criminal asylum. The girl becomes very upset and at that point the car stalls completely on the highway. The boyfriend gets out and tinkers around with the engine but can't get the car to start again. He decides that he is going to have to walk on up the road to a gas station and get a tow truck but wants his girlfriend to stay behind in the car. She is frightened and pleads with him to take her, but he says that she'll be safe on the floor of the car covered with a blanket so that anyone passing will think it is an abandoned car and not bother her. Besides he can sprint along the road and get back more quickly than if she comes with him in her high-heeled shoes and evening dress. She finally agrees and he tells her not to come out unless she hears his signal of three knocks on the window, kisses her goodbye, tucks her under the cover, locks the door, and sprints off down the road.

A half hour or so goes by although it seems like years to the girl. Suddenly she hears a knock and is about to get up when she remembers her boyfriend's warning of waiting for three knocks. She waits, and hears two, three, four, five, six, seven, and they continue! She remains motionless and it just continues. Finally it stops and she hears voices outside. She peeks out and the policemen are crowded around the car and call to her to come out, that it's all right. She opens a door, comes out, and the police lead her to one of their cars, cautioning her not to look back. Despite this she turns and sees her boyfriend hung from the limb of a tree above the car and his feet are barely touching the roof – that was the continuous knocking sound!

THE BABYSITTER
Told by Brian Smith, 14, Willowdale, 1973.

There was this babysitter that was in Montreal babysitting for three children in a big house. She was watching T.V. when suddenly the phone rang. The children were all in bed. She picked up the phone and heard this guy on the other end laughing hysterically. She asked him what it was that he wanted, but he wouldn't answer and then hung up. She worried about it for a while, but then thought nothing more of it and went back to watching the movie.

Everything was fine until about fifteen minutes later when the phone rang again. She picked it up and heard the same voice laughing hysterically at her, and then hung up. At this point she became really worried and phoned the operator to tell her what had been happening. The operator told her to calm down and that if he called again to try and keep him on the line as long as possible and she would try to trace the call.

Again about fifteen minutes later the guy called back and laughed hysterically at her. She asked him why he was doing this, but he just kept laughing at her. He hung up and about five seconds later the operator called. She told the girl to get out of the house at once because the person who was calling was calling from the upstairs extension. She slammed down the phone and just as she was turning to leave she saw the man coming down the stairs laughing hysterically with a bloody butcher knife in his hand and meaning to kill her. She ran out onto the street but he didn't follow. She called the police and they came and caught the man, and discovered that he had murdered all the children.

(Brian heard this story from a friend named Gordon Weidauer whose brother's girlfriend was the babysitter.)

BABYSITTER MISTAKES CHILD FOR TURKEY
Told by Jenny Nix, 16, Toronto, 1973.

This story was told to me by a friend who heard it on the news on the radio a year or so ago. It is a factual account.

There was a girl and she was babysitting. The parents had gone out to a very big party and had left this infant at home with this sixteen-year-old girl. So she was babysitting and they phoned just to see if everything was all right. She said, "Oh, fine. Everything's great. The turkey's in the oven." The mother went, "Oh, okay, fine," and she hung up. Then she looked at her husband and went, "The turkey's in the oven? We didn't have a turkey!" He said, "What's the matter?" So they decided they had better go home and see what was the matter. Maybe there was something wrong with the babysitter.

They excused themselves from the party and went home. So they walked in the house and saw the babysitter sitting in the chair freaking out. She had put the little infant in the oven and had thought it was a turkey.

THE DISAPPEARING HITCHHIKER
Told by Tanys Howell, 16, Toronto, 1973.

Well this happened to one of my girlfriend's best friends and her father. They were driving along a country road on their way home from the cottage when they saw a young girl hitchhiking. They stopped and picked her up and she got in the back seat. She told the girl and her father that she just lived in the house about five miles up the road. She didn't say anything after that but just turned to watch out the window. When the father saw the house, he drove up to it and turned around to tell the girl they had arrived – but she wasn't there! Both he and his daughter were really mystified and decided to knock on the door and tell the people what had happened. They told them that they had once had a daughter who answered the description of the girl they supposedly had picked up, but she had disappeared some years ago and had last been seen hitchhiking on this very road. Today would have been her birthday.

THE CADAVER'S ARM
Told by Brian Smith, 14, Willowdale, 1973.

There was this laboratory with ten scientists in it. All of them worked very hard at their work, but one girl especially worked hard. She never took time out for fun, always just working on science, science, science.

Well one day the other nine scientists decided that they were going to play a joke on her. They strung up an arm (a human arm) that was a specimen at the laboratory, in her bedroom while she was out. When she came home that night, the other nine were in a room next door to hers and listening. All of a sudden they heard a scream and they all chuckled to themselves. But then there was a strange silence and they decided to check in on her. They found her in the bathroom eating the arm: she had gone completely insane!

(*Brian heard this from John Briggs, a friend, who said the story was true.*)

GIRLFRIEND'S LEGS CUT OFF
Told by Carolynne Parker, 14, Toronto, 1973.

Two girls were staying overnight at a friend's house and the one decided to go down and get a glass of milk before bed. A while later the girl who was still in bed heard a thumping at the bottom of the steps. She looked down and there was her girlfriend and someone had cut off her legs.

HUMANS CAN LICK HANDS TOO!
Told by Diana Booth, 16, Toronto, 1973.

There was a girl who had this dog. In her house when she went to bed the dog slept beside her on the carpet. In the middle of the night if she ever heard anything or was wondering if everything was all right she would put her hand down and the dog would lick her hand.

So one night she heard a noise and she put her hand down and the dog licked her hand. Then in the morning she went to the washroom and saw the dog with his throat slit open and written on the wall in blood was: HUMANS CAN LICK HANDS TOO!

BLOODY FINGERS
Told by Diana Booth, 16, Toronto, 1973.

There was this babysitter and she was at home and the kids were all upstairs when she got this phone call. And it said: "I'm bloody fingers, I am a mile away." She didn't think anything about it. She thought it was a prank call. So she was just sitting there and the phone rang again. She answered it and it said: "I am bloody fingers. I am half a mile away." So then she started to get scared. And she was just sitting there and started to go crazy and the phone rang again. He said: "I am bloody fingers. I am five houses away." She almost went batty there. So again he phoned and said: "I am bloody fingers. I am one house away." She was just waiting, when she heard a knock on the door. She answered it and he said: "I am bloody fingers. Can I borrow a band-aid?"

CHILDREN'S GHOST STORIES

Among the favourite stories that children tell are several versions of a widespread international tale in which a man steals the heart of one who has been hanged and gives it to his wife to eat; the ghost comes to claim his property and carries the man off. The American folklorist Richard Chase calls these "jump tales" – "A tale which is brought to a dramatic climax when the tale-teller jumps at his listeners." He notes that Joseph Jacobs' "The Golden Arm" is the same type, and that it is "the ha'nt tale usually told at Boy Scout campfires." It is also popular among Canadian teen-agers as the version below indicates.

Two common variants are "The Big Toe" and "Give Me Back My Liver." Chase says the first is widely known in the Appalachians, and the second is popular among Toronto schoolchildren.

THE LADY WITH THE GOLDEN ARM
Collected by Susan Smith from Tanys Howell, 16, Toronto, 1973.

Well, there was this lady and she had a golden arm because her real arm had gotten cut off. And the golden arm was put on to replace it. And she married this old guy and he killed her because he wanted to get the golden arm from her. So after she died he kept the arm under his pillow because it was a great treasure being made of gold. So every night she'd come back and she'd stand before him with just one arm and say: "I want my arm back." But he didn't think anything of it. And so finally this had been going on for about a month, and she kept coming back and saying "I want my arm."

Finally one day the housekeeper came in and he was lying on the floor with the golden arm clutched around his throat.

THE GRANDFATHER'S LIVER
Collected by Susan Smith from Brian Smith, 14, Willowdale, 1973.

There once was a boy named Johnny. He was asked by his mother to go to the store and buy some liver for supper. He met some of his pals on the way and was persuaded to go with them to the ice-cream shop and spend his mother's money on an ice-cream cone. After finishing the cone and leaving his pals he realized he hadn't gotten the liver he had been sent for, and had spent all the money. He got an idea and went to the cemetery where his grandfather was buried and dug up the grave. Johnny brought his grandfather's liver home for supper instead of admitting to wasting the money. The whole family commented on how good the liver was at supper that night. That night in bed Johnny saw a ghostly figure and heard a wavering voice call: "Johnny, I want my liver back." And again: "Johnny, I want my liver back."

IV Canadian Mosaic

IV Canadian Mosaic

Although the French and British have long had pre-eminence as the two founding peoples of Canada, our population is becoming increasingly multi-cultural. At the time of Confederation the British and French made up some 3,000,000 of the total 3,500,000; all other groups totalled only 14 per cent. By 1971 some 27 per cent was of neither British nor French origin, and that segment is growing.

In the 1960s the Folklore Division of the National Museum of Man shifted its emphasis from Canada's native and founding cultures to the varied traditions that more recent immigrants had brought to this country. Special sections devoted to scientific research on ethnic group cultures were established, and in 1970 the name of the Folklore Division was changed to the Canadian Centre for Folk Culture Studies. It now has material collected from over seventy different groups.

Such research serves to emphasize the variety of Canada's cultural heritage, and the collections will be of value in future years. However, most of these groups represent an infinitesimal part of Canada's total population: some fifty of them together make up about 5 per cent. Also, a great many of them have come to Canada during the last quarter century so their traditions are typical of the countries from which they come, but have not yet taken root in our soil. Because of limits of space only a few of the ethnic groups can be represented in this anthology so our choice has been determined largely by two factors: the size of the group, and the length of time it has been established in Canada. Our aim is to emphasize the traditions that have been preserved, adapted, or created in this country.

The Germans and the Ukrainians rank next to the British and French in population, and both have been here for a number of generations. The Icelanders and Jews, while making up a smaller part of our population,

270

have each been here for several generations and have played a significant role in our cultural life. Therefore, these groups have been chosen to represent the Canadian mosaic.

1. SUPERSTITIONS AND POPULAR BELIEFS IN WATERLOO COUNTY
W.J. Wintemberg

German-Canadians form the third-largest group in our population. The 1971 census showed 1,317,000 Canadians of German descent. The earliest groups came direct from Europe, some settling in Lunenburg on the east coast as early as 1753. After the American Revolution many Loyalists of German origin moved from the United States to the Maritimes and what is now southwestern Ontario, and another wave of Germans from the old country came over in the first half of the nineteenth century.

The settlement that has been studied most extensively is that of the Pennsylvania Germans in Ontario's Waterloo County, some fifty miles southwest of Toronto. These people are often called "Pennsylvania Dutch" because of the word deutsch *meaning German. Many of them are Mennonites, including some Amish. Elmore G. Reaman's* The Trail of the Black Walnut *is a good general account of their migrations and settlements.*

The following folk treatments for various ailments, bad luck signs, and death signs which W.J. Wintemberg collected from his Waterloo County neighbours are typical of the beliefs found in many rural communities.

FOLK MEDICINE

Asthma. Boil the lung of a fox in water and drink the liquid. Obviously the lung of the fox was chosen because that animal can run long distances without its powers of respiration being impaired.

Bee Stings. If you can succeed in killing the bee that stings you the wound will not mortify. Mud applied to a bee sting will help to allay the pain. (2262)

Blood Purifier. Tea made from the leaves of the hemlock spruce is used as a blood purifier. (889)

Boils. Cow excrement is applied to a boil to bring it to a head. The inner white skin of an egg is also used. (919)

271

Cold Cures. Tea made from the flowers of the mayweed, the leaves of the catnip, the bark of the spice bush, or from the flowers of the common mullein. (1106, 1110)

Colic. If before breakfast on Easter morning you suck a raw egg that was laid on Good Friday it will keep you from getting the colic the rest of the year. (1151)

Consumption. Eat the leaf of a male dandelion for nine successive mornings.

Cure for Bad Temper. Pass the child head first through the left leg of its father's trousers.

Dog Bite. Take some hairs of the dog that bit you and place them in the wound. (1293)

Dysentery. Tea made from the leaves of the curled dock, the knotgrass, or the plaintain-leaved everlasting, or from the roots or leaves of the wild red raspberry, the black raspberry, and the high blackberry. The tea must be prepared in a pot that has not previously been used. (cf. 1305)

Dyspepsia. A tea made by boiling a handful of chips of ironwood in two pints of water until it boils down to one pint.

Earache. A poultice made from the wool of a black sheep. (1334)

Eyes. Wear earrings for sore eyes. Take the blood of a bat and bathe your eyes with it and you will be able to see as well in the dark as you can in the daytime. (cf. 1370)

Fits. Give the blood of a black hen as a drink to the patient. Some to cure a child thus afflicted took it into the woods, placed its back against a tree, and bored a hole into the tree above the child's head. They then cut off some of the child's hair and stuffed it into the hole, which they closed with a wooden plug. It was believed that as the child grew up above the hole the disease disappeared. (cf. 2341)

Freckles. To keep a child from getting freckles rub a live gosling over its face. Dew rubbed on the face before sunrise on any morning during the month of May will remove freckles and give one a beautiful complexion. (cf. 1508)

Goitre. Wind a black ribbon around the neck three times and then put the ribbon into a coffin with a corpse, but do it secretly. Or rub a live frog on it and then bury the animal alive with its head downward. It was believed that as the frog disappeared the growth would also disappear.

Hiccough. When anyone hiccoughs it is customary to say "*Du hosht eppes g'schtole,*" i.e., "You have stolen something." This, it is believed, will frighten the person and make him forget to hiccough. (1670)

Jaundice. Eat all the carrots you can.

Lumbago. Lie on the floor face downward and have your wife tread on the afflicted part.

Measles. A decoction prepared from sheep's excrement. (1809)

Rheumatism. Carry a horse chestnut in the pocket. (2001)

Rupture. Take the hand of a corpse and press the thumb on the rupture.

Side stitch. Spit on a pebble and throw it over your shoulder, and then walk away without looking back at it. Or overturn a stone and spit into the cavity in the soil caused by its removal and then replace the stone. (2104, 2107)

Sore Mouth. Use blacksmith's forge water as a wash.

Sore Throat. Take the sock off your left foot, turn it inside out, and wear it around your neck. It is said the cure will be more effectual if the sock is red. (2211)

Sore Umbilicus. Get a hen's egg from your neighbour and hold it on the child's umbilicus until the egg is warm, then bury it where the rain will not fall upon it, and as it decays the sore will heal. This must be done before sunrise, and during the performance you are not to speak to anyone.

Sprain. If you find a bone, rub it on the sprained hand or foot, and then throw it over your shoulder and do not look back.

Sties. Throw a pail of swill over your head without wetting yourself. Or rub the tail of a cat on the sty. (2277)

Stopping Flow of Blood. To stop nose bleeding put a key on the back of the neck, or tie a string of red yarn round the little finger. (1896, 1881) Cobwebs are used as a styptic for flesh cuts or wounds. (858)

Toothache. Put a piece of garlic in the ear on the same side as the aching tooth. The white limy particles in hen's feces were sometimes used. One was placed in the hollow of the aching tooth. Cut off a bunch of your hair and place it with a corpse in a coffin. This must be done secretly.

If a child chews a bread crust that has been gnawed by a mouse it will never be subject to toothache. A bone from a pig's skull, called *hernzahn* (i.e., "Brain-tooth"), is carried in the pocket as a preventive or suspended around a child's neck to assist in teething. (2348) A splinter from a tree that had been struck by lightning if used as a toothpick will prevent toothache. (2363)

Warts. Rub a piece of quartered apple on the wart and at the same time blow on it. Rub a copper coin on the wart and present it to some person who will thereupon get it. (cf. 2685) Go into a house and steal a dishcloth and bury it under a stone; as the cloth rots the wart will also disappear. (2604) Rub the wart with a piece of pork and bury it under the eaves. (2472) Take a potato and cut it in two and then rub one of the pieces on the wart. Take this and wrap it in a piece of paper and place it on the sidewalk or other place much frequented by the public. Whoever opens the package will get the wart. (2549)

Whooping Cough. Let the child eat a piece of bread from the hands of a woman whose maiden name was the same as her husband's surname. (2729) Or take the hair of a person who has never seen his or her father alive and put it on the child's breast.

A hairy caterpillar, put in a little bag and worn on the child's breast is a preventive of whooping cough. It must be left there nine days – presumably till the caterpillar dies.

Wounds. Poultices made from the leaves of the purslane, the giant plantain, the round-leaved mallow, or the common chickweed. The flowers of the great white lily preserved in white whisky are applied directly to the sore or wound.

To prevent blood poisoning, if you step on a rusty nail, immerse the nail in lard, then remove it and put it into the oven to remain there until the wound is healed. (1789)

BAD LUCK SIGNS

To sit on a table. (3049)

To sing while eating at the table. (2842)

To look into a mirror at night. (3058)

To open an umbrella in the house. (3062)

To cut your fingernails on Sunday. (597)

To sing or whistle while lying in bed. (3085, 3093)

To kill a spider that crawls on your person. (7378)

To leave a knife on the table after retiring.

To step over a grave. (cf. 185)

To draw the window blinds before lighting the lamps.

To hold a loaf of bread upside down while cutting it. (2773)

For children to play funeral.

To break a mirror – you will have no luck for seven years. (3060)

To collect birds' eggs. (7218)

To spill salt – the evil may be counteracted by burning the salt. (2880, 2883)

The crowing of a cock at sundown. (7190)

To eat any fruit growing in a graveyard. (cf. 5358)

To watch the moon go down.

To boast of good health – you will be sure to be ill soon after.

To take either a cat or a broom along when moving from one house to another. (2955, 2957)

To eat the fruit of a blackberry bush that has blossomed long after the other fruit has disappeared – the person who does so will not live long. (cf. 5370)

274

DEATH SIGNS

If a cat looks into a window at night. (cf. 5188)

Two forks on a table.

When a white spider crawls towards you or your house.

Three spiders crawling on a wall.

The hooting of an owl near a house. (5305)

When the corn shoots are of a whitish colour.

If the cabbage heads are white or covered with white spots. (5354)

A white bean plant.

When a bunch of apple blossoms appears late in the season. (cf. 5370)

When a wild bird enters an occupied house. (5280)

The howling of a dog. (5208)

If the clock strikes six or twelve while the head of the house asks the blessing.

If a cock crows before ten o'clock. (5262)

If roosters crow between sundown and midnight. (5263)

In whatever direction a star falls there will be a death; presumably of some relative or friend of the person who sees it fall. (5143)

A person passing over a mole working underground will die within a year.

The last person mentioned by a dying person will be the next to die. (cf. 5014)

2. LOCAL ANECDOTES FROM LUNENBURG

Helen Creighton

Lunenburg County, on Nova Scotia's southeast coast just below Halifax, was originally settled by German immigrants, largely from Hanover, who came out in the middle of the eighteenth century. George II of England was also Elector of Hanover, and the British government wanted Protestant settlers to offset the Catholic Acadians. Some French Huguenots and a few Swiss also came out about the same time. Helen Creighton notes that some of the Germans intermarried with the Huguenots and also to a lesser extent with the Acadians, Swiss, and British, but "in spite of fusion with other races, the primary German is predominant. Although many of their beliefs and customs are universal, others will be found closely allied with those of the Germans of Pennsylvania."

Dr. Creighton also tells us that "Of the total population of about

33,000 inhabitants, less than 3,000 live in the town of Lunen-
burg . . . . Settlements are for the most part along the sea, and it is
interesting that from an inland people there has grown up a sea-
faring tradition among fisherfolk unequalled in the world." The fol-
lowing anecdotes clearly reflect the atmosphere of the little fishing
communities.

1.   We fish a lot for albacore in St. Margaret's Bay, or tuna as they call
     them on the market. One day a greenhorn came down from Ottawa
     on official business, so I thought I'd have some fun with him. He
     asked me about fishing so I said, "I went out one day and found
     twenty albacore in my net, but the market was bad and I didn't
     want them. I took the net up because it had already been down for
     twenty days, and when I went back four days later, do you know
     what I found? The albacore were still running round and round in
     the same place, just as though the net was still there." He didn't
     know whether to believe me or not, so he went and asked my
     brother, and my brother said, yes, of course it was true. – *Fox
     Point.*

2.   Well, we had fun here one day. A man from Northwest Cove was
     fishing for albacore when he lost his balance and fell smack into the
     spiller. That's the net where we catch 'em, and they weigh up to
     eight hundred pounds and even more sometimes. He took hold of an
     albacore's fin and was twirled around no less than fifteen times, and
     we couldn't do a thing to help him. Water was flying everywhere,
     but he didn't dare let go in case another albacore got him. Boy, oh,
     boy, it was a time! – *Fox Point.*

3.   One way to catch albacore is with a sweep and a spiller. These are
     big box-like nets that act as a trap. When enough are in, the lines
     are drawn together and this forces the fish to the surface. We kill
     them with axes, and gaff them and draw them aboard our boats.
     Once we were doing this when an axe stuck in an albacore's head
     and pulled the fisherman overboard. The water was red with blood
     from the fish where the axe had gone in, and nobody knew what to
     do. Somehow or other the man got his foot into the head of the fish,
     and before any of us realized what was happening, the albacore had
     thrown him back into the boat again. That's a true story and no
     yarn. – *Fox Point* and *Hubbards.*

4.   Two men from Tancook were fishing for cod when they saw schools
     of albacore, but they hadn't brought hooks along for catching such
     large fish. Still, they knew albacore would come where herring

were, so what do you suppose they did? They took a thole pin and tied it to the end of a line and used the herring for bait. The first albacore swallowed the thole pin and was caught so they decided to try it again, and they caught three albacore that night. – *Hubbards*.

5. A Conservative Member of Parliament went to visit a Liberal friend. The Conservative was an influential man, and the Liberal wanted him on his side. The Liberal had a cat, which he showed to the Conservative saying, "My beautiful angora has kittens; five little Conservative kittens." The Conservative was pleased and thought the Liberal must have changed his views. The next time he went to the house the Liberal took him to see the kittens again. "Five little Liberals," he said. "What?" said his friend. "I thought you said they were Conservatives." "So they were," he said, "but they've got their eyes open now and they can see." – *Mahone Bay*. (X599.1*)

6. Years ago there was an American who stopped at St. Ann's, Cape Breton, to see Angus McAskill, the Cape Breton giant. Angus was ploughing and standing in a furrow so that the visitor didn't realize his size. He said, "Is that the house where Angus McAskill lives?" "No," said Angus, "there it is," and used the plough to point with. – *Tancook*. (F624.4; X941[b])

7. A sea captain from Lunenburg, or perhaps from some other part of the coast, was visiting Halifax when he got a long-distance call from one of his help who said, "Your wife fell overboard and was drowned. We found her body with eight lobsters attached. What will we do now?" To which he replied, "Ship me the lobsters and set her again." – *Halifax*.

8. One day while travelling through New Germany I stopped at a house and asked the woman who came to the door where Willie Wiggle lived. She said, "There's two Villy Viggles. One's name's Clary. He don't live where he does now. He's moved." – *Mahone Bay*.

9. A Lunenburg sea captain came to Halifax and was met at the station by a red cap who greeted him, thinking he might want to go to a hotel. "Lord Nelson, sir?" he said, "Lord Nelson?" "Lord Nelson? Hell no, I'm Captain C* from Lunenburg." – *Mahone Bay*. (Lord Nelson is the name of one of the Halifax hotels.)

10. In one particular season one person could only shoot one deer in and around Louisbourg. One day a man went into the woods and saw another man coming out with a beautiful deer. He stopped and said,

"That's a beautiful deer you have. Do they grow many here as fine as that?" The man nodded, "Yes, it's a nice deer all right. But you should see the one I got last week at Catalone." The man looked at him. "Do you realize who I am? No? Well, I'm Inspector of Mounted Police." "Well," came the prompt rejoinder, "Do you realize who I am? I'm the biggest liar in Catalone." – *Mahone Bay.* (J1155.1.*[b])

11. There was a Baptist deacon at Bass River who wanted to quiz the minister, so he asked him what hell was. At the moment the minister was chopping wood, so he looked up from his work and said, "Hell is ten cords of wood and a dull saw." – *Mahone Bay.*

12. Grandpa was at a wedding at Kingsburg and took so much dark fruit cake that the hostess thought she had better pass him something else. But he refused it and said, "No, thank you. This brown bread's good enough for me." – *Riverport.* (J1742.7*)

13. A Tancook woman went one day to a large town on the main [mainland] and saw this sign: Smith's Manufacturing Company. "Oh, my," she exclaimed. "I never knew before where all the Smiths came from." – *Tancook.*

14. A story is told of a guest who was visting in Lunenburg County and when they sat down at the table the host turned to him and said, "Eat welcome. God knows you're hearty." – *Mahone Bay.*

15. The story is told of a man who wanted the banns published and asked Father Cossman, a beloved Lutheran clergyman, to do it. The conversation ran like this: "Father Cossman, Father Cossman, holler me out to Hannah Tanner from Feltzen South. And how much will it cost me?" "Thirty cents and a good fat goose." – *Lunenburg and Riverport.*

16. Two men from Lunenburg met. "You know Izzy Spindler? Izzy Spindler's brudder's dead." "Is he?" "Oh, no, Izzy's brudder. Izzy's vell as I is." – *Lunenburg.*

17. At Gold River there was an Indian who was a great salmon fisherman. Every spring since he died, his wife brings a salmon in and puts it on his grave. – *Mahone Bay.*

18. Men used to train at Crescent Beach for the Fenian Raid and they got twenty cents while training. One man didn't know his right foot from his left, so they tied straw on his left foot and the sergeant would call, "Straw foot ahead!" – *Petite Rivière.*

19. A boy who had a toy boat left it on the shore, and when he went to

look for it in the spring it had grown into a four-masted schooner.
– *Mahone Bay.* (X1816)

20. An American was travelling with a Canadian and the American was boasting. Everything was bigger and better in the United States. The Canadian got fed up and thought he would go him one better, so as they started off to bed he found a turtle and put it in the American's bed. When the American turned back the bedclothes he said, "What's this?" "That's a Canadian bedbug," he replied. "Can you do any better than that?" – *Mahone Bay.*(1499.13*[d])

21. There are no rats on Tancook, but a story is told of a vessel putting in there once that had one on board. That was all right, but it was decided to put the vessel ashore at Little Tancook, a smaller island, and leave it there. When the rat realized that it would have to spend the rest of its life on Little Tancook, rather than end its days there, it jumped overboard and drowned itself. – *Tancook.*

22. One time I saw a squid as big as a dory. – *Gold River.*

3. UKRAINIAN-CANADIAN FOLKTALES
Robert B. Klymasz

Until recently, the Ukrainians formed the fourth largest ethnic group in Canada, after the British, French, and Germans. They have now been surpassed by the Italians, but their roots are deeper in this country. Most of them came here between 1890 and 1910 and settled mainly on the prairies from southeast Manitoba to Edmonton, with the largest concentration around Winnipeg.

In 1963 when Kenneth Peacock published A Survey of Ethnic Folkmusic across Western Canada, *he noted: "The survey confirmed what was suspected beforehand – that Ukrainian Canadians have the most widespread and flourishing folkmusic and folklore in western Canada. After French, English, and Indian, theirs is potentially the largest body of folklore in Canada. In fact, if the same amount of time and effort that have been spent on any of these three larger ethnic groups were devoted to Ukrainian research, the body of material would approach, or even surpass, that of the English or Indian collections at the National Museum."*

The following tales which Robert B. Klymasz collected in Alberta and Saskatchewan are typical of the many European folktales that were brought over to this country by the early settlers and handed

279

down through oral tradition. The first is a Ukrainian counterpart of the story best known in English through the old Scottish ballad of "The Twa Sisters" (Child 10). The riddles in the second can be compared with those in the "Pat and Mike" version of the same international tale (see p. 164), and the impossible tasks are similar to those found in the old British ballad of "The Elfin Knight" (Child 2). The third belongs to the same category of ribald stories as Chaucer's "The Miller's Tale" and such broadside ballads of adultery as "The Boatsman and the Chest" and "Will the Weaver" (Laws 08 and 09).

THE MAGIC FLUTE

This is just a little *bajochka* (story) that mother always used to tell us, about a little brother and sister and how they went to gather berries. The brother wanted her to give him that pitcher full of berries and he would give her a ring. But she didn't want to do this, and he killed her out of anger. And he went and covered her up with willow branches. He had a flute and he liked to play. But when he began to play on that flute, that flute would always sing the same thing for him:

> "Play slowly, my dear brother,
> Do not wound my little heart.
> You slew and covered me with willow
> For the pitcher of berries,
> For my beloved ring,
> For my dowry."

THE CLEVER DAUGHTER

This was still in the Old Country during serfdom, when the overlords had a great deal of power. They were the judges, they did with the poor people whatever they wanted. But one time, one of the lords gave out three riddles: what is the most nourishing, what is the sweetest, and what is the most agile? One man had a daughter who was eighteen years old. They were poor, and she says, "Father, go and solve those riddles!"

"How can I go there, my daughter? Such personages have gone there like the magistrate and the judge, those kind have gone. And the lord asks the gentlemen, 'Why have you come?' – those rich men. 'Why we have come, kind sir, to guess those riddles.' 'All right! If you guess them, you'll have a hundred ducats. But if you don't guess them, then you'll have a hundred lashes!' And so the lord says, 'What is the sweetest?' One says, 'I have mead which has been standing there for three years already. It seems to me that this is the sweetest.' And another says, 'What is the most nourishing? – I killed a big hog with so much bacon that I think that this is the most nourishing.' 'Fine. And what's the most agile?' And that third one speaks, saying, 'I have a very quick dog. He'll catch a hare no matter where it is.' 'Fine.' The lord summoned his servants. 'Give them each a hundred lashes!' They all got a hundred lashes each and went home."

But that girl says to her father, "Go, father!"

"How can I when they were such rich men and they each got a hundred lashes? When I get a hundred lashes I'll not even get home!"

"No, father. You know what, when he says what's the sweetest, you say that it's sleep; and when he asks you what's the most nourishing, you say that it's the earth, for she feeds everyone. And say that the most agile things are the eyes."

Well, the old man went. The old man comes, the lord comes out. "Why have you come, old man?"

"Why I have come to guess those riddles which your lordship has made up."

"Fine. There were some here already to guess them, perhaps you'll guess them. What is the sweetest?"

He thinks and thinks and says, "It seems to me, sir, that sleep, for no matter what, if sleep overpowers you, you leave everything else behind."

"Hm. And what is the most nourishing?"

"I think, sir, that the earth, for she is the most nourishing. She feeds all of us."

"Fine. And what is the most agile?"

"The most agile, sir, I think are the eyes, for when you close the eyes tight and open them, then you'll see stars so far away, and I think that that's the most agile."

"You've guessed them, old man! But you didn't answer them from your own head! Tell me, you'll get a hundred ducats, but tell me who induced you to do this. Your head couldn't have said this without help."

"Why I have, sir, a girl, I've got a daughter, she's eighteen years old already."

"Oh, so she's the wise one. Here's a dozen eggs for you. By tomorrow out of these eggs there must be chicks! Tell her to place a hen on them, so that there'll be chicks."

The poor man goes and worries, "How can this be?"

And the daughter runs out, "Father! Did you guess them?"

"Oh leave me in peace, daughter. I guessed them but what of it? You've gotten mixed up with such a lord and you'll not come out of it at the end. Look, he gave these eggs to be hatched into chicks for tomorrow."

"Oh, that's nothing, father! Come! I'm so hungry!" And those eggs were cooked, he was so smart that he had cooked them yet! And the girl took the bowl with those eggs, gave some to her father and herself and the two of them ate their fill. The girl took a handful of millet still in the ears, and says, "Father, go to the lord and tell him to thrash this millet and sow it, and then cut and flay it, for tomorrow morning I'll have to give it to the chicks to eat."

The old man comes. "Well? And are the chicks out already?"

"No, no, my lord. Look, my daughter has given you this millet for you to sow; it has to grow and you have to thrash and flay it, for tomorrow the chicks have to be fed."

"Oh, so that's how wise she is! You tell her to come to me herself, but she must come neither naked nor dressed, not riding nor walking, neither with a gift nor without one."

Well, the old man goes home and again he became worried. And the daughter runs out. "Well, father, what did the lord say?"

"Ah! Leave me in peace, daughter! You've begun with this lord and you'll not come out of it at the end. He said that you should come to him tomorrow yourself, and you're not to ride nor walk, nor naked nor dressed, neither with a gift nor without."

"Oh I'll do it, father. Go to town, father, and buy me ten yards of netting." The old man went and bought a net. And she sewed herself a kind of dress and put it on. She caught a dog – she had a big dog – and she got on it: she neither rides nor walks, for her legs drag along – she stands up a little. She caught herself two sparrows and rides along.

And when the lord saw that, he says, "Hey!" to his lackeys. "Let out the dogs!" And the lord let the dogs out, and those dogs went after her, and she took a kitten and let it go, and the dogs went after the kitten and the kitten went up onto a willow, and she rode onward to his chamber. She let go those two sparrows, saying, "My lord! Lord! Here's your gift! Catch it for yourself!" The gift is and isn't – it flies and the lord can't catch it.

And he says to her, "Sit down! You know, you're a smart girl. I wonder whether I should not marry you."

"And why not? If you want to, I'll marry you."

"Well then you go home and tomorrow I'll come and talk with your father. And we'll get married."

The daughter comes home. "Father, the lord wants to marry me!" And that lord wasn't very old. He was maybe thirty-five to forty years old, not older, for the lords once used to get married at that age.

Well, the lord comes, talks with the old man, "I want to marry your daughter!"

"I'm not forbidding you! Marry her!" and so they got married. And now, no matter where the lord went or what the problem, they would come to her, and she understands those people and she judges fairly, so that it was even pleasant.

But one time some kind (of men) were riding to the fair. One had a mare, another had the cart, and the third made jugs. And they harnessed up and were riding to the fair. Night fell and they spent the night near that manor. They get up in the morning – there's a colt! Now one says, "Look! My old mare had a colt!"

"You're lying! My cart did!"

And that third one says, "My jugs did!"

Well, they came to that lord's place, but the lord wasn't home. His lady came out. "What is the problem?"

"It's like this. This one had a cart, I made jugs, and this one had a mare. And we spent the night near his lordship's and a colt was born." "I say that it was my mare that gave birth to the colt, but this one says that it was his cart, and that third one says that his jugs, and we don't know. We have come to you for a judgement."

"His lordship isn't home, he's gone to chase the fish out of the grain."

"Oh, we've never heard about fish being in grain!"

"And I've never heard that a cart or jugs should have a colt! The mare had the colt. The colt is yours, my man. Go!"

And when the lord returned, he heard about this and he got very angry at her, for he had told her repeatedly that she was not to enter into any affairs without him. He wanted to laugh a little at those people. "From today you are no longer my wife! Get off with you so that I don't see you!"

But she says, "Wait a bit. At least let's have dinner together."

"Well, then, you shall have dinner with me."

The cooks brought the dinner, they sat down. And there was a flask of wine, as is the custom with wealthy people. And she poured him some wine into a glass and some for herself. They don't talk to one another, just eat, for she has to leave. But the lord drank his wine and finished his dinner, and so did his wife. It is the custom with the rich that after dinner one has to go to sleep. And he went and lay down to sleep and fell into a deep sleep. And the lady came out and summoned a lackey and says, "Go and call the coachman! Let him harness the horses and have him ride up before the chamber." And the coachman did so, he rode up, and she told the lackey to put the lord into the coach. They brought the lord out – the lord sleeps. She sat herself down by him and sits. And there the lord had a good sleep and woke up – but here he was in the coach.

"Where am I? Where am I going?"

"Well, where are you going? – You're going with me! You drove me out!"

"Well I drove you out alone. Why am I riding with you?"

"Well, because you are my husband. You said that I should take with

me that which is the most dear and the best. And you are my husband –
you are most dear to me, and therefore I took you, and I am going with
you."

"Aj, aj! Turn back you miserable one! We shall live on (together)!"
And so they lived and lived until they died.

THE LIVE STATUES

There was once a man, a young fellow, who got married to a girl. Well,
and they were poor, but he was a kind of artisan. He knew how to make
statues, crosses – like the saints, he was able to make things like this. But
there rode up a lady saying, "Master artisan! Would you be able to cast
the three saints for me: Ivan, Paul, and Gabriel?"

And he says, "Why not? But you know, I don't have any money. You
leave me some as a deposit and I'll buy some of that material." And the
lady left some.

And he then rode into town, and his wife was behind him saying, "I
need a dress! I need shoes!"

And he says, "Wife! For God's sake! I don't have any money, I only
have enough for that material that I must use to cast the saints!"

"Oh, that's nothing! I'll make the saints myself!"

"Well, if that's the way it is, let it be so. Let it be your word! and I'll
buy you both the shoes and the dress." And the money went.

But now they're coming home, and she says, "Husband, take a sack
and stuff some rags in there and go through the village saying that
you're going off to work." And he did this. He took the sack on his
shoulders and goes.

But here the priest comes out, "And where are you going, Ivan?"

"Why, I'm going away to work."

"But it's been only two weeks since you've gotten married, and already you're going off to work!"

"Well, I have to, there's nothing to live on, and that's that."

"Well then, I wish you a good journey – may you make a lot of
money!"

And he goes further. The cantor comes up. "Do you hear, Ivan –
where are you going?"

"Where I'm going? I'm going to work."

"Oh my, my! Why, it's only been two weeks since you got married!
Such a nice wife! How can you leave her behind?"

"Well, it's God's will. I'm going because I need the money."

"Well then, go, go, may you earn a lot of money!"

And he goes on. At the end of the village there's a smithy, and in that smithy there's a gypsy working as the blacksmith. And the gypsy asks him, "And are you leaving, Ivan?"

"Well, I'm going off to work."

"My, my, my, that's such a nice wife. It's been two weeks since you got married and you're leaving her behind?"

"Well, I have to."

"Well then, I wish you a good journey! Go, go! May you earn a lot of money!" And he went.

Now, she got all dressed up and came to the well to fetch water. And the priest came up. "Listen! Just wait, young woman! Why have you chased your husband off to work? Why, you just got married recently!"

"Well, I ask you, father, what is there to do? We are poor. Let him go and earn something."

"But won't you be afraid to sleep alone?"

"Well, I'll be a little afraid, but what can I do about it?"

"Listen, how would it be if I came to you?"

"Oh, well, I don't know, as long as no one saw. Come at eleven o'clock."

"Fine, fine, I'll come."

Well, the priest comes, brings a bottle of wine, puts it on the table, and he brought something to eat besides. And so they drink and eat. But suddenly someone thumped at the door. "Oh, who's that?"

"Oh, it's my husband's returned!"

"But listen, now, where am I to hide?"

"Here, crawl here into the cupboard!" But that's not all! He had even taken his clothes off and he stood there naked in the cupboard – it was the kind of cupboard with two doors. "You stay there in the cupboard!" And that husband came, drank a little wine, and again hid himself. But then after a while the cantor comes. He brought a bottle, brought a bottle of whisky and put it on the table; he brought some sausage.

"Well, my young woman, let's drink a little!" They drank a little, some of this, and so forth. And now she yawns. "Well now, do you want to sleep already? Well, then, let's lay down, let's lay down! And now I'll go and take off my clothes."

"Well then, take them off."

He had just taken off his clothes when there was a thump, thump, at the door. "That's my husband! That's my husband's come! What's to happen now? He'll probably beat us! I'll hide you in the cupboard. Crawl in here into the cupboard!" Well then and he got into the cupboard. He was touching that other one, there was something warm, and he just moved over a little further. And the husband drank up a little whisky and again he hid himself.

A little while later the gypsy comes. Again he brings a bottle of whisky. And the gypsies like garlic, so he brought some garlic and sausage. And again they began to make company there. And now she yawns – she's smart – she yawns.

"What, do you want to sleep?"

"Yes. But here, you take off your clothes."

"Oh my, my! I'm for that!" He had barely taken off his clothes when the husband was at the door, boom, boom. "And who's that!"

"Oh, that's my husband! He's returned from work!"

"And where'll I hide?" he says.

"Wait. I'll hide you here in that cupboard. Crawl into that cupboard!"

And now there's three of them. The husband walks around the house, and she lay down for she hadn't slept the whole night. She sleeps. And here it was summer, the sun had come up. And the lady rides up to get the saints.

"Glory to Jesus Christ!"

"Glory forever!"

"And so, master artisan, are the saints ready?"

"Yes, the saints are ready."

"Please show them to me."

"Right away, I'll show them to you." And he opened the doors just for a prank.

And as soon as she saw them, "O Mother of God! But they are just as though they were alive! Just as though they are alive!" And they had crossed their arms yet! But it happened that "Only one thing doesn't please me."

"What?"

"Well, why did you make them with those things there?"

"Well, what did you think, my lady, that the saints don't have them? I made them just as though they were alive. But if that displeases you somehow, then I'll right away take a knife and cut them off." When he said that he'll take a knife and cut them off, the priest, who was at the very front, jumped out of the cupboard and out through the door, and the cantor followed him, and the gypsy did likewise.

And she again, "O Mother of God! Why did I say that? The saints would have remained standing there!"

"Well, I'm not in debt to you, my lady, for that. They got frightened over that operation and so they had to flee!"

"Well then, I'll leave you some money again, but you are to make the very same kind, but now without this here."

"Well then, I'll make them." And he went to town, bought some of that cement, those moulds, made the saints, and placed them in the cupboard.

And then the lady came and paid him. She looked at those saints and said, "Nice saints, but not as good as those others were."

And the lady took the saints away, and the wife says, "You see! It is I who made the saints, not you!" And the *bajka* (story) is ended.

4. ICELANDIC PULAR

Magnús Einarsson

When the new Dominion of Canada acquired title to Rupert's Land in 1869, the Icelanders were the first ethnic group to take advantage of the opportunity to settle in the west. In 1875 a number who had temporarily settled in eastern Canada migrated to the western shore of Lake Winnipeg where they founded the town of Gimli, meaning "the great hall of Heaven." This was the first of a series of settlements that came to be known as New Iceland. From Manitoba they spread out through the western provinces, mostly settling on farms or engaging in commercial fishing on Lake Winnipeg.

Mr. Einarsson got these two items in 1966 from an 81-year-old woman, Sigridur Björnsson, in Gimli, Manitoba. She had recently lost her sight and amused herself by remembering rhymes, verses, and riddles from her childhood which she occasionally recited for visiting nephews and nieces.

Icelandic scholars define a pula as a rhapsodic enumerative nonstrophic poem, often nonsensical. That definition obviously fits "The First Night of Christmas." "The Bird Who Lost His Nose" is also classified as a pula, even though it is not a poem, because of its enumerative quality. They resemble two familiar English cumulative items: "The Twelve Days of Christmas" and "The Old Woman and Her Pig."

THE BIRD WHO LOST HIS NOSE

A farmer was pounding a fish out by a stone, and then came a little bird and wanted to get himself a crumb, so the farmer chopped off his nose. He asked him to give him a piece of red thread to tie about his nose, but the farmer directed him to the Old Lady. "That I will not do," says Old Lady.

"Then Moth shall come and eat your web. Moth come and eat Old Lady's web; Old Lady won't give me a piece of red thread to tie about my nose, because Farmer chopped off my nose."

"That I will not do," says Moth.

"Then Mouse shall come and eat you. Mouse come and eat Moth,

Moth will not eat Old Lady's web, Old Lady will not give me a piece of red thread to tie about my nose, but Farmer chopped off my nose."

"That I will not do," says Mouse.

"Then Cat shall come and eat you. Cat come and eat Mouse, Mouse will not eat Moth, Moth will not eat Old Lady's web, Old Lady will not give me a piece of red thread to tie about my nose, but Farmer chopped off my nose."

"That I will not do," says Cat.

"Then Dog shall come and tear you. Dog come and tear Cat, Cat will not eat Mouse, Mouse will not eat Moth, Moth will not eat Old Lady's web, Old Lady will not give me a piece of red thread to tie about my nose, but Farmer chopped off my nose."

"That I will not do," says Dog.

"Then Wand shall come and whip you. Wand come and whip Dog, Dog will not tear Cat, Cat will not eat Mouse, Mouse will not eat Moth, Moth will not eat Old Lady's web, Old Lady will not give me a piece of red thread to tie about my nose, but Farmer chopped off my nose."

"That I will not do," says Wand.

"Then Fire shall come and burn you. Fire come and burn Wand, Wand will not whip Dog, Dog will not tear Cat, Cat will not eat Mouse, Mouse will not eat Moth, Moth will not eat Old Lady's web, Old Lady will not give me a piece of red thread to tie about my nose, but Farmer chopped off my nose."

"That I will not do," says Fire.

"Then Water shall come and extinguish you. Water come and extinguish Fire, Fire will not burn Wand, Wand will not whip dog, Dog will not tear Cat, Cat will not eat Mouse, Mouse will not eat Moth, Moth will not eat Old Lady's web, Old Lady will not give me a piece of red thread to tie about my nose, but Farmer chopped off my nose."

"That I will not do," says Water.

"Then Bull shall come and drink you. Bull come and drink Water, Water will not extinguish Fire, Fire will not burn Wand, Wand will not whip Dog, Dog will not tear Cat, Cat will not eat Mouse, Mouse will not eat Moth, Moth will not eat Old Lady's web, Old Lady will not give me a piece of red thread to tie about my nose, but Farmer chopped off my nose."

"That I will not do," says Bull.

"Then Yoke shall come and hang you. Yoke come and hang Bull, Bull will not drink Water, Water will not extinguish Fire, Fire will not burn Wand, Wand will not whip Dog, Dog will not tear Cat, Cat will not eat Mouse, Mouse will not eat Moth, Moth will not eat Old Lady's Web, Old Lady will not give me a piece of red thread to tie about my nose, but Farmer chopped off my nose."

"That I will not do," says Yoke.

288

"Then Axe shall come and chop you. Axe come and chop Yoke, Yoke will not hang Bull, Bull will not drink Water, Water will not extinguish Fire, Fire will not burn Wand, Wand will not whip Dog, Dog will not tear Cat, Cat will not eat Mouse, Mouse will not eat Moth, Moth will not eat Old Lady's web, Old Lady will not give me a piece of red thread to tie about my nose, but Farmer chopped off my nose."

"That I will not do," says Axe.

"Then Whetstone shall come and sharpen you. Whetstone come and sharpen Axe, Axe will not chop Yoke, Yoke will not hang Bull, Bull will not drink Water, Water will not extinguish Fire, Fire will not burn Wand, Wand will not whip Dog, Dog will not tear Cat, Cat will not eat Mouse, Mouse will not eat Old Lady's Web, Old Lady will not give me a piece of red thread to tie about my nose, but Farmer chopped off my nose."

"That I shall do," says Whetstone.

Whetstone sharpened Axe, Axe chopped Yoke, Yoke hanged Bull, Bull drank Water, Water extinguished Fire, Fire burned Wand, Wand whipped Dog, Dog tore Cat, Cat ate Mouse, Mouse ate Moth, Moth ate Old Lady's web, Old Lady gave me a piece of red thread to tie about my nose, and then the nose healed.

THE FIRST NIGHT OF CHRISTMAS

Come to me the first night of Christmas
I shall give you one fish,
All upon one dish.

Come to me the second night of Christmas
I shall give you two chickens, one fish,
All upon one dish.

Come to me the third night of Christmas
I shall give you three cakes, two chickens, one fish,
All upon one dish.

Come to me the fourth night of Christmas
I shall give you four slaughtered sheep, three cakes, two chickens, one
    fish,
All upon one dish.

Come to me the fifth night of Christmas
I shall give you five fat ones, four slaughtered sheep, three cakes, two
    chickens, one fish,
All upon one dish.

Come to me the sixth night of Christmas
I shall give you a sow with six pigs, five fat ones, four slaughtered sheep,
    three cakes, two chickens, one fish,
All upon one dish.

Come to me the seventh night of Christmas
I shall give you seven salted fry for cooking, a sow with six pigs, five fat
    ones, four slaughtered sheep, three cakes, two chickens, one fish,
All upon one dish.

Come to me the eighth night of Christmas
I shall give you eight oxen with grain fields, seven salted fry for cooking,
    a sow with six pigs, five fat ones, four slaughtered sheep, three cakes,
    two chickens, one fish,
All upon one dish.

Come to me the ninth night of Christmas
I shall give you nine straight-horned goats, eight oxen with grain fields,
    seven salted fry for cooking, a sow with six pigs, five fat ones, four
    slaughtered sheep, three cakes, two chickens, one fish,
All upon one dish.

Come to me the tenth night of Christmas
I shall give you ten early-bearing cows, nine straight-horned goats, eight
    oxen with grain fields, seven salted fry for cooking, a sow with six
    pigs, five fat ones, four slaughtered sheep, three cakes, two chickens,
    one fish,
All upon one dish.

Come to me the eleventh night of Christmas
I shall give you eleven trusses of hay, ten early-bearing cows, nine
    straight-horned goats, eight oxen with grain fields, seven salted fry
    for cooking, a sow with six pigs, five fat ones, four slaughtered sheep,
    three cakes, two chickens, one fish,
All upon one dish.

5. YIDDISH TALES FOR CHILDREN
Ruth Rubin

The first sizable group of Jews came to Canada in the 1880s, fleeing from persecution in Russia and Poland. Some settled on farms in the west, but most found new homes in Montreal or Toronto. They preserved many of their old-world customs, and such world-renowned folklorists as Dov Noy and Ruth Rubin have collected songs and stories from the Canadian Jewish community.

Ruth Rubin, who was born in Montreal, remembered the following stories from her own childhood. As she put it, "They are part of my own baggage. That means I did not consciously collect them but have them in my memory." Designed for very small children, the Granny tales have an obvious didactic purpose, but the plots resemble familiar international types. They have elements found in "The Three Little Pigs," "Little Red Riding Hood," and "The Bremen City Musicians."

A GRANNY WHO HAD MANY CHILDREN

Once upon a time there was a Granny who had many, many children. One day Granny had to go into the woods to gather some kindling wood. She told the children that if anyone should come, they should not let him in, and warned them especially about the big bear who prowled about in the forest and sometimes came near the house.

When Granny left, the children latched all the windows, barred the door, and hid. One hid on top of the cupboard, one under the cupboard; one on the bed, one under the bed; one on top of the oven, one under the oven; one over the chimney, one under the chimney. But the tiny little Heshela just couldn't find a place to hide, so he slid into a little bottle and sat there, very still.

Just then the great big bear passed by the house and noticed that Granny had gone to the woods to gather some kindling wood. He thought: "I'll just go in and gobble up all those little children." So he knocked on the door and said: "Children, children, open the door."

No one answered.

So he said again: "Children, children, open the door and I'll give you some blackberries."

The children replied: "No. We have our own blackberries."

So the bear said: "Children, children, open the door and I'll give you some blueberries."

And the children said: "No. We have some blueberries too."

So the bear went off to the blacksmith's and had his rear end well shod, and returned. This time he said: "Children, children, if you don't open the door, I'll break it in!"

And the children answered: "We're not afraid of you! We'd rather listen to Granny!"

So the angry bear turned around and with his well-shod rear end broke the door down. He went into the house, searched out all the children, opened his great big mouth, and "hm, hm," he ate them all up!

But the tiny little Heshela, who was hiding inside the little bottle, saw everything. But the bear did not see him at all! Then the great big bear went back into the forest.

When Granny returned, she found the house very still. She called: "Children, dear children, where are you?"

No one answered. She called again: "Children, dear children, where *are* you?"

But no one answered. So she began to look everywhere for them. She looked in the corridor. No one was there. She looked in the attic. Nobody was there. So she called again and again: "Dear little children, where are you?"

Just then little Heshela crawled out of the little bottle and jumped into Granny's lap and told her the whole story: how the great big bear came out of the forest; how he broke the door down with his well-shod rear end; how he found all the children and ate them all up!

When Granny heard this, she took a great big knife. She went to the blacksmith's and had him sharpen it very well, and hid it under her apron. Then she went off into the forest and called: "Berele, Berele, come to me."

"I won't," grunted the bear.

Granny said again: "Berele, Berele, come and I will give you some delicious milk pudding."

"I won't come," growled the bear.

So Granny said, "Berele, Berele, if you come, I will tickle your ear!"

"Aha!" said the bear, "That's exactly what I like!"

And the great big bear came out of the forest and lay down on the ground and put his head in Granny's lap. Granny began to tickle his ears – first the right one and then the left one.

"Hmmmmm," said the bear, his eyes closed and his great big mouth smiling. "Hmmmmm," and he seemed to be dozing off with pleasure.

When Granny noticed this, she took the sharp knife from under her apron, and quick as anything she snipped open the bear's belly, and all the little children came tumbling out!

Granny took all the children home and washed them and scrubbed them; she combed their hair and put clean clothes on them: she let them wear their new shoes and pretty socks to match. Then she set them all on a great big shovel and said: "Whoops now, off with you – to school you go!"

Socks to wear, socks to mend,
Our little story is at an end.
Groats with milk to make you shine,
Don't you think this story's fine?

THE LITTLE OLD GRANDMOTHER WHO LIVED AT THE EDGE OF THE FOREST

Once there was a little old grandmother and she lived in a little hut at the edge of the forest. She used to teach naughty little children how to behave. One day a mother brought her little girl to the little old grandmother and said: "Teach my little girl how to behave. She won't help around the house at all."

The little old grandmother smiled, shook her head, and said: "I will teach her how to behave."

The mother of the little girl went away, and the little old grandmother began to teach the little girl. The next day they both went into the forest to gather kindling wood for the fire.

While they were gone, a little bear came up to old Granny's hut and began to walk around it. Just then a little dog came running up and said: "Little bear, why do you walk round and round the hut?"

"What's it to you?" answered the little bear. "You can do it too, if you want to."

So they both walked round and round Granny's little hut. Then a little deer approached slyly and said: "Little bear and little dog, why are you both walking round and round Granny's hut?" And they answered: "What's it to you? You can do the same."

So the three walked round and round Granny's hut, when a cock came hopping by and asked: "Little bear, little dog, and little deer, why do you walk round and round Granny's hut?" And they answered: "You can join us if you wish!"

So the four of them were walking round and round and round Granny's hut, when the lid of a kettle came by and said to them: "Little bear and little dog, little deer and cock-a-doodle-doo, why do you walk round and round in this way?" And they answered: "What's it to you? You can do it too!"

So the five of them went walking round and round Granny's hut. Just then a pin and a blob of tar came up and said: "Little bear and little dog, little deer and cock-a-doodle-doo, and lid of a kettle too, why in the

world are you all walking round and round and round Granny's hut?"
And they answered: "You can do it too, if you like!"

So now all seven of them were strutting round and round, and round and round little old Granny's hut at the edge of the forest. And they walked and they strutted until it got dark. And when it got dark, they wanted to go to sleep. So they went into Granny's hut and looked for a place to sleep.

Little bear got into Granny's bed. Little dog jumped into the cradle. Little deer climbed up onto the oven. The cock flew up on the shelf. The lid of the kettle rolled into the chimney. The blob of tar snuggled into the box of matches, and the pin not knowing where to go, stuck herself into the towel.

Just then Granny and the little girl returned from the woods and began to get ready for bed. When they tried to get into the bed, the little bear kicked them and frightened them so badly that they jumped away. Then they tried to get ino the cradle, but the little dog snarled and bit them until they shouted: "Ouch! Ouch! Who is there?"

They looked for a place on top of the oven, but the little deer charged at them with his little antlers, until they began to tremble with fear. Granny went over to the stove to warm herself, but the lid from the kettle fell on her hand and she jumped back, yelling: "Woe is me, what is happening in my little hut this night?"

Then she thought she'd light the lamp to see what was going on. But when she tried to open the box of matches to get a match, the blob of tar stuck to her fingers and simply would not let go. She hurried over the wash-basin and washed the tar off, but when she went to wipe her hands on the towel, the pin pricked her so hard that she shrieked with the pain.

Just then the cock-a-doodle-doo crowed down at her: "Bad luck to you! Bad luck to you!"

That frightened the little old Granny so much that she fell right down in a faint. It frightened the little girl too, so she ran home to her mother, and from that day on she did everything her mother told her to do. From that day on, all wise little girls began to listen to their parents and they knew how to behave.

I told you a story, you see,
And now you can tell one to me!

SOURCES, NOTES, AND REFERENCES

I THE NATIVE PEOPLES
1. THE SHAKING TENT

Alexander Henry, *Travels and Adventures in Canada and the Indian Territories between the Years 1760 and 1776* (New York: Riley, 1809; rpt. Toronto: Morag, 1901), pp. 167-72.

Lambert quotation: R.S. Lambert, *Exploring the Supernatural*, p. 14. He cites many reports of the shaking tent in his first two chapters.

Father Paul LeJeune described the shaking tent in his *Relation* for 1634: *The Jesuit Relations and Allied Documents* (Cleveland, 1896-1901), ed. Reuben Thwaites, vol. 6, chap. iv, pp. 163-77. Paul Kane's account is in *Wanderings of an Artist among the Indians of North America* (London: Longman, Brown, 1859; rpt. various editions), chap. xxv, entry for July 28, 1848. For a more general study see Alfred Irving Hollowell, *The Role of Conjuring in Saulteaux Society* (1942; rpt. New York: Octagon, 1970).

2. THE LAST SUN DANCE

Richard Hardisty, "The Last Sun Dance," *Alberta Folklore Quarterly*, 2(1946), 57-61.

Kurath quotation: *Standard Dictionary of Folklore, Mythology, and Legend*, ed. Maria Leach, p. 1088. For other accounts see the *Anthropological Papers of the American Museum of Natural History*: Pliny E. Goddard, "Notes on the Sun Dance of the Cree in Alberta," 16(1919), 295-310; Alanson B. Skinner, "The Sun Dance of the Plains-Cree," 16(1919), 283-93; Leslie Spier, "The Sun Dance of the Plains Indians: Its Development and Diffusion," 16(1921), 451-527. More recently Lloyd O'Brodovic described the "Plains Sun Dance" in the *Western Canadian Journal of Anthropology*: Cree Studies Issue, 1(1968), 71-87.

3. TAHLTAN TALES

Nos. 1, 5, 10, 21, and 33 of "The Raven Cycle" in James Teit, "Tahltan Tales," *JAF*, 32(1919), 198-226.

Franz Boas wrote the obituary of James Teit in *JAF*, 36(1923), 102-3. Boas analyzed the pattern of the Raven stories in *Tsimshian Mythology*, and Paul Radin analyzed the dual nature of the Indian culture hero in *The Trickster: A Study in American Indian Mythology*.

"The Birth of Raven" includes the motifs of A511.1, "Birth of the culture hero"; A522.2.2, "Raven as culture hero"; and D631.3.1, "Compressible canoe." "The Origin of Daylight" includes A721.1, "Theft of sun"; A1411.2, "Theft of light by being swallowed and reborn"; A1412.3, "Acquisition of daylight by culture hero"; and T512.3, "Conception by drinking water."

"Raven Paints the Birds" comes under A2217.1, "Birds painted their present colors"; and "The Origin of Birth and Death" includes A1335, "The origin of death." "Raven Loses His Nose" is A2335.2.3, "Why raven has nose marked as if it had been broken."

4. OJIBWA TALES

Diamond Jenness, *The Ojibwa Indians of Parry Island, Their Social and Religious Life* (Ottawa: National Museum, Bulletin 78, 1935), pp. 69-70 and 97-98. "Origin Legend" includes Motifs A515.1.1, "Twin culture heroes"; A1010, "Deluge"; A1021, "Deluge: escape on boat (ark)"; A812, "Earth Diver"; and A561, "Divinity's departure for the west."

5. MICMAC TALES

Silas T. Rand, *Legends of the Micmacs* (New York: Longmans, 1894), pp. 232-37. Motifs include A541, "Culture hero teaches arts and crafts"; A561, "Divinity's departure for west"; D1524.3.1, "Stone canoe"; D1551, "Waters magically divide and close"; A1152, "Boneless man turned over to produce seasons"; A575, "Departed deity grants requests to visitors"; C321, "Tabu: looking into box (Pandora)"; D1904, "Love-compelling man sickens of bargain"; C922, "Death by smothering for breaking tabu."
For comparative references, see Stith Thompson, *Tales of the North American Indians* (Bloomington: Indiana University Press, 1929; rpt. 1968), p. 274, note 10.

6. BLOOD INDIAN TALES

Collected by Kenneth Peacock, Blood Indian Reserve, Saskatchewan, June, 1968. Raconteur: Earl Willows; transcriber: Leo Fox.
Kenneth Peacock, who was born in Toronto in 1922, is best known as a musicologist. He received his Bachelor of Music degree from the University of Toronto in 1948 and from 1951 to 1971 worked in the Folklore Division of the National Museum in Ottawa, spending his summers on field trips. His major publication is his three-volume *Songs of the Newfoundland Outports*, and he has also collected music from various ethnic groups and transcribed songs for many National Museum publications.
"The Seven Stars." National Museum archival finding No.: PEA 427-2876. Motifs include A773, "Origin of the Pleiades"; D1526.1, "Magic arrow flight"; Z311, "Achilles heel"; E50, "Resuscitation by magic"; and R243, "Fugitives aided by helpful animal."
"Blueface." Archival finding No.: PEA 440-2925. Motifs include T531, "Conception from casual contact with man"; D300, "Transformation: Animal to person"; C600, "Unique prohibition"; H50, "Recognition by bodily marks"; H161, "Recognition of transformed person among identical companions"; and E35, "Resuscitation from fragments of body." For comparative references for both stories see Thompson, *Tales of the North American Indians*, p. 345, note 244, and p. 339, note 222.

7. ESKIMO TALES

Franz Boas, *The Central Eskimo* (Washington: Bureau of American Ethnology, 1888; rpt. Toronto: Coles, 1974), pp. 175-77 and 189-90.

Boas (1858-1942), the German-born scholar who taught at Columbia University from 1896 to 1936, was one of the most important figures in the development of anthropology. As collector, teacher, author, and theoretician he dominated the field for nearly fifty years. He collected extensively among the Eskimos and the Indians of the west coast and published numerous books of both texts and theory. For an account of his career and a complete bibliography see his obituary in *JAF*, 57(1944), 59-69.

"Sedna and the Fulmar" includes Motifs A310.1, "Goddess of the world of the dead"; B602, "Marriage to fulmar"; A1837, "Origin of seal"; and A2135, "Origin of whale."

"The Sun and the Moon" has Motifs A736.1.1, "Sun sister and moon brother"; H58, "Tell-tale hand-mark"; and T415, "Brother-sister incest."

For comparative references for both stories see Thompson, *Tales of the North American Indians*, p. 272, note 2, and p. 273, note 6. Also see H. Newell Wardle, "The Sedna Cycle: A Study in Myth Evolution," *American Anthropologist*, n.s., 2(1900), 569-80.

II CANADIENS

Quotation from Luc Lacourcière, "The Present State of French-Canadian Folklore Studies, *JAF*, 74(1961), 374.

1. THE BLIND SINGER

Condensed from C. Marius Barbeau, *The Kingdom of the Saguenay* (Toronto: Macmillan, 1936), pp. 89-103.

Later Barbeau published slightly different accounts of the same singer in *The Tree of Dreams* (1955), pp. 51-64, and in *Jongleur Songs of Old Quebec* (1962), pp. xviii-xxi. Alcock quotation: *JAF*, 63(1950), 129.

In 1947 Clarisse Cardin published a *Bio-Bibliographie de Marius Barbeau* listing some 578 items, *Archives de Folklore*, 2(1947), 7-96; and in 1970 Israel Katz gave a bibliography of his folk music writings in *Ethnomusicology*, 14(1970), 129-41.

2. CONTES POPULAIRES

"The Bee and The Toad." Translated from "L'Abeille et le crapaud," collected by Adélard Lambert from Mme J.-B. Lambert, *JAF*, 36(1923), 221-22. Motif A2286.2, "Animal characteristics result of contest between God and the devil."

"The Winter of the Crows." Translated from "L'Hiver des corneilles," collected by Adélard Lambert, *JAF*, 53(1940), 160-61. Motif A2234.1.1, "Raven does not return to ark in obedience to Noah; black color is resulting punishment."

"Ti-Jean and the Big White Cat." Translated from "Ti-Jean et la chatte blanche," collected by C. Marius Barbeau from Paul Patry, August, 1914, at Saint-Victor, Beauce, *JAF*, 29(1916), 45-49.

It is a form of AT 402, *The Mouse (Cat, Frog, etc.) as Bride*, and includes Motifs B313, "Helpful animal an enchanted person"; B422, "Helpful cat"; D700, "Person disenchanted"; H1210.1, "Quest assigned by father"; H1242,

"Youngest brother alone succeeds in quest"; H1301.1, "Quest for the most beautiful bride"; H1306, "Quest for the finest of linen"; H1308, "Quest for the finest of horses."

"Richard's Cards." Translated from "Les Cartes du nommé Richard," collected August, 1914, by Marius Barbeau from P. Sioui of Lorette, as learned from his father, *JAF*, 29(1916), 134. AT 1613, *Playing Cards are My Calendar and Prayerbook*, and Motif H603, "Symbolic interpretation of playing cards." The same type also circulates as a song: see "La Chanson des cartes," Anselme et Daniel, *Chansons d'Acadie*, II, pp. 1-2.

"The Calf Sold Three Times." Translated from "Le Veau vendu trois fois," collected by Adélard Lambert from Alexandre Poudrier, *JAF*, 36(1923), 253-55. AT 1585, *The Lawyer's Mad Client* (K1655) is a famous joke known in Europe as "Patelin" or "Pathelin." Thomas Edward Oliver discusses "Some Analogues of Maistre Pierre Pathelin" in *JAF*, 22(1909), 395-430, and W.J. Wintemberg gives a version told by his father in *Folklore of Waterloo County, Ontario*, p. 61.

"Jean Baribeau." Translated from "Facéties et contes canadiens," collected by Victor Morin, *JAF*, 30(1917), 146. This comes under "Formula Tales" which include AT 2320, *Rounds*: Stories which begin over and over again and repeat (Z17).

3. LEGENDES

"The Devil at the Dance." Translated from "Le Diable à la danse," communicated by Dr. J.-E.-A. Cloutier to Marius Barbeau in 1919, from people in l'Islet, especially the octogenarian widow of Joseph Caron, *JAF*, 33(1920), 274-78. Philippe-Aubert de Gaspé, fils, published this famous tale in 1837 in *L'Influence d'un livre*, which he re-issued in 1864 as *Le Chercheur de trésor, ou, L'Influence d'un livre*. He called the tale simply "L'Etranger" – "The Stranger" – and named the girl with whom the devil danced Rose Latulippe. He attributed it to an old farmer of the Montreal region, and he had probably heard some form of the tale from oral tradition. Certainly it was well known along the lower St. Lawrence, with minor variations. M. Godbout cites two other versions in *JAF*, 33(1920), 273, and Soeur Marie-Ursule gives three shorter ones that she collected in Sainte-Brigitte de Laval in *Civilisation traditionnelle des Lavalois*, pp. 187-88. Motifs include G303.3.1, "Devil in human form"; G303.4, "How the devil is dressed"; G303.5.2.1, "Devil appears at dance"; G303.7.1.1, "Devil rides a black horse"; G303.16.3.1, "Devils driven away by cross"; G303.16.7, "Devil is chased by holy water"; and G303.17.2, "Physical circumstances of devil's disappearance."

"The Black Dog at the Wicked Rock." Translated from "Le Chien noir, au Rocher-malin" collected by Marius Barbeau, July 1918, at Notre-Dame-du-Portage from Alcide Léveillé, who had heard it sixty years earlier, *JAF*, 33(1920), 193-94. Motifs include G303.9.9, "Pranks played by the devil," and G303.3.3.1.1, "Devil in form of dog."

"The Wizard's White Magic." Translated from "La Magie blanche du sorcier" collected by Marius Barbeau from Charles Barbeau, Sainte-Marie, Beauce,

1915, *JAF*, 33(1920), 221. Motifs include D1719.1, "Contest in magic" and D2031, "Magic illusion."

4. LA COMPLAINTE DE CADIEUX

Translated from Joseph-Charles Taché, *Forestiers et voyageurs* (Québec, 1863; rpt. Montréal: Fides, 1946), chapter xv, pp. 134-42.

J.-C. Taché (1820-1894) was a doctor who became professor of physiology at Laval University, member of the Lower Canada House of Assembly, and founder of *Les soirées canadiennes*, a literary magazine in which the sketches and tales that make up *Forestiers et voyageurs* first appeared in 1863. Ernest Gagnon quoted Taché's story in *Chansons populaires du Canada* (1865), pp. 200-5, and Marius Barbeau repeated it in "La Complainte de Cadieux, coureur-de-bois (ca. 1709)," *JAF*, 67(1954), 168-83, where he lists thirteen different versions of the song, and cites a study by Louvigny de Montigny who concluded that the hero of the legend was Jean Cadieu, who was born in Montreal or Boucherville on March 12, 1671, and died in May, 1709, at the age of thirty-eight.

5. CHANSONS D'ACADIE

"Où vas-tu, mon petit garçon?" Marius Barbeau, *Alouette!* (Montréal: Editions Lumen, 1946), pp. 161-63. This was one of 120 songs in a manuscript given to Dr. Barbeau by Father P. Arsenault in 1924 and seems to be the only report from tradition, although it has been often reprinted.

It is a form of AT 1178, *The Devil Outriddled* and of "The False Knight upon the Road" (Child 3), a rare ballad in Britain but known in Nova Scotia where Helen Creighton collected two versions: *Songs and Ballads from Nova Scotia*, p. 1, and *Traditional Songs from Nova Scotia*, p. 1.

"Le Vieux Sauvage." Père Anselme et Frère Daniel, *Chansons d'Acadie* (Pointe-aux-Trembles, Montréal: La Reparation, 1945), II, 27. Gagnon gave two versions as "Tenaouiche Tenaga, Ouich'ka!" in *Chansons populaires du Canada*. pp. 124-26.

"Le Sergent." *Chansons d'Acadie*, II, 22.

6. CHANSONS FRANCO-ONTARIENS

"Mon canot." Germain Lemieux, *Chansonnier franco-ontarien* (Sudbury: Université de Sudbury, 1974), I, 72-73. Collected from Wilfrid Clement, aged 66, of Timmins, Ontario, in 1967.

Many versions of this song have been collected throughout Canada. (For one see *JAF*, 21(1919), 78-79.) In the *Canadian Folk Music Journal*, 2(1974), 13-18, François Brassard traces it to three literary poems published in the 1860s.

"Vie penible des cageux." *Chansonnier franco-ontarien*, I, 70-71. Collected from Mme Paul Simon (Gracia Groulx) aged 45, of Warren, Ontario, who learned it in 1920 from her mother who was born in Quebec.

"Les Canayens sont là." Germain Lemieux, *Folklore Franco-Ontarien, Chansons II* (Sudbury: La Société Historique du Nouvel-Ontario, 1950), pp. 30-31. Collected from M. Aldéric Perrault of Sudbury who had learned it in his childhood at St. Théodore-de-Chertsey, Quebec, from his uncle, Ulric Perrault.

7. TALL TALES OF DALBEC

Selected from William Parker Greenough, *Canadian Folk-Life and Folk-Lore* (New York: George H. Richmond, 1897; rpt. Toronto: Coles, 1971), Chapter iv, pp. 45-66.
These are all "Tales of Lying" and draw their motifs from the section "Lie: Great Hunters and Fishermen." The first is AT 1890E, *Gun Barrel Bent to Make Spectacular Shot* (X1122.3); the second resembles AT 1900, *How the Man Came Out of a Tree Stump* (X1133.4); the third is an example of AT 1890F, *Lucky Shot: Miscellaneous Forms*, and X1122.1, "Lie: hunter shoots projectile great distance"; and the fourth is a fine version of AT 1881, *The Man Carried Through the Air by Geese* (X1258.1).

8. PARLOUR GAMES IN ILE VERTE

Maurice Tremblay, "Nous irons jouer dans l'isle(sic)," *JAF*, 63(1950), 163-70. (The first part of the article appeared in English; the descriptions of the games are translated from the French.)
M. Tremblay, who studied at Laval and Harvard before joining Laval's Faculty of Social Sciences in 1948, has published many articles and books relating to social questions in French Canada. In addition to the two articles about games that he cites, Carmen Roy published "Les Jeux en Gaspésie" (Ottawa: National Museum, Bulletin 147, 1957), pp. 67-83.

9. THE EARLY DEVELOPMENT OF FRENCH-CANADIAN FOODWAYS

Contributed by Jay Allan Anderson, the result of research inspired by summer vacations spent in Quebec.
Dr. Anderson was born in Buffalo in 1940, took his B.A. in the United States, then studied at Aberdeen University, and received a diploma in education in Uganda. He studied folklore at the University of Pennsylvania, receiving his Ph.D. in 1971 for a study of foodways, and became director of the Delaware County Folk Farm in Pennsylvania.

FOOTNOTES
[1]Max. Sorre: "La Géographie de l'alimentation,"*Annales de Geographie*, 61(1952), 185-86.
[2]Cited in Ewan Jones, "Sourdough and Hardtack," in*The American Heritage Cookbook* (New York, 1964), p. 49
[3]*Peter Kalm's Travels in North America: The English Version of 1770*, 2 vols., ed. Adolph B. Benson (New York: Dover, 1966), p. 511.

III ANGLO-CANADIANS
1. THE QUEST OF THE BALLAD

Condensed from W. Roy Mackenzie, *The Quest of the Ballad* (Princeton, N.J.:

Princeton University Press, 1919), pp. 42-62.

Leach quotation, *JAF*, 78(1965), 82-83.

Halpert quotation, *JAF*, 71(1958), 98-99.

In his "Foreword" to the reprint of Mackenzie's *Ballads and Sea Songs from Nova Scotia* (Hatboro, Pa.: Folklore Associates, 1963), J. Malcolm Laws, Jr., gives a colourful sketch of the collector. He notes that William Roy Mackenzie was a native of River John, Nova Scotia, graduated from Dalhousie University in 1902, and took graduate degrees at Harvard under George Kittredge who encouraged his interest in ballads. He began serious collecting in 1908 and continued it for a number of years from his summer cottage at River John after he had become an English professor at Washington University in St. Louis, Missouri. Dr. Laws praises Mackenzie's research into previously collected and broadside versions of his songs, noting that "the Mackenzie headnotes remain of unique value to anyone making a serious study of these songs" (p. viii).

In "The Discovery of Bob," the first ballad is "The Banks of Dundee," M25 in J. Malcolm Laws, Jr., *American Balladry from British Broadsides*; "The Little Fighting Chance" is J19; "The Female Warrior" is N4; "The Gaspard Tragedy" is P36A; and the last is a fine version of Child 7, "Earl Brand."

2. SUPERSTITIONS AND THE SUPERNATURAL IN NOVA SCOTIA

Selected from chapters 3, 4, 5, 6, 9, and 11, Mary L. Fraser, *Folklore of Nova Scotia* [Toronto: Catholic Truth Society, 1931]; rpt. Antigonish: Formac, 1975.

Miss Fraser entered the Congregation of Notre Dame in Sydney in 1901 and took her perpetual vows in 1909. Her name in religion was Mother St. Thomas of the Angels. *Folklore of Nova Scotia* was her Ph.D. thesis for Fordham University, New York, where she received her degree in 1928. She taught in Mount St. Bernard College, Antigonish, until 1951, and then returned to the Mother House of the Infirmary of the Congregation of Notre Dame in Montreal where she died in 1957.

Numbers in parentheses relate the superstitions to Wayland Hand's classification in Volumes 6 and 7 of *The Frank C. Brown Collection of North Carolina Folklore*, and the Thompson motif numbers have been added to the stories. The tale of "Donald MacNorman and the Fairy Child" resembles "Johnnie in the Cradle" which Hamish Henderson collected from Andra Stewart and issued on a School of Scottish Studies record (A.001/2) in 1960. In *Folklore of Lunenburg County, Nova Scotia*, pp. 33-34, Helen Creighton gives seven reports of a phantom ship which she identifies as the *Young Teazer*, a privateer that was set afire and exploded when it was trapped by British warships in Mahone Bay in 1812. She also has a chapter on "Phantom Ships and Sea Mysteries" (pp. 118-56) in *Bluenose Ghosts*.

3. CELTIC TALES FROM CAPE BRETON

Selected from MacEdward Leach, "Celtic Tales from Cape Breton," in *Studies*

in Folklore in Honor of Stith Thompson, ed. Edson Richmond (Bloomington: Indiana University Press, 1957), pp. 40-54.

Dr. Leach was the first head of the folklore graduate school at the University of
Pennsylvania and for twenty-five years the secretary-treasurer of the American Folklore Society. He collected in Newfoundland, Nova Scotia, and Labrador, and published *Folk Ballads and Songs from the Lower Labrador
Coast* in 1965. His Newfoundland song collection is in the folklore archives
at Memorial University.

Dr. Leach indicated motifs for each tale but as he was using the earlier edition
of the *Motif-Index* I have substituted motifs from the revised edition while
retaining his comments.

"Cornu and His Sons." Formulistic framework for tales, tale to avert execution
(Z19); man (and sons) hiding in bag in order to be carried into palace
(K1892.1); execution escaped by telling stories (J1185); giant cats
(B871.1.6) swallow cows (F911.2). Giant with only one eye (F531.1.1.1);
giant's eye destroyed by hot medicine (G511); escape from giant's cave by
hiding under goat (K603); magic ring adheres to finger (D2171.1); cutting
off finger to save one's life (S161.1); escape by shamming death (K522).

"The Magic Gifts." This tale is especially interesting because the mill that
grinds without ceasing is not the climax, as is usual in such stories, but also
because of the unique motif of the sod. Motifs: Magic object stolen at inn
(D861.1) – type 563. Gold-producing duck (B103.2.1); self-grinding gold
mill (D1601.21); sod wraps up enemy (D1413.21).

"The Marvelous Piper." The male Cinderella is a common enough story, but
the combination here found with the fairy helper is unique. This uses stock
motifs at the beginning: cruel stepmother (S31); male Cinderella (L101).
The motifs building up the remainder of the story are rare: boy learns to play
pipes by putting his fingers in fairy's mouth (D1723); magic music charms
birds from nest, fish from sea (D1441.1.2).

4. NEWFOUNDLAND RIDDLES

Elisabeth B. Greenleaf, "Riddles of Newfoundland," *Marshall Review* (Hun-
tington, W. Va.), 1:3 (March 1938), 5-20.

This article was one of the sources for Archer Taylor's *English Riddles from
Oral Tradition* and his reference numbers have been added in parentheses. As
that work deals only with "true riddles," references for some of the other
types: neck riddles, arithmetic riddles, and conundrums, have been drawn
from the section on "Riddles" in *The Frank C. Brown Collection of North
Carolina Folklore*, I, 285-328. These numbers are distinguished by the prefix
N.C.

5. NEWFIE JOKES

Condensed from an article and collection of jokes which Gerald Thomas prepared while working towards a graduate degree in folklore at Memorial
University.

Gerald Thomas was born in Wales in 1940, took an Honours degree in French

302

at the University of Wales, and came to teach in the French Department of Memorial University in 1964. In 1970 he obtained the first M.A. in Folklore in an English-language Canadian university. He is currently Associate Professor of French and his Ph.D. dissertation deals with the narrative tradition of French Newfoundlanders.

In his joke collection Mr. Thomas cited the relevant Aarne-Thompson tale types and Thompson and Baughman motifs, and referred to several commercial joke books. At that time he did not have access to William M. Clements, "The Types of the Polack Joke," *Folklore Forum*, Bibliographic and Special Series, No. 3 (November 1969), which is now the recognized classification system for such jokes. Accordingly his tale-type and motif numbers have been kept, the joke-book references dropped, the order changed to conform to Clements' grouping, and the Clements' numbers added.

Many of the jokes fit under J1730-1749, "Absurd ignorance"; J1930, "Absurd disregard of natural laws"; Z691, "Stories about characteristics attributed to various races or nationalities"; and Baughman's J2259*[p], "Fools' action based on pun." However, such motifs are not indicated unless Thompson or Baughman cites a similar joke. The parenthetical reference numbers beginning with J or X refer to the Thompson or Baughman index; those beginning with C, E, F, G, H, and L refer to Clements' classification.

Mr. Thomas supplied the following notes on his informants.

Informants

Of the 16 informants, 11 are Newfoundlanders and 5 from Great Britain.

Mr. Stuart Barr, 37, from Liversedge, Yorkshire, Associate Professor of French and Head of the Department of Romance Languages and Literature. His feelings about Newfoundlanders are mixed; respecting them in some ways, he tells Newfie jokes with a certain relish, an attitude common to many British immigrants to Newfoundland. Nos. (collected by dictation) 3, 4, 68.

Miss Elizabeth Cook, 22, born in St. John's but now living in Ottawa. Nos. (contributed in ms.) 6, 18, 31, 34, 44, 71.

Mr. John Crawley, 21, student, from Holyrood, Conception Bay. Nos. (ms.) 11, 12, 13, 25, 61, 76, 77.

Mr. Vic Du Pre, born in England but resident in St. John's for nearly 15 years, Language Laboratory Administrator. Nos. (dictation) 10, 22, 63, 69, 80.

Mr. Robert Edwards, 25, student, from St. John's. Nos. (ms.) 19, 53.

Mr. Graham Field, 23, student, from Deer Lake. Mr. Field has been by far my richest informant. Four years of University residence life have provided him with the bulk of his jokes. Nos. 1, 2, 5, 7, 8, 20, 21, 24, 33, 35, 43, 50, 51, 54, 57, 58, 62, 66, 72, 75, 82, 83.

Miss Carol Fitzgerald, 22, Lecturer in French, from St. John's. She got the jokes from her 16-year-old brother, John: mostly formulaic one-liners which have been in circulation in local high schools. Nos. (ms.) 14, 27, 59, 60, 65, 67, 74.

Miss Emma Green, 21, student, from St. John's. No. 73.

Dr. John Hewson, 37, born in England but resident in St. John's for over 10 years and a Canadian citizen. Associate Professor and Head of Department of Linguistics. Nos. (dictation) 26, 70, 79.

Miss Beverley Hudson, 18, student, from Western Bay, Conception Bay. No. 16.

Mr. Claude Kelly, Assistant Professor of French, from Ireland. No. 9.

Mr. Patrick Lundrigan, 28, student, from Lord's Cove, Placentia Bay, heard the jokes while working in Toronto. Nos. (ms.) 17, 28, 30, 32.

Miss Yvonne Matthews, 21, student, from Corner Brook. She got the jokes from a Newfoundland friend working in Ontario: mainly formulaic one-liners, they had been put on his desk by anonymous colleagues. Nos. 29, 36, 37, 38, 39, 40, 41, 42, 45, 46, 47, 48, 49, 52, 55, 56.

Mr. David Rowe, 25, Lecturer in French, from Llanelli, Wales. Nos. 23, 64.

Mr. Eugene Spurvey, 23, student, from Fox Harbour, Placentia Bay. He heard his jokes from Gordon Caines of Bird Cove, Ste. Barbe North. Nos. 15, 81.

Mr. Brendan Tilley, 21, student, from St. John's. No. 78.

6. A MUMMERS' PLAY FROM NEWFOUNDLAND

"The Savage Play," contributed by Barney Moss to *The Newfoundlander*, January, 1950, pp. 14-15.

The most extensive study of any Canadian folk custom is *Christmas Mumming in Newfoundland*, a collection of "Essays in Anthropology, Folklore, and History" edited by Herbert Halpert and G.M. Story. Its nine contributors describe and analyze the history and practices associated with mumming in detail. An appendix gives three printed texts of mummers' plays originally printed in St. John's newspapers; this was one of them. A related article is Richard Bauman's description of "Belsnickling in a Nova Scotia Community," *Western Folklore*, 31(1972), 229-43.

7. LARRY GORMAN AND THE CANTE FABLE

Selected from Edward D. Ives, *Larry Gorman: The Man Who Made the Songs* (Bloomington: Indiana University Press, 1964).

Dr. Ives produced his study of Larry Gorman as his Ph.D. dissertation at the University of Indiana. He teaches folklore at the University of Maine, edits *Northeast Folklore*, and collects in the Canadian Maritimes as well as in Maine. He has studied two other east-coast songmakers, Lawrence Doyle and Joe Scott, in detail.

The humorous graces attributed to Larry Gorman come under AT 1567G, *Good Food Changes a Song*, and Motifs J1341.11, "Hired men sing of displeasure with food; change song when food is improved"; and J1341.12, "Hired man shows in singing grace how better food has resulted from arrival of unexpected guests."

8. JOKES AND ANECDOTES

"Pat and Mike Jokes from Nova Scotia." Selected from "Pat and Mike Stories and Tall Tales," Arthur Huff Fauset, *Folklore from Nova Scotia* (American Folklore Society Memoir 24, 1931), pp. 52-77.

304

These include several widespread tale types. "The Riddle Test" is a form of AT 922, *The Shepherd Substituting for the Priest Answers the King's Questions*; "Three Dreams" is AT 1626, *Dream Bread*, and "Let Me Spit on My Hands," AT 1250, *Bringing Water from the Well*. Many of the others illustrate widespread motifs, mostly from the section J1700-1799, "Absurd ignorance." Where these apply they are indicated in parentheses at the end of each item.

"Ontario Yarns from Joe Thibadeau." Told to Edith Fowke by Joe Thibadeau, Bobcaygeon, Ontario, October 11, 1964, and Lindsay, Ontario, June 10, 1965. Motif numbers are indicated after each item. Joe also told his tales to Newbell N. Puckett, an American folklorist who collected songs and stories from him and other informants in the Bobcaygeon district during summer vacations in Ontario. His collection is now in the Memorial University of Newfoundland Folklore and Language Archive. For a discussion of the Bunyan tradition in Canada see Fowke, "In Defense of Paul Bunyan," *Folklore Preprint Series*, 3:3(1975).

An actual French-Canadian strong man who worked in the woods also became the subject of traditional anecdotes. Benjamin Sulte told of his career in *Histoire de Jos. Montferrand: L'Athlète canadien,* and the loggers transformed him into Joe Mufferaw. Like Paul Bunyan, Joe Mufferaw has been commercialized, largely through Bernie Bedore of Arnprior, Ontario, who published *Tall Tales of Joe Mufferaw* in 1966 and had a television series, "Mufferaw Land," in 1971.

"Tall Tales and Other Yarns from Calgary, Alberta." Article by Herbert Halpert in the *California Folklore Quarterly*, 4(1945), 29-49. It has been slightly condensed by omitting variants of some of the tales. Tale types and motifs have been added where applicable. However, Baughman's specific reference numbers for these particular tales are not listed as most items fit under Thompson's more general motifs.

Dr. Halpert is an outstanding authority on bibliographical references. He has annotated several volumes of folktales by Richard Chase, Vance Randolph, and others, and the extensive footnotes which follow illustrate his painstaking research.

FOOTNOTES

[1] Professor Robert E. Gard has been in Alberta for over a year on a Rockefeller Foundation Grant in charge of a folklore and history project in connection with the Extension Department of the University of Alberta. By extensive publicity and innumerable talks before various organizations he has induced Alberta people to contribute a large amount of material. A few newspaper columnists, like Robert Needham of the *Calgary Herald*, have occasionally published folk tales and other folklore. Some stories have appeared in newspapers in the Province in interviews and as "fillers." Compare the informant's comment on the last tale in this collection.

[2] " . . . The warmth of the Great Plains at the eastern foot of the Rockies is the result not only of proximity to the ocean, but also of the 'chinook' winds. These are dry and warm west winds blowing on the south side of depressions crossing the continent. They are warm and damp after their passage over the Pacific and in crossing the Western ranges lose their humidity as rain, and in favourable circumstances descend to the plains of the interior with föhn heat and dryness due to compression. Their

influence is greatest along the east foot of the range, where they rapidly melt and dry up the snow and make grazing possible all winter . . . . The rise in temperature when the chinook sets in is somewhat exceedingly rapid, as much as 40° in 15 minutes being occasionally recorded. As a rule the temperature does not exceed 40° but this appears very warm after the intense cold which may have prevailed during a preceding spell of anticyclonic weather. Alberta being close under the Rockies is especially favoured by chinooks, and Calgary has recorded 58° in January. When chinooks are strong and frequent the western Prairie Provinces have a comparatively open winter . . . . " W.G. Kendrew, *The Climates of the Continents* (3rd ed., New York, 1942), pp. 314-315.

[3]Cf. H. Halpert, "John Darling, A New York Munchausen,"*JAF*, 57(1944), 98.

[4]For his life see: John Maclean,*McDougall of Alberta: A Life of Rev. John McDougall, D.D., Pathfinder of Empire and Prophet of the Plains* (Toronto, 1927). Rev. McDougall's writings are listed on pp. 265-266.

[5]In a pamphlet by Edna Kells,*Elizabeth McDougall, Pioneer* (Toronto, n.d.) p. 48, we are informed: "Her eldest son, the Rev. John McDougall, passed on in 1917, and the second son, David McDougall, trader and rancher, died in 1928."

[6]" . . . In 1862 Mr (George) McDougall and his eldest son, John . . . travelled . . . as far west as the Rockies . . . " They returned to near Edmonton in 1863. (Kells,*op. cit.*, p.7). In 1873 " . . . on November first John McDougall, with his wife, his brother David, John's man, named Donald, and some native helpers, left Edmonton for the Bow Valley . . . . The mission was named Morley . . . . " (Maclean, *op. cit.*, p. 82).

[7]Several of my informants suggested that Dave, a good business man, was not above following the standard trade practice of early Indian traders of getting far more than he gave.

[8]This saying is used about two Montana liars in C.M. Russell,*Trails Plowed Under* (Garden City and New York, 1927), p. 191; also reprinted in B.A. Botkin,*A Treasury of American Folklore* (New York, 1944), p. 565.

[9]Maclean,*op. cit.*, soberly gives us some amusing descriptions of McDougall as a storyteller. "His stories about the buffalo sometimes seemed pure flights of the imagination . . . " (p. 122). On a Lake steamer he and another missionary sang a hymn in Cree to entertain the passengers, and McDougall reports "and then they asked for a wild west story and I gave them one" (p. 180). And his final summary is: "McDougall was a splendid story teller. We have sat around the camp-fire, heedless of the intense cold, listening spellbound to thrilling tales of adventure, surpassing any of the experiences narrated in his published letters and books" (p. 262).

[10]Cf. Russell,*op. cit.*, p. 103, and reprinted in Botkin,*op. cit.*, pp. 565-566.

[11]For another story of two seasons existing at the same time, see: Halpert,*op. cit.*, p. 104. Others from Pennsylvania and New York are in the Halpert mss.

[12]Compare this with the changeable weather which kills one ox by sunstroke and freezes the other to death: M. C. Boatright,*Tall Tales from Texas* (Dallas, Texas, 1934), p. 75; R.S. Boggs, "North Carolina White Folk Tales and Riddles,"*JAF*, 47(1934), 316.

[13]This is a variant of the Munchausen tale. See*The Travels of Baron Munchausen*, edited by W. Rose, Broadway Translations (London and New York, n.d.), p. 31; C. Neely and J. W. Spargo, *Tales and Songs of Southern Illinois* (Menasha, Wisconsin, 1938), p. 47; R. M. Dorson, "Jonathan Draws the Long Bow,"*New England Quarterly*, 16(1943), 275. In Paul Bunyan's camp a skid sled gets left in the treetops when the snow melts, E. Shephard,*Paul Bunyan* (New York, 1924), pp. 104-107. In another American version of this tale the horse is tethered to a tree on top of a sand dune and the wind blows the sand away: Dorson,*op. cit.*, p. 275, note 34; A. Garland, "Pipeline Days and Paul Bunyan,"*Publications of the Texas Folklore Society*, 7(1928), 61;

Boatright,*op. cit.*, pp. 41-43. Compare the horse tied to a limb that had been bent down by the weight of wild pigeons. Botkin,*op. cit.*, pp. 588-589 (quoted from "Skitt,"*Fisher's River Scenes and Characters).*

[14]This, the best known of Dave's yarns, is a variation on the Munchausen story of the horse and rider outracing a storm. For a text and references see: Halpert,*op. cit.*, p. 104, P. Moulton,*2500 Jokes for All Occasions* (New York, 1942), No. 1234. A very modern variant, mentioning a "Model T," is in E.E. Selby,*100 Goofy Lies* (Decatur, Illinois, 1939), p. 15.

[15]Cf. Garland,*op. cit.*, p. 61.

[16]See the following story.

[17]For another yarn telling of the gigantic size of the engines on the "Jerusalem Center Railroad," see Burlington Liars Club,*The 25 Best Lies of 1933* (Burlington, Wisconsin, 1934), p. 11.

[18]This should be compared with the stories of boiling liquid freezing.

[19]Lake Louise is noted for its amazingly beautiful blue-green color.

[20]Cf. "How to Make Rattlesnake Soup," Botkin,*op. cit.*, pp. 379-381; recipe for planking carp. J.W. Blakley,*Tall Tales* (Franklin, Ohio and Denver, Colo., 1936), p. 58.

[21]See: R.M. Dorson, "Just B'ars,"*Appalacia*, n.s. 8, 183; Boatright,*op. cit.*, pp. 65-67; H.W. Thompson,*Body, Boots and Britches* (Philadelphia, 1940), p. 291. There is a text from Pennsylvania in the Halpert mss. Compare: O.C. Hulett,*Now I'll Tell One* (Chicago, 1935), pp. 90-91, where wolves set beaver to cutting down a tree.

[22]The Englishman's remarks are given with an exaggerated imitation of an English accent. For another story of the remarkable clarity of Western atmosphere, compare F.H. Hart, *The Sazerac Lying Club* (San Francisco and New York, 1878), pp. 95-97.

[23]Compare this with "Outracing the Chinook," story 13.

[24]Cf. Federal Writers' Project of the Work Projects Administration,*Idaho Lore* (Caldwell, Idaho, 1939), p. 120; V. Randolph,*Funny Stories about Hillbillies* (Girard, Kansas, 1944), p. 8. A variant from Alaska is in the Halpert mss. For other stories about the wind, compare Botkin, *op. cit.*, pp. 512-520, 611 613; Boatright,*op. cit.*, pp. 40 48.

[25]For frogs several years old that can't swim, cf. Burlington Liars Club,*op. cit.*, p. (5); Botkin,*op. cit.*, pp. 313-338, 339; Mildred Meiers and Jack Knapp,*Thesaurus of Humor* (New York, 1940), No. 5565; Randolph,*op. cit.*, pp. 9-10. For shrinking hogs in water so they won't leak when fed swill, cf. Hulett,*op. cit.*, p. 22. For other dry land stories, cf. Hulett, *op. cit.*, pp. 22, 100, 103; Botkin,*op. cit.*, pp. 312-314, 332-340; Thomas,*op. cit.*, pp. 218 219.

[26]In the usual form of this widely known story, a man picks up a hat on a muddy road only to find a man sunk under it riding safely on a horse or mule or vehicle. He is on horseback in: Thompson,*op. cit.*, pp. 173-174; Boatright,*op. cit.*, p. 48; E.C. Beck, *Songs of the Michigan Lumberjacks* (Ann Arbor, 1942), p. 282; Moulton,*op. cit.*, No. 1221; on a mule in: M.J. Atkinson and J.F. Dobie, "Pioneer Folk Tales,"*Publications of the Texas Folklore Society*, 7(1928), 75-76; A.P. Hudson and P.K. McCarter, "The Bell Witch of Tennessee and Mississippi: A Folk Legend,"*JAF*, 47(1934), 56-57 (reprinted in Botkin,*op. cit.*, p. 706); on a load of hay in L. Thomas,*Tall Stories* (New York, 1931), pp. 210-213; Selby,*op. cit.*, p. 20; Dreamy Bill and Others,*The Arkansaw I Saw* (Baltimore, Md., 1919), p. 50; and most up-to-date, on a jeep: Sgt. Bill Davidson,*Tall Tales They Tell in the Services* (New York, 1943), p. 47.

[27]See Moulton,*op. cit.*, No. 1254. Cf. Hulett,*op. cit.*, pp. 12-13, and Botkin,*op. cit.*, p. 338, where it is told of a coyote chasing a jackrabbit, and Randolph,*op. cit.*, p. 7 (fox chasing a weasel). For other hot weather stories see: Z.N. Huston,*Mules and Man* (Philadelphia and London, 1935), pp. 132-133 (also reprinted in Botkin,*op. cit.*, pp. 606-607); Botkin,*op. cit.*, pp. 312, 339-341.

[28]For sounds freezing in the air and not heard till spring see: Thompson, *op. cit.*, pp.

307

132, 138, 272; Thomas,*op. cit.*, pp. 197-198, 199; Hulett,*op. cit.*, p. 18; Boatright,*op. cit.*, pp. 50-51; Shephard,*op. cit.*, pp. 100-101; texts from Alaska in Halpert mss. The theme is one of Munchausen's and is also in one of Joseph Addison's essays in *The Tatler*. Compare the following yarn for a variant form.

[29] For sounds freezing into chunks of ice, see: Thomas,*op. cit.*, p. 198, 199-201; Moulton, No. 1223; D. Lavender,*One Man's West* (New York, 1943), p. 16.

[30] For coffee boiling with ice on top, see Botkin,*op. cit.*, p. 508; Blakley,*op. cit.*, p. 49; Randolph,*op. cit.*, p. 17. A text from New Jersey is in the Halpert mss.

[31] For the split or chopped dog, see: Thompson,*op. cit.*, p. 295; Shephard,*op. cit.*, pp. 115-116; H. Zunser, "A New Mexican Village,"*JAF*, 48(1935), 173; H. Halpert, "Family Tales of a Kentuckian,"*Hoosier Folklore Bulletin*, 1(1942), 71; S. Gates, "Windy Yesterdays,"*Publications of the Texas Folklore Society*, 14(1938), 264-265; R.S. Boggs, "North Carolina Folktales Current in the 1820's,"*JAF*, 47(1934), 276-277 (reprinted from Skitt,*op. cit.*,) also reprinted in Botkin, op. cit., pp. 593-594. For other split animals, see Dorson,*op. cit.*,*New England Quarterly*, 16, 246; H. Halpert, "Folktales Collected in the Army,"*California Folklore Quarterly*, 3(1944), 118.

[32] See *Idaho Lore*,*op. cit.*, pp. 127-129. Compare riding a shark, Federal Writers' Project of the Works Progress Administration for the State of New Jersey,*New Jersey, A Guide To Its Present and Past* (New York, 1939), p. 129. See the latter for a comparable story of being towed by a fish, p. 129. Cf. also: Thomas,*op. cit.*, pp. 57-61, 75-76.

[33] For texts and references see H. Halpert, "Indiana Folktales,"*Hoosier Folklore Bulletin*, 1(1942), 17-18, and A.L. Gary, "Some Indiana Yarns,"*ibid.*, 2(1943), 45-46. Add: Blakley, *op. cit.*, p. 55; Davidson,*op. cit.*, p. 35, Cf. Federal Writer's Project in Indiana, *Hoosier Tall Stories* (Works Progress Administration, 1937), pp. 23-24.

[34] For a text and references see H. Halpert, "John Darling, A New York Munchausen,"*op. cit.*, pp. 103-104. Add: C.F. Arrowood, "'Well Done, Liar,'"*Publications of the Texas Folklore Society*, 17(1943), 80; Lavender,*op. cit.*, p. 150; Sgt. Bill Davidson,*op. cit.*, p. 64.

[35] For another team which drags out a hole, cf. Thompson,*op. cit.*, p. 146.

[36] Note the change from third to first person.

[37] Almost exactly the same story from New York State is in the Halpert mss.

[38] Cf. Botkin,*op. cit.*, p. 710.

[39] Cf. Randolph,*op. cit.*, p. 20.

[40] For texts and references, see H. Halpert, "Folktale and Wellerism – a Note,"*Southern Folklore Quarterly*, 7(1943), 75-76. Add: C.E. Brown, "Wisconsin Versions of 'Scissors!'" *Hoosier Folklore Bulletin*, 2(1943), 46-47.

[41] For a text and reference, see H. Halpert, "Three Tales from Gwent,"*JAF*, 58(1945), 52-53. Note how sincerely the informant believes that this old folk tale is a story he helped compose.

9. THE BALDOON MYSTERY

Neil T. McDonald, *The Baldoon Mysteries: A Wierd* (sic) *Tale of the Early Scotch Settlers of Baldoon*, 3rd ed. (Wallaceburg, Ontario: W. Colwell, 1910), pp. 32-36 and 40-42.

In *Exploring the Supernatural*, pp. 63-68, R.S. Lambert draws upon all the statements to give a more detailed account of "An Ontario Witch-Hunt," and he also describes several similar Canadian episodes. James H. Coyne gives another account in "David Ramsay and Long Point in Legend and History" in *Transactions of the Royal Society of Canada*, Section II, 1919, pp. 11-26, and E.A. Owen describes "Dr. Troyer and His Big 'Witch-Trap'" in *Pioneer Sketches of the Long Point Settlement*, pp. 123-26.

The statements quoted contain many traditional motifs, notably those indexed under F473, "Poltergeist." These include F473.1, "Poltergeist throws objects"; F473.2, "Poltergeist causes objects to behave contrary to their nature"; F473.2.4, "House burns for no apparent reason"; F473.3, "Poltergeist mistreats person"; and F473.6.5, "Spirit throws back shots fired at it." Other motifs are G211.3.3, "Witch in form of goose"; D1814.1, "Advice from magician"; D1825.2, "Magic power to see distant objects"; G259.1, "Witch recognized by looking in or through magic object"; D1385.4, "Silver bullet"; G271.4.8, "Breaking spell by shooting bewitched object"; and G275.12, "Witch in form of animal injured or killed as a result of the injury to the animal."

10. SONGS OF THE GREAT LAKES

Selected from a manuscript, "The Great Lakes," in the Ivan H. Walton collection of tapes and manuscripts in the Library of the University of Michigan, Ann Arbor. Mr. Walton had been a member of the Ann Arbor faculty, teaching English in the College of Engineering. His manuscript gave full descriptive notes and texts with variants for nearly a hundred Great Lakes songs. The ones chosen are some he collected from Canadians, most of which deal with Canadian ships. Some of his notes have been slightly condensed, and variants have been omitted.

C. H. J. Snider, a Canadian authority on naval history, collected a number of Great Lakes songs and published them in his column, "Schooner Days," in the Toronto *Evening Telegram*. He and his friend Stanley Bâby sang "The Wreck of the *Asia*," "The *Maggie Hunter*," and "The Loss of the *Antelope*," as well as other *Songs of the Great Lakes* on Folkways record FM 4018. Another version of "The Foundering of the *Asia*" appears in *More Folk Songs of Canada* by Fowke and Johnston, pp. 52-53, and a fragment of "It's Me for the Inland Lakes" appears in E.C. Beck, *Lore of the Lumber Camps* (Ann Arbor: University of Michigan Press, 1948), p. 75.

11. SQUARE DANCE CALLS

From an undated manuscript in the papers left by the late John D. Robins.

Dr. Robins, a native of Ontario, taught at Victoria College, University of Toronto, first in the German Department and later in the English Department. He published two books of humorous sketches about Ontario's vacation country, and his versions of some Ontario lumbering yarns appear in *Logging with Paul Bunyan*.

Helen Creighton gives some Nova Scotia calls in *Folklore of Lunenburg County, Nova Scotia*, pp. 154-63, and Lois Fahs published *Swing Your Partner: Old-Time Dances of New Brunswick and Nova Scotia*. Roy Clifton described some typical dance patterns in the booklets accompanying Folkways records FW 8825, 8826, and 8827.

12. FOLKWAYS

"Building Our Log House" and "Making Maple Sugar." From *George Stanley, or, Life in the Woods. A Boy's Narrative of the Adventures of a Settler's Family in Canada,* ed. Cunningham Geikie (London: Routledge, Warne, and Routledge, 1864), pp. 24-28 and 183-88. The book was later issued as *Life in the Woods: A True Story of the Canadian Bush* (London: Strahan, 1873), and *Adventures in Canada, or, Life in the Woods* (Philadelphia, c. 1882).

"A Winter in a Lumbercamp." Condensed from George S. Thompson, *Up to Date, or, The Life of a Lumberman* (Peterborough, Ontario: Times Printing Company, 1895), chapters 3 and 4, pp. 20-38.

"The Cattle Round Up, 1906." From a manuscript written in longhand by John O. McHugh in 1959-1960 and edited by Hugh A. Dempsey; in the archives of the Glenbow-Alberta Institute, Calgary.

13. AUTOGRAPH VERSES FROM SASKATCHEWAN

Selected from entries in four autograph albums filled between 1927 and 1933 in Lumsden and Regina, Saskatchewn.

Similar verses occur in such American collections as Lelah Allison, "Traditional Verse from Autograph Books," *Hoosier Folklore*, 8(1949), 87-94; Duncan Emrich, *Folklore on the American Land* (Boston: Little Brown, 1972), pp. 216-37; Duncan Emrich, *The Nonsense Book* (New York: Four Winds Press, 1970), pp. 155-77; Vance Randolph and May Kennedy McCord, "Autograph Albums in the Ozarks," *JAF*, 61(1948), 182-93.

14. WESTERN VERNACULAR

Condensed from John D. Higinbotham, "Western Vernacular," *Alberta Historical Review*, 10(Autumn 1962), 9-17. This article was from an unpublished manuscript entitled "Salad Days." Mr. Higinbotham had previously published some historical reminiscences in *When the West Was Young* (Toronto: Ryerson, 1933).

Research carried on by the Lexographical Centre for Canadian English resulted in *A Dictionary of Canadianisms on Historical Principles* in 1967, and the Centre's director, Matthew H. Scargill, produced *Modern Canadian English Usage: Linguistic Change and Linguistic Reconstruction* in 1974. The Scargill quotation is from "The Growth of Canadian English" in *The Literary History of Canada*, p. 251.

15. MONSTERS OF THE WEST: THE SASQUATCH AND THE OGOPOGO

Prepared by M. Carole Henderson for this anthology, 1976.

Dr. Henderson, who was born in Vancouver in 1944, took her Ph.D in folklore at the University of Pennsylvania, completing her dissertation, "Many Voices: A Study of Folklore Activities in Canada and Their Role in Canadian Culture," in 1975. She is currently an assistant professor in the Division of Humanities, York University.

FOOTNOTES

[1]Harvey Cox,*The Feast of Fools* (Cambridge: Harvard University Press, 1969), p. 11.

[2]See John R. Napier's scholarly study, *Bigfoot: The Yeti and Sasquatch in Myth and Reality* (London: Jonathan Cape, 1972) and Ivan T. Sanderson's popularly written book, *Abominable Snowman: Legend Come to Life*(Philadelphia and New York: Chilton Co., 1961).

[3]F. W. Holiday discusses this creature in particular, and others similar to Ogopogo in*The Great Orm of Loch Ness* (New York: Faber & Faber, 1968).

[4]This work was first published as J. B. Tyrrell, ed.,*David Thompson's narrative of his explorations in western America, 1784-1812* (Toronto: Champlain Society, 1916).

[5]A theory presented in a letter to the*Sunday Times*, London, published in the *Vancouver Sun*, September 26, 1960.

[6](Bloomington: Indiana University Press, 1955-8). Motifs applicable to the Sasquatch include B29.9, "Man-ape," found in Jewish tradition; F521.1, "Man covered with hair like an animal," found in Indian, Irish, Persian, and Welsh tradition; F531.1.6.3, "Giants with shaggy hair on their bodies"; F610.1, "Wild man of superhuman strength," found in Missouri French tales. For the Ogopogo, the motifs include B91.5.2, "Lake serpent (monster)" and G308.4, "Lake made dangerous by haunting serpent," both from Irish myth.

[7]p. 23.

16. URBAN TALES

Selected from "Modern Migratory Belief Legends," a project prepared by Susan Smith for English 430, "Canadian Folklore," at York University, 1973.

Linda Degh quotations: "Folk Narrative," in *Folklore and Folklife*, ed. Richard Dorson (Chicago: University of Chicago Press, 1972), p. 77, and "The Belief Legend in Modern Society" in *American Folk Legend: A Symposium*, ed. Wayland Hand (Berkeley and Los Angeles: University of California Press, 1971), p. 62.

For comparative versions and discussion of typical tales, see articles by Linda Degh in *Indiana Folklore*: "The Hook," 1(1968), 92-100; "The Boy Friend's Death," 1(1968), 101-6; and "The Roommate's Death and Related Dormitory Stories in Formation," 2(1969), 55-74.

"The Disappearing Hitchhiker" is Motif E332.3.3.1; Richard Dorson noted that it had been collected more than a hundred times and gave various references in *American Folklore* (Chicago: University of Chicago Press, 1959), pp. 250 and 299.

"The Cadaver's Arm" is Motif N384.0.1.1; Ernest Baughman cited thirteen variants in *Hoosier Folklore Bulletin*, 4(1945), 30-32.

In her article in *American Folk Legend: A Symposium*, Degh notes that narratives such as "The Hook" and "The Boyfriend's Death" "belong to the female type of legendry that has strong sexual overtones and reflects the function of dating, only to a lesser extent" (p. 66), and writing "On the Psychology of Legend" in the same symposium Alan Dundes suggests that they represent "teen-age girls' fears of parking with their boyfriends" (p. 30). Susan Smith's collection indicates that these tales are not exclusively female: both her versions of "The Hook" and five of her six versions of "The Boyfriend's Death" came from boys. Even with "The Babysitter," which seems particularly feminine, three of the seven narrators were male.

Richard Chase quotation, *American Folk Tales and Songs* (New York: Sig-net, 1956), p. 57.

"The Lady with the Golden Arm" is AT 366, *The Man from the Gallows*, and Motif E235.4.1, "Return from the dead to punish the theft of the golden arm from grave." John Burrison has traced this tale's many forms, citing thirty-eight different versions in *The Golden Arm: The Folk Tale and Its Literary Use by Mark Twain and Joel C. Harris* (Atlanta: Georgia State Arts and Sciences Research Series, No. 19, 1968).

"The Grandfather's Liver" comes under Motif E235.4.4, "Return from dead to punish theft of liver from man on gallows."

IV CANADIAN MOSAIC
1. SUPERSTITIONS AND POPULAR BELIEFS IN WATERLOO COUNTY

Selected from W. J. Wintemberg: *The Folklore of Waterloo County, Ontario* (Ottawa: National Museum, Bulletin 116, 1950), pp. 11-20.

William John Wintemberg (1876-1941), who was born in New Dundee, Waterloo County, was one of the first to explore the folklore of the Pennsylvania Germans in Canada. Under the influence of David Boyle he became an authority on Canadian archaeology and in 1912 joined the Geological Survey of Canada, later becoming associate archaeologist on the staff of the National Museum. He published many articles and reports on archaeological subjects in addition to several articles on Waterloo County folklore which appeared in the *Journal of American Folklore*. His National Museum Bulletin did not appear until after his death; it was edited by Diamond Jenness.

Where items are similar to those Wayland Hand classified in *Popular Beliefs and Superstitions from North Carolina*, vols. 6 and 7 of *The Frank C. Brown Collection of North Carolina Folklore*, the Hand numbers have been added in parentheses.

2. LOCAL ANECDOTES FROM LUNENBURG

Selected from Helen Creighton: *The Folklore of Lunenburg County, Nova Scotia* (Ottawa: National Museum, Bulletin 117, 1950), pp. 123-38.

Dr. Creighton's collection is a valuable study of the varied folklore of a community: in addition to anecdotes and tall tales it contains *Märchen*, superstitions, proverbs, riddles, and customs.

Motif numbers have been added in parentheses and listed in the "Index of Motifs."

3. UKRAINIAN-CANADIAN FOLKTALES

Nos. 4, 32, and 33 from Robert B. Klymasz, *Folk Narrative Among Ukrainian-Canadians* (Ottawa: Canadian Centre for Folk Culture Studies, Mercury Series No. 4, 1973), pp. 39 and 81-85.

Peacock quotation from Kenneth Peacock, *A Survey of Ethnic Folkmusic*

Across Western Canada (Ottawa: National Museum, Anthropology Paper No. 5, 1953), p. 11.

Dr. Klymasz, who was born in Winnipeg in 1936, now heads the Slavic and East European Section of the Canadian Centre for Folk Culture Studies. He began his field collecting in the prairie provinces while working for his Ph.D. in folklore at Indiana University, and continued it when he joined the National Museum. He has prepared an extensive bibliography of Ukrainian folklore in Canada and published two collections of Ukrainian-Canadian folk songs and various other studies in addition to his survey of folk narratives which formed part of his doctoral dissertation in 1970: "Ukrainian Folklore in Canada: An Immigrant Complex in Transition." In the chapter titled "Old World Narratives for a New Environment" (pp. 18-27) he discusses the way the stories have been adapted to their new home.

References (as given by R. B. Klymasz)

"The Magic Flute." Recorded in Vegreville, Alberta, July 20, 1965. Archival finding No.: KLY 74, item 7.

AT 780 (*The Singing Bone*). Motifs include D1817.0.3, "Magic detection of murder"; J514, "One should not be too greedy"; and E632, "Reincarnation as a magical instrument."

"The Clever Daughter." Recorded in Yorkton, Saskatchewan, June 24, 1964. Archival finding No.: KLY 48, c.25-2, item 25.

AT 875 (*The Clever Peasant Girl*). Among the many motifs found here, the following are the most important: J1111.4, "Clever peasant daughter"; H632.2, "What is swiftest? The eye"; H633.1, "What is sweetest? Sleep"; H1023.1.1, "Task: hatching boiled eggs; countertask: sowing cooked seeds and harvesting the crop"; H1053.2, "Task: coming neither on horse nor on foot (Comes sitting on animal but with feet reaching ground)"; H1054.1, "Task: coming neither naked nor clad (Comes wrapped in net or the like)"; H1056, "Task: coming neither with nor without a present (Lets bird fly as she reaches it toward king)"; J1191.1, "Reduction ad absurdum: The decision about the colt"; J1545.4, "The exiled wife's dearest possession."

"The Live Statues." Recorded in Yorkton, Saskatchewan, June 24, 1964. Archival finding No.: KLY 48, c24-b, item 1.

AT 1730 (*The Entrapped Suitors*) + AT 1829 (*Living Person Acts as Image of Saint*) + AT 1359C (*Husband Prepares to Castrate the Crucifix*). Motifs: J1112, "Clever wife"; K1218.1, "The entrapped suitors"; K1842, "Living person acts as image of saint"; and K1558, "The husband prepares to castrate the crucifix."

4. ICELANDIC PULAR

Recorded by Magnus Einarsson from Mrs. Sigridur Björnasson, Gimli, Manitoba, August 20, 1966. CCFCS archival number: MU 55. Mrs. Björnasson was born in Iceland in 1885, landed in Canada in 1894, married in 1918, and lived in Riverton and Winnipeg before moving to the Betel nursing home in Gimli.

Dr. Einarsson collected from Icelanders in Manitoba in 1966 and 1967 while he was working for his Ph.D. at Indiana University. He joined the National

Museum of Man in 1969 where he now heads the Germano-Scandinavian Section of the Canadian Centre for Folk Culture Studies. He is currently preparing a study of Icelandic folklore in North America.

"The Bird Who Lost His Nose" is a formula tale, closest in theme to AT 2034, *The Mouse Regains Its Tail* (Z41.4).

"The First Night of Christmas" is AT 2010B, *The Twelve Kinds of Food* (Motif Z22.1). Dr. Einarsson found close variants in *Islenzkar Gatur, Vikivakar, Skemmtanir og Pulur* by Jón Arnason and Olafur Davidsson (Copenhagen, 1898-1903), pp. 292-94 and 298-99.

5. YIDDISH TALES FOR CHILDREN

Personal communication from Ruth Rubin, February 15, 1959.

"The Little Old Grandmother Who Lived at the Edge of the Forest" is like AT 123, *The Wolf and the Kids*, and contains Motif F913, "Victims rescued from swallower's belly."

"The Granny Who Had Many Children" resembles AT 210, *Cock, Hen, Duck, Pin, and Needle on a Journey*, and contains Motif B296, "Animals go a-journeying."

A SELECTIVE BIBLIOGRAPHY

This bibliography is by no means complete, but it does contain most of the important books and articles dealing specifically with Canadian folklore. It lists several more extensive bibliographies on special areas; these are marked by the symbol # . Sources from which items in this anthology come are marked by an asterisk.

As the book is organized into sections dealing with the native peoples, Canadiens, Anglo-Canadians, and other cultural groups, the major sections of the bibliography use similar divisions. Other shorter sections list some important international journals and Canadian journals that contain considerable folklore, a few American texts useful for reference, and general items that do not fit under the group headings. A short final section gives some of the many books and articles dealing with material folk culture.

The bibliography is most complete for Anglo-Canadian lore; Indian, Eskimo, and French-Canadian materials are too extensive to be covered fully. Major sources used include the *Journal of American Folklore* (abbreviated to *JAF*), Laval's *Archives de Folklore*, and publications of the National Museum including the Canadian Centre for Folk Culture Studies (abbreviated to CCFCS). Most items deal with authentic folklore, but some secondary material is included where it relates to the subjects dealt with in the articles or mentioned in the notes.

PERIODICALS

Alberta Folklore Quarterly. University of Alberta, Edmonton, 1945-1946.
Alberta Historical Review. Historical Society of Alberta, Calgary, 1953-1974.
Alberta History. Historical Society of Alberta, Calgary, 1975 –
Archives de Folklore. Université Laval, Québec, 1946 –
Beaver: Magazine of the North. Hudson's Bay Company, Winnipeg, 1921 –
Canadian Folk Music Journal. Canadian Folk Music Society, 1973 –
Cape Breton's Magazine. Skir Dhu, Cape Breton, 1972 –
Ethnomusicology. Society for Ethnomusicology, 1955 –
Folklore Forum. Indiana University, Bloomington, 1968 –
Journal of American Folklore. American Folklore Society, 1888 –
Journal of the Folk-Song Society. Folk Song Society, London, 1899-1931.
Journal of the English Folk Dance and Song Society. English Folk Dance and
  Song Society, London, 1932 –
Journal of the Folklore Institute. Indiana University, Bloomington, 1963 –
Journal of the International Folk Music Council. International Folk Music
  Council, 1949 –
Northeast Folklore. University of Maine, Orono, 1958 –
Regional Language Studies . . . Newfoundland. Memorial University Folk-
  lore and Language Archive, 1968 –
Saskatchewan History. Provincial Archives, Saskatoon, 1948 –
Western Folklore (formerly *California Folklore Quarterly*). University of Cal-
  ifornia, Berkeley and Los Angeles, 1942-

REFERENCE

AARNE, Antti and Stith THOMPSON. *The Types of the Folktale.* Helsinki:
  Academia Scientiarum Fennica, 1961.

BAUGHMAN, Ernest W. *Type and Motif Index of the Folktales of England
  and North America.* The Hague: Mouton, 1966.
BRONSON, Bertrand H. *The Traditional Tunes of the Child Ballads.* 4 vols.
  Princeton, N.J.: Princeton University Press, 1959-1972.
BRIGGS, Katherine M. *A Dictionary of British Folk-Tales.* 2 vols. Blooming-
  ton: Indiana University Press, 1970.

CHILD, Francis James. *The English and Scottish Popular Ballads.* 5 vols.
  Boston: Houghton, Mifflin, 1882-1898.
CLEMENTS, William M. *The Types of the Polack Joke. Folklore Forum,*
  Bibliographic and Special Series No. 3, Bloomington, Indiana, 1969.
COFFIN, Tristram P., *The British Traditional Ballad in North America.*
  Philadelphia: American Folklore Society, 1963.

GOLDSTEIN, Kenneth S. *A Guide for Fieldworkers in Folklore.* Philadelphia: American Folklore Society, 1964.

HAND, Wayland D. *Popular Beliefs and Superstitions from North Carolina.*

315

Vols. 6 and 7 of *The Frank C. Brown Collection of North Carolina Folklore*. Durham, N.C.: Duke University Press, 1961.

HAYWOOD, Charles. *A Bibliography of North American Folklore and Folksong*. 2 vols. 1951; rpt. New York: Dover, 1961.

LAWS, G. Malcolm, Jr. *American Balladry from British Broadsides*. Philadelphia: American Folklore Society, 1957.

LAWS, G. Malcolm, Jr. *Native American Balladry*. Philadelphia: American Folklore Society, 1964.

LEACH, Maria, ed. *Standard Dictionary of Folklore, Mythology, and Legend*. 2 vols. New York: Funk and Wagnalls, 1949-1950.

TAYLOR, Archer. *English Riddles from Oral Tradition*. Berkeley and Los Angeles: University of California Press, 1955.

THOMPSON, *Stith. Motif-Index of Folk Literature*. 6 vols. Bloomington: Indiana University Press, 1966.

GENERAL

COSBEY, Robert C. "Proposal for a Saskatchewan Oral History Project." *Folklore Forum*, Bibliographic and Special Series, 12, pp. 36-55.

CREIGHTON, Helen. "Canada's Maritime Provinces: An Ethnomusicological Survey." *Ethnomusicology*, 16(1972), 404-14.

FOWKE, Edith. "Folktales and Folk Songs." *The Literary History of Canada*. Ed. Carl Klinck. Toronto: University of Toronto Press, 1967, 163-73.

_____ ed. "A Reference List on Canadian Folk Music." *Canadian Folk Music Journal*, 1(1973),46-56.

FOWKE, Edith and Carole HENDERSON, with Judith BROOKS. *A Bibliography of Canadian Folklore in English*. Downsview: York University, 1976.

HALPERT, Herbert. "Folklore and Newfoundland: An Informal Introduction to the Materials and Methods of Folklore." *Papers of the Bibliographical Society of Canada*, 8(1969), 10-22.

HALPERT, Herbert and Neil ROSENBERG. "MUNFLA: The Development of a Folklore and Language Archive at Memorial University." *Laurentian University Review*, 8:2 (Feb. 1976), 107-114.

HENDERSON, M. Carole. "Folklore Scholarship and the Socio-political Milieu in Canada." *Journal of the Folklore Institute*, 10(1973), 97-107.

LAMBERT, R.S. *Exploring the Supernatural: Ghosts in Canadian Folklore*. Toronto: McClelland and Stewart, 1955; rpt. 1966.

LANDRY, Renée. "A Descriptive List of Selected Manuscript Collections at the Canadian Centre for Folk Culture Studies, National Museum of Man. Ottawa." *Canaadian Ethnic Studies*, 7:2(1975), 72-89.

MacLENNAN, Gordon W. *Canadian Centre for Folk Culture Studies: Annual Review, 1974*. Ottawa: CCFCS, Mercury Series No. 12, 1975.

PEACOCK, Kenneth. *A Practical Guide for Folk Music Collectors*. Canadian Folk Music Society, 1966.

ROY, Carmen. *Canadian Centre for Folk Culture Studies: Annual Review, 1972.* Ottawa: CCFCS, Mercury Series No. 6, 1973.

—— *Canadian Centre for Folk Culture Studies: Annual Review, 1973.* Ottawa: CCFCS, Mercury Series No. 9, 1974.

—— *An Introduction to the Canadian Centre for Folk Culture Studies.* Ottawa: CCFCS, Mercury Series No. 7, 1973.

TAFT, Michael. "A Bibliography for Folklore Studies in Nova Scotia." *Three Atlantic Bibliographies* compiled by H.F. McGee, Jr., S.A. Davis, and Michael Taft. Halifax: St. Mary's University, 1975, pp. 106-205.

THE NATIVE PEOPLES

ABLER, Tom, Douglas SANDERS, and Sally WEAVER. *A Canadian Indian Bibliography 1960-1970.* Toronto: University of Toronto Press, 1974.

AHENAKEW, Edward. "Cree Trickster Tales." *JAF*, 41(1929), 309-53.

—— *Voices of the Plains Cree.* Toronto: McClelland and Stewart, 1973.

BARBEAU, C. Marius. "Bear Mother." *JAF*, 59(1946), 1-12.

—— *Haida Myths Illustrated in Argillite Carvings.* Ottawa: National Museum, Bulletin 127, 1953.

—— *Huron and Wyandot Traditional Narratives.* Ottawa: National Museum, Bulletin 165, 1960.

—— *Indian Days on the Western Prairies.* Ottawa: National Museum, Bulletin 163, 1960.

—— "Loucheux Myths. JAF, 28(1915), 249-57.

—— *Medicine Men on the North Pacific Coast.* Ottawa: National Museum, Bulletin 152, 1958.

—— *Totem Poles, Volume I, According to Crests and Topics. Volume II, According to Location.* Ottawa: National Museum, Bulletin 119, 1950.

—— "Totemic Atmosphere on the North Pacific Coast." *JAF*, 67(1954), 103-22.

—— *Tsimsyan Myths.* Ottawa: National Museum, Bulletin 174, 1961.

—— "Wyandot Tales Including Foreign Elements." *JAF*, 28(1915), 83-95.

BAUER, George W. *Cree Tales and Beliefs. Northeast Folklore*, 7, (1971).

BLOOMFIELD, Leonard. *Sacred Stories of the Sweet Grass Cree.* Ottawa: National Museum, Bulletin 60, 1930.

BOAS, Franz. *Bella Bella Tales.* American Folklore Society, Memoir 25, 1932.

—— *The Central Eskimo.* Washington: Bureau of American Ethnology, 1888; rpt. Toronto: Coles, 1974.

—— "Eskimo Tales and Songs". *JAF*, 7(1894), 45-50; 10(1897), 109-15.

—— "The Folk-lore of the Eskimo." *JAF*, 17(1904), 1-13.

—— ed. *Folktales of the Salishan and Sahaptin Tribes.* American Folklore Society, Memoir 11, 1917.

—— *Kwakiutl Culture as Reflected in Mythology.* American Folklore Society, Memoir 28, 1935.

—— *Kwakiutl Tales.* 1935; rpt. New York: AMS, 1969.

—— "Mythology and Folk-tales of the North American Indians." *JAF*, 27(1914), 380-423.

_____ *Tsimshian Mythology.* Washington: Bureau of American Ethnology, 1916.

BOAS, Franz and George HUNT. *Kwakiutl Texts.* New York: American Museum of Natural History, 1905.

BOCK, Philip K. *The Micmac Indians of Restigouche.* Ottawa: National Museum, Bulletin 213, 1966.

BURTON, Frederick R. *American Primitive Music; With Especial Attention to the Songs of the Ojibways.* New York: Moffat, Yard, 1909.

CAMSELL, Charles. "Loucheux Myths." *JAF,* 28(1915), 249-57.

\# CAVANAGH, Beverley. "Annotated Bibliography: Eskimo Music." *Ethnomusicology,* 16(1972), 137-52.

_____ "Imagery and Structure in Eskimo Song Texts." *Canadian Folk Music Journal,* 1(1973), 3-15.

CHAMBERLAIN, Alexander F. "Nanibozo Among the Algonkian Tribes." *JAF,* 4(1891), 192-213.

COMMITTEE OF THE CHIEFS, Six Nations of the Grand River. "Traditional History of the Confederacy of the Six Nations." *Transactions of the Royal Society of Canada,* Section II, 1911, 195-245.

DENSMORE, Frances. *Music of the Indians of British Columbia.* Washington, Bureau of American Ethnology, 1943.

DESBARATS, Peter. *What They Used to Tell About. Indian Legends from Labrador.* Toronto: McClelland and Stewart, 1969.

DEWDNEY, Selwyn. *The Sacred Scrolls of the Southern Ojibway.* Toronto: University of Toronto Press, 1975.

DICKASON, Olive Patricia. *Indian Arts in Canada.* Ottawa: Information Canada, 1973.

The Eskimo World. Special issue, *artscanada,* nos. 162-3, Dec. 1971/Jan. 1972.

GARFIELD, Viola E., Paul S. WINGERO, and C. Marius BARBEAU. *The Tsimshian: Their Arts and Music.* Washington: American Ethnological Society, 1951.

\# GUEDON, Marie-Francoise. "Canadian Indian Ethnomusicology: Selected Bibliography and Discography." *Ethnomusicology,* 16(1972), 465-78.

* HARDISTY, Richard. "The Last Sun Dance." *Alberta Folklore Quarterly,* 2(1946), 57-61.

HAWKES, E.W. *The Labrador Eskimo.* Ottawa: National Museum, Memoir 91, 1916.

HAWTHORN, Audrey. *Art of the Kwakiutl Indians and Other Northwest Coast Tribes.* Vancouver: University of British Columbia, 1967.

HELM, June and Nancy Oestreich LUREI. *The Dogrib Hand Game.* Ottawa: National Museum, Bulletin 205, 1966.

* HENRY, Alexander. *Travels and Adventures in Canada and the Indian Territories between the Years 1760 and 1776.* New York: Riley, 1809; rpt. Toronto: Morang, 1901.

HOUSTON, James. *Canadian Eskimo Art.* Ottawa: Queen's Printer, 1966.

JACK, Edward. "Maliseet Legends." JAF, 7(1895), 193-208.

JENNESS, Diamond. *The Corn Goddess, and Other Tales from Indian Canada.* Ottawa: National Museum, Bulletin 141, 1956.

____ *Eskimo Folk-Lore. Report of the Canadian Arctic Expedition, 1913-1918,* vol. 13. Ottawa: King's Printer, 1924.

____ "Eskimo String Figures." *JAF,* 36(1923), 281-94.

____ *The Indian Background of Canadian History.* Ottawa: National Museum, Bulletin 86, 1937.

____ *The Indians of Canada.* Ottawa: National Museum, Bulletin 65, 1932; rev. 1963.

____ *The Life of the Copper Eskimos. Report of the Canadian Arctic Expedition, 1913-1918,* vol. 12. Ottawa: King's Printer, 1922.

____ "Myths of the Carrier Indians of British Columbia." *JAF,* 47(1934), 97-257.

* ____ *The Ojibwa Indians of Parry Island, Their Social and Religious Life.* Ottawa: National Museum, Bulletin 78, 1935.

____ *The Sarcee Indians of Alberta.* Ottawa: National Museum, Bulletin 90, 1938.

____ *The Sekani Indians of British Columbia.* Ottawa: National Museum, Bulletin 84, 1947.

JONES, William. "Ojibwa Tales from the North Shore of Lake Superior." *JAF,* 29(1916), 368-91.

KOLINSKI, Mieczyslaw. "An Apache Rabbit Dance Song Cycle as Sung by the Iroquois." *Ethnomusicology,* 16(1972), 415-64.

KURATH, Gertrude Prokosch. *Dance and Song Rituals of the Six Nations Reserve, Ontario.* Ottawa: National Museum, Bulletin 220, 1968.

LANDES, Ruth. *Ojibwa Religion and the Midewiwin.* Madison: University of Wisconsin, 1968.

LARMOUR, W.T. *Innuit: The Art of the Canadian Eskimo.* Ottawa: Queen's Printer, 1970.

LEECHMAN, Douglas. *Native Tribes of Canada.* Toronto: Gage, 1956.

____ *Vanta Kutchin.* Ottawa: National Museum, Bulletin 130, 1954.

LOWIE, Robert H. "Franz Boas (1858-1942)." *JAF,* 57(1944), 59-69.

McCLELLAN, Catharine. *The Girl Who Married the Bear.* Ottawa: National Museum, Ethnology Paper 2, 1970.

MECHLING, W.H. *Malecite Tales.* Ottawa: National Museum, Memoir 49, 1914.

MELANCON, Claude. *Indian Legends of Canada.* Toronto: Gage, 1974.

MICHELSON, Truman. "Micmac Tales." *JAF,* 38(1925), 33-54.

MORRISSEAU, Norval. *Legends of My People: The Great Ojibway.* Toronto: Ryerson, 1965.

NUNGAK, Zebedee and Eugene ARIMA. *Eskimo Stories – Unikkaatuat.* Ottawa: National Museum, Bulletin 235, 1969.

PARSONS, Elsie. "Micmac Folklore." *JAF,* 38(1925), 55-133; "Micmac Notes." *JAF,* 39(1926), 460-85.

PETITOT, Emile. *Traditions indiennes du Canada nord-ouest.* Paris, 1886.

RADIN, Paul. *Literary Aspects of North American Mythology.* Ottawa: National Museum, Bulletin 16, 1915; rpt. Norwood, 1974.

——— *Some Myths and Tales of the Ojibwa of Southeastern Ontario.* Ottawa: National Museum, Memoir 48, 1914.

——— *The Trickster: A Study in American Indian Mythology.* 1945; rpt. New York: Greenwood 1969.

RADIN, Paul and Albert S. REAGAN. "Ojibwa Myths and Tales." *JAF*, 41(1928), 61-146.

* RAND, Silas T. *Legends of the Micmacs.* New York: Longmans, 1894.

RASMUSSEN, Knud. *Intellectual Culture of the Copper Eskimos. Report of the Fifth Thule Expedition, 1921-1924,* vols. 7, 8, 9. Copenhagen: Gyldendalski Boghandel, 1929-1932.

ROBERTS, Helen and Diamond JENNESS. *Songs of the Copper Eskimos. Report of the Canadian Arctic Expedition, 1913-1918,* vol. 14. Ottawa: King's Printer, 1925.

SCHAEFFER, Claude E. *Blackfoot Shaking Tent.* Calgary: Glenbow-Alberta Institute, 1969.

SCHOOLCRAFT, Henry Rowe. *Algic Researches, Comprising Inquiries Respecting the Mental Characteristics of the North American Indians.* 2 vols. New York: Harper, 1839.

SCHWARTZ, Herbert T. *Tales from the Smokehouse.* Toronto: McClelland and Stewart, 1974.

SKINNER, Alanson. "European Tales from the Plains Ojibwa." *JAF*, 29(1916), 330-40.

——— "Plains Cree Tales." *JAF*, 29(1916), 341-67.

——— "Plains Ojibwa Tales." *JAF*, 32(1919), 280-305.

SPECK, Frank G. "Montagnis and Naskapi Tales from the Labrador Peninsula." *JAF*, 38(1925), 1-32.

——— *Myths and Folklore of the Timiskaming, Algonquin and Timagami Ojibwa.* Ottawa: National Museum, Memoir 71, 1915.

Stones, Bones, and Skin: Ritual and Shamanic Art. Special issue, *artscanada,* nos. 82-87, Dec. 1973/Jan. 1974.

SWINTON, George. *Sculpture of the Eskimo.* Toronto: McClelland and Stewart, 1965.

SYMINGTON, Fraser. *The Canadian Indian: The Illustrated History of the Great Tribes of Canada.* Toronto: McClelland and Stewart, 1969.

TEIT, James. "European Tales from the Upper Thompson Indians." *JAF*, 29(1916), 301-30.

* ——— "Tahltan Tales." *JAF*, 32(1919), 198-250; 34(1921), 223-53; 335-56.

——— Traditions of the Lillooet Indians of British Columbia." *JAF*, 25(1912), 287-371.

——— *Traditions of the Thompson River Indians of British Columbia.* American Folklore Society, Memoir 6, 1898.

THOMPSON, Stith. *Tales of the North American Indians.* Bloomington: Indiana University Press, 1929; rpt. 1968.

\# ULLOM, Judith. *Folklore of the North American Indians: An Annotated Bibliography.* Washington: Library of Congress, 1969.

WALLIS, Wilson D. *The Micmac Indians of Eastern Canada.* Minneapolis: University of Minnesota Press, 1955.

WALLIS, Wilson D. and Ruth S. WALLIS. *The Malecite Indians of New Brunswick.* Ottawa: National Museum, Bulletin 148, 1957.

WEAVER, Sally. *Medicine and Politics Among the Grand River Iroquois.* Ottawa: National Museums, 1972.

WRIGHT, J.V. *The Ontario Iroquois Tradition.* Ottawa: National Museum, Bulletin 110, 1966.

CANADIENS

* ANSELME, Père (CHIASSON) et Frère DANIEL (BOUDREAU). *Chansons d'Acadie.* 3 vols. Montréal, Pointe-aux-Trembles: La Reparation, 1942-1948.

* BARBEAU, C. Marius. *Alouette.* Montréal: Editions Lumen, 1946.

* ____ "Anecdotes de Gaspé, de la Beauce, et de Temiscouta." *JAF*, 33(1920), 172-258.

____ "Blason, geographie et genealogie populaires de Québec." *JAF*, 33(1920), 346-66.

____ "Chants populaires du Canada." *JAF*, 32(1919), 1-89.

____ "La Complainte de Cadieux, coureur de bois (ca. 1709)." *JAF*, 67(1954), 163-83.

____ "Contes populaires canadiens." *JAF*, 29(1916), 1-136; 30(1917), 1-140; 32(1919), 112-67.

____ *Les Enfants disent.* Montréal: Editions Paysans, 1943.

____ "The Ermatinger Collection of Voyageur Songs (ca. 1830)." *JAF*, 67(1954), 147-61.

____ *Jongleur Songs of Old Quebec.* Toronto: Ryerson, 1962.

* ____ *The Kingdom of Saguenay.* Toronto: Macmillan, 1935.

____ *Quebec Where Ancient France Lingers.* Toronto: Macmillan, 1936.

____ *Romancero du Canada.* Toronto: Macmillan, 1937.

____ *Le Rossignol y Chante.* Ottawa: National Museum, Bulletin 175, 1962.

____ *Roundelays – Dansons à la ronde.* Ottawa: National Museum, Bulletin 151, 1958.

____ *The Tree of Dreams.* Toronto: Oxford, 1955.

____ "Trois beaux canards (92 versions canadiennes)." *Archives de Folklore*, 2(1947), 191-292.

____ "Voyageur Songs." *Beaver*, June 1942, 15-19.

BARBEAU, Marius and Michael HORNYANSKY. *The Golden Phoenix.* Toronto: Oxford, 1958.

BARBEAU, Marius and Edward SAPIR. *Folk Songs of French Canada.* New Haven: Yale University Press, 1925.

BEAUGRAND, Honoré. *La Chasse-Galerie and Other Canadian Stories.* Montréal: Pelletier, 1900.

——— *New Studies of Canadian Folk Lore.* Montréal: Renouf, 1904.

BERNIER, Helene. *La Fille aux mains coupées (conte-type 706). Archives de Folklore* 12(1971).

BOLDUC, Evelyn. "Contes de la Beauce." *JAF*, 32(1919), 90-101.

\# BRASSARD, François. "French-Canadian Folk Music Studies: A Survey." *Ethnomusicology*, 16(1972), 351-59.

——— "Refrains canadiens de chansons de France." *Archives de Folklore*, 1(1946), 41-59.

——— "Le Retour du Soldat et le Retour du Voyageur." *JAF*, 63(1950), 147-57.

——— "Le Voyageur." *Canadian Folk Music Journal*, 2(1974), 13-18.

\# CARDIN, Clarisse. "Bio-Bibliographie de Marius Barbeau." *Archives de Folklore*, 2(1947), 17-96.

CASS-BEGGS, Barbara. *Seven Métis Songs.* Toronto: BMI Canada, 1967.

CHIASSON, Anselme. *Chéticamp: Histoire et traditions acadiennes.* Moncton: Aboiteaux, 1962.

——— *Les Legendes des Iles-de-le-Madeleine.* Moncton: Aboiteaux, 1972.

* CLOUTIER, J.-E.-A. "Anecdotes de l'Islet." *JAF*, 33(1920), 273-94.

CORMIER, Charlotte. "Situation de la recherche en folklore acadien." *Canadian Folk Music Journal* 3(1975), 30-34.

DAVIAULT, Pierre. "Contes populaires canadiennes." *JAF*, 53(1920), 273-94.

DAWSON, Nora. *La vie traditionnelle à Sainte-Pierre (île d'Orleans). Archives de Folklore*, 8(1960).

DORSON, Richard. "Canadiens." *Blood-Stoppers and Bear-Walkers.* Cambridge: Harvard University Press, 1959, 69-102.

DOYON, Madeleine. "Jeux, jouets et divertissements de la Beauce." *Archives de Folklore*, 3(1948), 137-46.

DUPONT, Jean-Claude. *Le Monde fantastique de la Beauce Québecois.* Ottawa: CCFCS Mercury Series No. 2, 1972.

——— *Le Pain d'habitant.* Québec: Leméac, 1974.

——— *Le Sucre du pays* Québec: Leméac, 1975.

FOWKE, Edith and Richard JOHNSTON. *Chansons de Québec.* Waterloo, Ont.: Waterloo Music, 1957.

GAGNON, Ernest. *Chansons populaires du Canada.* 1865; rpt. Montréal: Beauchemin, 1947.

GASPE, Philippe Aubert de, fils. *L'influence d'un livre.* Québec: William Cowan, 1837; rpt. as *Le Chercheur de trésor ou l'influence d'un livre.* Québec: Desbarats, 1864.

GAUTIER, Dominique. *Chansons de Shippagan. Archives de Folklore*, 16(1975).

GIBBON, John Murray. *Canadian Folk Songs (Old and New).* Toronto: Dent, 1927.

* GREENOUGH, William Parker. *Canadian Folk-Life and Folk-Lore.* New York: Richmond, 1897; rpt. Toronto: Coles, 1973.

GRIGGS, Mary Ann. *La Chanson folklorique dans le milieu canadien-français traditionnel* (*The Folk-Song in the Traditional Society of French-Canada*). Sudbury: La Société historique du Nouvel-Ontario, 1969.

HARCOURT, Marguerite d' et Raoul d'HARCOURT. *Chansons folkloriques françaises au Canada*. Québec: Presses Universitaires Laval, 1956.

JOLICOEUR, Catherine. *Le Vaisseau Fantôme, Legende etiologique. Archives de Folklore*, 11(1970).

KATZ, Israel J. "Marius Barbeau, 1883-1969." *Ethnomusicology*, 14(1970), 129-42.

LACOURCIERE, Luc. "Comptines canadiennes." *Archives de Folklore*, 3(1948), 109-57.

___ "Les Ecoliers de Pontoise." *Archives de Folklore*, 1(1946), 176-200.

___ "The Present State of French-Canadian Folklore Studies." *JAF*, 74(1961), 373-82.

LA FOLLETTE, James E. *Étude linguistique de quatre contes folkloriques au Canada français. Archives de Folklore*, 9(1969).

LAFORTE, Conrad. *Le Catalogue de la chanson folklorique française*. Québec: Presses Universitaires Laval, 1958.

___ *Les Poetiques de la chanson traditionnelle française*. Québec: Presses Universitaires Laval, 1975.

* LAMBERT, Adelard. "Contes populaires canadiens" *JAF*, 36(1923), 205-72; 53(1940), 89-181.

LAMBERT, Adelard et Marius BARBEAU. "Jeux d'enfants." *JAF*, 53(1940), 163-81.

LANCTOT, Gustave. "Chansons et rondes de Laprairie." *JAF*, 33(1920), 336-45.

___ "Contes populaires canadiens." *JAF*, 36(1923), 205-73; 39(1926), 371-450; 44(1931), 225-89.

___ "Fables, contes, et formules." *JAF*, 29(1916), 141-51.

LARUE, F.-A.-H. "Les chansons populaires et historiques du Canada." Québec: *Le Foyer canadien*, 1(1863), 321-84.

* LEMIEUX, Germain. *Chansonnier franco-ontarien*. 2 vols. Sudbury: Université de Sudbury, 1974, 1975.

___ *Chanteurs franco-ontariens et leurs chansons*. Sudbury: Société historique du Nouvel-Ontario, 1963-1964.

___ *Contes populaires franco-ontariens*. 2 vols. Sudbury: Société historique du Nouvel-Ontario, 1953, 1958.

* ___ *Folklore franco-ontarien – Chansons*. 2 vols. Sudbury: Société historique du Nouvel-Ontario, 1949, 1950.

___ *De sumer au Canada français*. Sudbury: Société de historique du Nouvel-Ontario, 1968.

___ *Les Jongleurs du Billochet*. Montréal: Editions Bellarmin, 1972.

___ *Placide-Eustache, Sources et paralleles du conte-type 938. Archives de Folklore*, 10(1970).

___ *Les Vieux m'ont conte*. 6 vols. Montréal: Editions Bellarmin, 1973-75.

LEMOINE, James MacPherson. *The Legends of the St. Lawrence.* Quebec: Holiwell, 1898.

MacLEOD, Margaret Arnett. *Songs of Old Manitoba.* Toronto: Ryerson, 1960.

MAILLET, Antonine. *Rabelais et les traditions populaires en Acadie. Archives de Folklore,* 13(1972).

MARIE-URSULE, Soeur. *Civilization traditionnelle des Lavalois. Archives de Folklore,* 5-6(1951).

MASSICOTTE, E.-Z. "Croyances et dictons populaires des environs de Trois-Rivières (Canada)." *JAF,* 32(1919), 168-75.

——— "Formulettes, rimettes et divinettes du Canada." *JAF,* 33(1920), 299-320.

MONTEIRO, George. "*Histoire de Montferrand: L'Athlète Canadien* and Joe Mufraw." *JAF,* 73(1960), 24-34.

* MORIN, Victor. "Facéties et contes canadiens." *JAF,* 30(1917), 141-57.

ORKIN, Mark M. *Speaking Canadian French.* Toronto: General, 1967.

PROCTOR, George. "Musical Styles of Gaspe Songs." Ottawa: National Museum, Bulletin 190, 209-12.

RIOUX, Marcel. "Contes populaires canadiens." *JAF,* 63(1950), 199-230.

——— *Description de la culture de l'île Verte.* Ottawa: National Museum, Bulletin 133, 1954.

ROY, Carmen. *Contes populaires gaspésiens.* Montréal: Fides, 1952.

——— "Les Jeux en Gaspésie." Ottawa: National Museum, Bulletin 147, 1957, 67-83.

——— *Littérature orale en Gaspésie.* Ottawa: National Museum, Bulletin 134, 1955.

ROY, Raoul. *Le Chant de l'alouette.* Québec: Presses de l'Université Laval, 1969.

SCHMITZ, Nancy. *La Mensongèrie, conte-type 710. Archives de Folklore,* 14(1972).

SEGUIN, Robert Lionel. *Les Jouets anciens du Québec.* Québec: Leméac, 1969.

——— *La Sorcellarie au Canada français du XVIIe au XIXe siècle.* Montréal: Librairie Ducharme, 1961.

SULTE, Benjamin. *Histoire de Jos. Montferrand: l'athlète canadien.* Montréal: Beauchemin, 1905.

* TACHE, Joseph-Charles. *Forestiers et voyageurs.* 1884; rpt. Montréal: Fides, 1964.

TREMBLAY, Jules. "Anecdotes de la Côte-Nord, de Portneuf et de Wright." *JAF,* 33(1920), 259-72.

TREMBLAY, Malvina. "Contes de Chicoutimi et de la Malbaie." *JAF,* 32(1919), 101-12.

* TREMBLAY, Maurice. "Nous irons jouer à l'isle." *JAF,* 63(1950), 163-70.

WYMAN, Lorraine. "Songs from Percé." *JAF,* 33(1920), 321-35.

YOUNG, Russell Scott. *Vieilles Chansons de Nouvelle-France. Archives de Folklore*, 7(1956).

ANGLO-CANADIANS

ABRAHAMSON, Una. *God Bless Our Home.* Toronto: Burns and MacEachern, 1966.

ARMSTRONG, George H. *The Origin and Meaning of Place Names in Canada.* Toronto: Macmillan, 1930.

BAUMAN, Richard. "Belsnickling in a Nova Scotia Community." *Western Folklore*, 31(1972), 229-43.

BECK, Earl C. *Lore of the Lumber Camps.* Ann Arbor: University of Michigan Press, 1948.

BEDORE, Bernie. *Tall Tales of Joe Mufferaw.* Ottawa: Fenn-Graphic, 1966.

BLEAKNEY, F. Eileen. "Folklore from Ottawa and Vicinity." *JAF*, 31(1918), 158-69.

BOYLE, David. "Canadian Folklore." Weekly series in the *Globe*, Toronto, Nov. 15, 1897 – Jan. 8, 1898.

BROWN, Cassie, with Harold HORWOOD. *Death on the Ice.* Toronto: Doubleday, 1972.

BUTLER, Victor. *The Little Nord Easter: Reminiscences of a Placentia Bayman.* St. John's: Memorial University, 1975.

CAMERON LIBRARY. *The Alberta Folklore and Local History Collection.* Edmonton: University of Alberta, 1966.

CASS-BEGGS, Barbara. *Eight Songs of Saskatchewan.* Toronto: Canadian Music Sales, 1963.

CHAMBERLAIN, A.F. "Folklore of Canadian Children." *JAF*, 8(1895), 252-55.

CHAMBERS, J.K., ed. *Canadian English: Origins and Structures.* Toronto: Methuen, 1975.

COX, Gordon. "The Christmas Carolling Tradition of Green's Harbour, Trinity Bay, Newfoundland." *Canadian Folk Music Journal*, 3(1975), 2-10.

CREIGHTON, Helen, *Bluenose Ghosts.* Toronto: Ryerson, 1957.

____ *Bluenose Magic: Popular Beliefs and Superstitions in Nova Scotia.* Toronto: Ryerson, 1968.

____ "Cape Breton Nicknames and Tales." *Folklore in Action.* Ed. Horace Beck. Hatboro, Pa.: Folklore Associates, 1962.

____ "Folklore of Victoria Beach, Nova Scotia." *JAF*, 63(1950), 131-46.

____ *Folksongs from Southern New Brunswick.* Ottawa: CCFCS, 1971.

____ *A Life in Folklore.* Toronto: McGraw-Hill Ryerson, 1975.

____ *Maritime Folk Songs.* Toronto: Ryerson, 1962.

____ *Songs and Ballads from Nova Scotia.* Toronto: Dent, 1932; rpt. New York: Dover, 1966.

CREIGHTON, Helen and Edward D. IVES. *Eight Folktales from Miramichi. Northeast Folklore*, 4(1962).

CREIGHTON, Helen and Calum MacLEOD. *Gaelic Songs in Nova Scotia.* Ottawa: National Museum, Bulletin 117, 1950.

CREIGHTON, Helen and Doreen H. SENIOR. *Traditional Songs from Nova Scotia*. Toronto: Ryerson, 1950.

DEVINE, D.K. *Devine's Folk Lore of Newfoundland in Old Words, Phrases, and Expressions*. St. John's: Robinson, 1937.

DIBBLEE, Randall and Dorothy DIBBLEE. *Folksongs from Prince Edward Island*. Summerside, P.E.I.: Williams and Crue, 1973.

A Dictionary of Canadianisms on Historical Principles. Toronto: Gage, 1967.

DOERFLINGER, William Main. "Cruising for Ballads in Nova Scotia." *Canadian Geographical Journal*, 16(1938), 91-97.

—— *Shantymen and Shantyboys*. New York: Macmillan, 1951; rpt. as *Songs of the Sailor and the Lumberman*, 1973.

DOUCETTE, Laurel. "An Introduction to the Puckett Collection of Ontario Folklore." *Canadian Folk Music Journal*, 3(1975), 22-29.

DOYLE, Gerald S. *Old-Time Songs and Poetry of Newfoundland*. St. John's: G.S. Doyle, 1927, 1940, 1955, 1966.

DUNN, Charles W. *Highland Settler: A Portrait of the Scottish Gael in Nova Scotia*. Toronto: University of Toronto Press, 1953.

ENGLAND, George Allan. *Vikings of the Ice*. 1924; rpt. as *The Greatest Hunt in the World*. Montreal: Tundra, 1969.

ENGLISH, L.E.F. *Historic Newfoundland*. St. John's: Tourist Development Division, n.d.

FAHS, Lois. *Swing Your Partner: Old-time Dances of New Brunswick and Nova Scotia*. Truro, N.S., 1939.

* FAUSET, Arthur Huff. *Folklore from Nova Scotia*. American Folklore Society, Memoir 24, 1931.

FOWKE, Edith. "American Civil War Songs in Canada." *Midwest Folklore*, 13(1963), 133-62.

—— "American Cowboy and Western Pioneer Songs in Canada." *Western Folklore*, 21(1962), 247-56.

—— "Anglo-Canadian Folksong: A Survey." *Ethnomusicology*, 16(1972), 335-50.

—— "British Ballads in Ontario." *Midwest Folklore*, 13(1963), 133-62.

—— "Folk Music in Canada." *The Canada Music Book*, Spring/Summer, 1975, 53-57.

—— "Folk Songs in Ontario." *Canadian Literature*, 16(1963), 27-42.

—— "In Defense of Paul Bunyan." *Folklore Preprint Series*, 3:3 (1975).

—— "Labor and Industrial Protest Songs in Canada." *JAF*, 82(1969), 34-50.

—— *Lumbering Songs from the Northern Woods*. Austin: University of Texas Press, 1970.

—— *The Penguin Book of Canadian Folk Songs*. London: Penguin, 1973.

—— "'The Red River Valley' Re-Examined." *Western Folklore*, 23(1964), 247-56; rpt. *Alberta Historical Review*, 13(1965), 20-25.

—— *Sally Go Round the Sun: 300 Songs, Rhymes, and Games of Canadian Children*. Toronto: McClelland and Stewart, 1969.

_____ "A Sampling of Bawdy Ballads from Ontario." *Folklore and Society*. Ed. Bruce Jackson. Hatboro, Pa.: Folklore Associates, 1966, pp. 45-61.

_____ "Songs of a Manitoba Family." *Canadian Folk Music Journal*, 3(1975), 35-46.

_____ *Traditional Singers and Songs from Ontario*. Hatboro, Pa.: Folklore Associates, 1965.

FOWKE, Edith and Richard JOHNSTON. *Folk Songs of Canada*. Waterloo, Ont.: Waterloo Music, 1954.

FOWKE, Edith and Richard JOHNSTON. *More Folk Songs of Canada*. Waterloo: Waterloo Music, 1967.

FOWKE, Edith, Alan MILLS, and Helmut BLUME. *Canada's Story in Song*. Toronto: Gage, 1960.

FRASER, Alexander. "The Gaelic Folk Songs of Canada." *Transactions of the Royal Society of Canada*, 60, section 2(1903), 49-60.

FRASER, C.A. "Scottish Myths from Ontario." *JAF*, 6(1893), 185-98.

* FRASER, Mary L. *Folklore of Nova Scotia*. Toronto: Catholic Truth Society, 1931; rpt. Antigonish: Formac, 1975.

GARD, Robert. *Johnny Chinook: Tall Tales and True from the Canadian West*. Toronto: Longmans Green, 1945; rpt. Edmonton: Hurtig, 1967.

* GEIKIE, John Cunningham. *George Stanley, or, Life in the Woods*. London: Routledge, Warne and Routledge, 1863; rpt. as *Life in the Woods*, 1873, and *Adventures in Canada*, 1882.

GELLATY, Dorothy Hewlett. *A Bit of Okanagan History*. Westbank, B.C.: Kelowna Printing Co., rev. ed., 1958.

GLEDHILL, Christopher. *Folk Songs of Prince Edward Island*. Charlottetown: Square Deal, 1973.

GREEN, John. *On the Track of the Sasquatch*. Agassiz, B.C.: Cheam, 1969.

_____ *The Sasquatch File*. Agassiz: Cheam, 1973.

_____ *The Year of the Sasquatch*. Agassiz: Cheam, 1970.

* GREENLEAF, Elisabeth Bristol. "Riddles of Newfoundland." *Marshall Review*, 1(March 1938), 5-20.

GREENLEAF, Elisabeth Bristol and Grace Yarrow MANSFIELD. *Ballads and Sea Songs of Newfoundland*. 1933; rpt. Hatboro: Folklore Associates, 1968.

GROVER, Carrie. *A Heritage of Song*. Bethel, Maine, n.d.; rpt. Norwood, Pa.: Norwood, 1973.

GUILLET, Edwin C. *Early Life in Upper Canada*. 1923; rpt. Toronto: University of Toronto Press, 1963.

_____ *The Pioneer Farmer and Backwoodsman*. 2 vols. Toronto: University of Toronto Press, 1963.

HALIBURTON, Thomas C. *The Old Judge; or, Life in a Colony*. 1849; rpt. Toronto: Clarke Irwin, 1968.

HALPERT, Herbert. "Skipping Rhymes from Calgary, Alberta." *California Folklore Quarterly*, 3(1945), 154-55.

* _____ "Tall Tales and Other Yarns from Calgary, Alberta." *California Folklore Quarterly*, 4(1945), 29-45.

HALPERT, Herbert and G. M. STORY. *Christmas Mumming in Newfoundland.* Toronto: University of Toronto Press, 1969.

* HIGINBOTHAM, John D. "Western Vernacular." *Alberta Historical Review,* 10(Autumn 1962), 9-15.

HUNTER, Don and Rose DAHINDEN. *Sasquatch.* Toronto: McClelland and Stewart, 1973.

IVES, Edward D. "'Ben Deane' and Joe Scott: A Ballad and Its Probable Author." *JAF,* 72(1959), 53-66.

* ____ *Larry Gorman: The Man Who Made the Songs.* Bloomington: Indiana University Press, 1964.

____ *Lawrence Doyle: The Farmer Poet of Prince Edward Island.* Orono: University of Maine Press, 1964.

____ "A Man and His Song: Joe Scott and 'The Plain Golden Band.'" *Folksongs and Their Makers,* by H. Glassie, E. D. Ives, and J. F. Szwed. Bowling Green, Ohio: Bowling Green University Popular Press, 1970, 69-164.

____ "The Man Who Plucked the Gorbey." *JAF,* 74(1961), 1-8.

____ *Twenty-one Folksongs from Prince Edward Island. Northeast Folklore,* 5 (1963).

JONES, Michael. *Why Faith Healing?* Ottawa: CCFCS, Mercury Series No. 3, 1972.

KARPELES, Maud. "British Folk Songs from Canada." *Journal of the Folk Song Society,* 34(1934), 218-30.

____ *Folk Songs from Newfoundland.* London: Oxford University Press, 1934.

____ *Folk Songs from Newfoundland.* London: Faber and Faber, 1971.

KIRTLEY, Bacil F. "Unknown Hominids and New World Legends." *Western Folklore,* 23(1964), 77-90.

LANGDON, Eustella. *Pioneer Gardens at Black Creek Pioneer Village.* Toronto: Holt Rinehart and Winston, 1972.

* LEACH, MacEdward. "Celtic Tales from Cape Breton." *Studies in Folklore in Honor of Stith Thompson.* Ed. Edson Richmond. Bloomington: Indiana University Press, 1957, 40-54.

____ *Folk Ballads and Songs of the Lower Labrador Coast.* Ottawa: National Museum, Bulletin 201, 1965.

McATEE, W. L. *Folk Names of Canadian Birds.* Ottawa: National Museum, Bulletin 149, 1957.

McCAWLEY, Stuart. *Cape Breton Come-All-Ye,* Glace Bay, N.S.: Brodie Printing, 1929.

MacDONALD, Alphonse. *Cape Breton Songster.* Sydney, N.S., 1935.

* McDONALD, Neil T. *The Baldoon Mysteries: A Weird Tale of the Early Scotch Settlers of Baldoon.* Wallaceburg, Ont.: W. Colwell, 1871; 3rd ed., 1910.

* McHUGH, John O. "The Reminiscences of H2 Jack." MS, Glenbow-Alberta Foundation, 1960.

MACKENZIE, W. Roy. *Ballads and Sea Songs from Nova Scotia.* Cambridge: Harvard University Press, 1928; rpt. Hatboro, Pa.: Folklore Associates, 1963.

*____ *The Quest of the Ballad.* Princeton: Princeton University Press, 1919.

MacLEAN, R. P. *Ogopogo: His Story.* Kelowna: Kelowna Courier, July 31, 1952.

MANNY, Louise and James Reginald WILSON. *Songs of Miramichi.* Fredericton: Brunswick Press, 1968.

MERCER, Paul. *The Ballads of Johnny Burke: A Short Anthology.* St. John's: Newfoundland Historical Society, 1974.

MINHINNICK, Jeanne. *At Home in Upper Canada.* Toronto: Clarke Irwin, 1970.

MOODIE, Susanna. *Roughing It in the Bush; or, Life in Canada. 1852; rpt. Toronto: McClelland and Stewart, 1962.*

MOON, Mary. "I saw it this time as a great, writhing, eel-like mass." *B.C. Motorist*, Nov.-Dec., 1973, pp. 12, 14-16, 52-53, 59-60, 62.

MURPHY, James. *Songs and Ballads of Newfoundland, Ancient and Modern.* St. John's: James Murphy, 1902.

NAPIER, John R. *Bigfoot: The Yeti and Sasquatch in Myth and Reality.* London: Jonathan Cape, 1972.

ORKIN, Mark M. *Speaking Canadian English.* Toronto: General, 1970.

OWEN, E. A. *Pioneer Sketches of Long Point Settlement.* Toronto: Briggs, 1898.

PATTERSON, George. "Notes on the Dialect of the People of Newfoundland." *JAF*, 8(1895), 27-40; 9(1896), 19-37; 10(1897), 203-13.

____ "Notes on the Folklore of Newfoundland." *JAF*, 8(1895), 285-90; 9(1897), 214-15.

PEACOCK, Kenneth. "Folk and Aboriginal Music." *Aspects of Music in Canada.* Ed. Arnold Walter. Toronto: University of Toronto Press, 1969, 62-89.

____ "The Native Songs of Newfoundland." Ottawa: National Museum, Bulletin 190, 213-39.

____ "Nine Songs from Newfoundland." *JAF*, 67(1954), 123-36.

____ *Songs of the Newfoundland Outports*, 3 vols. Ottawa: National Museum, Bulletin 197, 1965.

PROCTOR, George. "Old-Time Fiddling in Ontario." Ottawa: National Museum, Bulletin 190, 172-208.

ROBERTSON, Marion. "Counting Out Rhymes from Shelburne County, Nova Scotia." *Northeast Folklore*, 3(Summer 1960), 27-32.

ROBINS, John D. *Logging with Paul Bunyan.* Toronto: Ryerson, 1957.

____ "Paul Bunyan." *Canadian Forum*, 61(1926), 146-49.

RUSSELL, L. A. *Everyday Life in Colonial Canada.* Toronto: Copp Clark, 1973.

SCARGILL, M. H. "The Growth of Canadian English." *Literary History of*

Canada. Ed. C. F. Klinck. Toronto: University of Toronto Press, 1965, 251-59.

- SEARY, E. R. *Place Names of the Avalon Peninsula of the Island of Newfoundland*. Toronto: University of Toronto Press, 1971.

SEARY, E. R., G. M. STORY, and W. J. KIRWIN. *The Avalon Peninsula of Newfoundland: An Ethno-Linguistic Study*. Ottawa: National Museum, Bulletin 219, 1968.

SENIOR, Doreen H. and Helen CREIGHTON. "Folk Songs Collected in the Province of Nova Scotia, Canada." *Journal of the English Folk Dance and Song Society*, 6(1951), 83-91.

SUTTLES, Wayne. "On the Cultural Track of the Sasquatch." *Northwest Anthropological Research Notes*, 6:1 (1972), 65-90.

SZWED, John F. "Paul E. Hall: A Newfoundland Song-Maker and His Community." *Folksongs and Their Makers*, by H. Glassie, E. D. Ives, and J. F. Szwed. Bowling Green, Ohio: Bowling Green University Popular Press, 1970, 147-69.

TAFT, Michael. *A Regional Discography of Newfoundland and Labrador, 1904-1972*. St. John's: Memorial University of Newfoundland Folklore and Language Archives, 1975.

THOMAS, Philip J. "B.C. Songs." *B.C. Library Quarterly*, July 1962, 15-19.

____ "Where the Rivers Flow." *Canadian Folk Music Journal*, 3(1975), 47-55.

*THOMPSON, George S. *Up to Date; or, The Life of a Lumberman*. Peterborough: Times Printing Co., 1895.

TRAILL, Catharine Parr. *The Backwoods of Canada*. 1836; rpt. Toronto: McClelland and Stewart, 1966.

TULK, Bob. *Newfie Jokes*. Dartmouth, N.S., 1971.

____ *More Newfie Jokes*. Dartmouth, N.S., 1972.

WALTON, Ivan H. "Marine Lore." *Michigan, A Guide to the Wolverine State*. New York: Oxford, 1941, pp. 113-34.

____ "Songs of the Great Lakes Sailors." *Journal of the International Folk Music Council*. 3(1951), 73-76.

WAUGH, F. W. "Canadian Folk-Lore from Ontario." *JAF*, 31(1918), 4-82.

WHITTON, Charlotte. *A Hundred Years A-Fellin': Some Passages from the Timber Saga of the Ottawa in the Century 1842-1952*. Ottawa: Runge, 1943.

WINTEMBERG, W. J. "Folklore Collected in the Counties of Oxford and Waterloo, Ontario." *JAF*, 31(1918), 135-53.

CANADIAN MOSAIC

BRUNVAND, Jan. *Norwegian Settlers in Alberta*. Ottawa: CCFCS, Mercury Series No. 8, 1974.

CARLISLE, Roxane. "Ethnomusicology in a Multicultural Society." *Western Canadian Journal of Anthropology*. 4(1974), 97-109.

*CREIGHTON, Helen. *Folklore of Lunenburg County, Nova Scotia*. Ottawa:

National Museum, Bulletin 117, 1950; Toronto: McGraw-Hill Ryerson, 1975.

DEGH, Linda. *People in the Tobacco Belt.* Ottawa: CCFCS, Mercury Series No. 13, 1975.

DOERING, J. Frederick. "More Folk Customs from Western Ontario." *JAF,* 58(1945), 150-53.

_____ "Pennsylvania German Folk Medicine in Waterloo County, Ontario." *JAF,* 49(1936), 194-98.

_____ "Some Western Ontario Folk Beliefs and Practices." *JAF,* 54(1941), 197-98.

DOERING, J. Frederick and Eileen Elita Doering. "Some Western Ontario Folk Beliefs and Practices." *JAF,* 51(1938), 60-68.

DYCK, Ruth. "Ethnic Folklore in Canada: A Preliminary Survey." *Canadian Ethnic Studies,* 7:2(1975), 90-101.

DZIOBKO, J. *My Songs. A Selection of Ukrainian Folksongs in English Translation.* Winnipeg: Ukrainian Canadian Pioneer's Library, 1958.

EINARSSON, Magnús. "Oral Tradition and Ethnic Boundaries: West Icelandic Verses and Anecdotes." *Canadian Ethnic Studies,* 7:2(1975), 19-32.

KLYMASZ, Robert B. *Bibliography of Ukrainian Folklore in Canada, 1902-1964.* Ottawa: National Museum, Anthropology Paper 21, 1969.

_____ *Continuity and Change: The Ukrainian Heritage.* Ottawa: CCFCS, 1975.

_____ "The Ethnic Joke in Canada Today." *Keystone Folklore Quarterly,* 15(1970), 167-73.

* _____ *Folk Narrative Among Ukrainian Canadians in Western Canada.* Ottawa: CCFCS, Mercury Series No. 4, 1973.

_____ *The Ukrainian Canadian Immigrant Folksong Cycle.* Ottawa: National Museum, Bulletin 236, 1970.

_____ *The Ukrainian Winter Folksong Cycle in Canada.* Ottawa: National Museum, Bulletin 236, 1970.

KLYMASZ, Robert B. and James Porter. "Traditional Ukrainian Balladry in Canada." *Western Folklore,* 33(1974), 89-132.

LYSENKO, Vera. *Men in Sheepskin Coats.* Toronto: Ryerson, 1947.

MARTENS, Helen. "The Music of Some Religious Minorities in Canada." *Ethnomusicology,* 16(1972), 360-71.

MILNES, Humphrey. "German Folklore in Ontario." *JAF,* 67(1954), 35-43.

PAULSEN, Frank M. *Danish Settlements on the Canadian Prairies: Folk Traditions, Immigrant Experiences, and Local History.* Ottawa: CCFCS, Mercury Series No. 11, 1975.

PEACOCK, Kenneth. *A Garland of Rue: Lithuanian Folksongs of Love and Betrothal.* Ottawa: CCFCS, 1971.

_____ *Songs of the Doukhobors.* Ottawa: National Museum, Bulletin 231, 1970.

_____ "A Survey of Ethnic Folkmusic Across Western Canada." Ottawa: National Museum, Anthropology Paper 5, 1963, 1-13.

_____ *Twenty Ethnic Songs from Western Canada*: Ottawa: National Museum, Bulletin 211, 1966.

PELINSKI, Ramón. "The Music of Canada's Ethnic Minorities." *The Canada Music Book*, Spring/Summer, 1975.

PERKOWSKI, Jan. L. *Vampires, Dwarves, and Witches Among the Ontario Kashubs.* Ottawa: CCFCS, Mercury Series No. 1, 1972.

QURESHI, Regula. "Ethnomusicological Research Among Canadian Communities of Arab and East Indian Origin." *Ethnomusicology*, 16(1972), 381-96.

REAMAN, Elmore G. *The Trail of the Black Walnut.* Toronto: McClelland and Stewart, 1957.

RUBIN, Ruth. "Yiddish Folk Songs Current in French Canada." *Journal of the International Folk Music Council*, 12(1960), 76-78.

RUDNYC'KYJ, J.B. *Readings in Canadian Slavic Folklore.* 2 vols. Winnipeg: University of Manitoba, 1958.

_____ *Ukrainian Canadian Folklore in English Translation.* Winnipeg: Ukrainian Free Academy of Sciences, 1960.

SALO, Matt T. *Roles of Magic and Healing: The Tietäjä in the Memorates and Legends of Canadian Finns.* Ottawa: CCFCS, 1973.

SONG, Bang-Song. *The Korean-Canadian Folksong: An Ethnomusicological Study.* Ottawa: CCFCS, Mercury Series No. 10, 1975.

STAEBLER, Edna. *Food That Really Schmecks.* Mennonite Country Cooking. Toronto: Ryerson, 1968.

_____ *Sauerkraut and Enterprise.* Toronto: McClelland and Stewart, 1969.

STONE, Kay. "I Won't Tell These Stories to My Kids." *Canadian Ethnic Studies*, 7:2(1975), 33-41.

TEIT, James. "Water-Beings in Shetlandic Folk-Lore as Remembered by Shetlanders in British Columbia." *JAF*, 31(1918), 180-201.

*WINTEMBERG, W.J. *Folklore of Waterloo County, Ontario.* Ottawa: National Museum, Bulletin 116, 1950.

WOODCOCK, George and Ivan AVAKUMOVIC. *The Doukhobors.* Toronto: Oxford, 1968.

MATERIAL FOLK CULTURE

ABRAHAMSON, Una. *Crafts Canada: The Useful Arts.* Toronto: Clarke, Irwin, 1974.

ADAMSON, Anthony and John WILLARD. *The Gaiety of Gables: Ontario's Architectural Folk Art.* Toronto: McClelland and Stewart, 1974.

ARTHUR, Eric. *Early Buildings of Ontario.* Toronto: University of Toronto, 1938.

ARTHUR, Eric and Dudley WITNEY. *The Barn: A Vanishing Landmark in North America.* Toronto: McClelland and Stewart, 1972.

BARBEAU, C. Marius. *Assomption Sash*. Ottawa: National Museum, Bulletin 93, 1939.

____ *I Have Seen Quebec*. Toronto: Macmillan, 1957.

BURNHAM, Harold B. and Dorothy K. BURNHAM. *'Keep Me Warm One Night': Early Hand-weaving in Eastern Canada*. Toronto: University of Toronto, 1972.

CLEMSON, Donovan. *Log Cabins and Log Fences of British Columbia*. Saanichton, B.C.: Hancock, 1974.

GAUTHIER-LAROUCHE, Georges. *Évolution de la maison rurale traditionnelle dans la region de Québec. Archives de Folklore*, 15(1974).

GREEN, Gordon H. *A Heritage of Canadian Handicrafts*. Toronto: McClelland and Stewart, 1967.

HANKS, Carole. *Early Ontario Gravestones*. Toronto: McGraw-Hill Ryerson, 1974.

HARPER, J. Russell. *A People's Art: Primitive, Naive, Provincial and Folk Painting in Canada*. Toronto: University of Toronto, 1974.

MacRAE, Marion. *The Ancestral Roof*. Toronto: Clarke, Irwin, 1963.

MINHINNICK, Jeanne. *Early Furniture in Upper Canada Village, 1800-1837*. Toronto: Ryerson, 1964.

PALARDY, Jean. *The Early Furniture of French Canada*. Toronto: Macmillan, 1963.

SEGUIN, Robert Lionel. *Les Granges du Québec*. Ottawa: National Museum, Bulletin 192, 1963.

____ *La Maison en Nouvelle France*. Ottawa: National Museum, Bulletin 226, 1968.

____ *Les Moules du Québec*. Ottawa: National Museum, Bulletin 188, 1963.

SHACKLETON, Philip. *The Furniture of Old Ontario*. Toronto: Macmillan, 1973.

SYMONS, Harry. *Fences*. Toronto: Ryerson, 1958.

SYMONS, Scott. *Heritage: A Romantic Look at Early Canadian Furniture*. Toronto: McClelland and Stewart, 1971.

TILNEY, Philip. *Artifacts from the CCFCS Collections: Sampling No. 1*. Ottawa: CCFCS, Mercury Series No. 5, 1973.

INDEX OF TALE TYPES

The numbers are from *The Types of the Folktale* by Antti Aarne and Stith Thompson (Folklore Fellows Communications 184, Helsinki, 1961).

I. ANIMAL TALES

II. ORDINARY FOLKTALES

III. JOKES AND ANECDOTES

INDEX OF MOTIFS

Motif numbers are from Stith Thompson: *Motif-Index of Folk Literature*, revised and enlarged edition (Bloomington: University of Indiana Press, 1966), and Ernest W. Baughman: *Type and Motif Index of the Folktales of England and North America* (The Hague: Mouton, 1966). Baughman motifs are indicated by asterisks and/or letters in parentheses.

A. MYTHOLOGICAL MOTIFS

B. ANIMALS

C. TABU

D. MAGIC

E. THE DEAD

F. MARVELS

G. OGRES

338

K. DECEPTIONS

L. REVERSAL OF FORTUNE

339

INDEX OF CONTRIBUTORS

INDEX OF INFORMANTS

GENERAL INDEX

Titles of stories and songs are in italics; general titles are in small capitals. Place names are grouped under the province or state.